TEST PREP SERIES

PRACTICE TESTS FOR THE GRE®

2025-2026

- ❯ 6 Full-Length Tests for Complete Prep
- ❯ 500+ Realistic GRE Questions
- ❯ High-Difficulty Bonus Sections Reflecting Adaptive Test Format
- ❯ Detailed Answer Explanations

Scan the QR Code to access Online Resources

bit.ly/PT-GRE

Practice Tests for the GRE®
First Edition

Copyright © 2025, by Vibrant Publishers LLC, USA. All rights reserved. No part of this publication may be reproduced or distributed in any form or by any means, or stored in a database or retrieval system, without the prior permission of the publisher.

Published by Vibrant Publishers LLC, USA, **www.vibrantpublishers.com**

Paperback ISBN 13: 978-1-63651-439-0
Ebook ISBN 13: 978-1-63651-564-9

Library of Congress Control Number: 2025939624

This publication is designed to provide accurate and authoritative information regarding the subject matter covered. The Author has made every effort in the preparation of this book to ensure the accuracy of the information. However, information in this book is sold without warranty, either expressed or implied. The Author or the Publisher will not be liable for any damages caused or alleged to be caused either directly or indirectly by this book.

All trademarks and registered trademarks mentioned in this publication are the property of their respective owners. These trademarks are used for editorial and educational purposes only, without intent to infringe upon any trademark rights. This publication is independent and has not been authorized, endorsed, or approved by any trademark owner.

Vibrant Publishers' books are available at special quantity discounts for sales promotions, or for use in corporate training programs. For more information, please write to **bulkorders@vibrantpublishers.com**

Please email feedback/corrections (technical, grammatical, or spelling) to **spellerrors@vibrantpublishers.com**

Vibrant publishes in a variety of print and electronic formats and by print-on-demand. Some material included with standard print versions of this book may not be included in e-books or in print-on-demand. To access the complete catalog of Vibrant Publishers, visit **www.vibrantpublishers.com**

GRE® is the registered trademark of the Educational Testing Service (ETS) which neither sponsors nor endorses this product.

GRE® Books in Test Prep Series

GRE® VERBAL PRACTICE QUESTIONS

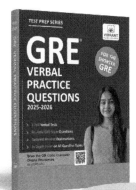

Paperback ISBN:
978-16365-144-1-3

GRE® QUANTITATIVE PRACTICE QUESTIONS

Paperback ISBN:
978-1-63651-440-6

GRE® WORDS IN CONTEXT: THE COMPLETE LIST

Paperback ISBN:
978-1-63651-206-8

GRE® MASTER WORDLIST: 1535 WORDS FOR VERBAL MASTERY

Paperback ISBN:
978-1-63651-196-2

For more practice, visit www.vibrantpublishers.com

Dear Test Taker,

Thank you for choosing *Practice Tests for the GRE®* by Vibrant Publishers. We are truly honored to support you in this significant stage of your academic and professional journey.

Preparing for the GRE is both a challenge and an opportunity—one that demands not just hard work but also the right guidance and resources. At Vibrant Publishers, we aim to be that reliable support system by creating books that are:

- **Content-rich** – Covers key GRE topics in a way that's clear, practical, and easy to absorb
- **Concise** – Designed to focus on what really matters, without unnecessary distractions
- **Approachable** – Written in a clear, accessible manner to ease your learning process
- **Strategic** – Built to mirror the test format and sharpen your skills for the actual GRE

How This Book Supports Your Success:

- Helps you identify strengths and areas for improvement
- Builds the confidence you need to tackle challenging questions
- Trains you to manage time effectively under test conditions
- Encourages a step-by-step approach to mastering the GRE

Tips for Getting the Most Out of This Book:

✓ Set a regular practice schedule and stick to it

✓ Take notes and track recurring errors or patterns

✓ Use the answer explanations as learning tools—not just to check accuracy

✓ Stay patient and persistent—progress comes with consistent effort

We also recognize that every learner's journey is unique. If you have questions, feedback, or suggestions as you work through this book, we warmly invite you to connect with us. Your input helps us create better resources for all learners.

Email us anytime at reachus@vibrantpublishers.com

As you take on this challenge, we hope this book proves to be a valuable companion and that your preparation opens doors to exciting new academic and professional opportunities.

Wishing you focus, clarity, and success on your GRE journey!

Warm regards,
The Vibrant Publishers Team

Table of Contents

How to Use This Book — vii

Focused Book Plan — xii

Chapter 1 Overview of the GRE General Test — 1

Chapter 2 Practice Test #1 — 13
- Section 1 - Analytical Writing   14
- Section 2 - Verbal Reasoning   16
- Section 3 - Quantitative Reasoning   19
- Section 4 - Verbal Reasoning (Easy)   22
- Section 4 - Verbal Reasoning (Hard)   26
- Section 5 - Quantitative Reasoning (Easy)   30
- Section 5 - Quantitative Reasoning (Hard)   33
- Answer Key   36
- Answers & Explanations   38

Chapter 3 Practice Test #2 — 61
- Section 1 - Analytical Writing   62
- Section 2 - Verbal Reasoning   64
- Section 3 - Quantitative Reasoning   67
- Section 4 - Verbal Reasoning (Easy)   70
- Section 4 - Verbal Reasoning (Hard)   74
- Section 5 - Quantitative Reasoning (Easy)   78
- Section 5 - Quantitative Reasoning (Hard)   81
- Answer Key   84
- Answers & Explanations   86

Chapter 4 Practice Test #3 — 109
- Section 1 - Analytical Writing   110
- Section 2 - Verbal Reasoning   112
- Section 3 - Quantitative Reasoning   115
- Section 4 - Verbal Reasoning (Easy)   118
- Section 4 - Verbal Reasoning (Hard)   122

For more practice, visit www.vibrantpublishers.com

Section 5 - Quantitative Reasoning (Easy)   126
Section 5 - Quantitative Reasoning (Hard)   129
Answer Key   132
Answers & Explanations   134

Chapter 5   Practice Test #4   159

Section 1 - Analytical Writing   160
Section 2 - Verbal Reasoning   162
Section 3 - Quantitative Reasoning   165
Section 4 - Verbal Reasoning (Easy)   168
Section 4 - Verbal Reasoning (Hard)   172
Section 5 - Quantitative Reasoning (Easy)   176
Section 5 - Quantitative Reasoning (Hard)   179
Answer Key   182
Answers & Explanations   184

Chapter 6   Practice Test #5   209

Section 1 - Analytical Writing   210
Section 2 - Verbal Reasoning   212
Section 3 - Quantitative Reasoning   215
Section 4 - Verbal Reasoning (Easy)   218
Section 4 - Verbal Reasoning (Hard)   222
Section 5 - Quantitative Reasoning (Easy)   226
Section 5 - Quantitative Reasoning (Hard)   229
Answer Key   232
Answers & Explanations   234

Chapter 7   Practice Test #6   259

Section 1 - Analytical Writing   260
Section 2 - Verbal Reasoning   262
Section 3 - Quantitative Reasoning   265
Section 4 - Verbal Reasoning (Easy)   268
Section 4 - Verbal Reasoning (Hard)   272
Section 5 - Quantitative Reasoning (Easy)   277
Section 5 - Quantitative Reasoning (Hard)   280
Answer Key   283
Answers & Explanations   285

How to Use This Book

Practice Tests for the GRE® is your complete guide to mastering the GRE General Test. Whether you're starting your GRE preparation or building confidence in the final weeks, this book offers the tools and practice you need to succeed. With six full-length practice tests, you'll gain experience that closely mirrors the official GRE in structure, content, and difficulty, helping you prepare effectively and approach the exam with confidence.

1. Why This Book?

Each test in this book is carefully crafted to reflect the format and feel of the real GRE. It covers all three core measures of the exam: **Analytical Writing, Verbal Reasoning**, and **Quantitative Reasoning**.

You can tailor your study plan in two effective ways:

- **Option 1:** Focus on individual sections to sharpen your skills in a targeted way.

- **Option 2:** Take a full-length test to discover where you stand, then direct your focus to the areas that need the most improvement.

2. Understand the Test Before You Start

The shorter GRE lasts just under 2 hours, but it still assesses the same essential skills as the actual test. Before diving into the practice tests, take a few minutes to familiarize yourself with the overall test format, timing, and question types. This foundation will help you approach each section with greater clarity and confidence.

Start with **Chapter 1**, where you'll get a quick overview of the GRE structure, scoring, and key test-taking strategies. It's the best way to ensure your preparation is focused and effective right from the start.

3. Simulate Real Testing Conditions

Take the 6 practice tests in the book at intervals. Taking practice tests is most effective when you simulate the actual test environment. This not only helps you become familiar with the test format but also builds the stamina and focus required for the real exam.

How to Create a Test-Like Environment?

- **Set aside time:** Allocate 1 hour 58 minutes to complete a full-length test, just as you would on test day.

- **Follow the official timing:** Stick to the time limits for each section. Use a timer to practice pacing yourself.

- **Avoid distractions:** Put away your phone, turn off notifications, and choose a quiet place where you won't be interrupted.

By consistently practicing under real testing conditions, you'll develop the confidence and endurance needed to perform well on the actual GRE.

To give you an adaptive testing experience **on paper**, each practice test in this book includes additional sections:

- **Section 2 (Verbal Reasoning)** and **Section 3 (Quantitative Reasoning)**
  These are the **first scored sections** and include a mix of easy, medium, and hard questions.

- **Section 4 (Verbal Reasoning)** and **Section 5 (Quantitative Reasoning)**
  These are adaptive follow-up sections—either **easier or harder**, depending on your earlier performance in that subject.

How to Simulate the Adaptive Test?

1. **Take Section 2 (Verbal Reasoning)** and **Section 3 (Quantitative Reasoning)** under timed conditions.
2. **Score your section** using the answer key.
3. **Determine your next section's difficulty:**

   Verbal Section:
   - Fewer than 7 correct → Take Section 4 (Easy)
   - 7 or more correct → Take Section 4 (Hard)

   Quantitative Section:
   - Fewer than 7 correct → Take Section 5 (Easy)
   - 7 or more correct → Take Section 5 (Hard)

4. Review Your Performance Thoroughly

After completing a practice test, it's tempting to move on to the next one. However, the most valuable part of your preparation lies in analyzing your results.

Steps to Review Your Test:

- **Check your answers:** Use the answer key to score your test. Note both correct and incorrect responses.
- **Understand mistakes:** For every incorrect answer, refer to the detailed explanations in this book. Identify whether the mistake was due to a lack of knowledge, a misinterpretation of the question, or a timing issue for the tests.
- **Revisit challenging questions:** Redo the questions you answered incorrectly without looking at the solutions. This helps reinforce your learning.
- **Identify patterns:** Look for recurring types of mistakes. For example, are you struggling more with algebra, grammar rules, or time management?

Use Mistakes as Learning Opportunities

Remember, mistakes are a normal part of the learning process. Treat them as opportunities to refine your skills and deepen your understanding of the test.

5. Focus on Your Weak Areas

One of the key benefits of using this book is the opportunity to improve in areas where you are less confident. After identifying your weak points from the subsequent practice tests, create a targeted study plan or follow the one given in this book.

How to Address Weak Areas?

- **Practice targeted questions:** Focus on similar types of questions in this book or from other GRE prep materials. The *GRE Verbal Practice Questions* and *GRE Quantitative Practice Questions* books are perfect for getting targeted practice on all types of questions.
- **Learn strategies:** For example, if Reading Comprehension passages feel overwhelming, practice skimming techniques or annotating key points.

Dedicate extra time to these areas while still maintaining a balance with overall test practice.

6. Track Your Progress

Preparation for the GRE is a journey, and tracking your progress helps you stay motivated and focused. Use this book as a tool to monitor your improvement over time.

Why Track Progress?

- It allows you to see tangible improvements in your scores.
- It helps you adjust your study plan based on your evolving needs.
- It builds confidence as you approach your target score.

How to Track Progress?

- **Maintain a score log:** Record your scores for each practice test, along with the number of correct answers per section.
- **Analyze trends:** Look for consistent improvements or recurring issues.
- **Set goals:** Break down your target score into smaller, achievable milestones.

Remember, progress may not always be linear. Some tests may feel harder than others, but consistency in practice is key.

7. Develop Effective Test-Taking Strategies

Success on the GRE isn't just about knowing the content; it's also about applying the right strategies. Use the practice tests in this book to hone your approach.

Key Strategies to Practice:

- **Time management:** Learn how to pace yourself to complete each section without rushing.
- **Eliminate wrong answers:** Narrow down your choices, especially on multiple-choice questions.
- **Guess wisely:** There's no penalty for guessing on the GRE, so make sure to answer every question.
- **Focus on high-value questions:** Prioritize questions you're more confident about before tackling harder ones.

By practicing these strategies during your preparation, you'll feel more prepared and less anxious on test day.

For more practice, visit www.vibrantpublishers.com

8. Prepare for the Real Exam

- **Review key concepts:** Spend extra time revising formulas, grammar rules, and other essential topics from the downloadable cheat sheet and vocabulary list provided with this book.
- **Practice pacing:** Take at least one full test under strict timed conditions.
- **Build confidence:** Use your previous successes to boost your morale. Remind yourself of how much you've improved.

The final days before the test should focus on reviewing rather than learning new material. This will help you feel calm and prepared.

9. Additional Tips for Success

Consistency is Key

GRE preparation is most effective when done consistently over time. Avoid cramming in the weeks leading up to the test. Instead, set aside regular study sessions and stick to a schedule.

Make Use of Answer Explanations

This book includes detailed explanations for every question, not only to show you the correct answer but also to help you understand why other options are incorrect. This insight is invaluable for developing critical reasoning skills.

A Final Word

This book is more than just a collection of practice tests—it's a comprehensive tool to help you achieve your best GRE score. By solving all the questions here, staying consistent in your practice, and reviewing your progress regularly, you'll be well on your way to success. With the right preparation and mindset, you can confidently approach this challenge and open doors to your future aspirations.

Good luck on your GRE journey!

Online Resources

With our test prep books, we also provide Online Resources to help you in your test prep journey! The online resources of this book include:

1. A Stress Management E-book

The book, titled *Conquer the GRE: Stress Management and a Perfect Study Plan*, is designed for test takers to manage the commonly experienced stress during GRE prep. It includes:

- Stress Management Techniques
- A 6-month Deep Study Plan
- An 8-week Sprint Plan
- Practical Tips to Get a Good Score on the GRE
- GRE Score Scale Parameters

2. Vocabulary List of Essential Words

Mastering vocabulary is key to scoring well on the GRE verbal section. This exclusive list features 75 high-frequency GRE words. It includes:

- **Part of Speech** – States if the word is a noun, verb, adjective, or more.
- **Meaning** – Defines the word clearly and concisely.
- **Usage** – Demonstrates how the word appears in real use.

3. GRE Quantitative Reasoning Cheat Sheet

A solid grasp of math fundamentals is essential for success in the GRE Quantitative section. This exclusive Cheat Sheet compiles the most important formulas, rules, and shortcuts. It includes:

- **Arithmetic rules** (number types, divisibility, GCF/LCM, absolute values)
- **Algebra essentials** (equations, inequalities, exponents, roots, identities)
- **Geometry formulas** (area, volume, angles, triangle properties, coordinate geometry)
- **Data analysis tools** (mean, median, mode, range, standard deviation, probability)

How to Access the Online Resources

Step 1: Scan the QR code

Step 2: Fill in your details and submit to request the online resources

Step 3: Check your email inbox to download the resources

bit.ly/PT-GRE

Have fun learning!

Focused Book Plan

Which Plan Is Right For You?

Want to study both Verbal and Quant quickly?
✓ **8-Week Sprint Plan (Online)**

Prefer a slower pace with deeper study?
✓ **6-Month Deep Study Plan (Online)**

Want a test-focused routine with 6 practice tests?
✓ **6-Week Focused Book Plan**

If you want a practice-heavy, test-focused plan that builds your skills through realistic exam simulations, this 6-week study plan is made for you. Whether you've already studied the basics or are looking to structure your final prep, this plan helps you build test stamina, sharpen strategies, and track your progress using 6 full-length practice tests. Each week offers a balance of testing, analysis, and targeted review, so you gain both accuracy and confidence.

Week 1: Foundation Review

Day 1-3: Review core concepts in math, grammar, and reading comprehension (1-2 hours per day).

Day 4: Take **Practice Test 1** under timed conditions.

Day 5-7: Analyze your results and identify strengths and weaknesses. Set improvement goals and track your current baseline score.

Week 2: Content Review

Day 1-3: Focus on Quantitative Reasoning: Review formulas, word problems, and problem-solving techniques.

Day 4: Switch to Verbal Reasoning: Review grammar, sentence structure, vocabulary-in-context, and reading strategies.

Day 5-7: Practice Analytical Writing (Argument Task): Understand the structure, practice outlines, and write at least one full essay.

Take **Practice Test 2** at the end of the week.

Week 3: Practice Questions and Timed Tests

Day 1-3: Practice GRE-style questions for math, grammar, and reading comprehension (1-2 hours per day).

Day 4: Take a timed subject test: Choose either Verbal or Quant to simulate real pressure.

Day 5-7: Review and analyze each section's results; identify areas for improvement.

Complete **Practice Test 3** by similarly simulating the real test environment.

Week 4: Strategy Development

Day 1-3: Learn and practice test-taking strategies for each section (1-2 hours per day). Use the *Online Resources* provided with this book to review key formulas and build vocabulary.

Day 4: Experiment with different strategies and approaches; find what works best for you.

Day 5-7: Continue practicing with **Practice Test 4**, focusing on implementing strategies effectively.

Week 5: Simulated Tests

Day 1-3: Take **Practice Test 5** and review thoroughly.

Day 4: Analyze results and use a notebook or spreadsheet to record frequent error types.

Day 5-7: Create your own "cheat sheet" of common mistakes and strategies.

Week 6: Final Review and Relaxation

Day 1-3: Prioritize a final review of key concepts and strategies (1-2 hours per day).

Day 4: Take a final full-length GRE test (**Practice Test 6**).

Day 5-7: Stay calm and confident; mentally prepare for the exam.

Adjust the study plan according to your individual needs and schedule, ensuring a balance between content review, practice, and relaxation. Stay committed, stay focused, and trust in your preparation as you approach the GRE.

Icons in this Book and Their Meanings:

 — Key points to remember

 — Quick glance

 — Solved examples

 — Expert tips to help you excel

Chapter 1
Overview of the GRE® General Test

The **Graduate Record Examinations (GRE) General Test** has traditionally been a key component in graduate admissions. While its role is now part of a broader evaluation process, a strong GRE score remains a valuable asset—it can serve as evidence of a strong scholarship on an application. This book is designed to prepare you thoroughly for the GRE General Test, formerly known as the GRE revised General Test (renamed in 2016). While the name has changed, the test's structure and scoring have remained consistent.

It's important to note that some graduate programs may also require GRE Subject Tests. These are designed to assess knowledge in specific academic disciplines and are not covered in this book. Before beginning your GRE preparation, review the admissions criteria of your target programs to determine whether a Subject Test is also required. For more information, visit the Subject Tests section on ets.org.

What the GRE Measures

The GRE General Test is not designed to measure your knowledge of specific fields. It does not measure your ability to be successful in your career or even in school. It does, however, give a reasonably accurate indication of your capabilities in certain key areas such as:

- Comprehending and analyzing complex written material
- Understanding basic mathematical concepts
- Interpreting and evaluating data
- Applying logical reasoning and critical thinking

By preparing for the GRE using this book, you'll not only enhance your test performance but also strengthen foundational skills that are crucial for success in graduate studies.

Format of the GRE General Test

The GRE General Test is offered as a computer-delivered test throughout the year. Post-COVID, ETS provides test-takers with the option to take the test from home. Whether you are taking the GRE General Test at the testing center or at home, the format of the test will essentially be the same. The total time for the test will be about **1 hour and 58 minutes**. The test consists of three main components:

- Analytical Writing
- Verbal Reasoning
- Quantitative Reasoning

Note: The unscored section has also been removed for the shorter GRE General Test, along with the 10-minute scheduled break, which was granted to the students after the 2-hour mark of the 3-hour 45-minute test.

Inside the GRE: What's Tested

The Verbal Reasoning and Quantitative Reasoning sections of the GRE General Test are **section-level adaptive**. This means that the computer will adapt the test to your performance. Since there are two sections, each for Verbal Reasoning and Quantitative Reasoning, the difficulty of the second section will depend on how well you did in the first section. The overall format of the GRE General Test will be as follows:

Measure	Number of Questions	Time Allowed
Analytical Writing (1 section)	1 Analyze an Issue	30 minutes
Verbal Reasoning (2 sections)	12 questions (first section) 15 questions (second section)	18 minutes (first section) 23 minutes (second section)
Quantitative Reasoning (2 sections)	12 questions (first section) 15 questions (second section)	21 minutes (first section) 26 minutes (second section)
		Total Time: 1 hour 58 minutes

1. Analytical Writing Measure

The first section of the GRE General Test is the Analytical Writing measure. This section of the GRE is designed to test your ability to use basic logic and critical reasoning to make and assess arguments. The Analytical Writing measure comprises a singular assignment, which must be completed within 30 minutes. You will be given an issue and a prompt with some specific instructions on how to approach the assigned issue. You will be expected to take a position on the issue and then write a clear, persuasive, and logically sound essay defending your position in correct English.

The tasks in the Analytical Writing measure are designed to reflect a wide range of subject areas—from the arts and humanities to the social and physical sciences—but they do **not require specialized content knowledge.**

To support your preparation, the GRE Program has published the complete pool of **Issue topics** from which the prompts are drawn—you can access this resource as a downloadable PDF from the official ETS website.

 Quick Glance at the Analytical Writing Measure

- **Duration:** The task must be completed within 30 minutes.

- **Task format:** A short essay must be written in response to an issue of general interest. The prompt should be addressed clearly and thoughtfully.

- **Skills measured:** This task assesses the ability to develop complex ideas coherently, structure writing in a focused and organized way, support claims with relevant evidence, and demonstrate a strong command of standard written English.

- **Subject knowledge:** The task is designed to measure reasoning, writing, and analytical skills, not familiarity with specific academic topics.

- **Evaluation criteria:** Responses are evaluated based on clarity of argument, depth of reasoning, use of evidence, organization, and language proficiency.

2. Verbal Reasoning Measure

The Verbal Reasoning measure of the GRE assesses your reading comprehension, ability to draw inferences, and vocabulary skills. You will encounter two Verbal Reasoning sections containing 12 and 15 questions, with time limits of 18 and 23 minutes, respectively.

Most questions are multiple-choice and fall into three main types:

- **Reading Comprehension (RC):** You will read a short passage (1 to 3 paragraphs) and answer questions that test your understanding of the content.

- **Text Completion (TC):** These questions present a brief passage with one to three blanks. You will select the best choices from multiple options to fill in the blanks appropriately.

- **Sentence Equivalence (SE):** You will complete a sentence by selecting two words that both fit the blank and produce sentences with similar meanings.

Together, these question types assess how well you understand and analyze written material, as well as your command of vocabulary in context.

Quick Glance at the Verbal Reasoning Measure

- **Duration:** The section is split into 12 questions with a 18-minute time limit and 15 questions with a 23-minute limit.

- **Question types:** This section includes Reading Comprehension, Text Completion, and Sentence Equivalence questions.

- **Choices:** RC questions may require selecting one or more correct answers or highlighting a relevant portion of the text. TC questions involve choosing the correct words to fill one or more blanks in a passage. SE questions ask for two answer choices that produce sentences with similar meanings.

- **Skills measured:** The section tests the ability to understand complex texts, apply vocabulary in context, and make logical inferences based on written material.

3. Quantitative Reasoning Measure

The Quantitative Reasoning section of the GRE tests your ability to apply basic math skills, interpret data, and reason with numbers. You'll face two sections: one with 12 questions in 21 minutes, and another with 15 questions in 26 minutes.

Questions may be set in real-world or purely mathematical contexts, with many presented as word problems that require mathematical modeling. The section covers **four** content areas: Arithmetic, Algebra, Geometry, and Data Analysis.

You'll encounter four types of questions:

- **Quantitative Comparison**
- **Multiple Choice — Select One Answer**
- **Multiple Choice — Select One or More Answers**
- **Numeric Entry**

Quick Glance at the Quantitative Reasoning Measure

- **Time Allotted:** The section is split into 12 questions with a 21-minute time limit and 15 questions with a 26-minute limit.

- **Question Types:** This section includes Multiple Choice, Numeric Entry, Quantitative Comparison, and Data Interpretation questions.

- **Skills Measured:** This section tests the ability to use Arithmetic, Algebra, Geometry, and Statistics, interpret and analyze quantitative data, and apply mathematical reasoning to real-world problems..

Features of the Computer-delivered Test

1. **Review and Preview Questions**
   Test takers can review and preview questions within a section, which allows them to manage their time effectively and focus on the most challenging questions first.

2. **Mark and Return to Questions**
   Questions can be marked within a section and revisited later. This enables moving past difficult questions and returning to them, as long as the time limit for the section is respected.

3. **Change or Edit Answers**
   Answers can be changed or edited within a section. If a mistake is noticed, test takers can correct their responses before the section time expires.

4. **On-Screen Calculator**
   An on-screen calculator is provided during the Quantitative Reasoning measure, facilitating quick and accurate calculations. However, you should only use the calculator for complex equations that will take a longer time to do manually, such as square roots, addition, subtraction, and multiplication of numbers with several digits.

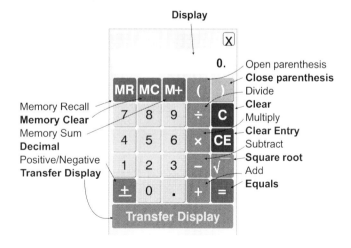

Guidelines for using the on-screen calculator

- The on-screen calculator follows the order of operations (PEMDAS). This means that it computes equations in the following order - parentheses, exponentiation (including square roots), multiplication and division (left to right), addition and subtraction (left to right). So, for an equation like 2 + 3 * 6, the on-screen calculator will give the answer 20 but some calculators will give the answer 30 as they first add 2 and 3 and get 5 which is multiplied by 6 to get the final answer 30.

- The Transfer Display button will be useful for Numeric Entry questions. The button will transfer the number on your calculator display to the numeric entry answer box. But remember to check the transferred answer as sometimes you may be required to round up your answer; adjust it accordingly.

- The Memory Recall (MR), Memory Clear (MC), and Memory Sum (M+) buttons work as per normal calculators.

Registering for the GRE

Before you register to take the GRE, be sure to consider your schedule and any special accommodations that you may need. Be aware that the availability of testing dates may vary according to your location. Be sure to give yourself plenty of time to prepare for the GRE and be sure that you know the deadlines for score reporting and application deadlines for all the schools you are applying to. For general information about deadlines and the GRE, visit the GRE section at ets.org. For more information on how to register for the GRE, visit the Registration section at ets.org. For information on special accommodations for disabled students, visit the Disability Accommodations section on ets.org.

If you are taking the GRE General Test at home, there are certain equipment, environment, and testing space requirements that you need to fulfill before you can start the registration process. For more information on these requirements, read the At Home Testing section on ets.org.

How the GRE General Test is Scored

Scoring for the Analytical Writing Section

In the Analytical Writing section, you will be scored on a scale of 0-6 in increments of 0.5. The Analytical Writing measure emphasizes your ability to engage in reasoning and critical thinking over your facility with the finer points of grammar. The highest scores of 5.5-6.0 are given to work that is generally superior in every respect - sustained analysis of complex issues, coherent argumentation, and excellent command of the English language. The lowest scores of 0.0-0.5 are given to work that is completely off-topic or so poorly composed as to be incoherent.

Scoring for the Verbal and Quantitative Reasoning Sections

The Verbal and Quantitative Reasoning sections are now scored on a scale of 130-170 in 1-point increments.

Preparing for Test Day

How you prepare for the test is completely up to you and will depend on your own test-taking preferences and the amount of time you can devote to studying for the test. At the very least, before you take the test, you should know the basics of what is covered on the test along with the general guidelines for taking the GRE. This book is designed to provide you with the basic information you need and give you the opportunity to prepare thoroughly for the GRE General Test.

Remember, you don't need to spend an equal amount of time on each of these areas to do well on the GRE - allot your study time to your own needs and preferences. Following are some suggestions to help you make the final preparations for your test, and help you through the test itself.

- In the time leading up to your test, practice, then practice some more. Practice until you are confident with the material.

- Know when your test is, and when you need to be at the testing center or in front of your computer at home.

- Make a "practice run" to your testing center, so that you can anticipate how much time you will need to allow to get there. For the at home test, make sure to sign in at least 15 minutes before the test.

- Understand the timing and guidelines for the test and plan accordingly. Remember that you are not allowed to eat or drink while taking the GRE, although you will be allowed to snack or drink during some of the short breaks during testing. Plan accordingly.

- Know exactly what documentation you will need to bring with you to the testing center. If you are testing at home, you will have to provide a valid government-issued identification document as well.

- Relax, especially on the day or night before your test. If you have studied and practiced wisely, you will be well prepared for the test. You may want to briefly glance over some test preparation materials but cramming the night before will not be productive.

- Eat well and get a good night's sleep. You will want to be well-rested for the test.

The Test Day

- Wake up early to give yourself plenty of time to eat a healthy breakfast, gather the necessary documentation, pack a snack and a water bottle, and make it to the testing center well before your test is scheduled to start.

- Have confidence; you've prepared well for the test, and there won't be any big surprises. You may not know the answers to some questions, but the format will be exactly like what you've been practicing.

- While you are taking the test, don't panic. The test is timed, and students often worry that they will run out of time and miss too many questions. The sections of the test are designed so that many students will not finish them, so don't worry if you don't think you can finish a section on time. Just try to answer as many questions as you can, as accurately as possible.

- If there's a question you're not sure of, don't panic—the GRE test allows you to skip and return to questions when you are ready, so take advantage of that. Remember, the value of each easy question is the same as the hard questions!

- Remember the strategies and techniques that you learn from this book and apply them wherever possible.

General Strategies for Taking the GRE

The following is a list of strategies that will help to improve your chances of performing well on the GRE:

- Learn the basics about the test - what is being tested, the format, and how the test is administered.

- Familiarize yourself with the specific types of questions that you will see on the GRE General Test.

- Review basic concepts in math, logic, and writing.

- Work through the test-taking strategies offered in this book.

- Work through mock GRE tests until you feel thoroughly comfortable with the types of questions you will see.

- As you are studying for the GRE, focus your energy on the types of questions that give you the most difficulty.

- Learn to guess wisely. For many of the questions in the Verbal and Quantitative Reasoning Sections, the correct answer is in front of you - you only need to correctly identify it. Especially for questions that you find difficult, you should hone your ability to dismiss the options that are clearly wrong and make an educated guess about which one is right.

- Answer every question. You won't lose any points for choosing the wrong answer, so even a wild guess that might or might not be right is better than no answer at all.

Frequently Asked Questions

General Questions

1. **What changes have been made to the GRE General Test after the announcement on May 31, 2023?**

    The main changes to the test are a reduction in the time (from 3 hours 45 minutes to 1 hour 58 minutes), and the removal of the "Analyze an Argument" essay task (which was a part of the Analytical Writing section) and the unscored section. The time has been curtailed by decreasing the number of questions in each section, reducing the total number of questions from 40 to 27. Furthermore, the removal of the "Analyze an Argument" task and the unscored section also aided in shortening the total duration. The official scores will also be delivered more promptly and will now take 8-10 calendar days, facilitating faster applications to their desired institutes by the students. For more information on the changes, visit the GRE section at ets.org.

2. **Can I take the GRE test at home?**

   Yes. ETS now provides students with the option to take the test from home. If your local test centers are closed or you prefer a familiar testing environment, you can take the GRE from home. You will have to check the equipment, environment, and testing space requirements for the at home test and whether it's an option for you. For detailed information on the requirements for the home test, check the At Home Testing section at ets.org.

3. **How do I get ready to take the GRE General Test?**

   To take the GRE General Test, there are several steps you'll need to take:

   - Find out what prospective graduate/professional programs require: Does the program you're interested in require additional testing beyond the GRE General Test? What is the deadline for receipt of scores?

   - Sign up for a test date. You need to sign up for any GRE testing. Act in a timely manner so that you have plenty of time to prepare and are guaranteed that your scores will be sent and received on time. For the in-center test, testing dates are much more restricted, so if you know that you will need to take the GRE General Test at the center, make arrangements well in advance of the application deadline for your program. There are additional requirements if you're taking the test at home, so make sure to check the requirements well in advance.

   - Use resources provided by ETS and Vibrant Publishers to familiarize yourself with the format of the GRE and the types of questions you will face. Even if you are confident about taking the test, it is essential to prepare for the test.

4. **Does the GRE General Test measure my proficiency in specific subject areas?**

   No. The GRE General Test is designed to measure general proficiency in reading, critical reasoning, and working with data, all abilities that are critical to graduate work. However, you won't be tested on your knowledge of any specific field.

5. **Where can I get additional information on the GRE General Test?**

   Educational Testing Service (ETS), the organization that administers the GRE, has an informative website entirely devoted to information about the test in the GRE section at ets.org. There, you can find links that further explain how to sign up for testing, fees, score reporting, and much more.

Preparing for the Test

1. **How should I start to prepare for the test?**

   The first thing you should do is thoroughly familiarize yourself with the format of the GRE General Test. Read about each section of the test, how many questions are there per section, and the required format for answers. You can find general information about the structure of the test earlier in this chapter.

2. **How do I prepare for the questions I will be asked on the GRE General Test?**

   There are plenty of resources by Vibrant Publishers, including this book to help you prepare for the questions you will face on the GRE General Test. A list of books is provided at the beginning of this book. For the most updated list, you may visit the Test Prep Series section on www.vibrantpublishers.com.

3. **How much should I study/practice for the GRE?**

   Study and practice until you feel comfortable with the test. Practice, practice, and practice some more until you feel confident about test day!

4. **Are there additional materials I can use to get even more practice?**

   Yes. ETS offers a free full-length practice test that can be downloaded from the GRE section at ets.org. Also, after you have signed up for testing through ETS, you are eligible for some further test preparation materials free of additional charge.

Test Content

1. **What skills does the GRE test?**

   In general, the GRE is designed to test your proficiency in certain key skills that you will need for graduate-level study. More specifically:

   - **The Analytical Writing section** tests your ability to write about complex ideas in a coherent, focused fashion as well as your ability to command the conventions of standard written English, provide and evaluate relevant evidence, and critique other points of view.

   - **The Verbal Reasoning section** is an assessment of your ability to understand, interpret and analyze complex passages, use reasoning to draw inferences about written material, and use sophisticated vocabulary in context.

   - **The Quantitative Reasoning section** is an assessment of basic, high school-level mathematical skills and knowledge, as well as your ability to analyze and interpret data.

2. **What level of math is required for the Quantitative Reasoning section?**

   You will be expected to know high school-level math: arithmetic, and basic concepts in algebra and geometry. You will also be expected to be able to analyze and interpret data presented in tables and graphs.

Scoring and Score Reporting

1. **How are the sections of the GRE General Test scored?**

   The GRE General Test is scored as follows:

   - **The scores of the Verbal Reasoning section** are done in 1-point increments on a scale of 130-170.

   - **The scores of the Quantitative Reasoning section** are done in 1-point increments on a scale of 130-170.

   - **The scores of the Analytical Writing section** are done in increments of 0.5 on a scale of 0-6.

2. **When will my score be reported?**

   It depends on when you decide to take the GRE General Test. In general, scores for the test are reported in 8-10 days. You can find your scores in your official ETS account. An email notification from ETS is sent when the test scores are made available. ETS will also send an official Institution Score Report to the institutions you've chosen to send the test scores to. Check the GRE section at ets.org for updates on score reporting and deadlines.

3. **How long will my scores be valid?**

   Your score for the GRE General Test will remain valid for five years.

Other Questions

1. **Do business schools accept the GRE instead of the GMAT?**

   An increasing number of business schools accept the GRE as a substitute for the more standard test for admission to an MBA program, the GMAT. Before you decide to take the GRE instead of the GMAT, make sure that the programs you are interested in applying to will accept the GRE. You can find a list of business schools that currently accept the GRE in the GRE section at ets.org.

2. **How is the GRE administered?**

   The GRE is administered continuously year-round at designated testing centers, where you can take the test free from distractions in a secure environment that discourages cheating. The GRE Test at home is also available for those who are more comfortable in a familiar environment. For information on testing centers in your area and important dates, visit the GRE section at ets.org.

3. **I have a disability that requires me to ask for special accommodation while taking the test - what sort of accommodation is offered?**

   ETS does accommodate test-takers with disabilities. For information on procedures, visit the GRE Disability Accomodations section at ets.org.

4. **Will there be breaks during testing?**

   No. There are no breaks. If you take an unscheduled break, testing time will not stop.

5. **Will I be given scratch paper?**

   Yes. The test administrator will provide you with scratch paper to use during the test, which has to be returned to the testing center staff without any pages missing.

   For the at home test, you cannot use regular notepaper. You may use either of the following materials:

   - One small desktop whiteboard with an erasable marker.
   - A sheet of paper placed inside a transparent sheet protector. You can write on this with an erasable marker.

   At the end of the test, you will need to show the proctor that all the notes you took during the test have been erased.

6. **Should I bring a calculator to the test?**

   No. There will be an on-screen calculator for you to use.

Before You Begin the Test

Please Read the Instructions Carefully

This practice test is designed to mirror the structure and rigor of the GRE. Treat it as a formal simulation. The more seriously you take this exercise, the more accurately it will reflect your current preparedness—and guide your next steps.

The number of questions and the time limits in each section are aligned with those on the actual GRE, providing you with a realistic and reliable measure of your readiness.

Once you complete the test, refer to the answer key to check your responses. You'll also find detailed instructions for calculating your Quantitative Reasoning score, along with explanations for each question. Be sure to review these explanations thoroughly—especially for the questions you got wrong—to gain insight into the reasoning behind the correct answers and to sharpen your test-taking strategies.

Set Up Your Testing Environment

To replicate real testing conditions:

- Choose a quiet, uninterrupted space to work in.
- Have the following materials at hand:
  - ❑ Rough paper
  - ❑ A few sharpened pencils
  - ❑ A timer, stopwatch, or clock to track your time (if you are simulating test-day pacing)
- Ensure that you remain free of distractions throughout the session.
- Avoid checking your phone, notes, or external resources during the test.

Why This Matters

Your performance on this test is more than just a score—it's a diagnostic tool. It will help you identify question types you excel at and those that need reinforcement. The explanations provided are a valuable resource—use them to deepen your understanding and refine your test-taking strategy.

Chapter 2
Practice Test #1

IMPORTANT
READ THE INSTRUCTIONS BEFORE BEGINNING THE TEST

1. Take this test under real testing conditions. Put away any distractions and sit in a quiet place with no disturbances. Keep a rough paper, some pencils, and a calculator beside you.
2. Begin with **Section 1** of the test on page 14. Write your essay in 30 minutes.
3. Next, move to **Section 2 - Verbal Reasoning** on page 16.
   - ❑ Attempt all questions and note the number of correct answers using the answer key on page 36.
   - ❑ If you get fewer than 7 correct, proceed to **Section 4 - Verbal Reasoning (Easy)** on page 22.
   - ❑ If you get 7 or more correct, proceed to **Section 4 - Verbal Reasoning (Hard)** on page 26.
4. After that, take **Section 3 - Quantitative Reasoning** on page 19.
   - ❑ Complete the section, then check your score using the answer key on page 37.
   - ❑ If you get fewer than 7 correct, proceed to **Section 5 - Quantitative Reasoning (Easy)** on page 30.
   - ❑ If you get 7 or more correct, proceed to **Section 5 - Quantitative Reasoning (Hard)** on page 33.
5. Complete Section 4 and Section 5, respectively, and note down the number of correct answers you got right in each section.
6. Calculate your **Scaled Score** on page 317 for the test.
7. Review **detailed explanations** for all questions beginning on page 38.

Section 1 - Analytical Writing

Analyze an Issue
30 Minutes

In order to become well-rounded individuals, all college students should be required to take courses in which they read poetry, novels, mythology, and other types of imaginative literature.
Write a response in which you discuss the extent to which you agree or disagree with the recommendation and explain your reasoning for the position you take. In developing and supporting your position, describe specific circumstances in which adopting the recommendation would or would not be advantageous and explain how these examples shape your position.

You may start writing your response here

Section 1 - Analytical Writing

Section 2 - Verbal Reasoning

18 Minutes | 12 Questions

For Questions 1 to 3, select one entry for each blank from the corresponding column of choices. Fill all blanks in the way that best completes the text.

1. _____ forensic scientist understands that the Hollywood interpretation of their field deliberately plays up the sensationalist aspects and that such an approach is not applicable in reality.

Ⓐ	A judicious
Ⓑ	A despondent
Ⓒ	An imprudent
Ⓓ	An asinine
Ⓔ	A daft

2. Calculating the habitability of distant planets is an inexact science. Because of the immense distances involved, astronomers are forced to rely on (i)_____ about distant solar systems. Moreover, the more astronomers look at these solar systems, the more they realize that the solar system around our Sun might not be the (ii)_____ it was assumed to be. This is because most neighboring solar systems actually reverse the structure of our own—their gas giants are close to the sun, while rocky planets are farther away.

Blank (i)	Blank (ii)
Ⓐ fauna	Ⓓ liability
Ⓑ inferences	Ⓔ archetype
Ⓒ ambiguities	Ⓕ recidivist

3. There has always been a strong parallel between religious (i)_____ and health benefits. Many students have shown that religious involvement increases life expectancy and decreases depression. These (ii)_____, of course, are not always so simple: the benefits of religious participation on health fluctuate depending on the religion, the sex of the individual, and many other factors. Still, there is (iii)_____ bond between general health benefits and religious participation.

Blank (i)	Blank (ii)	Blank (iii)
Ⓐ partaking	Ⓓ correlations	Ⓖ a fungible
Ⓑ renunciation	Ⓔ antagonisms	Ⓗ an incontrovertible
Ⓒ eloquence	Ⓕ contingencies	Ⓘ a rescindable

For Questions 4 and 5, select one answer choice unless otherwise instructed.

Question 4 is based on this passage.

Social media was initially created with the purpose of connecting users digitally with family members, friends, colleagues, and like-minded groups. The development of the smartphone led to the spread of social media beyond computers. The first iPhone, launched by Steve Jobs in 2007, helped shift online social connections to mobile devices. Further, phones with high-quality cameras promoted the sharing of images along with written messages.

The evolution of social media usage has led companies to place advertisements on social media platforms and grow a virtual community of customers. While formal social media advertising costs money, simply sharing content on a popular social media platform allows brands to grow authentically without a cost.

Section 2 - Verbal Reasoning

4. How is the argument presented in the second paragraph supported by the first paragraph?

    Ⓐ The second paragraph presents an argument that social media helps companies grow for free, while the first paragraph supports this by explaining how social media has rapidly evolved before companies used it for advertising.

    Ⓑ The second paragraph presents an argument that social media helps companies grow for free, while the first paragraph supports this by explaining how social media has always been cost-effective.

    Ⓒ The second paragraph presents an argument that social media helps companies grow for free, while the first paragraph supports this by explaining how social media was originally created strictly for connecting with friends.

    Ⓓ The second paragraph presents an argument that social media advertising is an easier way to build connections with customers, while the first paragraph supports this by explaining how social media was originally created strictly for connecting with friends.

    Ⓔ The second paragraph presents an argument that social media advertising is an easier way to build connections with customers, while the first paragraph supports this by explaining how social media has always been cost-effective.

Question 5 is based on this passage.

The quality and quantity of human social relationships have a drastic impact on overall mental health, health behavior, physical health, and even the risk of mortality. Sociologists have long worked to establish a link between interaction in social relationships and health outcomes. Much research has been conducted to find explanations for this link and the effects of social variations like race and gender. It has been concluded that social relationships have both short-term and long-term effects on health that can be negative or positive. These effects are evident in childhood and continue to develop throughout a person's life, leading to cumulative benefits or detriments.

5. Select the sentence that leads into the discussion about research on this topic.

For Questions 6 to 9, select the two answer choices that, when used to complete the sentence, fit the meaning of the sentence as a whole and produce complete sentences that are alike in meaning.

6. The prosecution had grandiose plans to spring a surprise witness and subvert the defense's narrative, but the vehement _____ of the formerly acquiescence witness rendered the plan useless.

    A aimlessness
    B obstinacy
    C simplicity
    D insinuations
    E recalcitrance
    F effervescence

7. The "profit at all cost" approach to businesses can, if left unchecked, introduce _____ at a fundamental level and undermine any legitimacy the company might have with the public.

    A villany
    B velocity
    C complaisance
    D turpitude
    E indolence
    F articulacy

Section 2 - Verbal Reasoning

8. Although financial solvency is a vital component of a healthy enterprise, a business will not survive for long with _____ leader; a strong, sound decision maker who is willing to enforce even fractious decisions is an imperative component for sustaining an enterprise through difficult times.

   - [A] a craven
   - [B] an impolitic
   - [C] a limpid
   - [D] a ribald
   - [E] a brusque
   - [F] a prosaic

9. Out of fear of _____ business growth — and a desire to remain competitive in a ferocious global marketplace—some nations decide to enact low business tax rates to encourage new investment and to incentivize existing foreign businesses to move their headquarters from their home countries to within their nations' borders.

   - [A] promulgating
   - [B] restricting
   - [C] obstructing
   - [D] averring
   - [E] congealing
   - [F] glowering

For Questions 10 to 12, select one answer choice unless otherwise instructed.

Questions 10 to 12 are based on this passage.

The liver is a human organ that is shaped like a cone, with the smaller end resting above the spleen and the larger end residing above the small intestine. This reddish-brown organ is located in the right upper abdomen and weighs around three pounds. The liver is required for survival and serves over 500 important functions in the human body.

The liver's duties include helping to remove waste products, regulating the blood, and creating and storing essential nutrients. One example of a way these functions are carried out is through the liver's production of bile, a fluid that is crucial to the digestion process. Another task handled by the liver is blood filtration by removing harmful toxins from blood as it leaves the stomach and intestines. This helps prevent infections because bacteria are eliminated from the bloodstream as well. Additionally, the liver stores a significant amount of vitamins and minerals including vitamins A, D, E, K, B12, iron, and copper. Thus, the liver is a vital, powerful, and busy organ!

10. Which of the following statements best summarizes the functions of the liver?

    - (A) The liver serves over 500 purposes including filtering toxins to prevent infections, producing bile, and creating and storing many vitamins and minerals.
    - (B) The liver serves a multitude of essential functions including regulating the blood, filtering it for toxins, and resisting bacterial infections.
    - (C) The liver is a reddish-brown organ in the right upper abdomen that serves a wide variety of essential functions.
    - (D) The liver serves over 500 vital functions such as the creation and storage of essential vitamins and minerals.
    - (E) The liver is a reddish-brown, cone-shaped organ that removes waste products and regulates the blood.

11. In the second paragraph, which of the following could best replace the phrase, "carried out"?

    - (A) Foregone
    - (B) Desecrated
    - (C) Accomplished
    - (D) Shown
    - (E) Sorted out

12. Which of the following words would the author most likely use to describe the human liver?

    - (A) Indolent
    - (B) Uninvolved
    - (C) Active
    - (D) Nugatory
    - (E) Inert

Section 3 - Quantitative Reasoning

18 Minutes | 12 Questions

1

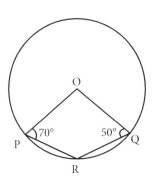

In the above figure, O is the center of the circle and ∠OPR = 70° AND ∠OQR = 50°

Quantity A	Quantity B
Reflex angle ∠POQ	240°

Ⓐ Quantity A is greater.
Ⓑ Quantity B is greater.
Ⓒ The two quantities are equal.
Ⓓ The relationship cannot be determined from the information given.

2

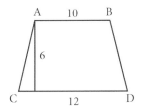 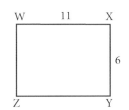

Quantity A	Quantity B
The area of trapezoidal region ABCD	The area of rectangular region WXYZ

Ⓐ Quantity A is greater.
Ⓑ Quantity B is greater.
Ⓒ The two quantities are equal.
Ⓓ The relationship cannot be determined from the information given.

3

$$x < 0 < y$$

Quantity A	Quantity B
$x^2 + y$	$x - y^2$

Ⓐ Quantity A is greater.
Ⓑ Quantity B is greater.
Ⓒ The two quantities are equal.
Ⓓ The relationship cannot be determined from the information given.

4

List A consists of the numbers x, $\sqrt{x}$, 4, and $\sqrt{10}$ where $x > 0$ and the range of the numbers in list A is 6.

Quantity A	Quantity B
x	3

Ⓐ Quantity A is greater.
Ⓑ Quantity B is greater.
Ⓒ The two quantities are equal.
Ⓓ The relationship cannot be determined from the information given.

5

If x is the unit digit of the product 14,042 × 6,313 and y is the tens digit of the product of 512,821 × 41,240, what is the value of $x + y$?

Ⓐ 6
Ⓑ 8
Ⓒ 10
Ⓓ 12
Ⓔ 14

Section 3 - Quantitative Reasoning

Questions 6 to 8 are based on the following data.

In a customer survey, three snack brands, brand A, B, and C, were reviewed and ranked in order of preference. Each of the snack brands were also rated in three categories on a scale of 1 to 5, with 5 being the best rating.

Survey Results

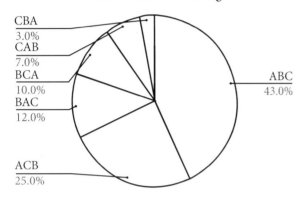

Distributions of Rankings
- CBA 3.0%
- CAB 7.0%
- BCA 10.0%
- BAC 12.0%
- ACB 25.0%
- ABC 43.0%

Note: The notation ABC means A ranked 1st, B ranked 2nd, and C ranked 3rd.

Average Rating

Category	Snack Brand A	Snack Brand B	Snack Brand C
Flavor	5.0	4.3	3.2
Price	2.8	4.0	4.8
Healthiness	2.2	4.5	1.0

6

The sum of the three average ratings was calculated for each of the snack brands. The snack brand with the highest sum was ranked last by what fraction of the customers?

Enter your answer as a fraction with the numerator and denominator in their lowest terms.

7

Snack brand A's average rating for flavor was approximately what percent greater than snack brand C's average rating for flavor?

- (A) 18%
- (B) 36%
- (C) 50%
- (D) 56%
- (E) 64%

8

If 100 customers were surveyed and each of the average ratings was the arithmetic mean of the ratings given by the customers, approximately how much greater was the total ratings given to all three snack brands for price than that for healthiness?

- (A) 100
- (B) 200
- (C) 300
- (D) 400
- (E) 500

9

A typist has x amount of words to type. The total word count is divided between different types of documents, some of which are 250 words long and some of which are 500 words long. If $\frac{1}{8}$ of the documents are 250 words long and the remaining 49 documents are 500 words long, what is the value of x?

- (A) 56
- (B) 1,750
- (C) 23,000
- (D) 24,500
- (E) 26,250

10

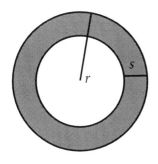

If r = 15 and s = 7, then what is the area of the shaded portion? Round to the nearest tenth.

[   ]

11

A cyclist travels the length of a bike path that is 225 *miles* long, rounded to the nearest *mile*. If the trip took him 5 *hours*, rounded to the nearest *hour*, then which of the following can be his average speeds?

Indicate all such answers.

- [A] 37
- [B] 39
- [C] 40
- [D] 41
- [E] 43
- [F] 44
- [G] 48
- [H] 50
- [I] 51
- [J] 52

12

The value of Quantity A is inversely related to the square of B. Both A and B are positive quantities. If the value of A decreased by 19%, then the value of B increased by what percent?

- (A) 11%
- (B) 19%
- (C) 25%
- (D) 50%
- (E) 81%

Section 4 - Verbal Reasoning (Easy)

23 Minutes | 15 Questions

For Questions 1 to 4, select one entry for each blank from the corresponding column of choices. Fill all the blanks in the way that best completes the text.

1. Literary techniques are _____ to creating a unique work of literature—two otherwise identical plots, if written with widely different literary devices, will not be recognizable to each other in any way.

A	indispensable
B	antagonistic
C	allegorical
D	anachronistic
E	insufficient

2. Even though his doctor warned him that running would not be good for his knees, the middle–aged man found that the emotional _____ of exercise justified any subsequent stiffness.

A	catharsis
B	indolence
C	exacerbation
D	calamity
E	inanity

3. Einstein's theory of relativity is so (i)_____ that it has not been disproven. It is the rare theory that crosses through many disciplines. (ii)_____, many of the experiments that have been conducted to challenge the theory of relativity have actually served to reinforce its validity. It has seen slight tweaks in recent years, but its central tenets are unequivocal.

Blank (i)	Blank (ii)
A axiomatic	D Disparagingly
B equivocal	E Ironically
C arcane	F Redundantly

4. The United States faces no greater economic (i)_____ today than healthcare reform. With roughly fifty million uninsured citizens in the country, medical care costs frequently drag families into bankruptcy. The numbers can (ii) _____: more than 60% of Americans filing for bankruptcy cite medical expenses as the cause. The problem is a (iii) _____one, as well—bankruptcy problems can poison the economic waters even for the financially solvent.

Blank (i)	Blank (ii)	Blank (iii)
A windfall	D corroborate	G reserved
B calamity	E mitigate	H counter–intuitive
C evolution	F exonerate	I communal

Section 4 - Verbal Reasoning (Easy)

For Questions 5 to 9, select one answer choice unless otherwise instructed.

Questions 5 and 6 are based on this passage.

The world is a different place because of electricity. Electricity is the flow of electrons between atoms. In sum, electricity is generated at power plants and transmitted through a network to reach buildings. There are many components that work together to help a switch turn on, but one crucial piece is a copper wire.

Copper wires serve as the conduit for electricity to flow. Of all conductive materials, copper is one of the greatest conductors of electricity, which means that it allows electrons to flow freely. Materials that do not allow for an easy electrical flow are known as insulators. Thus, copper has commonly been used for electrical wiring for hundreds of years. It can be easily manipulated, shaped, and cut into various sizes. Plus, copper resists erosion well, which means electrical systems last longer.

For the following question, consider each of the choices separately and select all that apply.

5. Based on the passage, which of the following assumptions can be made?

   A. Copper is the only conductive material and all others are categorized as insulators.
   B. The only reason copper is used in electrical systems is due to its excellent conductivity.
   C. Copper is one of the best conductive materials, but other conductive materials do exist.

6. Which of the following purposes is the passage most likely intended to serve?

   A. Explain to semi-seasoned electrician apprentices the purpose of using copper in electrical systems.
   B. Provide information to the public about the purpose of an electrician.
   C. Advertise for the sale of copper to an electrical company.
   D. Explain to new electrician trainees the purpose of using copper in electrical systems.
   E. Inform a group of students about the history of copper.

Questions 7 to 9 are based on this passage.

Candles have a rich cultural history that stretches far beyond the whimsical, decorative, and seasonal purposes they serve today. Wicked candles were used as early as 3,000 B.C. by the ancient Romans to provide light during night travels, brighten homes, and complete religious ceremonies. During this time, most candles were crafted from animal-based tallow. However, in other regions of the world ancient candles were made from a profusion of materials like rice paper, insect-derived wax, seeds, tree nuts, and boiled fruit.

Throughout the Middle Ages, candles were introduced to Europe and a major development took place. Beeswax became the primary ingredient in candles because it produced less smoke and emitted a sweet, pleasant smell. Beeswax candles became the most widely used type of candles for important church ceremonies but were still not often seen in commoners' homes because of their high price.

7. Based on the second paragraph of the passage, which of the following can most likely be concluded?

   A. Church ceremonies were not as important to common people as they were to the wealthy.
   B. The homes of poorer citizens were often smokier than the homes of wealthier citizens.
   C. Because of their use in church ceremonies, most people did not feel comfortable having beeswax candles in their homes.
   D. Wealthier citizens still used candles made from tallow to light their homes during the Middle Ages.
   E. Church leaders used beeswax candles to light their own homes during the Middle Ages.

8. Select the sentence from the passage that suggests candles were developed in other parts of the world independent of the invention in Rome.

Section 4 - Verbal Reasoning (Easy)

9. In the context of the first paragraph, which word could best replace the word "profusion"?

   Ⓐ Infusion
   Ⓑ Plethora
   Ⓒ Intimation
   Ⓓ Scanty
   Ⓔ Insipid

For Questions 10 to 12, select the two answer choices that, when used to complete the sentence, fit the meaning of the sentence as a whole and produce complete sentences that are alike in meaning.

10. Even authors of tremendous directness and incisiveness will sometimes use the guise of a fictional story, a technique known as a roman à clef, to tell details about themselves in what is ostensibly an attempt to overcome their own _____.

    A. reticence
    B. arrogance
    C. bombast
    D. reserve
    E. structure
    F. cynicism

11. Many scholars read ancient legal documents not because they want to adopt those antiquated judicial constructions directly into modern law, but rather because they want to glean the _____ properties of the works.

    A. didactic
    B. infallible
    C. educational
    D. argumentative
    E. vituperative
    F. preposterous

12. Despite memorizing every detail necessary for an Organic Chemistry test on polyannulated rings, it is still possible for the mind to wander upon hearing an indolent professor's _____ reading of testing center rules.

    A. meandering
    B. wily
    C. craven
    D. cacophonous
    E. rambling
    F. harrowing

For Questions 13 to 15, select one answer choice unless otherwise instructed.

Question 13 is based on this passage.

Clementine Hunter worked most of her life on the Melrose Cotton Plantation in Louisiana. She lived from 1887 to 1988 and was one of the most gifted and bold self-taught artists of her time. She painted during the night after a full day of labor. She used any surfaces she could find including wood, wine boxes, gourds, iron pots, and plastic milk jugs. She recalled memories of everyday life on the farm to create expressionless pictures void of perspective and scale.

13. Which of the following inferences can be made from the passage to best support the claim that Clementine Hunter was an intrepid artist?

    Ⓐ Hunter painted when she was surely exhausted after a day of work.
    Ⓑ Hunter experienced more inhumane treatment than other slaves who worked on the plantation.
    Ⓒ Hunter had a particularly strong memory, which made her able to recall even the smallest details from past environments.
    Ⓓ Hunter preferred to create unwonted pieces of art despite the fact that they pictured everyday experiences.
    Ⓔ Hunter lived a relatively long life for the demanding physical labor she was likely put through because she felt art gave her a purpose to live for.

Section 4 - Verbal Reasoning (Easy)

Questions 14 and 15 are based on this passage.

In the world of international business, developing a solid strategic approach for increasing export sales in foreign markets is crucial. An international business strategy is defined as a plan put in place to help a company make a larger international footprint. This should be an extension of a company's practices and values that have been altered in order to meet global needs.

One key aspect of developing a successful international business strategy is prioritizing a carefully selected market entry method. The right path of entering a market can be a launchpad for the success of a company in a foreign region. Companies should focus on target markets where products can be offered competitively.

14. Which word could best replace "launchpad" in the second paragraph?

    A) Division
    B) Kickstart
    C) Mission
    D) Compilation
    E) Reduction

15. How do the first and second paragraphs relate to one another?

    A) The first paragraph defines international business strategy and the second paragraph defines another type of strategy, which is market entry.
    B) The first paragraph outlines one aspect of developing an international business strategy and the second paragraph provides background information on domestic versus international businesses.
    C) The first paragraph provides background information on domestic versus international businesses and the second paragraph outlines one aspect of developing an international business strategy.
    D) The first paragraph provides background information on domestic versus international businesses and the second paragraph defines another type of strategy, which is market entry.
    E) The first paragraph defines international business strategy and the second paragraph outlines one aspect of developing an international business strategy.

Section 4 - Verbal Reasoning (Hard)

23 Minutes | 15 Questions

For Questions 1 to 4, select one entry for each blank from the corresponding column of choices. Fill all the blanks in the way that best completes the text.

1. Zoology broadens our understanding of the conditions that early humans lived in by explaining the adaptive measures taken by animals that existed _____ to them.

A	coetaneously
B	inventively
C	transcendentally
D	incredulously
E	mysteriously

2. Biogerontology, the study of the biological causes of aging, is a field in rapid development. The science continues to creep forward and caress answers out of formerly (i)_____ issues. Even if some of biogerontology's loftier goals are never reached, any (ii)_____ increases in our understanding of human aging will yield tremendous dividends in the fields of chemistry and biology.

Blank (i)	Blank (ii)
A intractable	D specious
B acquiescent	E substantive
C vituperative	F unexplainable

3. He (i)_____ his teachers. Any complex mathematical problem they put in front of him he solved immediately, but even the simplest of grade school calculations he found hopelessly (ii)_____. It was as if his mind was programmed to operate solely on an advanced level, and was incapable of slowing itself down for (iii)_____ work. He seemed to function in the exact opposite way as all of their other students.

Blank (i)	Blank (ii)	Blank (iii)
A conquered	D palliative	G rudimentary
B confounded	E esoteric	H rustic
C cohabitated	F pellucid	I invective

4. Airlines have seen a steady decrease not just in profits, but in (i)_____. Gone are the days when picturesque teams of stewardesses roamed plane aisles and when pilots enjoyed some of the highest professional salaries available. However, like any (ii)_____ enterprise, the industry has managed to evolve. (iii)_____ flying experiences have been toned down to functional affairs, promoting good value above all else.

Blank (i)	Blank (ii)	Blank (iii)
A eminence	D sprightly	G Regal
B loquaciousness	E brusque	H Immaterial
C ire	F indolent	I Nominal

For Questions 5 to 9, select one answer choice unless otherwise instructed.

Questions 5 and 6 are based on this passage.

The theory of plate tectonics explains how Earth's subterranean movements help to create major landforms such as volcanoes. This relatively young theory has transformed our understanding of Earth science by explaining events like earthquakes and mountain growth. However, for some time one nagging question continued to plague geologists: Why are most volcanoes found above subduction zones while others are located far from plate boundaries? In 1963 the question was answered, solidifying the validity of plate tectonics. John Tuzo Wilson, a Canadian geologist, proposed the idea that "hot spots" in the Earth's mantle create volcanic island chains, like the Hawaiian Islands. When a plate shifts over a hot spot, a volcano is formed.

For the following questions, consider each of the choices separately and select all that apply.

5. Based on the information in the passage, which of the following statements are most likely true about the theory of plate tectonics?

   A. The theory of plate tectonics changed how scientists predict how and when earthquakes will occur differently.

   B. The theory of plate tectonics changed the way scientists understand the development of clusters of volcanoes.

   C. The theory of plate tectonics changed the way scientists created hot spots.

6. Which of the following purposes could this passage most likely be used for?

   A. To explain to a group of students how plate tectonics changed the way scientists viewed major landforms.

   B. To begin an essay on the life of John Tuzo Wilson.

   C. To begin an essay about the genesis of volcanic island chains.

Questions 7 to 9 are based on this passage.

Throughout the nineteenth century, the population of Ireland plummeted severely, with only 4.7 million remaining at the end. In the 1820s difficult living conditions in Ireland led to many leaving their home nation and immigrating to America. Just over two and a half decades later a fungus destroyed the potato crops in Ireland, leading to a massive famine in the country. This Potato Blight is credited with kickstarting the second wave of Irish immigrants traveling to America. With starvation rampant, one million Irish people were dead within five years and half a million had found a new country of residence. During this period, Irish people made up almost half of all American immigrants. Previously, it was more common for men to immigrate from Ireland to America. However, during this period entire families were fleeing to the land of opportunity.

7. How does the first sentence of the passage contribute to the development of the passage?

   A. It states the main idea of the passage, which is the fact that the potato famine was incredibly difficult for the Irish population.

   B. It outlines the author's argument and introduces the opposing argument.

   C. It states the main idea of the passage, which is the fact that the reasons for the first wave of Irish immigration were different from the second.

   D. It provides a thesis statement that outlines the timeline and overall point of the passage.

   E. It poses a question to get the reader thinking about the message that the passage aims to prove.

Section 4 - Verbal Reasoning (Hard)

For the following question, consider each of the choices separately and select all that apply.

8. Based on the passage, which of the following is an accurate inference on Irish immigration to America in the nineteenth century?

   - [A] Irish immigrants were likely to return to Ireland following the resolution of the potato famine.
   - [B] Irish men were less likely to immigrate to America near the end of the nineteenth century than Irish women.
   - [C] The drastic decrease in the population of Ireland matched a drastic increase in the population of America.

9. What does the last sentence of the passage suggest about the possible alternative reasons for Irish people immigrating to America?

   - (A) There were fewer international threats to America.
   - (B) The culture and art scene were richer in America.
   - (C) There were more ways to earn a living in America.
   - (D) There was less crime in America.
   - (E) There were fewer restrictive laws in America.

For Questions 10 to 12, select the two answer choices that, when used to complete the sentence, fit the meaning of the sentence as a whole and produce complete sentences that are alike in meaning.

10. Although its name is synonymous with high science and the consequences of its role in the universe require massive cross-disciplinary studies in order to fully appreciate, the String Theory can still be _____ into simple principles by a good teacher.

    - [A] fulminated
    - [B] condensed
    - [C] inverted
    - [D] interpolated
    - [E] reduced
    - [F] expanded

11. While he was familiar with the complexities of magnetic flux, the relationship between alternating and direct currents, and the study of electromagnetism, he still found the Earth's abilities to combine these principles in its geomagnetic reversal to be _____.

    - [A] impenetrable
    - [B] opaque
    - [C] pellucid
    - [D] clear
    - [E] self-effacing
    - [F] insidious

12. Even the most cunning of corporate executives will try to mask his _____ with an effervescent personality in order to remain in the public's good graces.

    - [A] guile
    - [B] acquiescence
    - [C] wiliness
    - [D] obstinacy
    - [E] friendliness
    - [F] vicariousness

For Questions 13 to 15, select one answer choice unless otherwise instructed.

Question 13 is based on this passage.

The purpose of genetic testing for cancer is to examine genes that may increase the risk of certain cancers. About 5 to 10 percent of cancers are most likely hereditary. However, cancer can sometimes appear to be hereditary when it is actually a result of other shared risk factors like toxins in the home or tobacco use. Genetic testing via blood or saliva analysis can help to clarify whether or not an individual possesses a cancer gene that could lead to health problems in the future.

13. Which of the following is the greatest weakness in the author's argument for genetic cancer testing?

    A. The author provides an approximation of 5 percent to 10 percent of cancers being most likely hereditary instead of providing a clear statistic.
    B. The author does not define genetic testing or explains how it works.
    C. The author does not state the purpose of genetic testing for cancer.
    D. In the final sentence, the author reveals that genetic testing is only preventative and cannot be cured with treatment.
    E. The author does not explain which type of cancers can be caught with genetic testing.

Questions 14 and 15 are based on this passage.

In the United States, it is hard to imagine additional political parties existing beyond the Democratic and Republican parties today. However, in the nineteenth century, the American political system included a multitude of parties encompassing an array of philosophies and missions.

Parties such as the Federalist Party were able to put presidents in power. Other parties, such as the Anti-Masonic Party campaigned for social and moral interests. Some political parties only existed briefly before being overtaken by the more dominant parties. A combination of the historical political parties in the United States has formed the basis for the Democratic and Republican parties that are known today. The Democratic-Republican Party and the Whig Party are considered the most relevant predecessors of the current political system. In order to fully understand these parties and the roots of American democracy, one must learn about past political leaders and their ideological positions.

For the following question, consider each of the choices separately and select all that apply.

14. Based on the second paragraph, which of the following can be assumed about American political parties in the nineteenth century?

    A. The Democratic-Republican Party was one of the more dominant political parties of this time period
    B. The Federalist Party was not known for being concerned with social issues.
    C. The Democratic and Republican Parties did not exist at the inception of the United States.

15. How do the first and second paragraphs relate to one another?

    A. The first paragraph explains more about specific political parties and the second paragraph provides a conclusion.
    B. The first paragraph discusses modern political parties before the second paragraph delves into historic political parties.
    C. The first paragraph is an introduction to historic political parties and the second paragraph explains what those political parties were.
    D. The first paragraph delves into historic political parties before the second paragraph discusses modern political parties.
    E. The first paragraph is an introduction to historic political parties and the second paragraph explains how they all faded away over time.

Section 5 - Quantitative Reasoning (Easy)

26 Minutes | 15 Questions

1

List A consists of all odd numbers between 1 and 10 inclusive. List B consists of all even integers between 1 and 10 inclusive.

Quantity A	**Quantity B**
The standard deviation of the numbers in list A	The standard deviation of the numbers in list B

A) Quantity A is greater.
B) Quantity B is greater.
C) The two quantities are equal.
D) The relationship cannot be determined from the information given.

2

If $8y - 4x = 5$ and $y > 800$

Quantity A	**Quantity B**
The least integer value of x	1600

A) Quantity A is greater.
B) Quantity B is greater.
C) The two quantities are equal.
D) The relationship cannot be determined from the information given.

3

Quantity A	**Quantity B**
The perimeter of a rectangle with an area of 24 cm³	22

A) Quantity A is greater.
B) Quantity B is greater.
C) The two quantities are equal.
D) The relationship cannot be determined from the information given.

4

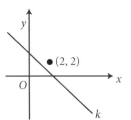

Quantity A	**Quantity B**
The slope of a line perpendicular to line k	The slope of a line parallel to line k

A) Quantity A is greater.
B) Quantity B is greater.
C) The two quantities are equal.
D) The relationship cannot be determined from the information given.

5

Two dice are thrown and the numbers facing up are added.

Quantity A	**Quantity B**
Probability of getting a sum of 5	Probability of getting a sum of 9

A) Quantity A is greater.
B) Quantity B is greater.
C) The two quantities are equal.
D) The relationship cannot be determined from the information given.

Section 5 - Quantitative Reasoning (Easy)

6

How many ways can you arrange the numbers 1, 3, 5, and 7 to get distinct positive four digit numbers?

- (A) 4
- (B) 16
- (C) 24
- (D) 28
- (E) 40

7

In 2022, there were 1,340 residents who voted in the town election. In 2023, there were 1,072 residents who voted in the town election. What was the percent decrease in voters from 2022 to 2023?

- (A) 12.25%
- (B) 20.00%
- (C) 25.00%
- (D) 55.55%
- (E) 80.00%

8

An isosceles triangle has a side length of 4 and a side length of 6. Which of the following could be its perimeter?

Indicate all such answers.

- [A] 14
- [B] 15
- [C] 16
- [D] 17

9

A person that is 6 feet tall is casting a 10 foot shadow. The person is standing x feet away from a tree that is 24 feet tall and is casting a shadow that overlaps with the person's shadow. If the lengths of the shadows are proportional to the heights of the person and the tree, what is the value of x, in feet?

- (A) 5
- (B) 10
- (C) 15
- (D) 20
- (E) 30

10

If a is the sum of all two digit prime numbers and b is the product of prime numbers less than 10, then $a - b = ?$

- (A) 830
- (B) 833
- (C) 1010
- (D) 1026
- (E) 1043

11

A list consists of the values $x - 2$, x, and y where $y > x$. If the median is equal to 18 and the average (arithmetic mean) is 19, what is the value of the greatest number in the list?

☐

Section 5 - Quantitative Reasoning (Easy)

12

A science teacher had x boxes of beakers, each containing 6 beakers. Each student was given b beakers for a class experiment and n beakers were left over. Which of the following represents the number of students in the class?

- A) $\dfrac{6-n}{b}$
- B) $6x - nb$
- C) $\dfrac{6x - n}{b}$
- D) $\dfrac{6x - b}{n}$
- E) $\dfrac{6x + n}{b}$

13

If $x^2 + 2x - 8 = 0$ and $x > \dfrac{1}{3}$, what is the value of x^{-2}?

- A) $-\dfrac{1}{16}$
- B) $-\dfrac{1}{4}$
- C) $\dfrac{1}{16}$
- D) $\dfrac{1}{4}$
- E) 4

14

If a and b are integers, and ab is odd, which of the following must also be odd?

- A) $2a - b$
- B) $ab + b$
- C) $a - ab$
- D) $2b - 2a$
- E) $2ab$

15

A baker needs 2 cups of flour for a cake and 3 cups of flour for a dozen cookies. If they have at most 20 cups of flour, which of the following is a possible combination of cupcakes and cookies they could make?

Indicate all such answers.

- A) 5 cakes and 6 dozen cookies
- B) 3 cakes and 2 dozen cookies
- C) 10 cakes and 0 dozen cookies
- D) 6 cakes and 1 dozen cookies

Section 5 - Quantitative Reasoning (Hard)

23 Minutes | 15 Questions

1

Angelique needs to buy new pans and the pan set she wants has a retail price of *x* dollars. Store *A* is selling the pan set for $25 under the retail price and is having a sale for 15% off. Angelique has a 10% off coupon for Store *B* which is selling the pans for $35 off retail price.

Quantity A	**Quantity B**
The price of the pan set at Store *A* with the sale.	The price of the pan set at Store *B* with the coupon.

Ⓐ Quantity A is greater.
Ⓑ Quantity B is greater.
Ⓒ The two quantities are equal.
Ⓓ The relationship cannot be determined from the information given.

2

Quantity A	**Quantity B**
The numbers of integers between 0 and 500 that contain a 7	95

Ⓐ Quantity A is greater.
Ⓑ Quantity B is greater.
Ⓒ The two quantities are equal.
Ⓓ The relationship cannot be determined from the information given.

3

a and *b* are negative integers.

Quantity A	**Quantity B**
$\dfrac{a-5}{b-5}$	$\dfrac{a}{b}$

Ⓐ Quantity A is greater.
Ⓑ Quantity B is greater.
Ⓒ The two quantities are equal.
Ⓓ The relationship cannot be determined from the information given.

4

In triangle *ABC*, angle *A* is twice as large as angle *B*.

Quantity A	**Quantity B**
The degree measure of Angle *B* plus Angle *C*	The degree measure of Angle *A*

Ⓐ Quantity A is greater.
Ⓑ Quantity B is greater.
Ⓒ The two quantities are equal.
Ⓓ The relationship cannot be determined from the information given.

5

The width of rectangle *A* is 25% greater than the width of rectangle *B*. The length of rectangle *A* is 25% less than the length of rectangle *B*.

Quantity A	**Quantity B**
The perimeter of rectangle *A*	The perimeter of rectangle *B*

Ⓐ Quantity A is greater.
Ⓑ Quantity B is greater.
Ⓒ The two quantities are equal.
Ⓓ The relationship cannot be determined from the information given.

Section 5 - Quantitative Reasoning (Hard)

6

Homes Sold in City A

Price	Number of Homes Sold
Under $150,000	3
$150,000 to $249,999	4
$250,000 to $349,999	6
Over $350,000	4

The prices of homes sold last month in City A are summarized in the table. Which of the following amounts could be the median of the prices?

Indicate all such amounts.

- [A] $125,000
- [B] $165,000
- [C] $235,000
- [D] $265,000
- [E] $345,000
- [F] $385,000

7

If a, b, and c are positive integers and the expression $(bc)(a - b)$ is an even number, which of the following numbers can be even?

  I. $b + c$

  II. $a + b + c$

  III. $a + b$

- (A) None
- (B) I only
- (C) II only
- (D) I and II only
- (E) I, II, and III

8

A theater has a sequence of rows where each row has 6 more seats than the previous row. The first row has r amount of seats and there are a total of 15 rows. Which of the following represents the number of seats that are neither in the 3rd nor the 10th row?

- (A) $r + 630$
- (B) $13r + 105$
- (C) $13r + 564$
- (D) $15r + 90$
- (E) $15r + 630$

9

A race car can travel at a rate of 200 miles per hour. A car race has a 185 mile circuit. Approximately how many minutes would it take the race car to finish the circuit?

- (A) 1
- (B) 2
- (C) 45
- (D) 55
- (E) 60

10

What is the greatest integer n such that $\dfrac{1}{5^n} > 0.0003$?

- (A) 4
- (B) 5
- (C) 8
- (D) 10
- (E) 15

Section 5 - Quantitative Reasoning (Hard)

11

A regular 12-sided polygon has exterior angles all of value $x°$. What is the value of x?

[   ]

12

If $5 \leq d \leq c \leq b \leq a$ and the average (arithmetic mean) of a, b, c, and d is 30, what is the greatest possible value of a?

A) 10
B) 30
C) 80
D) 100
E) 130

13

A shoemaker makes a certain type of shoe for a cost of d dollars. The shoe store pays the shoemaker for the shoe at a price 35% higher than the cost. The shoe store then sells the shoe to the customer for 60% more than the store paid the shoemaker. What did the shoe cost the customer, in dollars?

A) $0.95d$
B) $1.90d$
C) $2.16d$
D) $2.25d$
E) $2.95d$

14

The function f is defined by all numbers x by $f(x) = x(x + 3)(x - 2)$. If t is a number such that $f(t + 1) = 0$. Which of the following could be the number t?

Indicate all such answers.

A) -4
B) -1
C) 0
D) 1
E) 2

15

A teacher found in her morning class of 30 students, the average (arithmetic mean) score on the most recent exam was x. Her afternoon class of 25 students scored an average of 86. Which of the following is the average score of all students in the morning and afternoon classes?

A) $\dfrac{x + 86}{2}$
B) $\dfrac{x + (25)(86)}{2}$
C) $\dfrac{(30)(25) + 86x}{55}$
D) $\dfrac{30x + (25)(86)}{55}$
E) $\dfrac{30x}{55}$

Answer Key

VERBAL REASONING

Section 2		
Q. No.	Correct Answer	Your Answer
1	A	
2	B, E	
3	A, D, H	
4	A	
5	Sociologists... health outcomes.	
6	B, E	
7	A, D	
8	A, B	
9	B, C	
10	A	
11	C	
12	C	

Section 4 (Easy)		
Q. No.	Correct Answer	Your Answer
1	A	
2	A	
3	A, E	
4	B, D, I	
5	C	
6	D	
7	B	
8	However,... boiled fruit.	
9	B	
10	A, D	
11	A, C	
12	A, E	
13	D	
14	B	
15	E	

Section 4 (Hard)		
Q. No.	Correct Answer	Your Answer
1	A	
2	A, E	
3	B, E, G	
4	A, D, G	
5	A, B	
6	A, C	
7	D	
8	C	
9	C	
10	B, E	
11	A, B	
12	A, C	
13	B	
14	A	
15	C	

Answer Key

QUANTITATIVE REASONING

Section 3		
Q. No.	Correct Answer	Your Answer
1	C	
2	C	
3	A	
4	A	
5	C	
6	$\frac{8}{25}$	
7	D	
8	D	
9	E	
10	505.8	
11	D, E, F, G, H	
12	A	

Section 5 (Easy)		
Q. No.	Correct Answer	Your Answer
1	C	
2	B	
3	D	
4	A	
5	C	
6	C	
7	B	
8	A, C	
9	E	
10	B, D, F	
11	23	
12	C	
13	D	
14	A	
15	B, C, D	

Section 5 (Hard)		
Q. No.	Correct Answer	Your Answer
1	D	
2	C	
3	D	
4	D	
5	D	
6	D, E	
7	E	
8	C	
9	D	
10	B	
11	30	
12	E	
13	C	
14	A, B, D	
15	D	

Analytical Writing — Answers & Explanations — Section 1

Analyze an Issue

The sample essay that follows was written in response to the prompt that appeared in the question.

For most young people, setting long-term, realistic goals is the route to lifetime success. Those who choose this route are less likely to experience failure and become discouraged. However, setting long-term, realistic goals is not the best choice for some, and notable exceptions exist today and throughout history that demonstrate the wisdom of their choices. Those with special talents may be better served by seeking immediate fame and recognition.

The world of professional sports is populated by stellar athletes who made the decision to seek immediate fame and recognition. It used to be that those seeking careers as professional athletes would first complete a college degree and, then, enter the draft. In recent years, it has become more common for those with high-level skills to leave college early or never attend at all and be drafted right out of high school. Kobe Bryant and LeBron James went directly from high school to the NBA. At the ripe old age of eighteen, each was making millions of dollars per year. Would four years of college hoops have made them better players? Perhaps not. They may have run the risk of career-ending injuries, ultimately ending any chance of signing multi-year, multi-million dollar contracts. Seeking immediate fame and recognition was the right decision for these two superstars, both of whom have won multiple NBA championships with their teams.

Examples abound in the world of the arts of those whose talents may not have been recognized or rewarded had they been advised to set realistic goals. Every year, hundreds of thousands of hopefuls audition for American Idol. Rather than testing their talents in small clubs or enduring rounds of auditions, these young singers take a single shot at the big time. Only one of them can win the prize, relegating the remainder to the ranks of also-rans. In the case of the winner and a select few of the top ten, great success ensues. In 2012, Phil Phillips won, and the song written for him to sing in the finale became the theme of the American gymnastics team at the London Olympics.

Still a teenager, Phillips gained immediate fame and recognition. Had he not taken a chance on American Idol, he may have continued to sing in church and the school choir, and singing might have become a pleasant pastime in his adult life.

Situations do exist where long-term, realistic goals are more likely to insure success. Medical research comes to mind. As scientists search for cures or treatments for serious, even deadly, diseases or genetic conditions, they must meticulously test and retest, create scientific trials, and seek FDA approval before releasing new drugs on the market. This process can take many years, and virtually none of those individual scientists gains fame or recognition.

A young woman from my home town set a long-term goal for her life when she was a small child. She wanted to be an astronaut when she grew up. Toward that end, Jessica Meir worked hard in school and graduated as valedictorian of her class. She went on to Brown University and obtained her first degree. She completed research at the Scripps Oceanographic institute, becoming an aquanaut. Eventually, she attended the International Space University in Strasbourg, France. At the time of her selection as one of eight in the newest class of NASA astronauts she was an assistant professor of anesthesiology at Harvard. Now in her mid-thirties, Jessica has reached her lifelong goal by systematically setting a course that would lead her there. It is important to note that Jessica was not selected the first time she applied to become an astronaut, but she stayed the course and, eventually, reached her destination.

In reality, the vast majority of us benefit from setting long-term goals. The finish line is far in the future, and we will get there one step at a time. Making long-term, realistic goals will keep us from becoming discouraged or quitting altogether. Even very talented individuals sometimes spurn the chance for early fame and recognition in order to avoid the stress and public scrutiny that attend them. Young people should be encouraged to take the path that best suits their talents and circumstances.

Verbal Reasoning — Answers & Explanations — Section 2

1 **Choice A is correct** because the sentence states that Hollywood exaggerates the flashier aspects of forensic science. It also says that certain types of forensic scientists are smart enough to avoid believing in the sensationalist depiction of their work. Therefore, we want a word that stresses this quality of reservation and common sense. The word "judicious" means sensible. A sensible forensic scientist is the exact type that would not allow himself to get caught up in Hollywood sensationalism.

Choice B is incorrect because "despondent" means depressed. Being depressed would not cause a forensic scientist to ignore Hollywood sensationalism. **Choice C** is incorrect because "imprudent" means irresponsible. Being irresponsible would increase a forensic scientist's chance of getting caught in Hollywood sensationalism. **Choice D** is incorrect because "asinine" means foolish. Once again, if anything, this would increase a forensic scientist's chance of getting caught up in Hollywood sensationalism. **Choice E** is incorrect because "daft" means unintelligent. An unintelligent forensic scientist would have a greater chance of being caught up in Hollywood sensationalism.

2 **Choice B and Choice E are correct** because the passage states that understanding the habitability of distant planets is an "inexact science." Therefore, scientists cannot rely on precise data. The word "inferences" means extrapolations. It makes sense that, in lieu of exact data, scientists would base their predictions of habitability on logical interpretations of observable facts. The passage also suggests that the structure of our own solar system might not represent the usual or typical model that astronomers previously assumed. An "archetype" serves as a recognized model or standard for comparison. It makes sense that our solar system is no longer considered a standard model if scientists keep finding other systems with different structures.

Choice A is incorrect because "fauna" means wildlife. This answer makes no sense in the context of the question. **Choice C** is incorrect because "ambiguities" means contradictions. Scientists would not base their understanding on contradictions. **Choice D** is incorrect because "liability" means responsibility which does not fit the context of the sentence. **Choice F** is incorrect because "recidivist" means a repeated offender. It has no relevance to the scientific study of solar systems or making conclusions based on observational data.

3 **Choice A, Choice D, and Choice H are correct** because the passage states that there is a direct relationship between religious involvement and good health. "Partaking" means involvement. The passage states that involvement in religion provides health benefits. "Correlations" means connections. This makes sense because the passage talks about the factors that affect the connection between health and religion. Finally, for the third blank, the passage states that despite slight complications in the relationship, there is definitely a connection between religion and health. "Incontrovertible" means undeniable. This makes sense because the passage says that in spite of some problems that arise, there is still an undeniable relationship between religion and health.

Choice B is incorrect because "renunciation" means rejection. The passage says that it is religious involvement that increases health benefits, so rejection would mean the opposite. **Choice C** is incorrect because "eloquence" means articulacy. The passage makes no reference to how eloquence within one's religion affects health benefits. **Choice E** is incorrect because "antagonisms" mean resentments. The passage is not talking about resentments between religion and health, it is talking about connections. **Choice F** is incorrect because "contingencies" means emergencies which does not align with the context of the passage. **Choice G** is incorrect because "fungible" means exchangeable which also does not align with the context of the passage. **Choice I** is incorrect because "rescindable" means reversible. As the passage does not highlight the reversal of a connection between religion and health, it does not align with the context of the passage.

4 **Choice A is correct** because the first paragraph explains how social media progressed following the development of the smartphone, the development of the iPhone specifically, and the development of cameras in phones. Then, the second paragraph argues that formal advertising costs money, but simply posting on social media is free for companies. Since the second paragraph claims that social media helps companies grow for free, the first paragraph supports this by explaining how social media has become so widely used. The argument in the second paragraph would be weaker if the initial background information about how social media has become so popular was not provided. If social media was not widely used, advertising on social media would be pointless.

Choice B is incorrect because the first paragraph does not explain how social media has always been cost-effective. Rather, it discusses the evolution of social media since its inception. **Choice C** is incorrect because the first paragraph does not say that social media was originally created strictly for connecting with friends. The first paragraph states that users could connect with family members, colleagues, and like-minded groups as well. Additionally, this information would not support the argument in the second paragraph. **Choice D** is incorrect because the second paragraph does not argue that social media is an easier way to build connections with customers. The ease of use for social media advertising is not discussed, nor is it compared with any other methods of advertising. Additionally, the first paragraph states that users could connect with family members, colleagues, and like-minded groups as well, not just friends. **Choice E** is incorrect because the second paragraph does not make the case that establishing connections with customers through social media is simpler. There is no comparison or discussion of social media advertising's simplicity of use to other forms of advertising. Furthermore, the first paragraph fails to clarify how social media has consistently remained affordable. Instead, it talks about how social media has changed since it first started.

5 **"Sociologists have long worked to establish a link between interaction in social relationships and health outcomes."**

This sentence is correct because it first mentions that sociologists have researched the connection between "social relationships and health outcomes." The previous sentence does not mention any type of research and only presents the fact that relationships impact health. More information regarding the research is provided in the consequent sentences, where it is said that researchers are attempting "to find explanations for this link."

6 **Choice B and Choice E are correct** because the sentence states that the prosecution plans to unveil a witness whose testimony will surprise the defense, but is instead surprised at the witness' unwillingness to cooperate. Thereforefore, we want words that establish a lack of cooperativeness from the witness. Both "obstinacy" and "recalcitrance" fit this context. Both mean stubbornness or resistance. This is exactly the type of behavior that would surprise the prosecution, especially coming from a formerly helpful witness.

Choice A is incorrect because "aimlessness" means pointless, which does not help the prosecution. **Choice C** is incorrect because "simplicity" means straightforwardness, a quality that would help the prosecution, therefore it would not be correct. **Choice D** is incorrect because "insinuations" means allusions or references. You can't make vehement allusions, therefore this answer is wrong. **Choice F** is incorrect because "effervescence" means enthusiastic, which would help rather than hurt the prosecution, therefore it is wrong.

7 **Choice A and Choice D are correct** because the sentence says that if companies focus entirely on making money, then certain ill-desired traits might crop up and hurt their public standing. Therefore, we want to answer choices that describe these ill desired traits. "Villany" and "turpitude" mean depravity or wickedness. These are basic human instincts that can crop up in a "profit at all cost" environment.

Choice B is incorrect because "velocity" means swiftness, which does not describe a negative trait that could be associated with a company because it obsesses too much over money. **Choice C** is incorrect because "compliance" means the tendency to be agreeable. Again, this characteristic would actually be a good thing for the company and would not undermine its legitimacy with the public. **Choice E** is incorrect because "indolence" means laziness, which does not align with the "profit at all cost" ethos described in the passage. **Choice F** is incorrect because "articulacy" means the ability to explain oneself, which is not a bad thing and does not hurt a company in the public eye.

8 **Choice A and Choice B are correct** because this question sets up a pair of opposites. The business will not survive with one type of leader, but it will survive with a strong leader who has enough grit to make tough decisions. Therefore, the type of leader under which the business will not survive must be the opposite of strong and sound. "Craven" which refers to a lack of even the rudiments of courage, and "impolitic" which refers to being unwise or failing to display prudence both fit with the context provided.

Choice C is incorrect because "limpid" means transparent or easily understood, which does not align with the context of the passage. **Choice D** is incorrect because "ribald" which means humorously vulgar or coarse, does not provide an opposite meaning to "strong" or "brave."

Choice E is incorrect because "brusque" means curt, rough, or abrupt in manner, but does not provide an opposite meaning to "strong" or "brave." Choice F is incorrect because "prosaic" meaning uninspired, flat, or dull, likely defines a poor leader but does not reflect an opposite meaning of strong and sound.

9 **Choice B and Choice C are correct** because the sentence points out that some nations have implemented low tax rates to bring businesses into their countries. As they are attempting to encourage more business growth, they would fear the opposite action – discouraging business investment. The correct answers must reflect the idea of stopping business investment. The correct answers are therefore Choice B, "restricting" because it refers to placing limitations, and Choice C, "obstructing" refers to blocking the natural progression of something.

Choice A is incorrect because "promulgating" means putting a law into effect by formal declaration, which does not align with the context of the passage. Choice D is incorrect because "averring" refers to formally declaring something to be true, which does not align with the context of the passage. Choice E is incorrect because "congealing" means to change from a fluid to a solid state by freezing, which does not align with the context of the passage. Choice F is incorrect because "glowering" refers to staring angrily or sullenly, which does not align with the context of the passage.

10 **Choice A is correct** because all facts regarding the liver's functions are stated in the sentence and are accurate based on the passage. The information is well summarized because it does not offer excessive details regarding the liver's other characteristics.

Choice B is incorrect because although the sentence is true, it omits some of the liver's most critical functions, such as generating bile and storing vitamins and minerals. As a result, it only mentions one function of the liver rather than offering a thorough overview of its functions. Choice C is incorrect because although the sentence is true, it does not summarize the functions of the liver well. It includes unnecessary details, such as its color and location, while leaving out important details, like the functions of the liver. Choice D is incorrect because it fails to mention some of the other important functions of the liver like the production of bile and the filtration of blood. Therefore, it does not provide a concise summary but a detailed restatement of one aspect of the liver. Choice E is incorrect because it does not include some of the liver's other vital functions, such as "producing bile" and "creating nutrients." Furthermore, it contains extraneous information, such as the color and shape of the liver.

11 **Choice C is correct** because "carried out" in this context means that a task is completed or performed. The word, "accomplished" also means completed or performed. Therefore, "accomplished" could replace, "carried out" without changing the meaning of the sentence.

Choice A is incorrect because "foregone" means something has passed. It does not connect well with the idea of actively performing a task. Choice B is incorrect because "desecrated" means to treat something sacred with disrespect or to violate it. It has a negative connotation that does not match the neutral or positive action implied by "carried out." Choice D is incorrect because "shown" means to display or reveal something. While it involves an action, it does not capture the sense of execution or completion that "carried out" conveys. In addition, since the liver's functions take place inside the human body, they cannot be shown. Choice E is incorrect because "sorted out" is a phrase that suggests organizing or resolving something, which may involve a task but lacks the broader implication of a completed action. It is too specific and does not fit the same context as "carried out" as sorting is not a part of the liver's function of producing bile.

12 **Choice C is correct** because the author describes all of the functions of the liver and calls it a "vital, powerful, and busy organ." Therefore, the author would most likely use the term "active" to describe the liver, which refers to engaging in energetic activities on a daily basis.

Choice A is incorrect because "indolent" means lazy or inactive. Describing the liver as indolent would be inaccurate, as it performs numerous critical functions in the body. Choice B is incorrect because "uninvolved" means a lack of participation or engagement. Since the author states that the liver is heavily involved in many biological processes, such as filtering blood and aiding digestion, the author would be unlikely to use the term "uninvolved" to characterize the liver. Choice D is incorrect because "nugatory" means something of little value or importance. The author states that the liver is "vital" for survival and bodily function, so describing it as nugatory would be misleading. Choice E is incorrect because "inert" means lacking the power to move or get things done quickly. The author states that the liver is quite the opposite, showcasing significant activity and involvement in various bodily functions. Hence, using the term "inert" would be inappropriate.

Quantitative Reasoning — Answers & Explanations — Section 3

1 **Choice C is correct** because the reflex angle ∠POQ can be found by identifying that the central angle ∠POQ is equivalent to the addition of the angles ∠OPR and ∠OQR. This is because the central angle is always equal to the sum of the angles subtended by the same arc PQ. Therefore, ∠POQ = ∠OPR + ∠OQR which equals 70° + 50° = 120°. The reflex angle is 360° minus this angle so 360° − 120° = 240°. This means the two quantities are equal.

Choice A is incorrect because the reflex angle ∠POQ equals 240°. **Choice B** is incorrect because the reflex angle ∠POQ equals 240°. **Choice D** is incorrect because it is possible to solve for the reflex angle ∠POQ.

2 **Choice C is correct** because the area of the trapezoidal region and the area of the rectangular region are equal to 66.

1. To find the area of the trapezoidal region, use the formula $A = \frac{b_1 + b_2}{2} h$. Plugging into this formula you would get $A = \frac{10 + 12}{2}(6)$ which equals 66.
2. To find the area of the rectangular region, use the formula $A = bh$. Plugging into this formula you would get $A = 6(11)$ which equals 66.
3. Therefore, both areas are equal to 66 which means that the two quantities are equal.

Choice A is incorrect because the area of the two regions are equal. **Choice B** is incorrect because the area of the two regions are equal. **Choice D** is incorrect because it is possible to solve for the areas of the two regions.

3 **Choice A is correct** because Quantity A will always give a positive answer and Quantity B will always be negative. Since a positive number will always be greater than a negative number, Quantity A is greater. For Quantity A, the value of x is negative based on the given inequality that shows x is less than 0. A negative number squared will always be positive. The value of y is also positive given the inequality shows it is greater than 0. So $x^2 + y$ is always positive. For Quantity B, y squared will always be positive and x will always be negative. A negative minus a positive will always result in a negative.

Choice B is incorrect because Quantity B would result in a negative based on the inequality relationship given. **Choice C** is incorrect because it is not possible for the two quantities to be equal. **Choice D** is incorrect because it is possible to use the given information to make a comparison between Quantity A and Quantity B.

4 **Choice A is correct** because x is equal to 9. To solve for x, use the range given and work backward. It can be determined that x and $\sqrt{x}$ must be the smallest and largest number since there is no possible way to get a range of 6 using 4 and $\sqrt{10}$. To solve for x, arrange the numbers in order as $\sqrt{x}$, $\sqrt{10}$, 4, and x. If the range is 6, $x - \sqrt{x}$ must be equal to 6. The only possible values for $\sqrt{x}$ would be 1, 2, or 3 since $x > 0$ and $\sqrt{x}$ has to be less than $\sqrt{10}$ which is a little more than 3. Therefore, the $\sqrt{x}$ must be 3 and that would make $x = 9$ and $9 - 3 = 6$.

Choice B is incorrect because $x = 9$ which is greater than 3. **Choice C** is incorrect because $x = 9$ and is not equal to 3 so the two quantities are not equal. **Choice D** is incorrect because it is possible to solve for x and compare.

5 **Choice C is correct** because $x + y = 10$. To find x, find the product of 14,042 and 6,313 which is 88,647,146. The unit digit of this product is 6. To solve for y, find the product of 512,821 and 41,240 which is 21,148,738,040. The tens digit of this product is 4. Therefore, $x = 6$ and $y = 4$ so $x + y = 10$.

Choice A is incorrect because this would be the answer if you found the unit digit for both numbers and said $x = 6$ and $y = 0$. **Choice B** is incorrect because this would result from a miscalculation error. **Choice D** is incorrect because this would result from a miscalculation error. **Choice E** is incorrect because this would result from a miscalculation error.

6 The correct answer is $\frac{8}{25}$ because the snack brand with the highest sum of the three average ratings was snack brand B. Snack brand A's sum of the rankings was 10 (5.0 + 2.8 + 2.2), snack brand B's sum of the rankings was 12.8 (4.3 + 4.0 + 4.5), and snack brand C's sum of the rankings was 9 (3.2 + 4.8 + 1.0). Snack brand B was ranked last in ratings ACB and CAB. ACB is 25% of the ranks and CAB is 7% of the rankings. If you add 25% and 7% you get 32%. 32% as a fraction of all rankings is $\frac{32}{100}$ which can be simplified to be $\frac{8}{25}$.

7 **Choice D is correct** because you can find the percent snack brand A's average flavor rating is greater than snack brand C's average flavor rating by using the percent

42 | Practice Tests for the GRE

1 Quantitative Reasoning   Answers & Explanations   Section 3

increase formula $\left|\frac{final - initial}{initial}\right| \times 100$. The initial value will be snack brand *C*'s average flavor rating and the final value will be snack brand *A*'s average flavor rating. Plugging these into the equation you would get $\left|\frac{5.0 - 3.2}{3.2}\right| \times 100$ which would equal to 56.25% which is approximately 56%.

Choice A is incorrect because you might choose this number if you subtracted the ratings and attempted to convert it to a percent which would be the incorrect way to solve. **Choice B** is incorrect because this answer would result if you took the difference of the two ratings and divided by snack brand *A*'s rating which would not give you the correct answer. **Choice C** is incorrect because this would result from a calculation error. **Choice E** is incorrect because this is what percent snack brand *C*'s average rating of flavor is of snack brand *A*'s average rating of flavor, not the percent increase.

8 **Choice D is correct** because the difference between the total price rating and the total healthiness rating is 390 which is approximately 400. To find how much greater the total price rating is compared to the total healthiness rating, follow these steps:

1. Use the average value to find the sum of all values for price rating. Average = $\frac{sum\ of\ values}{number\ of\ values}$ so the sum of the values can be found by multiplying each average by the number of values which we are told is 100 customers. Plugging each of the given averages into the formula for price rating, you would get 280 for snack brand *A*, 400 for snack brand *B*, and 480 for snack brand *C* for a total of 1160.

2. Doing the same calculations for healthiness ratings gives you 220 for snack brand *A*, 450 for snack brand *B*, and 100 for snack brand *C* which gives a total of 770.

3. The difference of these totals would get us the answer, 1160 – 770 = 390 which can round to 400.

Choice A is incorrect because this is just the total number of customers and does not account for the averages. **Choice B** is incorrect because 200 is not the difference in ratings for all three snack brands. **Choice C** is incorrect because this answer might result from a rounding or calculation error. **Choice E** is incorrect because 500 is not the difference in ratings for all three snack brands.

9 **Choice E is correct** because there are 7 documents that are 250 words long and 49 documents that are 500 words long. You can figure out how many documents are 250 words long by determining that $\frac{7}{8}$ of the documents at 500 words long. Set up the proportion $\frac{7}{8} = \frac{500}{total}$ to find the total documents to be 56. If 49 of the documents are 500 words long, the remaining 7 must be 250 words long. Multiply 7 by 250 to get 1750 words and multiply 49 times 500 to get 24,500 words. Add these together to get 26,250 words total.

Choice A is incorrect because this is the total number of documents, not words. **Choice B** is incorrect because this is the total words for the 250-word count documents and does not include the total for the 500-word count documents. **Choice C** is incorrect because this number would result from a calculation error. **Choice D** is incorrect because this is just the number of words for the 500-word count documents. It does not include the 250-word count documents.

10 **The correct answer is 505.8**

The area of the entire figure is πr^2, and the area of the unshaded portion is $\pi(r - s)^2$. The area of the shaded area is $\pi(r^2 - (r - s)^2)$.

Therefore, $\pi(15^2 - (15 - 7)^2) = 161\pi$ which is approximately 505.8.

11 **Choices D, E, F, G and H are correct.**

If the cyclist rode 225 *miles*, rounded to the nearest *mile*, and took 5 *hours*, rounded to the nearest *hour*, he traveled between 224.5 *miles* and 225.5 *miles*, and took between 4.5 and 5.5 *hours*. The maximum speed can be obtained by dividing the largest possible number of *miles* (225.5) by the SMALLEST (4.5) number of *hours*. Similarly, the minimum speed can be obtained by dividing the smallest number of *mile* (224.5) by the LARGEST number of *hours* (5.5):

$$\text{Maximum speed} = \frac{225.5}{4.5} = \frac{225.5(2)}{4.5(2)} = \frac{451}{9} = 50\frac{1}{9} mph$$

$$\text{Minimum speed} = \frac{224.5}{5.5} = \frac{224.5(2)}{5.5(2)} = \frac{449}{11} = 40\frac{9}{11} mph$$

Therefore, the cyclist speed must be between 40 and 51 *mph*. So out of all the given options 41, 43, 44, 48 and 50 are valid.

Choice A is incorrect because 37 is not in the range of 40 to 51 mph. **Choice B** is incorrect because 39 is not in the range of 40 to 51 mph. **Choice C** is incorrect because the speed cannot equal 40 mph. **Choice I** is incorrect because the speed cannot equal 51 mph. **Choice J** is incorrect because 52 is not in the range of 40 to 51 mph.

12 **Choice A is correct** because based on the relationship between *A* and *B*, if *A* decreases by 19%, *B* has to increase in a manner that follows the defined relationship. To solve:

- First, write out the equation to show how *A* and *B* are related. Since *A* is inversely related to the square of *B*, $A = \frac{k}{B^2}$ where *k* is an unknown constant.
- If *A* is decreased by 19%, that means we are left with 81% of the original value of *A*. We can denote this as 0.81*A*.
- Since *k* is a constant and would remain the same no matter what happens to *A* and *B*, we can rearrange the original equation to be $k = AB_1^2$, and then from the changes to *A*, we also know $k = 0.81 AB_2^2$.
- Since *k* is the same in both statements, you can set the equations equal to each other to get: $AB_1^2 = 0.81 AB_2^2$. Divide both sides by *A* to get $B_1^2 = 0.81 B_2^2$.
- Divide both sides by 0.81 to get $B_2^2 = \frac{B_1^2}{0.81}$. Square both sides to get $B_2 = 1.11 B_1$. This means *B* was increased by 11%.

Choice B is incorrect because the proportions are not directly related so the percent decrease will not equal the percent increase. **Choice C** is incorrect because you would get approximately this answer if you only used the inverse relationship and forgot to square *B*. **Choice D** is incorrect because this does not relate to the relationship between *A* and *B*. **Choice E** is incorrect because you do not get the percent decrease by subtracting 19% from 100%.

1 Verbal Reasoning (Easy)   Answers & Explanations   Section 4

1 **Choice A is correct** because this sentence expresses the importance of literary devices. It says that stories with identical plots can look very different if different literary techniques are used. "Indispensable" means essential. Given the effects that literary devices can have on a story, they can accurately be described as essential.

Choice B is incorrect because "antagonistic" means opposed. Literary devices help to create a unique work of literature, so this word is wrong. **Choice C is incorrect** because "allegorical" means symbolic. This answer might be tempting because an allegory is a literary device, but literary techniques are not described as being symbolic of anything in this sentence. **Choice D is incorrect** because "anachronistic" means out of chronological order. Literary devices are never described as being out of chronological order, so this answer is wrong. **Choice E is incorrect** because "insufficient" means lacking. Literary devices are described as being very useful in crafting stories, so this answer is wrong.

2 **Choice A is correct** because the sentence states that something good that occurs emotionally outweighs the physical strain of running. Choice A is correct because "catharsis" means purification, which makes sense as the man would consider emotional purification to be worth the physical pain that would result from running.

Choice B is incorrect because "indolence" means laziness. The middle-aged man would not exert his body in order to become emotionally lazy. **Choice C is incorrect** because "exacerbation" is the act of making something worse. Again, the man would not insist on running if it made him feel worse emotionally. **Choice D is incorrect** because "calamity" means disaster. The man would not exert himself to achieve an emotional disaster. **Choice E is incorrect** because "inanity" means pointlessness. This, also, is not something the man would be striving for.

3 **Choice A and Choice E are correct** because upon reading the entire passage, it becomes apparent that Einstein's theory of relativity is the foundation on which modern science is built. This, of course, leads to ironic situations when physicists try to disprove it, because the very experiments designed to disprove it are based on the tenets established in the theory. The first blank talks about the theory of relativity's relation to science. "Axiomatic" means "accepted." The passage stresses that the "central tenets" of the theory of relativity are "unequivocal" so the theory can safely be called "axiomatic." The second sentence comments on the inherent contradiction of trying to disprove a theory while using the same tenets that have been established by the theory. Choice E best fits the answer as "ironically" means paradoxically as it would be paradoxical to try to disprove a theory using that same theory as an intellectual foundation.

Choice B is incorrect because "equivocal" means vague. If the theory is so definite then it cannot be vague. **Choice C is incorrect** because "arcane" means mysterious. If the theory is so universally accepted then it cannot be mysterious. **Choice D is incorrect** because "disparagingly" means disapprovingly. This answer does not make sense in the context of the sentence. **Choice F is incorrect** because "redundantly" means superfluously. Once again, this answer does not make sense in the context of the sentence.

4 **Choice B, Choice D, and Choice I are correct** because the passage states how healthcare costs in the United States are threatening the country's entire economy. Choice B is correct because "calamity" means "disaster" which makes sense given that the healthcare industry in the United States is causing so many problems that it can accurately be described as a "disaster." For the second blank, the passage presents data supporting the assertions being made, and "corroborate" essentially means support. Thus, Choice D is correct. For the third blank, the passage talks about how healthcare costs are a problem for the entire country. The term "communal" means collective and it fits well with the context because the healthcare problems in the United States affect the entire country, making it a "collective" concern.

Choice A is incorrect because "windfall" means unexpected gains resulting from lucky circumstances. Obviously, if the healthcare industry is costing the country so much money, it cannot be considered a payout. **Choice C is incorrect** because "evolution" means progress. The passage talks about how pervasive the problems are in the healthcare industry. It does not mention what progress is being made to deal with it. **Choice E is incorrect** because "mitigate" means lessen. The data that the passage provides in regard to American healthcare does not lessen the argument being made. They support it. **Choice F is incorrect** because "exonerate" means forgive. The numbers do not forgive the argument being made. Again, they support it. **Choice G is incorrect** because "reserved" means detached or distant. Obviously, if the problem affects so many individuals, it cannot be distant. **Choice H is incorrect** because "counter-intuitive" means going against intuition. There is nothing in the passage to

For more practice, visit www.vibrantpublishers.com

suggest that the damaging effects of healthcare costs go against anybody's intuition about healthcare.

5 **Choice C is correct** because the author explains that copper is an outstanding conductive material because it allows electrons to flow easily. The author mentions that copper is one of the greatest conductors of electricity out of all the conductors so it is clear that other conductive materials exist.

Choice A is incorrect because the passage does not state that copper is the only conductive material. It explains copper's usefulness as a conductor but also introduces the concept of insulators, which implies that other materials, besides copper, can conduct electricity. **Choice B** is incorrect because the author expresses that copper, "can be easily manipulated, shaped, and cut into various sizes" and that copper "resists erosion well." Therefore, copper is used in electrical systems for more than just its conductive characteristics.

6 **Choice D is correct** because the passage explains very basic concepts such as the definitions of "electricity" "conductor" and "insulator." It is unlikely that electricians with experience would need this information, but new trainees might. The passage also describes why copper is often used in electrical systems by stating it is an excellent conductor that resists erosion and can be easily manipulated.

Choice A is incorrect because a semi-seasoned electrician apprentice would know the meaning of "electricity" "conductor" and "insulator." This passage is clearly targeting a less experienced audience. **Choice B** is incorrect because the passage does not provide any information about the purpose of an electrician's services. Rather, it discusses the basics of electrical systems and the purpose that copper serves. **Choice C** is incorrect because the passage is written in an informative style and does not use any persuasive tactics. Also, if the audience were an electrical company the basic concepts of electricity, conductors, and insulators would not need to be described. **Choice E** is incorrect because this passage does not explain the history of copper beyond stating that it has been used in electrical systems for "hundreds of years." Contrarily, the passage discusses why copper is so useful in electrical systems today.

7 **Choice B is correct** because beeswax candles are described as, "not often seen in commoners' homes because of their high price." In other words, commoners or ordinary people were likely to still use lower-priced candles to brighten their homes. Beeswax candles were said to produce less smoke. Therefore, the tallow candles used by poorer citizens would create smokier air in homes.

Choice A is incorrect because there is no reason to assume the importance of church ceremonies to common people or wealthy people. The sentence simply states that beeswax candles were used for church ceremonies, so this is not relevant. **Choice C** is incorrect because the passage does not suggest that people did not feel comfortable using beeswax candles in their homes, but states that the high price of beeswax candles deterred them from using them at home. **Choice D** is incorrect because beeswax candles are described as, "not often seen in commoners' homes because of their high price." In other words, wealthy people would be able to use this superior type of candle in their homes. **Choice E** is incorrect because the passage does not suggest that church leaders lit their own homes with beeswax candles, but only that they were used in church ceremonies. The type of candles that church leaders used in their own homes cannot be assumed unless their financial status was revealed.

8 **"However, in other regions of the world ancient candles were made from a profusion of materials like rice paper, insect-derived wax, seeds, tree nuts, and boiled fruit."**

This sentence mentions various places of the world producing ancient candles with different ingredients than the Romans. As a result, candles evolved independently of Rome's creation.

9 **Choice B is correct** because "profusion" means an abundance or large quantity of something, and "plethora" means a large amount of something. These definitions are very similar, and both describe the multitude of ingredients that went into the creation of ancient candles around the world.

Choice A is incorrect because "infusion" means an extract is introduced into something. However, this is not how ancient candles were made, and it cannot be assumed that any infusions were used. "Profusion" simply means a large amount of something. These two words do not mean the same thing. **Choice C** is incorrect because "intimation" means an indication or hint. This word would not apply in the context of the sentence because a "hint" of ingredients would not make sense. Additionally, a hint describes a small quantity, which would be the opposite of a profusion. **Choice D** is incorrect because "scanty" means a small or insufficient amount. This is the opposite of "profusion" which means an abundance or large quantity of something. There were many ingredients used in ancient candles, not a scanty amount. **Choice E** is incorrect because "insipid" means lacking flavor or vigor. This word cannot be applied to describe candles, but it also does not match the many diverse ingredients described in the sentence.

10 **Choice A and Choice D are correct** because this sentence says that authors will sometimes write fictional stories in which they embed the truth because of a certain personality trait they possess. If they are hesitant to tell direct information about themselves it can be inferred that they are shy. "Reticence" and "reserve" both mean a restraint or silence. An author would definitely want to use a roman à clef to overcome their own personal restraint in divulging autobiographical details.

Choice B is incorrect because "arrogance" means conceit or egotism. This doesn't make sense because an arrogant person would want to write about themselves. **Choice C** is incorrect because "bombast" is the desire to talk frequently and fiercely. This doesn't make sense because a bombastic person would want to talk about themselves. **Choice E** is incorrect because "structure" means order, which does not fit the context as an author cannot overcome his or her own sense of order. **Choice F** is incorrect because "cynicism" means suspicion. This also doesn't make sense because writing a roman à clef would not necessarily help a writer overcome their own cynicism.

11 **Choice A and Choice C are correct** because the scholars who read ancient documents are trying to take something instructive away from the experience, not trying to adopt the documents wholesale. Therefore, we want words that establish these scholars as trying to learn something. "Didactic" and "educational" both mean instructive. It makes sense that, even though the scholars don't want the word–for–word adoption of ancient law, they do want to learn from it for the benefit of modern law.

Choice B is incorrect because "infallible" means unfailing. If these documents were unfailing then scholars would want to adopt them directly, so this can't be an answer. **Choice D** is incorrect because "argumentative" means challenging. This answer does fit (because the scholars could want to see how ancient cultures argued for legal concepts) but there is no second choice that matches it. **Choice E** is incorrect because "vituperative" means scathing or malicious. Reading the malicious properties of ancient works would not be of any benefit to modern scholars. **Choice F** is incorrect because "preposterous" means absurd or outrageous. Scholars looking to learn new ideas from old documents would not be concerned with the absurd properties of said documents.

12 **Choice A and Choice E are correct** because the proctor's style of reading the testing information has distracted a focused student. Therefore, we want words that talk about lack of focus for our answer. The words "meandering" and "rambling" both mean long-winded and tedious. A reading that fits this description would bore a student, especially one who entered the testing center with such determination.

Choice B is incorrect because "wily" means clever or crafty, often in a way that is deceitful. This does not fit the context because the reading of testing center rules is not something that is typically clever or crafty—it is straightforward information. **Choice C** is incorrect because "craven" means cowardly or timid, which is not applicable in describing a professor's reading style. It doesn't relate to the act of reading itself. **Choice D** is incorrect because "cacophonous" means harsh or jarring. While a monotonous or harsh voice might be annoying, this word does not directly convey the sense of boredom or distraction due to lengthiness, which is the focus of the sentence. **Choice F** is incorrect because "harrowing" means extremely upsetting or distressing. While a harrowing reading could distract students, it does not accurately depict the reading of procedural rules, which are usually straightforward rather than distressing.

13 **Choice D is correct** because "intrepid" is defined as bold and unabashed. A bold artist would be an artist who confidently takes risks in art. Therefore, painting on surfaces that were unusual and unpredictable is an example of Hunter being a bold artist.

Choice A is incorrect because painting after a long day of work is not necessarily what made Hunter a bold artist. This would make her a tireless or resilient artist. Additionally, this is not an inference but is explicitly stated in the text. **Choice B** is incorrect because the text implies that she worked as a slave, but does not indicate that her fellow slaves were treated any differently. In addition, this fact would not necessarily support the claim that she was a bold artist. **Choice C** is incorrect because

Verbal Reasoning (Easy) — Answers & Explanations — Section 4

painting from memory is not necessarily a bold thing to do. Additionally, the passage implies that she had a superb enough memory to paint without physical stimuli, but it cannot be assumed that her memory was strong enough to recall even the smallest details. **Choice E is incorrect** because the long life that Hunter lived is irrelevant to the fact that she was a bold artist.

14 **Choice B is correct** because "launchpad" in this context means something that sets an enterprise in motion. Similarly, "kickstart" refers to starting something.

Choice A is incorrect because "division" means separating something into parts. This is not something that would be desired by a business looking to expand, and this word does not mean the same thing as "launchpad." **Choice C** is incorrect because "mission" means an important assignment. Following the right path to enter a market is not the mission of a company, but the starting point, which the word "launchpad" refers to. **Choice D** is incorrect because "compilation" means assembling different items. This is not relevant in the context of the passage because nothing is being brought together. **Choice E** is incorrect because "reduction" means making something smaller. This is the opposite of what a business would be trying to do when expanding globally.

15 **Choice E is correct** because the first paragraph provides background information and a definition of the term, "international business strategy." Then, the second paragraph discusses one aspect of developing an international business strategy, which is selecting a method to enter the market.

Choice A is incorrect because although the first paragraph does define international business strategy, the second paragraph does not define a different type of strategy. Rather, it discusses one aspect of developing an international business strategy. This aspect is selecting a method for market entry. **Choice B** is incorrect because it switches the main arguments in the first and second paragraph. The second paragraph outlines one aspect of developing an international business strategy, not the first. Neither the first or second paragraphs provide any information on domestic businesses or compare them to international businesses. **Choice C** is incorrect because although the second paragraph does outline one aspect of developing an international business strategy, the first paragraph does not provide any information on domestic businesses or compare them to international businesses. **Choice D** is incorrect because the first paragraph does not provide any information on domestic businesses. Also, the second paragraph does not define a different type of strategy. Rather, it just discusses one aspect of developing an international business strategy.

Verbal Reasoning (Hard) — Answers & Explanations

1 **Choice A is correct** because "coetaneously" means existing or occurring at the same time. In the context of the sentence, it suggests that zoology helps us understand the conditions that early humans lived in by studying the adaptive measures taken by animals that were alive during the same period or era.

Choice B is incorrect because "inventively" means creatively. This answer does not make sense in the context of the question. **Choice C** is incorrect because "transcendentally" means supernaturally. This answer also does not fit well. A supernatural quality wouldn't shed light on the conditions that distant humans lived in. **Choice D** is incorrect because "incredulously" means disbelievingly but this answer does not explain why studying these animals would help in understanding early humans. **Choice E** is incorrect because "mysteriously" means strangely. This answer does not make sense in the context of the question.

2 **Choice A and Choice E are correct** because the first two sentences talk about how biogerontology has managed to develop rapidly and solve issues. If these issues weren't solved before then they must have been difficult, so the word needs to fit that description. The word "intractable" in fact, means difficult or complex. This term perfectly describes formerly unresolved issues. For the second blank, Choice E is correct as the word "substantive" refers to significant or meaningful increases, which aligns with the idea that even small advancements in understanding human aging can lead to "tremendous" benefits in related fields.

Choice B is incorrect because "acquiescent" means "amenable" but the correct answer should be the opposite of this term. **Choice C** is incorrect because "vituperative" means insulting. This answer does not make sense as it is not close enough to the desired definition of "difficult." **Choice D** is incorrect because "specious" means misleading. Misleading research would not benefit the scientific community. **Choice F** is incorrect because "unexplainable" means incapable of being accounted for. Of course, unexplainable increases in our understanding would not benefit the scientific community, nor would they be an adequate substitute for "lofty" ones.

3 **Choice B, Choice E, and Choice G are correct** because this passage states that the student's teachers don't understand how his mind operates. "Confounded" means "confused." For the second blank, the passage says how the young man finds difficult questions easy, but finds ostensibly easy questions difficult. "Esoteric" means puzzling. If the young man is not able to answer a question, he must find it to be cryptic and confusing. For the third blank, the passage describes the type of problem that the young man cannot solve. The passage has already stated that his mind works "solely on an advanced level" so it must be simple questions that confuse him. "Rudimentary" means "basic." If the young man is only capable of working "on an advanced level" then he would have a hard time with basic work.

Choice A is incorrect because "conquered" means dominated. There is no indication in the passage that the young man uses his genius to dominate his teachers. **Choice C** is incorrect because "cohabitated" means lived together, which does not fit the context of the question. **Choice D** is incorrect because "palliative" means calming. The young man would not find questions that confuse him to be calming. **Choice F** is incorrect because "pellucid" means clear. The young man would not find difficult questions to be clear, or else he would be able to solve them. **Choice H** is incorrect because "rustic" means "rural" which does not fit the context of math problems. **Choice I** is incorrect because "invective" means diatribe. This word does not make sense in the context of the question.

4 **Choice A, Choice D, and Choice G are correct** because the passage states how airlines haven't just lost their financial standing, but the prestige of the people working within the industry. "Eminence" means "prestige." This makes sense. From "picturesque teams of stewardesses" to pilots enjoying high salaries, there clearly used to be prestige within the airline industry. For the second blank, the passage is talking about how the airline industry has managed to evolve. It takes an agile industry to evolve. "Sprightly" means "lively" or "agile." Being lively and agile would allow an industry to evolve and fix itself. For the third blank, the passage is talking about how flying experiences have been toned down and become more functional. Therefore, we can infer that they focused on other approaches to the flying experience before toning it down. "Regal" means "magnificent." If the flying experience has been toned down to "functional" then it must have been something better than functional before. "Regal" fits this description.

Choice B is incorrect because "loquaciousness" means "talkativeness." There's no mention in the passage about talkativeness in relation to the airline industry. **Choice C** is incorrect because "ire" means "anger." The article

Verbal Reasoning (Hard) — Answers & Explanations — Section 4

doesn't make any reference to any anger that the airline industry used to have. **Choice E** is incorrect because "brusque" means "rude." This is not a quality that would help an industry evolve. **Choice F** is incorrect because "indolent" means "lazy." This is not a quality that would help an airline evolve, either. **Choice H** is incorrect because "immaterial" means "unimportant." It would be hard to tone down further a flying experience that is "unimportant." **Choice I** is incorrect because "nominal" means minor. Again, it would be hard to tone down a flying experience from "minor" and get it to "functional." If anything, it would have to be toned up.

5 **Choice A is correct** because the passage states that plate tectonics helped geologists learn why earthquakes were occurring. Therefore, scientists would most likely predict how and when earthquakes would occur differently. **Choice B is correct** because the passage states that plate tectonics helped geologists understand volcanic island chains and how they were created on hot spots. Therefore, scientists would most likely understand the reason behind the development of clusters of volcanoes.
Choice C is incorrect because scientists do not create hot spots. According to the passage, hot spots are naturally occurring phenomena in the Earth's mantle that lead to the creation of volcanic island chains. However, the theory did help geologists understand hot spots better.

6 **Choice A is correct** because the passage is written in an informative style and the main idea of the passage is how plate tectonics changed geologists' perspective on the formation of volcanoes. **Choice C is correct** because the second half of the passage discusses how plate tectonics impacted scientists' understanding of volcanic island chains. This could lead to an essay that provides further information on the genesis of volcanic island chains.
Choice B is incorrect because the mention of Wilson only serves the purpose of explaining how an understanding of hot spots contributed to the theory of plate tectonics. If an essay were to be written about Wilson's life, it would likely begin with background information on him such as his hometown and birth year, rather than the theory of plate tectonics.

7 **Choice D is correct** because the definition of a thesis is a statement put forward to be proved. This sentence states the idea that the population of Ireland plummeted severely, which is then proved by the remainder of the passage. It also outlines the timeline of the period that is discussed during the rest of the passage. **Choice A** is incorrect because though the first sentence states the main idea of the passage, it does not talk about the potato famine. Rather, the main idea is that the population of Ireland plummeted in the nineteenth century. **Choice B** is incorrect because the author does not explain any counterarguments made. **Choice C** is incorrect because though the first sentence states the main idea of the passage, the difference in the reasons between the first and second waves of immigrants is not the main idea of the passage. Rather, the main idea is that the population of Ireland plummeted in the nineteenth century. **Choice E** is incorrect because the first sentence does not pose any question.

8 **Choice C is correct** because the passage focuses on the dramatic decrease in the population of Ireland during the first and second wave of immigrants in the nineteenth century. It also states that the immigrants came to America. Thus, the population of America increased.
Choice A is incorrect because the passage does not mention anything about Irish immigrants returning to their homeland or planning to return to their homeland. There is no information from which this could be assumed. **Choice B** is incorrect because families were more likely to immigrate to America in the second wave of immigration. This would include men and women, so it cannot be assumed that women were more likely to immigrate.

9 **Choice C is correct** because the last sentence says, "However, during this period entire families were fleeing to the land of opportunity." Referring to America as the "land of opportunity" suggests there were more ways to make a living than simply farming potatoes.
Choice A is incorrect because the passage does not mention or imply anything about international threats or America being safer from external conflicts. The focus is on economic hardship and famine in Ireland, not on safety or threats in America. **Choice B** is incorrect because there is no mention of culture, art, or any cultural scene influencing Irish immigration. The passage focuses on survival and economic opportunity, not on cultural reasons for immigration. **Choice D** is incorrect because crime rates or safety concerns are not discussed in the passage. The reason for Irish immigration is linked to famine and economic hardship, not crime or law

50 | Practice Tests for the GRE

enforcement conditions in either country. **Choice E** is incorrect because the passage does not mention restrictive laws in Ireland or suggest that legal conditions were a significant factor for immigration. The focus is on the famine and economic factors, not on legal restrictions or freedoms.

10 **Choice B and E are correct** because this passage is saying that String Theory is a tremendously complicated topic, but still one that can be made simpler. Therefore we want answer choices that relate to reduction and streamlining. "Condensed" and "reduced" both mean to abbreviate or summarize. This is exactly what a good teacher would need to do to the String Theory in order to make it accessible to students.

Choice A is incorrect because "fulminated" means ranted or raved. This does not complete the sentence in any logical fashion. **Choice C** is incorrect because "inverted" means reversed. This answer looks tempting because it describes the material being manipulated in some way, but it's not being done in a way that is conducive to teaching. **Choice D** is incorrect because "interpolated" means added or inserted. This barely makes sense in the context of the question, and even if it did it would mean String Theory had been made more complex, which is the opposite of what we want. **Choice F** is incorrect because "expanded" means to make something larger or more detailed—opposite of what the sentence suggests, which is simplification.

11 **Choice A and B are correct** because this sentence is saying that the student has tremendous knowledge of magnetism and electric currents but he still finds something frustrating about the geomagnetic reversal of the Earth's poles. For a well-read student this frustration would come from not understanding. "Impenetrable" and "opaque" both mean unclear or difficult to understand. This is exactly how an overwhelmed student would find a topic such as geomagnetic reversal to be.

Choice C is incorrect because "pellucid" means easily understood, which does not align with the context of the passage. **Choice D** is incorrect because "clear" means easily understood, which does not align with the context of the passage. **Choice E** is incorrect because "self-effacing" means humble. This makes no sense in the context of the question. The process doesn't have a personality. **Choice F** is incorrect because "insidious" means sinister or treacherous. Once again, this answer makes no sense in the context of the question. A natural process can't be sinister.

12 **Choice A and C are correct** because this sentence is saying that executives need to play both sides of the game: they need to appear friendly while also masking an undesirable characteristic. This undesirable characteristic can be inferred from the context to be craftiness or sneakiness. "Guile" and "wiliness" both mean slyness and craftiness. This is the exact personality type that the executive would try to mask from the public.

Choice B is incorrect because "acquiescence" means passive assent. This doesn't make any sense as that's what the executives would want to show publicly, so it's not the quality they would want to mask. **Choice D** is incorrect because "obstinacy" means stubbornness. This is a flimsy fit as there are much better examples of qualities that executives would want to mask from the public. Moreover, there is no other answer choice that means "stubborn." **Choice E** is incorrect because "friendliness" means openness and sociability. This doesn't work for the same reason as "acquiescence" as this is the facade that the executive must put on in public. It does the executive no good to try to mask this characteristic. **Choice F** is incorrect because "vicariousness" means the quality of experiencing something indirectly. This does not complete the sentence in a logical way.

13 **Choice B is correct** because the author is making an argument for genetic testing for cancer but has not defined or explained the term. In order to convince the reader of the benefits, the author should clearly explain the concept first.

Choice A is incorrect because even though a specific statistic is not provided, the approximation of the statistic is still sufficient to make the point that some cancers are hereditary. **Choice C** is incorrect because the author clearly states in the first sentence that the purpose of genetic testing for cancer is to examine genes that may increase the risk of certain cancers. **Choice D** is incorrect because the fact that genetic testing is preventative is not a flaw in the author's argument, but simply a characteristic of the test. The author is not suggesting that genetic testing could be used for treatment, so it is subjective whether preventative care matters to the patient. **Choice**

E is incorrect because describing the specific type of cancers that can be caught with genetic testing would not be necessary in order to make the point that some cancers can be detected through genetic testing.

14 **Choice A is correct** because the passage says that the Democratic-Republican party greatly contributed to the modern political system and that some parties only existed briefly before being overtaken by more dominant ones. Therefore, the Democratic-Republican Party must have been a more dominant political party. **Choice B is correct** because the passage says that the Federalist Party was concerned with putting presidents in power and the Anti-Masonic Party campaigned for social interests. Thus, the Federalist Party was not likely known for its concern with social issues. **Choice C is correct** because this passage discusses historic political parties and how they have contributed to the existence of the two dominant political parties today. Therefore, the two political parties that dominate today did not always exist in the United States.

15 **Choice C is correct** because the first paragraph is brief. It begins with a hook, and then mentions the multitude of parties that made up the nineteenth-century political system. Then, the second paragraph discusses the specific political parties by name.

Choice A is incorrect because the first paragraph does not discuss specific political parties, but simply introduces the topic. Also, the second paragraph is not a conclusion; it rather provides new information on specific political parties. **Choice B** is incorrect because the first paragraph does not discuss modern political parties, but simply introduces the topic of historic political parties. **Choice D** is incorrect because the first paragraph does not delve into historic political parties, but simply introduces the topic. Also, the second paragraph does not only discuss modern political parties but goes into detail about historic political parties as well. **Choice E** is incorrect because the second paragraph does not explain how historic political parties faded away, but simply mentions that they did. The focus of the second paragraph is on specific historic political parties and how they contributed to the modern political system in the United States, not on how parties dissolved.

Quantitative Reasoning (Easy) — Answers & Explanations — Section 5

1 **Choice C is correct** because if you were to calculate the standard deviation of both data sets by hand, List A and list B both have a standard deviation of around 2.83. However, it is not necessary to use the standard deviation formula to solve this question. Since standard deviation is a numerical way to measure the spread of the data, you can use other predictors to make estimates about it. For example, data sets with equally spaced progressions are more likely to have similar standard deviations if their range is similar. List A consists of the numbers 1, 3, 5, 7, and 9. List A therefore has a spacing of two digits and a range of 8. List B consists of the numbers 2, 4, 6, 8, and 10. List B also has a spacing of two digits and a range of 8. This would be a strong indication that the standard deviation is the same for both list A and list B.

Choice A is incorrect because list A's spacing and range is similar to list B's. **Choice B** is incorrect because list B's spacing and range is similar to list A's. **Choice D** is incorrect because it is possible to compare the values and calculate the standard deviations of list A and list B.

2 **Choice B is correct.**

Given $8y - 4x = 5$

$8y = 4x + 5$

$y = \dfrac{4x + 5}{8}$

Now $y > 800$

$\therefore \dfrac{4x + 5}{8} > 800$

$\therefore 4x + 5 > 6400$

Hence $4x > 6395$

$\therefore x > \dfrac{6395}{4}$

$\therefore x > 1598.75$

So the least integer value of $x = 1599$

Choice A is incorrect because the least integer value of x is less than 1600. **Choice C** is incorrect because Quantity A and Quantity B are not equal. **Choice D** is incorrect because it is possible to solve for the least integer value of x.

3 **Choice D is correct** because there are multiple solutions depending on what side lengths are used for the rectangle. The side lengths of the rectangle can be found by first identifying all factor pairs for 24. Since the area of a rectangle equals base times height, an area of 24 can be achieved through side length pairs of 1 and 24, 2 and 12, 3 and 8, and 4 and 6. This leaves four options for the perimeter of the rectangle. Option one would be using 1 and 24 as side lengths which using the perimeter formula of two times the length plus two times the width would yield 50 cm as the perimeter. Option two would be using 2 and 12 as side lengths for a perimeter of 28. Option three would be using 3 and 8 for a perimeter of 22. Option four would be using side lengths 4 and 6 for a perimeter of 20. Options one and two give us a Quantity A value greater than Quantity B. Option three gives a Quantity A value equal to Quantity B. Option four gives us a Quantity A value less than Quantity B. Therefore, the relationship cannot be determined.

Choice A is incorrect because Quantity A is not always greater than Quantity B. **Choice B** is incorrect because Quantity B is not always greater than Quantity A. **Choice C** is incorrect because Quantity A and Quantity B are not always equal.

4 **Choice A is correct** because a line perpendicular to line k would have a positive slope since perpendicular lines have slopes that are negative reciprocals of each other. Line k has a negative slope so the negative reciprocal of a negative would be a positive. A line parallel to line k would have a negative slope since parallel lines have the same slope and line k has a negative slope. A positive number would always be greater than a negative number so Quantity A is greater than Quantity B.

Choice B is incorrect because the slope of a parallel line would be negative which would not be greater than a perpendicular line's slope which would be positive. **Choice C** is incorrect because the two slopes would not be equal. **Choice D** is incorrect because it is possible to compare Quantity A and Quantity B.

5 **Choice C is correct.**

A sum of 5 is obtained from the following combinations: 1–4, 2–3, 3–2, 4–1. That means a probability of 4 out of 36. A sum of 9 is obtained from the following combinations: 3–6, 4–5, 5–4, 6–3, which is also a probability of 4 out of 36. Therefore, the two quantities presented are equal.

Choice A is incorrect because the probabilities are equal. **Choice B** is incorrect because the probabilities are equal. **Choice D** is incorrect because it is possible to solve for both probabilities.

Quantitative Reasoning (Easy) Answers & Explanations   Section 5

6 **Choice C is correct** because you can find the solution by using a permutation instead of writing out all options. If you use a permutation you would solve 4! since there are four distinct digits to fill without repeats. To solve rewrite 4! as 4 × 3 × 2 × 1 which equals 24.

Choice A is incorrect because this would not account for all options. **Choice B** is incorrect because this would not account for all options. **Choice D** is incorrect because there are not more than 24 possible options. **Choice E** is incorrect because there are not more than 24 possible options.

7 **Choice B is correct** because you can find the percent decrease using the formula $\left|\frac{final - initial}{initial}\right| \times 100$ to determine the percent decrease in voters in 2022 to 2023 was 20.00%. The final value would be 1,072 and the initial value would be 1,340. Plugging these in would yield $\left|\frac{1340 - 1072}{1340}\right| \times 100$ which equals 20.00%.

Choice A is incorrect because this answer would result from a calculation error. **Choice C** is incorrect because this answer would result if you divided by 1340 when solving for a percent decrease. **Choice D** is incorrect because this answer would result from a calculation error. **Choice E** is incorrect because this would be if you found what percent 1072 is of 1340.

8 **Choices A and C are correct.** An isosceles triangle has two equivalent sides. This means the two options for the other side length are 4 or 6.

Choice A is correct because this is the perimeter if the other leg has a side length of 4 since adding up all the sides would get you 4 + 4 + 6 = 14. **Choice C is correct** because this is the perimeter if the other leg has a side length of 6 since adding up all the sides would get you 4 + 6 + 6 = 16.

Choice B is incorrect because this perimeter would not be possible for the given isosceles triangle. **Choice D** is incorrect because this perimeter would not be possible for the given isosceles triangle.

9 **Choice E is correct** because you can draw a diagram and use a proportional relationship to determine the value of x is 30.

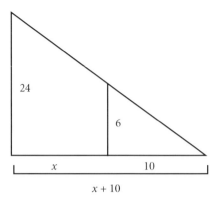

1. To create a diagram, draw two proportional triangles, one inside the other. Then label the known information such as the height of the tree (24 feet), the height of the person (6 feet), the distance the person is standing from the tree (x feet), and the length of the person's shadow (10 feet).

2. You can then label the length of the shadow of the tree as $x + 10$ since the distance the person is from the tree plus the length of the person's shadow would make up the entire length of the tree's shadow.

3. Next create a proportion based on the known information comparing the ratio of the person's height to their shadow to the tree's height to its shadow. You would get $\frac{6}{10} = \frac{24}{x+10}$.

4. Cross multiply to get the equation $6(x + 10) = 240$. Now distribute to get $6x + 60 = 240$ and then solve for x. Subtracting 60 on both sides and then dividing by 6 would give us $x = 30$.

Choice A is incorrect because the length of the tree's shadow would not be proportional if the person was only 5 feet away from the tree. **Choice B** is incorrect because the length of the tree's shadow is not double the person's shadow. **Choice C** is incorrect because this would not create a proportional relationship. **Choice D** is incorrect because this distance would not make the tree's shadow proportional to the person's shadow.

10 **Choice B is correct** because the sum of all two-digit prime numbers is 1043 (11 + 13 + 17 + 19 + 23 + 29 + 31 + 37 + 41 + 43 + 47 + 53 + 59 + 61 + 67 + 71 + 73 + 79 + 83 + 89 + 97) and the product of all primes less than 10 is 210 (2 × 3 × 5 × 7). Subtract to get 1043 − 210 = 833.

Choice A is incorrect because this answer would result from a calculation error. **Choice C** is incorrect because this answer would result from a calculation error. **Choice D** is

1 Quantitative Reasoning (Easy) Answers & Explanations Section 5

incorrect because this answer would result from adding all prime numbers under 10 instead of multiplying them. **Choice E is incorrect** because this is just the sum of all two-digit numbers and does not find the difference.

11 **The correct answer is 23.** because you can use the median and average to solve for x and y to determine $x = 18$ and $y = 23$ which makes 23 the greatest value in the list. To solve for these values use these steps:

1. If the median equals 18, that would mean x equals 18.
2. Using $x = 18$, you can set up the equation for the average (average = $\frac{\text{sum of numbers}}{\text{amount of numbers}}$) to solve for y. Plugging in you would get $\frac{(x-2)+x+y}{3} = 19$ and then substituting in 18 for x would get you $\frac{(18-2)+18+y}{3} = 19$.
3. Solve for y by simplifying $\frac{34+y}{3} = 19$. Then cross multiply to get $34 + y = 57$. Subtracting 34 would get you $y = 23$.

12 **Choice C is correct** because this represents the amount of students in the class by correctly organizing the ideas from the question.

1. You can first write out an equation to relate the amount of beakers available to those handed out and left over. Using s for students, that equation would be $sb + n = 6x$, which can be read as the number of students (s) times the number of beakers (b) they each received plus the leftover beakers (n) would equal the amount of boxes (x) times six beakers per box. Both sides of the equation would give us the amount of beakers.
2. Next, you can rearrange this statement to isolate s. Subtracting n and dividing by b would give you the final equation $s = \frac{6x-n}{b}$.

Choice A is incorrect because this does not account for x number of boxes. **Choice B is incorrect** because this would incorrectly multiply the number of beakers left over by the number of beakers per student. **Choice D is incorrect** because this answer mixes up the relationship between n and b. **Choice E is incorrect** because you would not add the total number of beakers in all boxes to the number of beakers left over because that would double account for beakers.

13 **Choice D is correct** because when you factor $x^2 + 2x - 8 = 0$, you would get $(x + 4)(x - 2) = 0$. Setting each factor equal to 0 is how you would get x equals –4 and 2. Since $x > \frac{1}{3}$, x^{-2} must be solved using $x = 2$. A negative exponent indicates turning the number into a fraction and then squaring the denominator which would mean $2^{-2} = \frac{1}{4}$.

Choice A is incorrect because you cannot get a negative from inputting a value into the equation x^{-2}. **Choice B is incorrect** because you cannot get a negative from inputting a value into the equation x^{-2}. **Choice C is incorrect** because this would be found using $x = -4$ as a solution which does not work because –4 is not greater than $\frac{1}{3}$. **Choice E is incorrect** because this would be the answer if you just squared 2, but this ignores the negative exponent.

14 **Choice A is correct** because the only way to get an odd number when multiplying integers is if the two numbers are both odd. If you double an odd number you will get an even number so $2a$ is even. An even minus an odd is always an odd number, so $2a - b$ will always be odd.

Choice B is incorrect because both a and b must be odd, we know ab is odd, and an odd plus an odd would give you an even. **Choice C is incorrect** because both a and b must be odd, we know ab is odd, and an odd minus an odd is always an even. **Choice D is incorrect** because both a and b must be odd and multiplying an odd by two makes it an even. An even minus an even is always even. **Choice E is incorrect** because if you double an odd number it will always be even.

15 **Choices B, C and D are correct.** Since the most amount of flour available is 20 cups, the expression $2x + 3y \leq 20$ can be created to establish the number of cups of flour used for x amounts of cake and the number of cups of flour for y amount of dozens of cookies has to be less than or equal to 20. **Choice B is correct** because this would be $2(3) + 3(2) = 12$ which is less than 20. **Choice C is correct** because this would be $2(10) + 3(0) = 20$. **Choice D is correct** because this would be $2(6) + 3(1) = 15$ which is less than 20.

Choice A is incorrect because this would not work as a combination since $2(5) + 3(6) = 28$ which is not less than or equal to 20.

Quantitative Reasoning (Hard) Answers & Explanations — Section 5

1. **Choice D is correct** because without knowing the original price of the pans, it is not possible to determine if the $10 difference in retail price is enough to offset the 5% difference in discount. If you want to try to solve it, you can represent each store's price with an equation. For store A, the price of the pan would be $0.85(x - 25)$ which can be read as 15% off store A's price (or 85% of the price) times the $25 off of retail price x. For store B, the price of the pan could be represented as $0.90(x - 35)$ which can be read as 10% off store B's price (or 90% of the price) times the $35 off of retail price x. If you expand the equations you would get $0.85x - 21.25$ and $0.90x - 31.5$. We would not be able to determine if these expressions are equal or not without an x value.

Choice A is incorrect because we cannot determine a relationship between Quantity A and Quantity B. **Choice B** is incorrect because we cannot determine a relationship between Quantity A and Quantity B. **Choice C** is incorrect because we cannot determine a relationship between Quantity A and Quantity B.

2. **Choice C is correct** because there are 95 numbers between 0 and 500 that contain a 7. To find this quickly, use the repeated occurrences of 7, 17, 27, 37, 47, 57, 67, 87, 97, and numbers 70-79 for every 100. There are 19 values with 7 in it per hundred and between 0 and 500 there are 5 sets of these. Multiply 5 by 19 to get 95 numbers that have a 7.

Choice A is incorrect because both Quantity A and Quantity B are 95. **Choice B** is incorrect because both Quantity A and Quantity B are 95. **Choice D** is incorrect because it is possible to determine both Quantity A and Quantity B.

3. **Choice D is correct** because in most cases, any value of a and b, where $a \neq b$, Quantity A would be larger in some scenarios where $a > b$, and Quantity B would be larger in some scenarios where $a < b$. Then, if $a = b$, the two quantities would both equal 1. Therefore, without knowing more restrictions on a and b, the relationship cannot be determined. Here are both scenarios worked out:

Scenario One: $a \neq b$

We know that a and b are negative integers. Plugging any negative integer into Quantity A's and Quantity B's equation would give you a negative number over a negative number which makes a positive. If $a > b$ then the numerator would be greater than the denominator making Quantity A larger. If $a < b$ then the numerator would be less than the denominator making Quantity B larger.

Scenario Two: $a = b$

If $a = b$, then both answers would be equal to 1. This would be because both Quantity A and Quantity B would have the same numerator and denominator. Dividing a number by itself will always give you 1.

Choice A is incorrect because Quantity A is not always greater than Quantity B. **Choice B** is incorrect because Quantity B is not always greater than Quantity A. **Choice C** is incorrect because Quantity A and Quantity B are not always equal.

4. **Choice D is correct** because there are multiple possibilities based on the information given that would result in Quantity A sometimes being larger, Quantity B sometimes being larger, and some instances where the quantities would be equal. For all circumstances, keep in mind that Angle C would be 180 − (Angle A + Angle B).

Quantity A is larger if Angle B is less than 45 degrees. For example, if Angle B is 40 degrees, then Angle A would be 80 degrees and Angle C would be 60 degrees $(180 - (60 + 40) = 80)$. This would mean that Quantity A equals $40 + 60 = 100$ which is greater than Quantity B.

Quantity B is larger if Angle B is greater than 45 degrees. For example, if Angle B is 46 degrees, then Angle A would be 92 degrees and Angle C would be 42 degrees $(180 - (46 + 92) = 42)$. This would mean that Quantity A equals $46 + 42 = 88$ which is less than Quantity B.

The quantities are equal if Angle B is 45 degrees because that would make Quantity A equal to $45 + 45 = 90$ and Quantity B 90 since $45 \times 2 = 90$.

Choice A is incorrect because Quantity A is not always greater than Quantity B. **Choice B** is incorrect because Quantity B is not always greater than Quantity A. **Choice C** is incorrect because Quantity A is not always equal to Quantity B.

5. **Choice D is correct** because we would have to know the relationship between the length and width of the two rectangles to determine if Quantity A or Quantity B is larger or if they are equal. If the value added to the width was equivalent to the value taken from the length the perimeters would be equal. We cannot determine this just from the percentages, however. You can construct equations to represent the perimeter of each rectangle based on what

Quantitative Reasoning (Hard) Answers & Explanations — Section 5

is given. Denote rectangle B's width as *x* and its length as *y*. The equation for the perimeter of rectangle B would be $2x + 2y$ since the perimeter equals two times the width plus two times the length. Rectangle A's width would be represented by $1.25x$ since it is 25% greater than rectangle B's width. The length of rectangle A would be denoted as $0.75y$ since it is 25% less than rectangle B's length. The equation for the perimeter of rectangle A would be $2(1.25x) + 2(0.75)y$ which simplifies to be $2.5x + 1.5y$. It is not possible to determine the relationship between these two equations without an *x* and *y* value.

Choice A is incorrect because it is not possible to determine the relationship between Quantity A and Quantity B. **Choice B** is incorrect because it is not possible to determine the relationship between Quantity A and Quantity B. **Choice C** is incorrect because it is not possible to determine the relationship between Quantity A and Quantity B.

6 **Choices D and E are correct.**

To find the median add up all the house amounts and divide by 2 to determine the place value where the median falls. Adding up the number of houses sold (3 + 4 + 6 + 4) equals 17. Divide 17 by 2 to get 8.5 which means the median lies at place value 9. Counting up the numbers in each category shows place value 9 is in the range of $250,000 to $349,999.

Choice D is correct because it falls in the range of the median. **Choice E is correct** because it falls in the range of the median.

Choice A is incorrect because it does not fall between $250,000 and $349,999. **Choice B** is incorrect because it does not fall between $250,000 and $349,999. **Choice C** is incorrect because it does not fall between $250,000 and $349,999. **Choice F** is incorrect because it does not fall between $250,000 and $349,999.

7 **Choice E is correct** because for the value of $(bc)(a - b)$ to be even, one of the statements *bc* or $a - b$ has to be even. If *bc* is even, then *b* and/or *c* have to be even. If $a - b$ is even the numbers both have to be even or both have to be odd.

From this, $b + c$ can be confirmed to be even based on the constraints as you would get an even number with both evens or both odds.

The value $a + b + c$ can also be even if all numbers are even which is possible.

Then $a + b$ can also be even because *a* and *b* both must be even or both must be odd which would always add to an even.

Choice A is incorrect because all answers are true. **Choice B** is incorrect because all answers are true. **Choice C** is incorrect because all answers are true. **Choice D** is incorrect because all answers are true.

8 **Choice C is correct** because if you find the total number of seats and then remove the 3rd and 10th row you will end up with $13r + 564$. To solve follow these steps:

1. First, you need to create an expression to determine the amount of seats per row. This can be calculated by using *r* as your first row and $6(n - 1)$ to determine how many seats are being added each time. So the number of seats in the nth row is equal to $r + 6(n - 1)$.

2. To find the total number of seats in all 15 rows, you can use the sum of an arithmetic sequence equation as a shortcut. The sum equals $\frac{n}{2}(2a_1 + (n - 1)(d))$ where *n* is the number of terms, a_1 is the first term in the sequence, and *d* is the common difference. Plugging into this equation you would get $\frac{15}{2}(2r + (15 - 1)(6))$. Solving this would yield $15r + 630$ as the total seats in all 15 rows.

3. Now, subtract the seats in rows 3 and 10 using the formula found in step 1. Row 3 would have $r + 12$ and row 10 would have $r + 54$ seats. $15r + 630 - (r + 12) - (r + 54) = 13r + 564$.

Choice A is incorrect because this does not account for *r* seats per row. **Choice B** is incorrect because this results from a math error calculating total seats. **Choice D** is incorrect because this results from a math error removing the amount of seats. **Choice E** is incorrect because this is the total of all seats and does not remove the 3rd and 10th row of seats.

9 **Choice D is correct** because you can determine the number of minutes by first determining the amount of hours it takes to complete the circuit and then multiplying by 60 to convert it to minutes. It would take the race car approximately 0.925 hours to complete the race as determined by dividing 185 miles by 200 miles per hour. Multiply 0.925 by 60 to get 55.5 minutes which is closest to 55.

Quantitative Reasoning (Hard) Answers & Explanations — Section 5

Choice A is incorrect because this would be the answer if you forgot to convert miles per hour to miles per minute. Choice B is incorrect because this answer results from a calculation error. Choice C is incorrect because this answer results from a calculation error. Choice E is incorrect because this answer results from a calculation error.

10 Choice B is correct because $\frac{1}{5^5}$ equals 0.00032 which is greater than 0.0003. As the exponent n gets larger from there, the result gets smaller and smaller since you would be dividing by a larger number each time. You can also solve the equation to determine the value by first multiplying each side by 5^n to get $1 > 0.0003(5^n)$. Next, divide both sides by 0.0003 to get $3333.\overline{33} > 5^n$. You can then use a logarithm to solve. Rewrite as $\log_5 3333.\overline{33} > n$. Plugging this into a calculator yields approximately $5.04 > n$. This confirms 5 as the greatest integer value of n.

Choice A is incorrect because while $\frac{1}{5^4}$ is greater than 0.0003, 4 is not the largest value of n that is possible. Choice C is incorrect because $\frac{1}{5^8}$ would be significantly smaller than 0.0003. Choice D is incorrect because $\frac{1}{5^{10}}$ would be significantly smaller than 0.0003. Choice E is incorrect because $\frac{1}{5^{15}}$ would be significantly smaller than 0.0003.

11 The correct answer is 30 because all regular polygons have exterior angles that add up to 360. To find the value of each angle, divide 360 by the number of sides which in this case is 12. The result is 30°.

12 Choice E is correct because to get the greatest possible value for a, you have to find the lowest possible values for d, c, and b. Based on the inequality, the lowest values for d, c, and b would have to be 5. Use the average formula to now solve for the greatest value of a. The equation for average is average = $\frac{sum\ of\ the\ numbers}{amount\ of\ numbers}$. Plugging in you would get $30 = \frac{5+5+5+5+a}{5}$. Simplifying would give you $30 = \frac{20+a}{5}$. Cross multiply to get $150 = 20 + a$. Subtract 20 from both sides to determine $130 = a$.

Choice A is incorrect because this would be the answer if the sum of the numbers was 30, but the average is 30 so this would not work. Choice B is incorrect because this is not the greatest value of a possible. Choice C is incorrect because this is not the greatest value of a possible. Choice D is incorrect because this is not the greatest value of a possible.

13 Choice C is correct because you can find the total percent markup by adding 1 to both percentages and multiplying them together. The price the shoe store paid the shoemaker would be $1.35d$ (35% higher than the cost means 135% of the cost). The price the consumer paid would be 1.60 times $1.35d$ since the consumer is paying 160% of what the shoe store paid the shoemaker. Multiplying 1.60 by 1.35 yields 2.16 which can be represented as $2.16d$.

Choice A is incorrect because this would be just adding the percentages together and this would overall result in a price decrease. Choice B is incorrect because this answer results from a calculation error. Choice D is incorrect because this answer results from a calculation error. Choice E is incorrect because this would just be adding 1.35 and 1.60 together which is the incorrect way to combine percentages.

14 Choices A, B and D are correct. To solve for t, plug the statement $t + 1$ into for x in the original $f(x)$ statement and then set the whole equation equal to 0 to get $0 = (t + 1)(t + 1 + 3)(t + 1 - 2)$. Simplify the expression to get $0 = (t + 1)(t + 4)(t - 1)$. Set each factor equal to 0 to solve for t and you would get $t + 1 = 0$, $t + 4 = 0$, and $t - 1 = 0$. This would give you $t = -1$, $t = -4$, and $t = 1$ as your final answers.

Choice A is correct because t can equal -4. Choice B is correct because t can equal -1. Choice D is correct because t can equal 1.

Choice C is incorrect because this value of t does not work for the equation. Choice E is incorrect because this value of t does not work for the equation.

15 Choice D is correct because to get the new average you need to multiply the average of each class by the number of students in each class, add those numbers together, and then divide by the total number of students to get an accurate average for both classes. The formula for average is Average = $\frac{sum\ of\ values}{total\ values}$. In this scenario, the sum of the values would be all the morning class scores and all the afternoon class scores. This can be found by multiplying the total values by the average to get the sum of all values. For the morning class, this would be $30x$ (30 students with an average of x) and for the afternoon class, this would be $(25)(86)$ (25 students with an average of 86). These two values would be added for the sum of all values. The total values would be the number of students in both the morning and afternoon class which would be $25 + 30 = 55$ students. The average formula with this information plugged in would be Average $= \dfrac{30x + (25)(86)}{55}$ which matches answer D.

Choice A is incorrect because you cannot use the average of two averages as it does not account for the sum of all students. **Choice B** is incorrect because this does not account for all students. **Choice C** is incorrect because this does not follow the numerical formula to find average. **Choice E** is incorrect because this does not account for the average of the afternoon class.

This page is intentionally left blank

Chapter 3
Practice Test #2

IMPORTANT
READ THE INSTRUCTIONS BEFORE BEGINNING THE TEST

1. Take this test under real testing conditions. Put away any distractions and sit in a quiet place with no disturbances. Keep a rough paper, some pencils, and a calculator beside you.

2. Begin with **Section 1** of the test on page 62. Write your essay in 30 minutes.

3. Next, move to **Section 2 - Verbal Reasoning** on page 64.
   - Attempt all questions and note the number of correct answers using the answer key on page 84.
   - If you get fewer than 7 correct, proceed to **Section 4 - Verbal Reasoning (Easy)** on page 70.
   - If you get 7 or more correct, proceed to **Section 4 - Verbal Reasoning (Hard)** on page 74.

4. After that, take **Section 3 - Quantitative Reasoning** on page 67.
   - Complete the section, then check your score using the answer key on page 85.
   - If you get fewer than 7 correct, proceed to **Section 5 - Quantitative Reasoning (Easy)** on page 78.
   - If you get 7 or more correct, proceed to **Section 5 - Quantitative Reasoning (Hard)** on page 81.

5. Complete Section 4 and Section 5, respectively, and note down the number of correct answers you got right in each section.

6. Calculate your **Scaled Score** on page 317 for the test.

7. Review **detailed explanations** for all questions beginning on page 86.

Analyze an Issue
30 Minutes

Claim: Any piece of information referred to as a fact should be mistrusted, since it may well be proven false in the future.

Reason: Much of the information that people assume is factual actually turns out to be inaccurate. Write a response in which you discuss the extent to which you agree or disagree with the claim and the reason on which that claim is based.

You may start writing your response here

Section 2 - Verbal Reasoning

18 Minutes | 12 Questions

For questions 1 to 3, for each blank, select one entry from the corresponding column of choices. Fill all blanks in the way that best completes the text.

1. While the number of motor vehicle fatalities per year has decreased substantially over the past decade, airline passage is still the _____ to which all forms of transportation aspire.

   - (A) exemplar
   - (B) contrarian
   - (C) subversion
   - (D) reprobate
   - (E) scoundrel

2. Early attempts at studying human anatomy relied on (i)_____ more than anything. Lacking advanced technologies like x-rays and MRI, early doctors simply dissected corpses to understand placement and function of organs. Although great strides were made with this approach from the macroscopic level, the details of microscopic human anatomy escaped surgeons for generations. The pathogeneses of diseases like cancer were too (ii)_____ to be detected in these early days of surgery.

Blank (i)	Blank (ii)
(A) fortitude	(D) diminutive
(B) artifice	(E) convoluted
(C) precision	(F) inconsequential

3. Political science, like the entire field of social science, faces challenges in conducting accurate studies. Unlike the physical or natural sciences, which are focused on (i)_____ observations, political science must deal with the biases of the human mind. These inconsistencies have lead political scientists to (ii)_____ their research approaches in order to mitigate the shortcomings of any one approach. In spite of these obstacles, the field of political science has (iii)_____ significantly in recent years.

Blank (i)	Blank (ii)	Blank (iii)
(A) dispassionate	(D) coalesce	(G) regressed
(B) preconceived	(E) inundate	(H) proliferated
(C) psychological	(F) diversify	(I) fulminated

For Questions 4 and 5, select one answer choice unless otherwise instructed.

Question 4 is based on this passage.

Watercolor is a water-based artistic medium that is applied by brush to a paper revealing transparent and radiant colors. Watercolor paints are typically packaged as dry cakes in a paint pan or in tubes of condensed paint. This paint is made of finely ground pigment that is mixed with gum arabic and, finally, water. A typical watercolor palette includes a variety of shades derived from resins, minerals, and vegetables. Traditionally, earthy colors came from azurite, terre verte, gamboge, and madder root. More artificial colors usually came from vermilion, cadmium yellow, and lead white. Today, man-made colors can be synthesized to create bright hues.

Section 2 - Verbal Reasoning

For the following question, consider each of the choices separately and select all that apply.

4. Which of the following statements can be assumed based on the passage?
   - [A] Watercolor paints can be used to paint a variety of pictures.
   - [B] Dry watercolor paints are typically sold in sets of multiple colors.
   - [C] The production process of watercolor paints has hardly changed over time.

Question 5 is based on this passage.

Nowadays, it is a well-known fact that smoking cigarettes negatively impacts physical health. When smoke is inhaled, it moves from the mouth through the upper airway and to the alveoli. It then progresses further into the respiratory tract, where soluble gasses are absorbed, and particles are left behind. Great amounts of toxins and carcinogens make their home and place the smoker at risk of serious diseases.

Tobacco smoke is made up of thousands of chemicals, most of which are in the gas phase. Most of these chemicals (not only nicotine) can cause damage to the smoker's respiratory system. Some chemicals injure the lungs while others harm the host's defenses. Plus, cigarette smoke contains high concentrations of free radicals.

5. If the remainder of this passage described the benefits of smoking cigarettes, which of the following purposes would this passage serve overall?
   - (A) To provide background information on the primary ingredients in cigarettes.
   - (B) To explain reasons for opposition before rebuking them.
   - (C) To introduce the respiratory system and its weakness.
   - (D) To convince the reader of the dangers of cigarette smoking.
   - (E) To introduce the concept of free radicals before explaining their health benefits.

For Questions 6 to 9, select the two answer choices that, when used to complete the sentence, fit the meaning of the sentence as a whole and produce complete sentences that are alike in meaning.

6. When the particular epoch and theoretical structure of two disparate genres of music are thrown away and all that is considered is the emotional import of the material, one finds that any two genres of music have made essentially _____ contributions to the elevation of the human emotional state.
   - [A] fungible
   - [B] unequal
   - [C] confusing
   - [D] unnecessary
   - [E] interchangeable
   - [F] enlightening

7. Preparing for a complex reaction synthesis such as the sharpless epoxidation often overwhelms the mind of an organic chemistry lab student and causes him or her to forget more _____ yet still–necessary things such as proper distillation apparatus setup.
   - [A] perfunctory
   - [B] riveting
   - [C] sympathetic
   - [D] adroit
   - [E] mechanical
   - [F] inexplicable

8. Because of the prevalence of the Medieval theory of "spontaneous generation" Darwin's attempt to modernize the alternate "descent with modification" theory had to endure years of _____ before the scientific community would warm to it.
   - [A] contempt
   - [B] derision
   - [C] companionship
   - [D] competition
   - [E] egotism
   - [F] relief

9. The invention and adoption of Magnetic Resonance Imaging in delineating the soft tissues of the heart and brain have made _____ the high quality spatial resolution maps that only a few years ago seemed unattainable.

- A ubiquitous
- B inconceivable
- C relatable
- D prevalent
- E extreme
- F essential

For Questions 10 to 12, select one answer choice unless otherwise instructed.

Questions 10 to 12 are based on this passage.

Great scientific advances have resulted in longer and more fulfilling human lives. While extended lifespans suggest wonderful accomplishments in medical and social fields, they also pose significant problems to society as a whole. Societal aging has a drastic impact on the economy, the provision of social resources, and the prevalence of chronic disease and disability. However, the United States trails behind other developed nations with respect to human longevity. Within the past thirty years, Americans have gained approximately five years in life expectancy while citizens of comparable nations have gained approximately eight years.

When comparing life spans across developed nations, harmonized surveys have shown the powerful role that longer work lives play in cognitive function. Additionally, there is evidence that suggests that alterations in economic incentives and social support programs can increase the use of preventative services. Striving to live a longer life begins with decisions that are made during mid-life.

10. Based on the author's perspective, which of the following statements would the author most likely disagree with?

- A The sole focus of the study of longevity should be extending the lifespan.
- B Ways to extend human lifespans should be researched more extensively.
- C Longevity should be the priority of most people throughout the lifespan.
- D Aging is a problematic societal accomplishment that impacts the economy.
- E Aspiration for longevity has not made enough progress in the United States when compared with other developed nations.

11. How does the first sentence of the passage best contribute to the development of the passage?

- A It serves as a thesis presenting the author's overall argument.
- B It provides background information on societal aging.
- C It introduces the concept of scientific advancements in the area of aging.
- D It acts as a hook that introduces the topic being discussed in the passage.
- E It introduces two sides of the argument being presented in the passage.

12. Based on the information provided in the passage, which of the following could be a possible negative effect of societal aging?

- A An increased workload for lawyers developing legal wills and trusts
- B A greater number of people capable of joining the workforce and remaining in the workforce for many decades
- C The cost of social support programs designed to care for elderly people with diseases
- D The innovation and development of social support programs designed to care for elderly people with diseases
- E A greater number of people driving on public roads

Section 3 - Quantitative Reasoning

18 Minutes | 12 Questions

1.

If $x > 0$, then

Quantity A	Quantity B
$\dfrac{2x}{3}$	x

Ⓐ Quantity A is greater.
Ⓑ Quantity B is greater.
Ⓒ The two quantities are equal.
Ⓓ The relationship cannot be determined from the information given.

2.

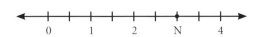

Quantity A	Quantity B
$\dfrac{1}{N}$	$\dfrac{1}{4}$

Ⓐ Quantity A is greater.
Ⓑ Quantity B is greater.
Ⓒ The two quantities are equal.
Ⓓ The relationship cannot be determined from the information given.

3.

The mean of a group of 10 numbers is 83. A different group of 20 numbers has a mean of 65. When k is added to the first 10 numbers, the new mean is 82.

Quantity A	Quantity B
The mean of the 30 numbers	k

Ⓐ Quantity A is greater.
Ⓑ Quantity B is greater.
Ⓒ The two quantities are equal.
Ⓓ The relationship cannot be determined from the information given.

4.

$$4x + 2y = 5$$
$$2ax + ay = 5$$

The system of equations shown has an infinite number of solutions, where a is a constant.

Quantity A	Quantity B
a	2

Ⓐ Quantity A is greater.
Ⓑ Quantity B is greater.
Ⓒ The two quantities are equal.
Ⓓ The relationship cannot be determined from the information given.

5.

Determine the interest rate of the bank if $2,250 is realized from a deposit of $1,500 after 5 years, if it earned simple interest at a rate calculated semi annually.

Ⓐ 2.5%
Ⓑ 3.3%
Ⓒ 5%
Ⓓ 6.7%
Ⓔ 10%

Questions 6 to 8 are based on the following data.

Tourism Revenue Summary for Region R

Summary of Tourism Revenue for 2015, 2018, and 2021
(in millions of dollars)

Activity	2015	2018	2021
Sightseeing	$82	$104	$118
Adventure Sports	$51	$60	$83
Cultural Tours	$36	$42	$55
Total	$169	$206	$256

Revenue from Sightseeing by Type of Tour, 2021

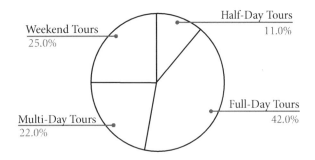

6

For sightseeing tours in 2021, which of the following is closest to the ratio of the dollar amount of the revenue of full-day tours to the dollar amount of the revenue of half-day tours?

Ⓐ 5 to 2
Ⓑ 4 to 2
Ⓒ 4 to 1
Ⓓ 3 to 2
Ⓔ 3 to 1

7

For 2015, if the revenue of water rafting accounted for 22 percent of the dollar amount of the revenue of adventure sports, then the revenue of water rafting accounted for what percent of the dollar amount of the revenue of all tourism activities in 2015?

Give your answer to the nearest whole percent.

[ ] %

8

If the revenue of weekend sightseeing tours accounted for 18% percent of sightseeing tours revenue in 2018, by approximately what percent did the dollar amount of the revenue of this type of tour increase from 2018 to 2021?

Ⓐ 25%
Ⓑ 35%
Ⓒ 45%
Ⓓ 55%
Ⓔ 65%

9

The circular bases of a right circular cylinder are circumscribed around two opposite faces of a cube. If the volume of the cube is 64, which of the following is the closest to the volume of the cylinder?

Ⓐ 50
Ⓑ 64
Ⓒ 81
Ⓓ 92
Ⓔ 100

10

Salary Interval	Number of Employees
900-1000	6
800-899	7
700-799	8
600-699	4

All of the employees in a company earned a weekly salary that was a whole number between 600 and 1000 dollars, inclusive. The table shows the number of employees who earned a weekly salary in each of the four salary intervals. Which of the following numbers could be the median weekly salary for all of the employees?

Indicate all such numbers.

- [A] 655
- [B] 725
- [C] 798
- [D] 800
- [E] 860
- [F] 975

11

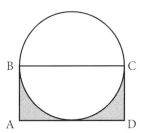

Circle X is inscribed with half of its area contained in rectangle ABCD. The area of the shaded region can be represented as $96 - 18\pi$. What is the circumference of Circle X?

Ⓐ 6π
Ⓑ 12π
Ⓒ 18π
Ⓓ 36π
Ⓔ 48π

12

If $|2x - 7| < 5$, then which of the following represents all possible values of x?

Ⓐ $-5 < x < 5$
Ⓑ $-6 < x < 6$
Ⓒ $1 < x < 6$
Ⓓ $-13 < x < 13$
Ⓔ $5 < x < 13$

Section 4 - Verbal Reasoning (Easy)

23 Minutes | 15 Questions

For Questions 1 to 4, select one entry for each blank from the corresponding column of choices. Fill all the blanks in the way that best completes the text.

1. Its cross–discipline application and depth of study has caused organic chemistry to receive a level of importance in the biological sciences that is _____ to the role of physics in the physical sciences.

A subservient
B sequestered
C correspondent
D variable
E unconnected

2. Marine biologists experience tremendous obstacles when creating their models of aquatic life. They are not granted the (i) _____ that workers in most branches of science take for granted. Their subjects of study travel greater distances and greater depths, and often settle in regions of the ocean that are completely inaccessible to humans. (ii) _____ those problems are the difficulties faced when trying to construct tracking devices that can withstand the environments that subjects will be swimming through.

Blank (i)	Blank (ii)
A amenities	D Insinuating
B recalcitrance	E Exacerbating
C biliousness	F Alleviating

3. Although its name would suggest it is (i) _____, the Kiss-Kiss, a leech with a predilection for human blood, (ii) _____ infiltrates homes and ensconces itself among the bedding to ambush its prey—us! Once thought to be rare, recent Kiss-Kiss inventories confirm that the Kiss-Kiss bug, a vector of Chagas disease, is (iii) _____ in the southwestern US, Mexico, and most parts of Central America.

Blank (i)	Blank (ii)	Blank (iii)
A innocuous	D surreptitiously	G ubiquitous
B portentous	E precipitously	H exiguous
C accumbent	F quintessentially	I anomalous

4. Although the Salem witch trials remain a (i) _____ passage of American history, there is no shortage of speculation as to their cause. Although the hallucinations purportedly experienced by the victims may have resulted from something as simple as moldy bread, it seems likely that socio-economic tensions and the (ii) _____ religious climate created an atmosphere in which mass hysteria could (iii) _____.

Blank (i)	Blank (ii)	Blank (iii)
A clandestine	D austere	G convene
B enigmatic	E vitriolic	H fester
C infamous	F pristine	I languish

Section 4 - Verbal Reasoning (Easy)

For Questions 5 to 7, select one answer choice unless otherwise instructed.

Questions 5 to 7 are based on this passage.

Pollen allergies are incredibly common in spring, summer, and fall. Pollen allergies are often referred to as, "hay fever" though experts call them "seasonal allergic rhinitis." During certain times of the year pollen grains are released from plants and travel by wind to fertilize other plants of the same species. These pesky particles can enter eyes, noses, and lungs, leading to coughing, sneezing, and irritation.

Most of the pollen that leads to allergic reactions comes from trees, grasses, or weeds. Tree pollen typically occurs earliest in the year in the United States, making it the primary culprit behind springtime allergies. Grass pollen emerges in spring and summer months, though in the southern states grasses may release pollen year-round. There are countless varieties of grasses, but only a handful actually cause allergic reactions. Furthermore, ragweed pollen allergies plague approximately 15% of Americans. This type of pollen is prevalent in summer and fall and grows all over the country. It can travel hundreds of miles in the air, making it nearly impossible to escape.

5. Which of the following can best be assumed based on the information in the passage?

   A) Pollen particles typically travel across states rather than affecting those in their immediate vicinity.
   B) Pollen particles are not small enough to enter the human body.
   C) Pollen allergies are uncommon in the winter in northern states.
   D) Grass pollen causes more problematic symptoms than tree pollen.
   E) Pollen allergies can be avoided by staying away from fields and farms.

6. Which of the following conclusions about seasonal allergies can be drawn from the passage?

   A) Seasonal allergies come at unexpected times.
   B) Seasonal allergies contribute to the mortality of many Americans.
   C) Seasonal allergies cannot be treated or prevented.
   D) Seasonal allergies are uncommon in certain parts of the country.
   E) Seasonal allergies are a common problem for many Americans.

7. Based on the second paragraph alone, which of the following can best be inferred?

   A) There is no overlap between the release of pollen between trees, grasses, and weeds.
   B) Pollen can come from other plants besides trees, grasses, and weeds.
   C) Many types of grasses lead to allergic reactions.
   D) Ragweed is the only type of weed that releases pollen.
   E) The purpose of pollen being released is for the fertilization of other plants.

For Questions 8 to 10, select the two answer choices that, when used to complete the sentence, fit the meaning of the sentence as a whole and produce complete sentences that are alike in meaning.

8. Office managers who had long concerned themselves with procedural efficacy were thrilled to witness the global technological revolution in which computers _____ written documents and left them in the wastebasket of history.

   A. fulminated
   B. ousted
   C. integrated
   D. prioritized
   E. galvanized
   F. superseded

Section 4 - Verbal Reasoning (Easy)

9. In order to lure his business rival into a false sense of security, the corporate executive would ask deliberately _____ questions during the rival's presentation even while relentlessly prodding it for holes.

   A refractory
   B benign
   C transparent
   D gentle
   E insensitive
   F meandering

10. Casual observers of chemistry wouldn't be quick to _____ such an innocuous element like carbon if they knew that it was the foundation of the most complex creations ever seen in organic systems.

    A question
    B vilipend
    C denigrate
    D corroborate
    E endorse
    F invigilate

For Questions 11 to 15, select one answer choice unless otherwise instructed.

Question 11 is based on this passage.

The nineteenth century was a time of great social reform in the United States, particularly in the category of women's rights. In November of 1872, women were not permitted to vote in presidential elections. However, civil rights activist Susan B. Anthony cast a vote for republican candidate Ulysses S. Grant. Following her vote, Anthony was given a fine of $100 and placed under arrest. She refused to pay her fine and boldly asserted, "I shall never pay a dollar of your unjust penalty." This took place over four decades before the 19th Amendment was passed, allowing women the right to vote in the United States.

11. Although described as a bold activist in this passage, how would Susan B. Anthony most likely be described in the nineteenth century?

    A combative
    B shiftless
    C befuddled
    D conformist
    E delinquent

Questions 12 and 13 are based on this passage.

Children's stories were originally based on oral tradition as myths and fairytales were verbally passed down through generations. Stories have long been told to entertain, educate, and instill morals in young people. Literature makes up an important aspect of cultural heritage and community building. Stories have been used to help children understand their role in society, as well as the perspectives of others.

Books have the unique capability of being able to deliver information, strengthen vocabulary, enhance language skills, and improve listening endurance. Plus, by creating fictional scenarios that align with real-world dilemmas, children can learn to problem-solve in a safe environment with the emotional support of an adult. Characters from these fictional tales can serve as role models demonstrating correct and righteous behaviors.

12. Based on the information in the passage, which of the following would best serve as an example of a child learning to solve problems through a book?

    A A child asking a parent to join Sewing Club after reading a fictional tale titled, "The Seamstress of the Farley Plantation"
    B A child asking for help from a teacher after reading a fictional tale titled, "The Silent Bully"
    C A child befriending a new student at school using a few words from their native language after reading a fictional tale titled, "My Abuela's Backyard"
    D A child asking a parent for more resources on their family's heritage after reading a fictional tale titled, "And That's The Way It Was"
    E A child stealing colored pencils from school to give to a less fortunate peer after reading a fictional tale titled, "Rebel Do Good"

13. In the second paragraph, what does the author most likely mean by, "listening endurance?"

   A. Children who read stories will learn how to listen for longer periods of time.
   B. Children who read stories will learn how to make it through more intense stories calmly.
   C. Children who read stories will learn vocabulary and language skills.
   D. Children who read stories will learn how to listen to various voices and tones.
   E. Children who read stories will be able to make it through more sorrowful and serious tales.

Questions 14 and 15 are based on this passage.

Archaeology and anthropology are often confused for one another due to their similar names and areas of study. However, these are two distinct disciplines with some overlapping purposes. Firstly, archaeology is the study of the remains of different organisms and their cultures through the examination of artifacts. Artifacts are objects that humans have used like money, pottery, and jewelry. Archaeologists also analyze "features" like human dwellings. The main specializations within archaeology are prehistoric, historic, underwater, aerial, and bioarcheology.

On the other hand, anthropology is the study of humans in societies and cultures including human biology and companionship. In the United States, archaeology is considered a sub-discipline under anthropology. However, in the United Kingdom anthropology is classified as a sub-discipline of archaeology.

14. Which of the following is the most indistinct difference between anthropology and archaeology given in the passage?

   A. Archaeologists study artifacts while anthropologists do not.
   B. Archaeologists study multiple organisms, while anthropologists study only humans.
   C. Archaeology has different specializations from anthropology.
   D. Anthropologists focus on how humans interact with one another, while archaeology does not address human interactions.
   E. Anthropology and archaeology both study humans.

15. Which of the following statements best summarizes how archaeology and anthropology relate to one another?

   A. They are both fields that study humans and their biology, but with different approaches to handling artifacts.
   B. They are both fields that study humans, but anthropology includes many more subtopics than the specific study of archaeology.
   C. They are both fields that study humans and their cultures, but with slightly different emphasis areas.
   D. They are both fields that study humans and their biology, but anthropology includes many more subtopics than the specific study of archaeology.
   E. They are both fields that study humans and other organisms, but with different approaches to handling artifacts.

Section 4 - Verbal Reasoning (Hard)

23 Minutes | 15 Questions

For Questions 1 to 4, select one entry for each blank from the corresponding column of choices. Fill all the blanks in the way that best completes the text.

1. Predicting which way a body should move when acted on by outside forces sounds easy, but the _____ way in which these forces often act makes the process significantly more challenging.

A	unequivocal
B	callow
C	tepid
D	disparate
E	engorged

2. The concept of uncertainty dominates the field of economics. Simply put, uncertainty is the unknown potential for gain or loss in a given transaction. This simple concept has tremendous ramifications, however. Potential risk for gain or loss cannot be easily (i) _____. As a result, the governments and households that want to have a concrete idea of the risk involved in a given endeavor don't always have data to go by. But this uncertainty is a necessary (ii) _____ that must be made in order to enjoy the benefits of a market economy.

Blank (i)	Blank (ii)
A perturbed	D frankness
B enumerated	E flaccidity
C aggrieved	F price

3. The topic of public sector finance has long been (i) _____. Issues such as who to tax, the cost–benefit models of government institutions, and income distribution have polarized political parties and private citizens alike. The sheer size of public finance means that every citizen, regardless of social status, has a tremendous stake in the structure of the economy. (ii) _____, the number of voices participating in public debate often overwhelms any attempt at (iii) _____ engagement.

Blank (i)	Blank (ii)	Blank (iii)
A acrimonious	D Equally	G sardonic
B acquiescent	E Ruinously	H sagacious
C frank	F Pensively	I rancorous

4. He never expected to find any semblance of (i) _____ between his two favorite activities. He always viewed basketball and guitar as being totally separate endeavors. But when he stopped playing at full speed and instead focused on establishing a (ii) _____, he began to play basketball better. (iii) _____, when he viewed guitar as a series of discrete skills that could be developed through repetition, he became a better musician, too.

Blank (i)	Blank (ii)	Blank (iii)
A delusion	D conjecture	G Refreshingly
B synergy	E clout	H Analogously
C deprecation	F cadence	I Exceedingly

For Questions 5 to 9, select one answer choice unless otherwise instructed.

Questions 5 and 6 are based on this passage.

The efficiency of bike riding is impacted by multiple factors such as wind resistance and gravity. Rolling resistance is one example of a physical phenomenon that can create problems for the rider. Rolling resistance is the dragging force that is felt when a bike tire is not sufficiently inflated leading to the deformation of the tire against the ground. This results in a loss of momentum and the need for more force to be exerted by the rider. Additionally, rolling resistance can increase when a bike has a heavy frame or a heavy rider. It takes more energy to increase the speed of a weightier object. Hence, competitive bicyclists try to stay skinny and inflate their tires well.

For the following question, consider each of the choices separately and select all that apply.

5. Based on the information in the passage, which of the following would likely be reasons to avoid the creation of rolling resistance?

   A. To increase the amount of force exerted by the rider, thereby improving the overall workout

   B. To abate momentum during a bike ride when wind resistance is present

   C. To conserve energy throughout a long-distance ride

6. Select the sentence in the passage that best states the main idea.

Questions 7 to 9 are based on this passage.

The earliest theater productions in England were born from church services in the tenth and eleventh centuries. Theater greatly increased in popularity in the middle of the fourteenth century when religious leaders began to encourage the production of Bible stories and tales of the saints. These plays were written and performed in the language of commoners for the purpose of educating the illiterate masses about Christianity. Unlike most plays today, these productions took place on wagons that circulated the city and parked at designated sites. For this reason, many towns dedicated specific spaces to public theater.

The sixteenth century brought hostility toward the Roman Catholic Church and its authority. This led to the suppression of religious theater productions. Nobleman-approved licenses became a requirement for any groups that wished to perform publicly.

7. Which of the following statements is best supported by the main idea of the first paragraph?

   A. Theater has always been a prominent part of arts and culture.

   B. Storytelling is an effective teaching method.

   C. Theater wagons parked at pre-assigned sites.

   D. Distaste for the authority of the Roman Catholic Church led to a decline in public theater productions.

   E. Early theater productions were used to educate common people about Christianity, but hostility toward the church in the sixteenth century resulted in fewer theater productions.

8. Which point best supports the author's argument that the church played a significant role in the popularity of public theater?

- A) The author states that religious leaders made suggestions for topics of theater productions, such as Bible stories.
- B) The author explains how the church facilitated a rise in public theater productions in order to educate commoners.
- C) In the sixteenth century, noblemen had to approve licenses before plays could be performed.
- D) Those who needed to be educated about Christianity were illiterate, so theater was the best way to reach them meaningfully.
- E) The author discusses the sharp decrease in the popularity of theater due to hostility toward the Roman Catholic Church.

9. If this passage continued, based on the format of the first two paragraphs what would the third paragraph most likely be about?

- A) How the popularity of theater changed in the seventeenth and eighteenth centuries.
- B) How the Roman Catholic church responded to public hostility.
- C) How theater productions changed from wagons to stationary production areas.
- D) Background information on the original plays of the tenth century.
- E) Information on the most well-known playwrights of the fourteenth century.

For Questions 10 to 12, select the two answer choices that, when used to complete the sentence, fit the meaning of the sentence as a whole and produce complete sentences that are alike in meaning.

10. The flavored–water company made sure to avoid the use of any specific language in their advertising campaign so they could make _____ claims about the supposed vitamin content of their product.

- A) disingenuous
- B) obdurate
- C) factual
- D) duplicitous
- E) lucid
- F) trivial

11. The interplay of supply and demand in a marketplace is not _____ to any one culture or class; the buying and selling of fabrics in a village square and the buying and selling of stocks on Wall Street are both examples of the reciprocal forces of supply and demand at work.

- A) anomalous
- B) unorthodox
- C) incongruous
- D) apocryphal
- E) tendentious
- F) sententious

12. There has never been a consensus on what constitutes "good" writing and that would explain the _____ of written works.

- A) incisiveness
- B) plethora
- C) variety
- D) visibility
- E) multiplicity
- F) incoherence

For Questions 13 to 15, select one answer choice unless otherwise instructed.

Question 13 is based on this passage.

Down syndrome is the most well-known form of trisomy, but there are other versions of chromosomal trisomy such as Patau syndrome, Klinefelter syndrome, and Edwards syndrome. Trisomy occurs when a person has three of a specific chromosome instead of the typical two. Various trisomies can lead to distinct symptoms and physical defects. Some are life-threatening, while others are very survivable.

To understand trisomies, one must first understand the nature of human chromosomes. Chromosomes are located in the nucleus of a cell and are thread-like structures that store genetic information. They are composed of genes that carry DNA. Usually, human cells contain 46 chromosomes, half from our mothers and half from our fathers. Sometimes, a cell divides abnormally during embryogenesis.

13. If the purpose of this essay was to argue for the inclusion of students with Down Syndrome in typical classrooms, how would the second paragraph contribute to the essay?

   A. The second paragraph would strengthen the argument because it provides critical background information on chromosomes so that the author's point can be made.
   B. The second paragraph would strengthen the argument because it shows the author's strong understanding of the science behind chromosomal issues.
   C. The second paragraph would weaken the argument because it contains information that is unnecessary for the argument.
   D. The second paragraph would weaken the argument because it is written in a way that is not consumable to the desired audience.
   E. The second paragraph would strengthen the argument because it explains that there are different types of trisomies with various symptoms, not only Down syndrome.

Questions 14 and 15 are based on this passage.

Contemporary art is simply art that is crafted in modern times by living artists. While many consumers appreciate aged pieces, contemporary art is special because it reflects the issues and social movements of today's dynamic world. Contemporary art examines prominent institutions, offers cultural critiques, and makes attempts to redefine art altogether. Deep questions and stimulating conversations are provoked through modern art pieces, making contemporary artists an important part of the cultural progression of society.

For the following questions, consider each of the choices separately and select all that apply.

14. Based on the passage, which of the following statements is true about the impact contemporary art has on society?

   A. Contemporary art propels movements that fight against injustices.
   B. Contemporary art is used to complement efficacious aspects of modern culture.
   C. Contemporary art facilitates changes to cultural understandings of art.

15. Based on the passage, which of the following is likely an objective of a contemporary artist?

   A. To imitate styles of art used in aged pieces
   B. To reflect social issues that occurred throughout history
   C. To create a dialogue between art consumers

Section 5 - Quantitative Reasoning (Easy)

26 Minutes | 15 Questions

1.

$$|x - a| = |x + a| \text{ where } a \geq 0$$

Quantity A	Quantity B
x	0

- (A) Quantity A is greater.
- (B) Quantity B is greater.
- (C) The two quantities are equal.
- (D) The relationship cannot be determined from the information given.

2.

Quantity A	Quantity B
The remainder when x is divided by 5.	The remainder when $x + 3$ is divided by 5.

- (A) Quantity A is greater.
- (B) Quantity B is greater.
- (C) The two quantities are equal.
- (D) The relationship cannot be determined from the information given.

3.

Quantity A	Quantity B
Area of a circle when the circumference is 12π	Area of a circle when the radius is 6.

- (A) Quantity A is greater.
- (B) Quantity B is greater.
- (C) The two quantities are equal.
- (D) The relationship cannot be determined from the information given.

4.

The ratio of the number of apples to oranges in Basket A is 3:2, and the ratio of apples to oranges in Basket B is 4:3. Basket A has 18 apples.

Quantity A	Quantity B
The number of oranges in Basket A.	The number of oranges in Basket B when there are 20 apples.

- (A) Quantity A is greater.
- (B) Quantity B is greater.
- (C) The two quantities are equal.
- (D) The relationship cannot be determined from the information given.

5.

$$f(x) = 3x + 2$$

Quantity A	Quantity B
The value of $f(4)$.	The value of $f(2) + 5$.

- (A) Quantity A is greater.
- (B) Quantity B is greater.
- (C) The two quantities are equal.
- (D) The relationship cannot be determined from the information given.

Section 5 - Quantitative Reasoning (Easy)

6

Consider the expression $2n^2 - 5n + 3$. For which of the following values of n does the expression yield the greatest value?

- A) 0
- B) 1
- C) 2
- D) 3
- E) 4

7

A bag contains red, blue, and green marbles. The probability of randomly selecting a red marble is $\frac{3}{10}$, and the probability of selecting a blue marble is $\frac{1}{2}$. If the bag contains 30 marbles in total, how many green marbles are in the bag?

- A) 3
- B) 6
- C) 9
- D) 12
- E) 15

8

What is the least common multiple (LCM) of $|15|$ and $|-20|$?

Indicate all such answers.

- A) 5
- B) 15
- C) 35
- D) 60
- E) 300

9

In a school, 35% of the students participate in sports activities. If there are 840 students in total, how many students do not participate in sports activities?

- A) 252
- B) 294
- C) 546
- D) 840
- E) 1,386

10

A map is drawn with a scale where 1 inch represents 5.5 miles. If the distance between two landmarks on the map is 3 inches, what is the actual distance between the landmarks?

Indicate all such answers.

- A) $\frac{33}{2}$
- B) 16.5
- C) $16\frac{1}{2}$
- D) 17.2
- E) $\frac{35}{2}$
- F) 18.5
- G) $18\frac{1}{2}$

11

$$2^{3y} \times 2^2 = 64$$

What is the value of y?

- A) 1
- B) $\frac{4}{3}$
- C) $\frac{5}{3}$
- D) 2
- E) $\frac{7}{3}$

12

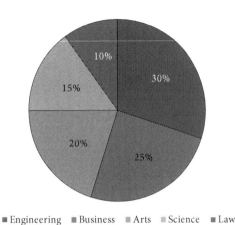

■ Engineering ■ Business ■ Arts ■ Science ■ Law

The pie chart above shows the distribution of students in a college based on their major. The total number of students is 1,200. If 80% of the Engineering and Business students are male, how many female students are there in these two majors combined?

- A) 132
- B) 300
- C) 360
- D) 528
- E) 660

13

Which of the following points lie on the same horizontal line as the point (3, 5)?

Indicate all such answers.

- A (1, 5)
- B (2, 6)
- C (4, 5)
- D (5, 4)
- E (3, 4)
- F (8, 6)
- G (7, 5)

14

The midpoint of the line segment connecting points $C(5, -1)$ and $D(x, 4)$ is $M(7, 1.5)$. What is the missing coordinate x of point D?

- A) 5
- B) 7
- C) 9
- D) 11
- E) 13

15

The difference between the squares of two consecutive integers is 31. What is the product of the integers?

[   ]

Section 5 - Quantitative Reasoning (Hard)

23 Minutes | 15 Questions

1

The following are the ages (in years) of five employees at a company: 24, 26, 30, 28, and 32.

Quantity A	Quantity B
Mean age of the employees.	30

A) Quantity A is greater.
B) Quantity B is greater.
C) The two quantities are equal.
D) The relationship cannot be determined from the information given.

2

Quantity A	Quantity B
$\|-7x+3\| + \|-9-x\|$	$\|14-4x\| + \|3x+5\|$
Where $x = -2$	Where $x = -2$

A) Quantity A is greater.
B) Quantity B is greater.
C) The two quantities are equal.
D) The relationship cannot be determined from the information given.

3

In an arithmetic progression, the first term is 3, and the common difference is 5.

Quantity A	Quantity B
5th term in the progression.	23

A) Quantity A is greater.
B) Quantity B is greater.
C) The two quantities are equal.
D) The relationship cannot be determined from the information given.

4

In an isosceles triangle $\triangle ABC$ with base angles B and C, the measures of the angles are $\angle A = 2x + 10°$, $\angle B = 3x - 5°$ and $\angle C$.

Quantity A	Quantity B
$\angle C + 10°$	$\angle A$

A) Quantity A is greater.
B) Quantity B is greater.
C) The two quantities are equal.
D) The relationship cannot be determined from the information given.

5

In a regular octagon, the length of one side is s. The distance between two opposite vertices (the diameter of the circumscribed circle) is D.

Quantity A	Quantity B
$\dfrac{D}{s}$	$2 + \sqrt{2}$

A) Quantity A is greater.
B) Quantity B is greater.
C) The two quantities are equal.
D) The relationship cannot be determined from the information given.

Section 5 - Quantitative Reasoning (Hard)

6

A bookshelf contains 5 distinct books: 2 fiction books, 2 non-fiction books, and 1 mystery book. Three books are to be selected to form a reading list, but at least one fiction book and one non-fiction book must be included. How many different ways can the reading list be formed if the order of selection does not matter?

- A) 4
- B) 6
- C) 8
- D) 10
- E) 12

7

The perimeter of a square is 20 meters. What is the area of the square?

- A) 5
- B) 9
- C) 16
- D) 20
- E) 25

8

A tank is filled with water at a rate of 3 gallons per minute. After 12 minutes, the tank is $\frac{3}{4}$ full. How many gallons of water does the tank hold when full?

- A) 12
- B) 24
- C) 36
- D) 48
- E) 60

9

Let x and y be integers such that $x^2 - y^2$ is odd, and xy is divisible by 3. If $x = 9$ and $y = m$, which of the following must be true for m?

- A) m is odd.
- B) m is divisible by 3.
- C) m is even.
- D) m is divisible by 2 but not 3.
- E) m is odd and divisible by 3.

10

John's salary was $50,000 last year, and he received a 12% raise this year. He is required to pay 20% of his new salary in taxes. What is his take-home pay after taxes?

- A) $11,200
- B) $44,800
- C) $50,000
- D) $56,000
- E) $60,000

11

If x is increased by 20% and then decreased by 25%, the resulting value is 15 less than the original value of x. What is the original value of x?

- A) 135
- B) 150
- C) 180
- D) 195
- E) 210

82 | *Practice Tests for the GRE*

Section 5 - Quantitative Reasoning (Hard)

12

The sum of the first 7 terms of an arithmetic progression is 119, and the sum of the first 10 terms is 230. What is the common difference d of the sequence?

- (A) 4
- (B) 6
- (C) 8
- (D) 10
- (E) 12

13

$$x + y \leq 10$$
$$x - y \geq 2$$
$$x \geq 3$$
$$y \geq 1$$

What is the minimum possible value of xy within the feasible region defined by the given inequalities?

[ ]

14

Month	City X	City Y
January	5	8
February	6	9
March	9	12
April	12	15
May	17	20
June	20	23
July	23	26
August	22	25
September	19	22
October	14	17
November	10	12
December	6	9

Consider the table above that shows the average monthly temperatures (in °C) for two cities over a year. Which city had the greater average temperature for the year?

- (A) City X
- (B) City Y
- (C) Both City X and Y
- (D) Neither City X and Y
- (E) Cannot be determined from the information.

15

$$2x - 3y = z$$
$$4x + y = 2z$$

Which of the following statements is true if x, y, and z are integers?

Indicate <u>all</u> such answers.

- [A] $x = 2z - y$
- [B] $y = 2x - z$
- [C] $x = \dfrac{3z + y}{2}$
- [D] $y = \dfrac{2z - 4x}{-1}$
- [E] $x = -z - y$
- [F] $y = 4x - 2z$

Answer Key

VERBAL REASONING

Section 2		
Q. No.	Correct Answer	Your Answer
1	A	
2	A, D	
3	A, F, H	
4	A, B	
5	B	
6	A, E	
7	A, E	
8	A, B	
9	A, D	
10	A	
11	D	
12	C	

Section 4 (Easy)		
Q. No.	Correct Answer	Your Answer
1	C	
2	A, E	
3	A, D, G	
4	B, D, H	
5	C	
6	E	
7	B	
8	B, F	
9	B, D	
10	B, C	
11	E	
12	B	
13	A	
14	D	
15	C	

Section 4 (Hard)		
Q. No.	Correct Answer	Your Answer
1	D	
2	B, F	
3	A, E, H	
4	B, F, H	
5	C	
6	Rolling...for the rider.	
7	B	
8	E	
9	A	
10	A, D	
11	A, E	
12	C, E	
13	C	
14	A, C	
15	C	

Answer Key

QUANTITATIVE REASONING

Section 3

Q. No.	Correct Answer	Your Answer
1	B	
2	A	
3	B	
4	C	
5	C	
6	C	
7	7%	
8	D	
9	E	
10	D, E	
11	B	
12	C	

Section 5 (Easy)

Q. No.	Correct Answer	Your Answer
1	C	
2	D	
3	C	
4	B	
5	A	
6	E	
7	B	
8	D	
9	C	
10	A, B, C	
11	B	
12	A	
13	A, C, G	
14	C	
15	240	

Section 5 (Hard)

Q. No.	Correct Answer	Your Answer
1	B	
2	A	
3	C	
4	A	
5	B	
6	C	
7	E	
8	D	
9	C	
10	B	
11	B	
12	A	
13	3	
14	B	
15	B, D, F	

Analytical Writing — Answers & Explanations — Section 1

Analyze an Issue

The sample essay that follows was written in response to the prompt that appeared in the question.

A healthy dose of skepticism is recommended when digesting a meal of facts delivered by someone else. In most cases, however, one should trust that those who have expertise in a specific field have done due diligence before making claims they presume to be true. Over time and with improved technology, new discoveries may appear that alter or contradict the current facts, but that doesn't mean they weren't true for the time and conditions under which they were espoused.

Some facts are true in the context in which they appear, but the reporters of such facts have cherry-picked them to serve their own purposes. This is never more obvious than during a presidential election. Social media makes these "facts" spread like wildfire, and the uninformed willingly accept them as gospel, especially if they coincide with their own political leanings. One of the most pervasive claims during the last presidential election was based on a chart depicting the yearly salaries of the President and members of Congress. The chart intended to inflame readers by stating that those individuals get that salary for life. While the dollar amounts were correct, the duration of said salaries was not. The President, senators and representatives get a pension based on their salaries. Another fact intended to shame Michelle Obama for having 26 assistants. What a waste of taxpayer money! A little research reveals that Laura Bush and other First Ladies had similar numbers of assistants. Displaying a little mistrust concerning facts presented for political purposes is wise.

Gossip is, perhaps, the most egregious misuse of facts. Generally repeated sotto voce, gossip can easily be misheard or misinterpreted. The listener then hurries off to spread the facts as he or she understood them. By the time the inflammatory remarks return to the subject of them, there is little truth remaining. In the case of gossip, the issue's original claim and reason hold true, not just for the sake of accuracy but for the protection of those subjected to vicious gossip. Rumors have characteristics in common with gossip. However, while gossip is never intended to spread good news, rumors may be used to disseminate both good and bad information, and their effect can be just as harmful as gossip. I live in a small city that was devastated when a nearby Air Force base closed. It had been rumored that the base would close several times over the years. Each time that the rumors began, local citizens would become despondent with worry over their futures. A Save Loring Committee worked tirelessly to keep the base from closing and succeeded twice. When the rumors began the third time, the locals refused to believe them, and believed the more positive rumors that, once again, the base would remain open. It was like the little boy who cried wolf. As in the fable, the wolf, in the form of BRAC, did finally make an appearance, and the citizens of Some facts that have been disproved have little or no effect, either positive or negative, on the course of human development. In recent history, Pluto has lost its status as a planet. It was always a little suspect, anyway. So our solar system is reduced to eight planets. This fact reversal has no effect on the way the world proceeds or stands as an argument that one should mistrust factual information. A much earlier astronomical reversal, however, did have an impact on the world. The Catholic Church believed the Earth to be the center of the universe. Since God had created the Earth and all of the creatures in it, it must be the most important of His creations. Hence, the sun and other planets must be inferior and show obeisance to the Earth by revolving around it. In the sixteenth century, Copernicus developed a model that disproved the geocentric theory and validated the heliocentric theory that had been proposed centuries before. Even though the Church was wrong about the solar system, one should not necessarily mistrust everything that the Church proclaims to be fact.

Every day begins with the immutable fact that the sun will rise in the East and ends when the sun sets in the West. Much of what happens in that span of time is open to interpretation, but the average human will not question the events that occur or the facts they hear. Those who do so relinquish the ability to simply enjoy the day that they have been given. The habit of mistrusting those in authority leads to a life filled with uncertainty.

Verbal Reasoning — Answers & Explanations — Section 2

1 **Choice A is correct** because this passage is saying that while motor vehicle transportation has become safer over the past decade, "all forms of transportation aspire" to be more like airline passage. Therefore, we can infer that airline passage must be safer than other forms of transportation, and thus the ideal that they strive for. "Exemplar" means "ideal." If airline passage is what all other forms of transportation aspire to be like, then it can be safely called an "ideal."

Choice B is incorrect because "contrarian" means someone who rejects popular opinion. The sentence does not suggest that airline travel is rejecting popular opinion in any way. **Choice C** is incorrect because "subversion" means rebellion, and again, there is no indication that airline travel is rebelling against anything. It is presented as an ideal, not as a rebel. **Choice D** is incorrect because "reprobate" means troublemaker. The sentence does not suggest that other forms of transportation would aspire to resemble a troublemaker. **Choice E** is incorrect because "scoundrel" means villain. Similarly, the sentence does not imply that other modes of transportation would aspire to be like a villain. Instead, airline travel is portrayed as an ideal to be emulated.

2 **Choice A and D are correct** because upon reading the first sentence we learn that early doctors did not have the benefit of modern science and technologies, so they had to teach themselves using something else. Considering they "simply dissected corpses" this "something else" can be inferred to be great determination. "Fortitudes" means "determination." To simply cut into a corpse and investigate would require determination. The last blank refers to the small details that early doctors overlooked. Therefore, we need a word that conveys smallness. "Diminutive" means 'small' and aligns with the overall message of the sentence, as it discusses "microscopic human anatomy."

Choice B is incorrect because "Artifice" means "deception." The doctors did not use deception to aid their learning, so this is wrong. **Choice C** is incorrect because "Precision" means "accuracy." The doctors did not have the benefit of precise, modern technology so this answer is wrong as well. **Choice E** is incorrect because "Convoluted" means "complicated." Even though the pathogeneses of diseases may very well have been complicated, this is not what the passage is trying to express. It is clearly focusing on size. **Choice F** is incorrect because "Inconsequential" means "unimportant." Just because something is small does not mean it is unimportant, so this answer is wrong.

3 **Choice A, F, and H are correct** because the first blank is comparing the subjects of study of the natural sciences versus political science. Since political science is described both as having to deal with "biases" and as being "unlike" the natural sciences, we know that natural sciences must not have "biases." "Dispassionate" means "unemotional." This makes sense. Physical scientists deal with the natural world. Therefore, they don't have to worry about emotions creeping into their research; they work in quantifiable data. The second blank tells of how political scientists need to "mitigate the shortcomings of any one approach." This indicates that one approach to research is inadequate. Therefore, multiple approaches are most likely taken. "Diversify" means "vary." This makes sense. In order to mitigate the shortcomings of any one research method, scientists would vary their research methods. The third blank talks of how political science has managed to do "something" in spite of obstacles. "Proliferated" means "thrived." It makes sense that if the field of political science was doing "something" in spite of obstacles, it would be thriving.

Choice B is incorrect because "Preconceived" means "predetermined." If physical sciences had "predetermined" observations then they would have bias, so this answer is wrong. **Choice C** is incorrect because "Psychological" means "of or relating to the mind." Political science, not natural science, is described as dealing with the human mind, so this answer cannot be correct. **Choice D** is incorrect because "Coalesce" means "merge." This is the opposite of what is desired for answers to the passage. **Choice E** is incorrect because "Inundate" means "overwhelm." "Overwhelming" their research methods would not aid scientists conducting research. **Choice G** is incorrect because "Regressed" means "backslid." The field of political science would not do this in spite of obstacles; it would do it because of them. This answer is incorrect. **Choice I** is incorrect because "Fulminated" means "ranted." This answer makes no sense in the context of the question.

Verbal Reasoning — Answers & Explanations — Section 2

4 **Choice A is correct** because watercolor paints come in a variety of colors. Thus, there is no reason given in the passage that would lead to the belief that a variety of pictures could not be painted using watercolor paints. **Choice B is correct** because the passage states paints are, "typically packaged as dry cakes in a paint pan." Because multiple cakes are discussed in a singular cake pan, it is likely that multiple colors of paint are sold together simultaneously.

Choice C is incorrect because the passage explains that traditional colors came from a variety of natural sources but, today, man-made colors are synthesized. Therefore, the production of paint colors has evolved over time.

5 **Choice B is correct** because this passage outlines the negative side effects of smoking. So, if the rest of the essay was in support of smoking then this passage must serve the purpose of explaining the opposing sides, or reasons not to smoke, before rebuking them.

Choice A is incorrect because this passage is written using a persuasive approach in opposition to cigarette smoking. It focuses on the negative side effects of smoking and the dangers of cigarette ingredients. If the remainder of this essay was in support of cigarette smoking, it would not make sense for the ingredients to be explained in such a negative manner. **Choice C is incorrect** because the passage does not explain what the respiratory system is or how it functions. Rather, it simply discusses how smoking can harm the respiratory system. Also, simply being able to be damaged does not necessarily make the respiratory system weak. **Choice D is incorrect** because if this passage attempted to convince the reader of the dangers of cigarette smoking it would not align with the remainder of the essay which aimed to convince the reader of the opposite. **Choice E is incorrect** because this passage is written using a persuasive approach in opposition to cigarette smoking. It focuses on the negative side effects of smoking and the dangers of cigarette ingredients. Based on this introduction, it would not make sense for the passage to go on explaining the health benefits of free radicals. The context of the term, "free radicals" in the passage suggests that they are damaging to the body.

6 **Choice A and E are correct** because this sentence is saying that although the period and structure of music changes its superficial qualities, all music elevate the human spirit in the same way. This sameness is the operative idea. We want words that stress the interchangeable effects of these genres. "Fungible" and "Interchangeable" both mean substitutable. This is the exact sentiment we want. When all of the superficial structures are torn away all genres of music have substitutable contributions to emotional elevation; i.e. the same contributions.

Choice B is incorrect because "Unequal" means uneven distribution. This answer cannot work because the whole idea of the sentence is that the emotional elevation of the material is equal. **Choice C is incorrect** because "Confusing" means unclear. This word does not in any way complete the sentiment of sameness between disparate genres of music. **Choice D is incorrect** because "Unnecessary" means not needed. Again, the sentence is not trying to argue of the necessity of these emotional elevations, it's trying to say that they can come from different sources. Therefore "Unnecessary" is incorrect. **Choice F is incorrect** because "Enlightening" means informative. Again, "Enlightening" does not complete the sentiment of the passage. We're trying to establish a quality of computability between these two hypothetical genres, not discuss their philosophical import.

7 **Choice A and E are correct** because this sentence talks about difficult intellectual concepts in the laboratory causing students to overlook more bland procedural concepts, so the correct answer should establish how distillation apparatus setup is less interesting than the mechanism of sharpless epoxidation. "Perfunctory" and "mechanical" mean routine or automatic. It would make sense that routine, automatic procedures are overlooked by students who are focusing on a more complex topic.

Choice B is incorrect because "riveting" means exciting. This word does not complete the sentiment of the sentence because we want to show the apparatus being less interesting than the sharpless epoxidation. **Choice C is incorrect** because "sympathetic" means compassionate. This word does not complete the sentence in any logical way. It doesn't address the relative intrigue of the two

Practice Tests for the GRE

topics at hand. **Choice D** is incorrect because "adroit" means skillful. If the distillation technique is given less consideration by the students, then it cannot require more skill than the epoxidation. **Choice F** is incorrect because "inexplicable" means mysterious. If the setting up of a distillation apparatus was mysterious then students would be less likely to forget it, not more.

8 **Choice A and B are correct** because Darwin is described as going against Medieval and Christian theory; therefore his ideas were presumably not quickly adopted. To this end we want answer choices that focus on the conflict he experienced. "Contempt" and "Derision" mean scorn or mockery. It makes sense that Darwin and his theory would experience scorn and mockery from the scientific establishment, who had held the same ideas for hundreds of years.

Choice C is incorrect because "Companionship" means company or friendship. Nothing about this sentence implies that Darwin's ideas granted him exceptional amounts of company or friendship. **Choice D** is incorrect because "Competition" means rivalry. This answer choice does work, as there were obviously rival theories on this matter, but there is no matching answer choice for it. Therefore it cannot be chosen. **Choice E** is incorrect because "Egotism" means arrogance. Like "Competition" this answer choice works on its own. Darwin certainly had to deal with the egos of other scientists who scoffed at his theory. However, much like "Competition" this answer choice does not have a pair in the answer choices. **Choice F** is incorrect because "Relief" means respite. If Darwin had to fight so hard against entrenched theories, then he could not have had too much respite.

9 **Choice A and D are correct** because this sentence is trying to say that something (the high-quality spatial resolution maps) that used to be difficult to obtain is now easier to obtain. Therefore, we want words that stress how something has become commonplace. "Ubiquitous" and "Prevalent" both mean widespread. They both work in the sentence because they state how the imaging maps that used to be difficult to obtain are now commonplace in a medical setting.

Choice B is incorrect because "Inconceivable" means unthinkable or implausible. This is the exact opposite sentiment that we want to express in this sentence. The sentence is trying to say that high quality spatial maps have become less unattainable – calling them inconceivable means they've become more unattainable. **Choice C** is incorrect

because "Relatable" means relevant or applicable. There's no reason to believe that high quality spatial resolution maps were not applicable to medicine before the MRI was invented. The difficulty was making the maps easier to obtain. **Choice E** is incorrect because "Extreme" means risky or dangerous. There's no reason to believe that the MRI would render the imaging maps risky or dangerous. **Choice F** is incorrect because "Essential" means vital or crucial. Again, we want answers which show that the imaging maps have become less difficult to obtain. "Essential" if anything, has the opposite effect.

10 **Choice A is correct** because the author would likely disagree with this statement. The author expresses that there are many social problems presented with aging. Therefore, simply extending the lifespan should not be the only focus.

Choice B is incorrect because although the author does feel that longevity is a great societal accomplishment, the author does not indicate a desire for further research at any point. The author explains that some research has been done to compare countries and understand the impacts of economic incentives. No other information about research is given. **Choice C** is incorrect because the author states that living a longer life depends on decisions made during mid-life, not after retirement. Additionally, the author states that a longer work life can improve cognitive function. Therefore, there is no reason to believe the author feels that longevity should only become a priority after retirement. **Choice D** is incorrect because the author feels that aging poses societal problems and would therefore agree with this statement. **Choice E** is incorrect because the author does state that longevity in the United States has not progressed as much as longevity in other developed nations. However, the author does not indicate that this is not enough progress or that only gaining five years is insufficient.

11 **Choice D is correct** because it is a simple sentence that introduces the concept of longer human lives without stating the author's overall argument. The purpose of this sentence is to pique the reader's interest in the topic before delivering a thesis statement.

Choice A is incorrect because this sentence does not present the author's overall argument. It only states that scientific developments have led to longer human lives. The following sentence serves as a thesis and presents the author's overall argument to be proven in the remainder of the passage. **Choice B** is incorrect because it does not provide any background information on societal aging, but simply introduces societal aging as a concept before diving into more detail throughout the rest of the passage. **Choice C** is incorrect because although the sentence does mention scientific advancements in the area of aging, this is not the purpose of the sentence. The remainder of the passage does not discuss what these scientific advancements are, so that would not contribute to the development of the passage. The passage is focused on the repercussions of societal aging, not the advancements that have led to societal aging. **Choice E** is incorrect because it does not introduce the two sides of the argument presented in the passage. This sentence only presents the positive side of longevity without mentioning the negative social consequences that come with it.

12 **Choice C is correct** because the author explains that negative side effects of societal aging impact the economy, provision of social resources, and prevalence of disease and disability. Therefore, using more resources to care for those with diseases could be one negative impact of societal aging.

Choice A is incorrect because this is not necessarily a negative effect. Having more work available for lawyers could be considered a benefit to the economy. Also, this does not fall under any of the described categories of concern. **Choice B** is incorrect because having a greater number of people in the workforce is not a negative thing for society. Also, the author expresses that being in the workforce can contribute to greater cognitive function. Therefore, the author does not feel negatively about older adults remaining in the workforce. **Choice D** is incorrect because innovation and the development of social programs would not be a negative thing for society. It would be a benefit for social resources, not a detriment. **Choice E** is incorrect because although more people do drive on public roads as a result of societal aging, this does not fall under the categories of negative impacts provided by the author. The author explains that there are problems in relation to economic, social resource, and disease prevalence concerns. Public infrastructure is not a part of any of these categories.

Quantitative Reasoning — Answers & Explanations — Section 3

1 **Choice B is correct.**

Set up the initial comparison:

$\frac{2x}{3}$? x

Then simplify:

Multiply both sides by 3 to get $2x$? $3x$

To compare $2x$ and $3x$, basically, we compare 2 and 3, and it is clear that 2<3. We need to compare Quantity A and Quantity B to answer the question, not 2 and 3. To do so we need to start from $2x < 3x$ and divide this inequality by 3:

$\frac{2x}{3} < x$.

So, Quantity A is less than Quantity B.

Thus, the correct answer is Choice B, Quantity B is greater.

Choice A is incorrect because $x > 6$, then after simplification, we conclude that $x > 5$. **Choice C** is incorrect since we find that $x > 5$. **Choice D** is incorrect because we can compare quantities from the given information.

2 **Choice A is correct.** From the number line, we determine that N = 3.

Hence, we need to compare $\frac{1}{3}$ and $\frac{1}{4}$. Since 4 > 3, then $\frac{1}{3} > \frac{1}{4}$.

So, Quantity A is greater than Quantity B.

Thus, the correct answer is Choice A, Quantity A is greater.

Choice B is incorrect because $\frac{1}{3} > \frac{1}{4}$, not otherwise.

Choice C is incorrect because $\frac{1}{3}$ is not equal to $\frac{1}{3}$.

Choice D is incorrect because we can determine and compare given quantities.

3 **Choice B is correct** because you can use the mean to evaluate the value of k to be 72. To solve, multiply the mean by the number of terms in each group. For the first 10 numbers, the mean times the number of terms would yield a sum of $10 \times 83 = 830$. For the group of 20 numbers, $20 \times 65 = 1300$. The mean of the 30 numbers can be found by adding these two sums and then dividing by 30 to get $\frac{(830+1300)}{(10+20)} = \frac{2130}{30} = 71$.

To find k, use the same idea of multiplying the mean by the number of terms to find the sum. The mean of the numbers with k is 82 and there are 11 numbers so $82 \times 11 = 902$. Subtract the original sum of 830 to get the value of k that was added. This would get you $902 - 830 = 72$.

This means k is greater than the mean of all 30 numbers so Quantity B is greater than Quantity A.

Choice A is incorrect because k is greater than the mean. **Choice C** is incorrect because the two quantities are not equal. **Choice D** is incorrect because it is possible to solve for k and the mean.

4 **Choice C is correct.**

The system of linear equations has infinitely many solutions when equations are equal. So, $4x = 2ax$, $2y = ay$, $5 = 5$. From the first two equations, we find that $a = 2$. Thus, the correct choice is C, the two quantities are equal.

Choice A is incorrect because $a = 2$. **Choice B** is incorrect because $a = 2$. **Choice D** is incorrect because a can be determined and equal to Quantity B.

5 **Choice C is correct.**

Amount = $2,250

Deposit/ principal (P) = $1,500

Simple interest (I) = Total amount − Principal = $2,250 − $1,500 = $750

Interested is computed semi–annually, or twice a year, so in 5 years it is calculated 10 times.

Time (t) = 10

$I = Prt$

$r = \frac{I}{Pt} = \frac{750}{1500 \times 10} = 0.05 = 5\%$

Choice A is incorrect because this would result if the rate was halved incorrectly. **Choice B** is incorrect because this would be the result if the rate was calculated incorrectly. **Choice D** is incorrect because this results from a miscalculation. **Choice E** is incorrect because this results in a miscalculation.

6 **Choice C is correct.** The data on the pie chart shows the revenue from full-day tours is 42% and the revenue from half-day tours is 11%.

42:11 is close to the ratio 4:1. Thus, Choice C is correct.

Choice A is incorrect because the ratio of 42:11 is not close to 5 to 2. **Choice B** is incorrect because the ratio of 42:11 is not close to 4 to 2. **Choice D** is incorrect because the ratio of 42:11 is not close to 3 to 2. **Choice E** is incorrect because the ratio of 42:11 is not close to 3 to 1.

7 **The correct answer is 7%.** First, we find the dollar amount of 22 percent of the revenue accounted for water rafting in 2015.

It is given in the table that the dollar amount of adventure sports in 2015 was 51 million dollars. Hence, the dollar amount of water rafting is 51 · 22/100 =11.22 million dollars. From the table data, we see that the total dollar amount in 2015 is 169 million dollars.

Hence, we need to find what percent of 169 is 11.22.

11.22/169 · 100 = 6.64%

which is 7% to the nearest whole percent.

8 **Choice D is correct.** The table shows that the revenue from sightseeing tours in 2018 was $104 million. Then the review from weekend tours is 104 · 18/100 = 18.72 million dollars.

The table shows that the revenue from sightseeing tours in 2021 was $118 million. Then the review from weekend tours is 118 · 25/100 = 29.5 million dollars.

The percent increase in the revenue from weekend tours between 2018 and 2021 is (29.5 – 18.72)/ 18.72 · 100 = 57.6

The nearest value is 55%. Thus, the Choice D is correct.
Choice A is incorrect because 25% is far from 57.6 %.
Choice B is incorrect because 35% is far from 57.6 %.
Choice C is incorrect because 45 % is far from 57.6 %.
Choice E is incorrect because 65% is far from 57.5 %.

9 **Choice E is correct.** A volume of a cube with side a is a^3. Hence, we can find the side of the cube

$$64 = a^3, a = \sqrt[3]{64} = 4.$$

It is given that the base circle of the cylinder is circumscribed around a square with side 4. It means that the diameter of the circumscribed circle is equal to the diagonal of the square around which this circle is circumscribed.

The diagonal, d, of the square of side 4 by the Pythagorean Theorem is

$d = \sqrt{4^2 + 4^2} = 4\sqrt{2}$.

Hence, the radius of this circle is $2\sqrt{2}$.

Since we found that the side of the cube is 4, then the height of the cylinder is also 4 and we can find the volume of the cylinder.

The volume of the cylinder is equal to the product of the base area and the height, hence we get

$$V = \left(2\sqrt{2}\right)^2 \cdot \pi \cdot 4 = 8 \cdot 3.14 \cdot 4 = 100.48$$

Thus, the closest value is 100, Choice E is correct.
Choice A is incorrect because 50 is much less than 100.48.
Choice B is incorrect because 64 is much less than 100.48.
Choice C is incorrect because 81 is much less than 100.48.
Choice D is incorrect because 92 is much less than 100.48.

10 **Choices D and E are correct.** The middle observation is (4 + 8 + 7 + 6)/2 = 12.5, which is 13. It means that the middle class is ranged between 800 and 899. Thus, all values in this class could be median alues, namely 800 and 860. Hence, **Choices D and E are correct.**

Choice A is incorrect because 655 does not belong to the median class. **Choice B** is incorrect because 725 does not belong to the median class. **Choice C** is incorrect because 798 does not belong to the median class. **Choice F** is incorrect because 975 does not belong to the median class.

11 **Choice B is correct** because the radius of the circle can be found to be 6 which would mean the circumference is 12π. To find the radius of the circle, recognize that the 18π in the given expression must be the area of the semi-circle since the shaded area is the area of the rectangle (96) minus the area of the semi-circle (18π).

If half of the area of the circle is 18π, then doubling it would give you an area of 36π. Since the area of a circle equals A = πr² then you can find the radius of the circle by setting the area equal to the equation. This would get you πr² = 36π. Divide both sides by π to get r² = 36. Square root both sides to get r = 6.

To get the circumference of a circle, use the formula C = 2πr. Plugging in 6 for the radius will get you C = 2π(6) which equals 12π.

Choice A is incorrect because 6 is the radius, not the diameter. **Choice C** is incorrect because this would be using the numbers from the formula provided and not accounting for it being the area of half a semicircle. **Choice D** is incorrect because this would be the area of the circle, not the circumference. **Choice E** is incorrect because this is larger than the actual circumference.

12 **Choice C is correct** because to solve an absolute value inequality, you need to break the statement into two different equations. The first equation would be $2x - 7 < 5$. Add 7 to both sides and divide by 2 to get $x < 6$.

The second solution is found by setting the expression equal to −5 and flipping the direction of the inequality to get $2x - 7 > -5$. Add 7 and divide by 2 to get $x > 1$.

This means the possible solutions would be $1 < x < 6$.

Choice A is incorrect because this would be the answer if you ignored the 2 and the 7 in the original problem. **Choice B** is incorrect because only half of the statement is accurate. **Choice D** is incorrect because this is the result of a calculation error. **Choice E** is incorrect because this is the result of a math error.

2 Verbal Reasoning (Easy) — Answers & Explanations — Section 4

1 **Choice C is correct** because the sentence is setting up a simple comparison. Therefore, a word that facilitates the comparison of biological sciences to physical sciences is desired. "Correspondent" means "similar." This completes the comparison that is being set up in the sentence.

Choice A is incorrect because "subservient" means "deferential to." The two sciences are described as being very important. There is no implication that biological sciences are subservient to physical sciences. **Choice B** is incorrect because "sequestered" means "seized". This answer does not make sense in the context of the question. **Choice D** is incorrect because "variable" means "flexible". If the sentence is implying a similar level of importance between the two sciences then a "variable" level of importance for the biological sciences does not make sense. **Choice E** is incorrect because "unconnected" means "distinct". This is the opposite of what we want.

2 **Choice A and E are correct** because the second sentence says that marine biologists are not given something that other scientists take for granted. The passage then goes on to talk of the difficulties in working in an aquatic environment. Therefore, we can infer this "something" that marine biologists are not granted is convenience. "Amenities" means "conveniences." A lack of conveniences would explain why working in an aquatic environment is more difficult than on land. The last sentence lists even more difficulties that marine biologists face. Therefore, the second blank must be introducing issues that make a situation worse. "Exacerbating" means "making worse." This is exactly what added difficulties do to a situation. They make them worse.

Choice B is incorrect because "Recalcitrance" means "stubbornness." Marine biologists would not be suffering for lack of stubbornness, so this answer is wrong. **Choice C** is incorrect because "Biliousness" means "sickness." This answer makes no sense in the context of the question. **Choice D** is incorrect because "Insinuating" means "implying." This answer does not make sense in the context of the question. The difficulties faced in making durable tracking devices do not "insinuate" problems, they make them. **Choice F** is incorrect because "Alleviating" means to "assuage." This is the opposite of what we want. These problems make matters worse, not better.

3 **Choice A, D, and G are correct** because the word "although" is critical to this sentence, suggesting that the name belies the true nature of the Kiss-Kiss bug. The passage tells us the Kiss-Kiss bug is a dangerous and prevalent pest vector of Chagas disease. If its name suggests it is the opposite of its true nature, we can assume that its name suggests it is "innocuous." For the second blank, Choice D is correct because based on the description of how the Kiss-Kiss bug enters homes, including words like "infiltrates" and "ensconce" we can safely infer that the bug enters homes surreptitiously. As the Kiss-Kiss bug enters furtively and hides itself, surreptitiously is the correct answer. For the third blank, Choice G is correct because the phrase "Once thought to be rare" that opens the second sentence suggests that it is now known that the Kiss-Kiss bug is the opposite of rare, or highly prevalent. We must consequently look for a synonym for "highly prevalent." Ubiquitous means everywhere, and if the bug is highly prevalent it is everywhere.

Choice B is incorrect because the name is suggestive but not portentous, that is, foreboding, which does not align with the context of the passage. **Choice C** is incorrect because the name is not accumbent, or reclined, as this would make little sense in the passage. **Choice E** is incorrect because precipitously, or abruptly, does not account for the secretive qualities of the bug and must consequently be eliminated as an option. **Choice F** is incorrect because quintessentially means representing the ultimate or perfect example, leaving us to wonder, "example of what?". It does not fit within the context of the passage. **Choice H** is incorrect because exiguous, meaning scanty, does not align with the context of the passage. **Choice I** is incorrect because anomalous, meaning atypical, does not align with the context of the passage.

4 **Choices B, D, and H are correct** because this passage primarily provides possible explanations for the Salem witch trials. For the first blank, "enigmatic" fits well because the sentence highlights that there is "no shortage of speculation" about the cause of the trials, implying that they remain mysterious or perplexing. For the second blank, "austere" accurately describes the religious climate mentioned in the sentence. Since this climate is said to have contributed to an atmosphere where mass hysteria could develop, a word meaning strict or harsh (like "austere") suits the context. For the third blank, "fester" works well because the sentence suggests that socio-economic tensions and religious severity allowed mass hysteria to take hold and intensify. "Fester" which means to grow worse or become more intense over time, fits that idea perfectly.

Choice A is incorrect because "clandestine" (secretive or hidden) doesn't make sense—there's no suggestion in the sentence that the trials or their causes were concealed. **Choice C** is incorrect because while the trials were "infamous", the sentence is focused on explaining their cause, not judging their reputation. **Choice E** is incorrect because "vitriolic" (bitter or scathing) implies maliciousness, which overstates the nature of the religious climate described—it was strict, not hateful. **Choice F** is incorrect because "pristine" has positive connotations and contradicts the idea that the religious environment contributed to hysteria. **Choice G** is incorrect because "convene" (to bring people together) doesn't apply to an emotional state like hysteria and implies intentionality, which doesn't fit here. **Choice I** is incorrect because "languish" means to weaken or fade, which is the opposite of what the sentence implies—mass hysteria didn't diminish; it grew.

5   **Choice C is correct** because the passage states that pollen allergies are common in the spring, summer, and fall. Also, it discusses tree pollen coming in spring, grass pollen coming in spring and summer, and ragweed pollen coming in summer and fall. The passage states that only in southern states can pollen be released year-round. Thus, pollen allergies are not common in winter in any other state.

Choice A is incorrect because although pollen particles can travel hundreds of miles, there is no reason to believe they would cross states instead of affecting those in their immediate vicinity. They will likely impact anyone they encounter. **Choice B** is incorrect because pollen particles can enter the eyes, nose, and lungs. Therefore, they are small enough to enter the human body. **Choice D** is incorrect because there is no reason to believe grass pollen is more problematic than tree pollen. The specific symptoms resulting from different types of pollen are not discussed. **Choice E** is incorrect because the author explains that, because pollen particles can travel, they are nearly impossible to escape. Therefore, they can't simply be avoided by staying away from certain areas.

6   **Choice E is correct** because the author states that seasonal allergies are common and that pollen exists all over the country. Therefore, seasonal allergies to pollen are a common problem for Americans.

Choice A is incorrect because the passage outlines when certain plants release pollen throughout the year. Therefore, seasonal allergies to pollen do not come at unexpected times but on a well-understood schedule. **Choice B** is incorrect because there is no mention of mortality in this passage or any serious side effects of allergies beyond coughing and sneezing. There is no reason to assume that allergies contribute to mortality. **Choice C** is incorrect because there is no mention of the treatment or prevention of allergies. Although the passage explains that pollen is inescapable, there is no reason to assume that no treatments exist. **Choice D** is incorrect because seasonal allergies exist all over the country and pollen can travel hundreds of miles. Although pollen is only released in the southern states in the winter, pollen is released nationwide in spring, summer, and fall.

7   **Choice B is correct** because the first sentence of the second paragraph states, "Most of the pollen that leads to allergic reactions comes from trees, grasses, or weeds." In other words, not all pollen that leads to allergic reactions comes from these three sources. Therefore, pollen can come from other plants, though less often.

Choice A is incorrect because there is an overlap between the release of pollen of trees, grasses, and weeds. Trees release pollen in the spring, but grasses release pollen in the spring as well. Grasses also release pollen in the summer, alongside ragweed. **Choice C** is incorrect because the passage states, "There are countless varieties of grasses, but only a handful actually cause allergic reactions." Therefore, only a few grasses cause allergic reactions, not many types. **Choice D** is incorrect because the passage states that allergic reactions from pollen can stem from weeds, not a singular type of weed. The passage goes on to detail that many Americans are affected by ragweed, but there is not sufficient information to assume that ragweed is the only type of weed that releases pollen. This makes Choice B the better answer option. **Choice E** is incorrect because this is a conclusion that can be drawn from the passage, but this information comes from the first paragraph, not the second paragraph.

2 Verbal Reasoning (Easy)   Answers & Explanations   Section 4

8 **Choice B and F are correct** because the words should establish the competition between computers and written documents. "Ousted" and "superseded" both mean to succeed or replace something else. This completes the sentence because the sentence is trying to express how computers have made office work easier by abandoning a vestigial idea.

Choice A is incorrect because "fulminated" means raged against or criticized. Computers obviously did not criticize paper documents. They surpassed them. **Choice C** is incorrect because "integrated" means unified or combined. Computers can unify and combine written documents, but this sentence is stressing that computers are destroying written documents, not rendering them more efficient. **Choice D** is incorrect because "prioritized" means ordered or ranked. Again, computers can certainly order and rank written documents but this answer doesn't stress the way in which computers have "defeated" written documents. **Choice E** is incorrect because "galvanized" means spurred or roused. This is a completely wrong sentiment. Computers have not "roused" written documents into life.

9 **Choice B and D are correct** because this sentence is saying that the corporate executive isn't just asking questions, he's asking them in a certain way to lure his rival into a false sense of security. Therefore, we want words that characterize the questions as being kind, because a question that appears kind would not arouse the suspicion of the person being interrogated. "Benign" and "gentle" both mean kind and friendly. Asking questions in a seemingly gentle way would be a good way to catch a presenter off-guard and subvert their presentation.

Choice A is incorrect because "refractory" means headstrong. The executive is going for a quiet attack, therefore this does not work. **Choice C** is incorrect because "transparent" means clear and easily seen through. This sentiment is the opposite of what the sentence is trying to convey: the executive is working quietly, not clearly. **Choice E** is incorrect because "insensitive" means cruel or not regarding one's emotions. Insensitive questions would attract attention and it would not succeed in being subtle and subversive. **Choice F** is incorrect because "meandering" means unfocused. This looks like a good answer. But there's no other answer to pair it with.

10 **Choice B and C are correct** because this sentence says that carbon is responsible for much more in the natural world than casual viewers give it credit for. If credit is being denied to carbon, then these "casual observers of chemistry" must be talking down to it in some way. Therefore, we want words that stress degrading language. "Vilipend" and "denigrate" both mean to bitterly speak against something. It makes sense that the speaker in the sentence is telling people not to bitterly speak against carbon because it is the foundation for complex creations.

Choice A is incorrect because "question" means to doubt. While this answer seems like it might work it doesn't have the same import as some other choices. To "question" isn't nearly as severe as to insult or degrade. **Choice D** is incorrect because "corroborate" means to uphold or support. This sentence states that people degrade carbon as being an unimportant element. To degrade something is the opposite of corroborating it. Therefore, "corroborate" makes no sense as an answer. **Choice E** is incorrect because "endorse" means to support or approve, and thus fails for the same reason as "corroborate" does. The point is that casual observers are speaking against carbon, not for it. **Choice F** is incorrect because "invigilate" means to observe or check. Again this doesn't indicate anybody speaking ill of carbon, so it doesn't work.

11 **Choice E is correct** because a person who is delinquent is one who commits crimes, or illegal, immoral acts. Because Susan B. Anthony engaged in illegal behavior as women were not given the right to vote, she could be described as delinquent.

Choice A is incorrect because "combative" means ready and eager to fight. Susan B. Anthony did not engage in any aggressive behavior or make any threats to do so. Although she broke the law, she did so calmly without any personal attacks. **Choice B** is incorrect because "shiftless" means a person is lazy and lacks ambition. Susan B. Anthony was not lazy because she took action to make a move toward women's rights when it was not socially accepted to do so. **Choice C** is incorrect because "befuddled" means someone is unable to think clearly. Susan B. Anthony had a clear motive in her action and desired for women to be able to vote in presidential elections. She was not confused about her intent or behavior. **Choice D** is incorrect because a "conformist" is one who follows the rules to be accepted by society or a group. By voting illegally, despite the social unacceptability, Susan B. Anthony did not conform.

Verbal Reasoning (Easy) — Answers & Explanations — Section 4

12 **Choice B is correct** because the text explains that children can learn to solve real-world dilemmas through the ways characters respond in fictional scenarios. Also, the text states that characters can act as role models engaging in correct behaviors. So, if a child did not experience a bully firsthand, but read a story in which a bullying scenario was handled well, the child could learn how to correctly ask for help in the face of bullying in real life.
Choice A is incorrect because learning to sew is not a problem-solving skill. The child simply became interested in sewing after reading the story. **Choice C** is incorrect because learning another language is not a problem-solving skill, nor is making a new friend. Although these are both valuable skills, they are not used to overcome an obstacle. So, learning words from the way characters in a book speak does not count as learning to navigate real-world dilemmas through a fictional role model. **Choice D** is incorrect because learning about cultural heritage is not necessarily a problem-solving skill. Although learning about one's own heritage can be valuable, it is not used to overcome an obstacle in this scenario. **Choice E** is incorrect because although this may count as a child imitating the behavior of a fictional character, this would not be problem-solving in a righteous way. Also, this would show a negative effect of learning from a story, which is in direct opposition to the rest of the passage.

13 **Choice A is correct** because "endurance" means being able to continue with great stamina. So, "listening endurance" would mean being able to continue listening for a longer amount of time.
Choice B is incorrect because the author is expressing that vocabulary, language, and listening skills will improve through reading books. "Making it through more intense stories" does not fit contextually in this list of skills. Also, there is no mention in the passage of helping kids learn to get through difficult stories. **Choice C** is incorrect because this is another part of the text and is not what the term, "listening endurance" refers to. In other words, it would be redundant to say that reading books can, "strengthen vocabulary, enhance language skills, and learn vocabulary and language skills." **Choice D** is incorrect because there is no mention of striving to help kids learn how to listen to various voices and tones in the remainder of the passage. Also, the word, "endurance" is not at all related to the sound of a voice. **Choice E** is incorrect because the passage does not suggest that paying attention to sorrowful and serious tales is the goal. The passage aims to express that children can listen better for longer periods of time, but does not discuss the nature of the specific stories.

14 **Choice D is correct** because the author mentions, "anthropology is the study of humans in societies and cultures including human biology and companionship." From the word, "companionship" one can derive that anthropologists examine how humans interact with one another. This reason is not directly stated as the other reasons are, making it the most indistinct.
Choice A is incorrect because the fact that archaeologists study artifacts is explicitly stated in detail, so it is one of the more major differences between the two disciplines. **Choice B** is incorrect because the fact that archaeologists study different organisms is explicitly stated, so it is one of the more major differences between the two disciplines. **Choice C** is incorrect because the fact that archaeologists have different specializations is explicitly stated in detail, so it is one of the more major differences between the two disciplines. **Choice E** is incorrect because this is a similarity between the two fields, not one of the differences described.

15 **Choice C is correct** because both fields do study humans and their cultures, as stated in the text. However, archaeology emphasizes remains and artifacts to understand history, while anthropology emphasizes human biology and companionship.
Choice A is incorrect because it is never stated in the text that anthropologists handle artifacts in their studies. **Choice B** is incorrect because the text never indicates that anthropology includes more subtopics. Oppositely, there is more information provided on the subspecialties involved in archaeology. Also, in the United Kingdom archaeology is considered the broader umbrella discipline over anthropology. **Choice D** is incorrect because the text never indicates that anthropology includes more subtopics. Oppositely, there is more information provided on the subspecialties involved in archaeology. Also, in the United Kingdom archaeology is considered the broader umbrella discipline over anthropology. **Choice E** is incorrect because it is never stated in the text that anthropologists study any other organisms besides humans. Also, it is never stated in the text that anthropologists handle artifacts in their studies.

2 Verbal Reasoning (Hard)   Answers & Explanations   Section 4

1 **Choice D is correct** because this sentence says that making a prediction of where a body will move seems easy, but in reality, it is not. It specifically says that it's not easy because of a certain way in which forces act on the body in question. This "certain way" must be a discordant way of acting. If they moved in a uniform way, predictions would be easier. "Disparate" means unequal, or unlike. Forces acting in an unequal fashion would be difficult to make predictions about because they would be interacting with each other in a variety of confusing ways.

Choice A is incorrect because if they moved in an uniform way predictions would be easier. "Unequivocal" means "clear." Forces interacting in a "clear" way would not make the prediction process more difficult. **Choice B** is incorrect because "callow" means "inexperienced" or "immature." Physical forces cannot act in an "immature" way, so this answer is wrong. **Choice C** is incorrect because "tepid" means lacking in intensity. Again, the tepid action of forces would make the prediction process easier. **Choice E** is incorrect because "engorged" means enflamed. This word does not make sense in the context of the question.

2 **Choice B and F is correct** because the first blank can best be understood by reading the sentence that comes after it. The sentence says that households don't always have "data to go by" when it comes to assessing risk. Therefore, it must be difficult to quantify risk. "Enumerated" means "tallied" or "computed." This answer makes sense. If we cannot generate data by which to assess risk then risk must not be easily "enumerated." For the second blank, we must first analyze the last sentence carefully. The word "uncertainty" is described as something we must accept or pay in exchange for economic freedom or reward—so we're looking for a word that means cost, trade-off, or sacrifice. "Price" is a metaphor for sacrifice or cost and hence it makes perfect sense to say "uncertainty is the price we pay for the benefits of a market economy."

Choice A is incorrect because "perturbed" means "worried." The concept of the potential for gain or loss being "worried" does not make any sense in this context. **Choice C** is incorrect because "aggrieved" means "distressed." This answer suffers from the same problem as "perturbed." **Choice D** is incorrect because "frankness" means "honesty." This word does not express any idea of giving things up. **Choice E** is incorrect because "flaccidity" means "slackness." Again, this word does not express the idea of giving things up.

3 **Choice A, E, and H are correct** because after reading the whole passage, we learn that the topic of public sector finance has "polarized" private citizens. Therefore, we can infer that the topic does not lend itself to friendly conversation. "Acrimonious" means "hostile." This is an accurate description of a topic that leads to "polarized political parties." The second blank starts off a sentence in which it is said that the number of voices participating in public debate overwhelms certain types of engagements. If public engagement is being overwhelmed then it is certainly a bad thing. "Ruinously" means "disastrously." It would be disastrous if too many voices were allowed to overwhelm public engagement on an issue. The last blank can better be understood after the second has been filled. Now that we know that excessive amounts of voices are "ruinously" overwhelming a certain type of public discourse, we can safely infer that this type of discourse must be preferred "Sagacious" means "wise" or "learned." It would be "ruinous" if sagacious public engagement was overwhelmed by too many public voices.

Choice B is incorrect because "acquiescent" means "submissive." Given the description of "polarized political parties" this is not a good answer. **Choice C** is incorrect because "frank" means "honest." Although the topic of public sector finance is never specifically described as dishonest, there is no evidence given that it is honest, either. Furthermore, the idea of "polarized political parties" invokes the notion of potential dishonesty far more than honesty. **Choice D** is incorrect because "equally" means "alike." The number of voices participating in public debates is not described as being equal to anything else, so this is wrong. **Choice F** is incorrect because "pensively" means "thoughtfully." There is nothing thoughtful about voices overwhelming social engagement. **Choice G** is incorrect because "sardonic" means "mocking" or "sarcastic." This is not a type of public engagement that we would lament being rid of. **Choice I** is incorrect because "rancorous" means "bitter." Once again, this is not a type of public engagement that we would lament being rid of.

4 **Choice B, F, and H are correct** because this passage is saying that a person can find a connection between basketball and guitar. "Synergy" means cooperation, and since each activity helps improve the other, there is cooperation between them. For the second blank, the passage states that a skill from music helped a person get better at basketball. "Cadence" means rhythm, which is something one learns from playing guitar. By applying

98 | *Practice Tests for the GRE*

this rhythm—and not always playing at full speed—the person can improve at basketball. For the last blank, the passage suggests that basketball can help with guitar in the same way that guitar helps with basketball. "Analogously" means similarly. The way in which playing guitar has improved by basketball is similar to how basketball is improved by playing guitar.

Choice A is incorrect because "delusion" means misapprehension. There is nothing delusional about the connection between basketball and guitar; one activity clearly helps improve the other. **Choice C** is incorrect because "deprecation" means scorn. There is no scorn involved—basketball and guitar benefit each other. **Choice D** is incorrect because "conjecture" means guess. Guessing doesn't contribute to the improvement described in the passage. **Choice E** is incorrect because "clout" means influence. Influence alone would not explain how one skill enhances the other. **Choice G** is incorrect because "refreshingly" means in a way that is invigorating. There is no indication in the passage that the experience is invigorating—only that it leads to improvement. **Choice I** is incorrect because "exceedingly" means to a great extent. The passage doesn't suggest that the actions must be repeated often—only that they are effective.

5 **Choice C is correct** because rolling resistance slows the rider down and requires more force to be exerted by the rider. Therefore, rolling resistance should be avoided for any riders wishing to save energy for a great distance.

Choice A is incorrect because this goes against the passage. The passage says rolling resistance makes the ride harder and requires more force, but competitive cyclists try to reduce it. The focus is on efficiency, not exercise intensity. **Choice B** is incorrect because rolling resistance decreases momentum. So, avoiding rolling resistance would not decrease, or abate momentum, but increase momentum.

6 **"Rolling resistance is one example of a physical phenomenon that can create problems for the rider."** The sentence prior to this discusses other factors that can impact biking efficiency. This sentence introduces rolling resistance in a concise format before discussing it in detail for the remainder of the paragraph, including a definition, examples, and an additional detail about competitive bicyclists.

7 **Choice B is correct** because the main point of the first paragraph is that public theater was used to share religion with common people. This supports the idea that people can learn by hearing stories.

Choice A is incorrect because the main point of the first paragraph is that public theater was used to share religion with common people. This does not necessarily support the statement that theater has always been a prominent part of arts and culture. Therefore, Choice B is the best option. **Choice C** is incorrect because this is a minor point in the first paragraph. We know this because it is only mentioned in two sentences in the first paragraph and is completely irrelevant in the second paragraph. On the other hand, the topic of religion continues into the second paragraph, making Choice B the better option. **Choice D** is incorrect because this is the main point of the second paragraph, not the first one. **Choice E** is incorrect because it includes information from both the first and second paragraphs, not just the first paragraph.

8 **Choice E is correct** because this point reveals how much influence the church had over the fall of the public theater after it had just risen to such popularity. If theater suffered because of hostility toward the church, the two were obviously very closely tied. This is a stronger point than the church increasing the popularity of theater, to begin with, because it proves that theater had become popular because of the church rather than any other reasons.

Choice A is incorrect because the fact that religious leaders wished to contribute to topics for theater production does not necessarily prove that the church played a significant role in the popularity of theater. This only proves that religious leaders wanted to be involved in theater productions. **Choice B** is incorrect because although this does support the author's argument, it does not support the author's argument as strongly as Choice E. The church worked to increase theater productions, but without the information about the decline due to conflict with the Roman Catholic Church, it cannot be assumed that this was the sole reason for the rise of theater. **Choice C** is incorrect because the fact that noblemen had to approve plays is not relevant to the topic of the church's role in the popularity of theater. **Choice D** is incorrect because although this is a true statement, it does not support the author's argument that the church played a significant role in the popularity of public theater.

2 Verbal Reasoning (Hard)   Answers & Explanations   Section 4

9 **Choice A is correct** because the first paragraph discusses theater in the tenth to fourteenth centuries and the second paragraph discusses theater in the sixteenth century. Therefore, it would make sense for the third paragraph to continue this pattern and discuss theater in the seventeenth and eighteenth centuries.

Choice B is incorrect because the first paragraph talks about the rise of theater popularity in the tenth to fourteenth centuries and the second paragraph discusses how it decreased in the sixteenth century. It would not make sense for the passage to discontinue this pattern and pivot to a focus on how the church responded, rather than focusing on theater history. **Choice C** is incorrect because it would not make sense for the passage to discontinue the established pattern and revert to a focus on wagon productions, rather than progressing on theater history. **Choice D** is incorrect because the first and second paragraphs progress through time periods discussing the history of theater. It would not make sense for the third paragraph to revert back to the tenth century to discuss well-known plays. **Choice E** is incorrect because it would not make sense for the passage to discontinue this pattern and revert back to focus on playwrights of the fourteenth century, rather than progressing with theater history.

10 **Choice A and D are correct** because this sentence is saying that the flavored–water company is trying to get away with claiming something that ostensibly isn't true, so the answer should refer to deceit. "Disingenuous" and "duplicitous" both mean deceitful, which correctly characterizes the quality of their advertising campaign.

Choice B is incorrect because "obdurate" means stubborn. They are not trying to make stubborn claims about their water; they are trying to make deceitful ones. **Choice C** is incorrect because "factual" means accurate. The entire aim of the company is to use language that allows them to avoid making accurate claims, so this cannot be true. **Choice E** is incorrect because "lucid" means coherent. This is the opposite of what they are doing. They're not being clear, they're being vague. **Choice F** is incorrect because "trivial" means minor or unimportant. Considering that the company is trying to get away with making these claims they must be a big deal in the advertising campaign and therefore not trivial.

11 **Choice A and E are correct** because the process of supply and demand is present in such different cultural spaces as village squares and stock exchanges. The message is that the forces of supply and demand is not limited to or not unique to any one type of environment; since the missing word comes after "not" the correct answer will mean similarly to limited or unique. Thus, the answers that fit the intended meaning and are grammatically correct are "anomalous" (meaning peculiar or unique) and "tendentious" (meaning biased or promoting a specific point of view).

Choice B is incorrect because "unorthodox" (meaning deviating from the norm) is not grammatically correct when inserted into the sentence. **Choice C** is incorrect because "incongruous" (meaning out of place or absurd) do have the connotations needed but the choice is not grammatically correct when inserted into the sentence. **Choice D** is incorrect because "apocryphal" (meaning being of doubtful authenticity or fictional) does not align with the context of the passage. **Choice F** is incorrect because "sententious" (meaning given to pompous moralizing) is off-topic for this sentence.

12 **Choice C and E are correct** because this passage is saying that there is a lack of consensus on what qualifies as "good" writing, therefore implying that written works are often vastly different from one another. Therefore, we want answers that stress how different written works can be. "Variety" and "multiplicity" both mean a varied assortment. It makes sense that a lack of consensus on what constitutes "good" writing would lead to a variety of different works, because people would always be writing to fit their particular definition of "good."

Choice A is incorrect because "incisiveness" means brutality. Written works might sometimes be brutal, but a lack of consensus on what is "good" writing would not cause this to happen. **Choice B** is incorrect because "plethora" means an excess. It's plausible that a divided public might produce a wide range of written works, each reflecting differing opinions. However, this requires assumptions to be made; namely, that people would write not just different works but a lot of them in order to forward an opinion. Because this answer relies on assumptions not explicitly stated in the passage it is not a good one. **Choice D** is incorrect because "visibility" means prominence or clarity. This word does not fit with the sentiment of the passage. How would lack of consensus make written works more prominent? It could happen, but it's not a strict requirement. **Choice F is incorrect** because "incoherence" means unintelligibility. Again, it's possible that changing public perception could render some written works incoherent, but a clear line of cause and effect cannot be drawn.

13 **Choice C is correct** because the second paragraph explains the biological intricacies of chromosomes that lead to the development of genetic conditions. This information would not be relevant to arguing for the inclusion of students with Down syndrome. This paragraph is not needed and includes scientific information that may be challenging to understand. An argument for children with Down syndrome to be included would focus more heavily on the social factors and benefits than on the genetic explanation of the disorder. Thus, this paragraph would be superfluous.

Choice A is incorrect because scientific information on chromosomes does not contribute to an argument for students with Down syndrome being included. It is irrelevant to the argument, so it would act as a weakness in the argument. **Choice B is incorrect** because the author's understanding of chromosomal issues is not necessary in order to make an argument for inclusion of students with Down Syndrome. The author would need to show expertise in other areas, such as symptoms of Down Syndrome and how inclusion benefits individuals with Down syndrome. However, the scientific breakdown of chromosomes weakens the argument by adding unnecessary and distracting information. **Choice D is incorrect** because this is a subjective statement about the scientific understanding of the audience. The audience being targeted is not specified. There is not sufficient information to assume that the audience would not understand this paragraph or that it would be a weakness in the argument due to its wording. Therefore, Choice C is the better option. **Choice E is incorrect** because the first paragraph explains this, not the second. Also, this does not contribute to the argument that students with Down Syndrome should be included. Rather, it provides more information on different trisomies.

14 **Choice A is correct** because the passage explains that contemporary art reflects the issues and social movements of today's world and offers cultural critiques. Therefore, one can infer that social injustices are reflected and critiqued in contemporary art, propelling movements against them. **Choice C is correct** because the passage states that contemporary art makes attempts to redefine art and plays an important role in the cultural progression of society. Therefore, one can infer that the way society understands art is altered over time with the help of contemporary art pieces.

Choice B is incorrect because although art may be used to complement aspects of culture, this is not expressed anywhere in the passage. Oppositely, the passage states that contemporary art reflects issues, offers critiques, and helps with cultural progression.

15 **Choice C is correct** because the passage states, "Deep questions and stimulating conversations are provoked through modern art pieces." Therefore, contemporary artists likely want to make people speak about their pieces and what they represent.

Choice A is incorrect because the passage explains that contemporary artists try to redefine art. In other words, the passage does not include any information about repeating styles. **Choice B is incorrect** because the passage thoroughly discusses the fact that contemporary art reflects the social issues and culture of modern times. The passage does not indicate anywhere that contemporary art examines historical events.

Quantitative Reasoning (Easy) Answers & Explanations — Section 5

1 **Choice C is correct** because no matter what value of a is inputted, the only solution to the expression can happen when $x = 0$ since $|0 - a| = |0 + a|$ which simplifies to be $a = a$.

Choice A is incorrect because the two quantities are equal.
Choice B is incorrect because the two quantities are equal.
Choice D is incorrect because the two quantities are equal.

2 **Choice D is correct.** The value of x can be any integer, thus the possible remainders when x is divided by 5 are 0, 1, 2, 3, or 4. Adding 3 to any remainder will cycle through the possible remainder of dividing by 5.

If the remainder of x is 1, $x + 3$ has a remainder of 4.

If the remainder of x is 3, $x + 3$ has a remainder of 1.

The relationship between the quantities depends on x and therefore, cannot be determined from the given information.

Choice A is incorrect. The example above shows that Quantity A is not always greater. **Choice B** is incorrect. The example above shows that Quantity B is not always greater. **Choice C** is incorrect. The quantities are not equal in any case.

3 **Choice C is correct.** The formula for the circumference is given by $C = 2\pi r$. It is given that the circumference of Quantity A is 12π. Substituting the value of C into the formula yields $12\pi = 2\pi r$. Dividing both sides by 2π yields $6 = r$.

The formula for the area of a circle is given by $A = \pi r^2$. Substituting $r = 6$ into the formula yields $A = \pi(6)^2 = 36\pi$ for Quantity A.

It is given that the radius for Quantity B is also 6, therefore, the areas of both Quantity A and Quantity B are equal.

Choice A is incorrect. The two quantities are equal; therefore, neither quantity is greater. **Choice B** is incorrect. The two quantities are equal; therefore, neither quantity is greater. **Choice D** is incorrect. There is enough data to determine the relationship between the two.

4 **Choice B is correct.** Let x be the number of apples and y be the number of oranges.

In Basket A, the ratio of apples to oranges is 3:2, thus let the number of apples and oranges be $3x$ and $2x$, respectively. It is also given that there are 18 apples in Basket A, thus $3x = 18$. Dividing both sides by 3 yields $x = 6$. Substituting 6 for x to get the number of oranges yields $2x = 2(6) = 12$.

In Basket B, the ratio of apples to oranges is 4:3, thus let the number of apples and oranges be $4x$ and $3x$, respectively. It is also given that there are 20 apples in Basket B, thus $4x = 20$. Dividing both sides by 4 yields $x = 5$. Substituting 5 for x to get the number of oranges yields $3x = 3(5) = 15$.

Therefore, Quantity B has a greater number of oranges than Quantity A.

Choice A is incorrect. Quantity A has 12 oranges which is less than Quantity B. **Choice C** is incorrect. The two baskets have different numbers of oranges. **Choice D** is incorrect. There is enough data to determine the relationship between the two.

5 **Choice A is correct.** In Quantity A, to find the value of $f(4)$, substitute $x = 4$ into the given function $f(x) = 3x + 2$. This results in $f(4) = 3(4) + 2 = 14$.

In Quantity B, to find the value of $f(2)$, substitute $x = 2$ into the given function $f(x) = 3x + 2$. This results in $f(2) = 3(2) + 2 = 8$. Adding 5 to this value yields $f(2) + 5 = 8 + 5 = 13$.

Therefore, Quantity A has a greater value than Quantity B.

Choice B is incorrect. Quantity B has 13 which is less than Quantity A. **Choice C** is incorrect. The two values have different quantities. **Choice D** is incorrect. There is enough data to determine the relationship between the two.

6 **Choice E is correct.** To solve, calculate the value of the given expression $2n^2 - 5n + 3$ by substituting each value of n.

For $n = 0$, $2(0)^2 - 5(0) + 3 = 3$.
For $n = 1$, $2(1)^2 - 5(1) + 3 = 0$.
For $n = 2$, $2(2)^2 - 5(2) + 3 = 1$.
For $n = 3$, $2(3)^2 - 5(3) + 3 = 6$.
For $n = 4$, $2(4)^2 - 5(4) + 3 = 15$.

Therefore, the greatest value is 15 when n=4.

Choice A is incorrect. This results in 3 which is less than 15. **Choice B** is incorrect. This results in 0 which is less than 15. **Choice C** is incorrect. This results in 1 which is less than 15. **Choice D** is incorrect. This results in 6 which is less than 15.

2 Quantitative Reasoning (Easy) Answers & Explanations   Section 5

7 **Choice B is correct.** Let r be the number of red marbles, b be the number of blue marbles, and g be the number of green marbles.

The probability of selecting a red marble is $\frac{r}{30} = \frac{3}{10}$, thus $r = \frac{3}{10} \times 30 = 9$.

The probability of selecting a blue marble is $\frac{b}{30} = \frac{1}{2}$, thus $b = \frac{1}{2} \times 30 = 15$.

It is given that the total number of marbles is 30, thus the number of green marbles is $30 - 9 - 15 = 6$. Therefore, there are 6 green marbles in the bag.

Choice A is incorrect. This may result if the total marbles in the bag is 18. **Choice C is incorrect.** This is the number of red marbles. **Choice D is incorrect.** This is twice the number of green marbles. **Choice E is incorrect.** This is the number of blue marbles.

8 **Choice D is correct.** The absolute value of the given numbers are $|15| = 15$ and $|-20| = 20$.

Using prime factorization to find LCM of 15 and 20 yields $15 = 3 \times 5$ and $20 = 2^2 \times 5$.

LCM is the product of the highest power of all prime factors which are 3, 2^2, and 5.

Thus, LCM $= 2^2 \times 3 \times 5 = 60$.

Choice A is incorrect. This is the difference in the absolute value of the given numbers. **Choice B is incorrect.** This is the absolute value of $|15|$. **Choice C is incorrect.** This is the sum of the absolute value of the given numbers. **Choice E is incorrect.** This is the product of the absolute value of the given numbers.

9 **Choice C is correct.** It is given that 35% of students participate in sports activities and there are a total of 840 students. Calculating the number of students participating in sports yields $35\% \times 840 = \frac{35}{100} \times 840 = 294$.

Therefore, the number of students who did not participate in sports is $840 - 294 = 546$.

Choice A is incorrect. This is the difference between the number of students who did not participate and who did participate in sports. **Choice B is incorrect.** This is the number of students who participate in sports. **Choice D is incorrect.** This is the total number of students. **Choice E is incorrect.** This is the sum of the number of students who did not participate and the total number of students.

10 **Choices A, B, and C are correct.** It is given that the map scale is 1 inch and represents 5.5 miles.

The actual distance corresponding to 3 inches is Actual distance $= 3 \times 5.5 = 16.5$.

Therefore, the options that represent or equal to 16.5 are A: $\frac{33}{2}$, B: 16.5, and C: $16\frac{1}{2}$.

Choice D is incorrect. This option is 17.2 and not equal to 16.5. **Choice E is incorrect.** This option is 17.5 and not equal to 16.5. **Choice F is incorrect.** This option is 18.5 and not equal to 16.5. **Choice G is incorrect.** This option is 18.5 and not equal to 16.5.

11 **Choice B is correct.** Using the exponent rule $a^m \times a^n = a^{m+n}$, simplify the left-hand side of the given equation $2^{3y} \times 2^2 = 64$ to get $2^{3y+2} = 64$. Expressing 64 as a power of 2 yields $64 = 2^6$. The equation is now $2^{3y+2} = 2^6$, where the bases are equal.

Setting the exponents equal to each other yields $3y + 2 = 6$. Subtracting 2 from both sides yields $3y = 4$. Dividing both sides by 3 yields $y = \frac{4}{3}$. Therefore Choice B is the correct answer.

Choice A is incorrect. This may result if the given is $2^{3y} \times 2^2 = 32$. **Choice C is incorrect.** This may result if the given is $2^{3y} \times 2^2 = 128$. **Choice D is incorrect.** This may result if the given is $2^{3y} \times 2^2 = 256$. **Choice E is incorrect.** This may result if the given is $2^{3y} \times 2^2 = 512$.

12 **Choice A is correct.** To solve this, find the number of students in Engineering and Business.

The number of Engineering students is $30\% \times 1{,}200 = 0.30 \times 1{,}200 = 360$.

The number of Business students is $25\% \times 1{,}200 = 0.25 \times 1{,}200 = 300$.

The students in Engineering and Business are $360 + 300 = 660$.

It is given that 80% of the students in these two majors are male, thus $80\% \times 660 = 0.8 \times 660 = 528$.

Therefore, the female students in these two majors are $660 - 528 = 132$.

Choice B is incorrect. This is the number of Business students. **Choice C is incorrect.** This is the number of Engineering students. **Choice D is incorrect.** This is the number of male students in Engineering and Business. **Choice E is incorrect.** This is the total number of Engineering and Business students.

13 **Choices A, C, and G are correct.** For points to be on the same horizontal line, the y-coordinate must be the same. The given point $(3, 5)$ has a y-coordinate of 5.

Therefore, the points with the same y-coordinate as $(3, 5)$ are $(1, 5)$, $(4, 5)$, and $(7, 5)$.

Choice B is incorrect. This option has a y-coordinate of 6 instead of 5. **Choice D** is incorrect. This option has a y-coordinate of 4 instead of 5. **Choice E** is incorrect. This option has a y-coordinate of 4 instead of 5. **Choice F** is incorrect. This option has a y-coordinate of 6 instead of 5.

14 **Choice C is correct.** Use the midpoint formula $M(x_m, y_m) = (\frac{x_1 + x_2}{2}, \frac{y_1 + y_2}{2})$ to solve.
Substitute the given points $C(5, -1)$ and $D(x, 4)$, and midpoint $M(7, 1.5)$ into the formula.

This results in $7 = \frac{5 + x}{2}$ and $1.5 = \frac{-1 + 4}{2}$. Solve the x-coordinate of the midpoint $7 = \frac{5 + x}{2}$.
Multiplying both sides by 2 yields $14 = 5 + x$. Subtracting 5 from both sides yields $9 = x$.

Therefore, the missing coordinate x of the point D is 9.

Choice A is incorrect. This may result if the given midpoint is $M(5, 1.5)$. **Choice B** is incorrect. This may result if the given midpoint is $M(6, 1.5)$. **Choice D** is incorrect. This may result if the given midpoint is $M(8, 1.5)$. **Choice E** is incorrect. This may result if the given midpoint is $M(9, 1.5)$.

15 **The correct answer is 240.** Let the two consecutive integers be n and $n + 1$.

The difference between the squares of these integers can be expressed as $(n + 1)^2 - (n)^2 = 31$.

Applying the difference of squares formula $a^2 - b^2 = (a - b)(a + b)$ yields $((n + 1) - n)((n + 1) + n) = 31$ or $2n + 1 = 31$.

Subtracting 1 from both sides yields $2n = 30$. Dividing both sides by 2 yields $n = 15$.

Thus, the two consecutive integers are 15 and 16.

Therefore, the product is $15 \times 16 = 240$.

2 Quantitative Reasoning (Hard)   Answers & Explanations   Section 5

1 Choice B is correct. To solve, find the sum of the ages which results in 24 + 26 + 30 + 28 + 32 = 140.

Dividing the sum by the number of employees which is 5 yields $\frac{140}{5} = 28$.

Since Quantity B is 30, therefore, Quantity B is greater than Quantity A.

Choice A is incorrect. Quantity A has a mean of 28 which is less than Quantity B. **Choice C** is incorrect. The two have different quantities. **Choice D** is incorrect. There is enough data to determine the relationship between the two.

2 Choice A is correct. Finding the value of Quantity A when $x = -2$ yields

$|-7(-2) + 3| + |-9 - (-2)| = |14 + 3| + |-9 + 2|$. Simplifying yields $|17| + |-7|$.

Getting the absolute value yields 17 + 7 = 24.

Finding the value of Quantity B when $x = -2$ yields $|14 - 4(-2)| + |3(-2) + 5| = |14 + 8| + |-6 + 5|$.

Simplifying yields $|22| + |-1|$.

Getting the absolute value yields 22 + 1 = 23.

Since 24 > 23, therefore Quantity A is greater than Quantity B.

Choice B is incorrect. Quantity B has a value of 23 which is less than Quantity A. **Choice C** is incorrect. The two values have different quantities. **Choice D** is incorrect. There is enough data to determine the relationship between the two.

3 Choice C is correct. Use the formula $a_n = a_1 + (n - 1) \cdot d$ to get the n-th term of an arithmetic progression where $a_1 = 3$, $d = 5$, and $n = 5$.

Substituting the given results in $a_5 = 3 + (5 - 1) \cdot 5 = 23$.

Since 23 = 23, therefore Quantity A is equal to Quantity B.

Choice A is incorrect. The two quantities are equal; therefore, neither quantity is greater. **Choice B** is incorrect. The two quantities are equal; therefore, neither quantity is greater. **Choice D** is incorrect. There is enough data to determine the relationship between the two.

4 Choice A is correct. To solve, calculate the measure of $\angle C$.

The sum of the angles in a triangle is 180°, thus $\angle C = 180 - \angle A - \angle B = 180 - (2x + 10) - (3x - 5) = 175° - 5x$.

To compare the quantities, set up the equation $\angle C = \angle B$ to get $175 - 5x = 3x - 5$.

Adding $5x + 5$ to both sides yields $180 = 8x$.

Dividing both sides by 8 yields $22.5 = x$.

Substituting the value of x into $\angle A = 2x + 10°$ yields $\angle A = 2(22.5) + 10° = 55°$.

Substituting the value of x into $\angle C + 10° = (175° - 5x) + 10°$ yields $\angle C + 10° = (175° - 5(22.5)) + 10° = 72.5°$.

Since 72.5° > 55°, therefore, Quantity A is greater than Quantity B.

Choice B is incorrect. Quantity B has an angle value of 55° which is less than Quantity A. **Choice C** is incorrect. The two angles have different quantities. **Choice D** is incorrect. There is enough data to determine the relationship between the two.

5 Choice B is correct. For a regular octagon, the side length s and the diameter D of the circumscribed circle are related by the formula $D = s(1 + \sqrt{2})$.

In Quantity A, $\frac{D}{s}$, substitute the relationship between D and s into the formula to get $\frac{D}{s} = \frac{s(1 + \sqrt{2})}{s}$. Simplifying yields $\frac{D}{s} = 1 + \sqrt{2}$.

Comparing the two quantities results in Quantity A = $\frac{D}{s}$ = $1 + \sqrt{2} \approx 2.414$ and Quantity B = $2 + \sqrt{2} \approx 3.414$.

Since 3.414 > 2.414, therefore, Quantity B is greater than Quantity A.

Choice A is incorrect. Quantity A has a value of 2.414 which is less than Quantity B. **Choice C** is incorrect. The two values have different quantities. **Choice D** is incorrect. There is enough data to determine the relationship between the two.

6 Choice C is correct. To determine the possible combinations, 3 books need to be selected with the condition that at least 1 fiction book and 1 non-fiction book must be included.

It is given that there are 2 fiction books, 2 non-fiction books, and 1 mystery book.

Checking Case 1: 1 fiction, 1 non-fiction, and 1 mystery yields 2 × 2 × 1 = 4 ways to form the reading list.

Checking Case 2: 2 fiction and 1 non-fiction yields 2 × 1 = 2 ways to form the reading list.

Checking Case 3: 1 fiction and 2 non-fiction yields $1 \times 2 = 2$ ways to form the reading list.

Therefore, the total number of combinations is $4 + 2 + 2 = 8$.

Choice A is incorrect. This option only considers Case 1 or Case 2 and 3. **Choice B** is incorrect. This option may result if only Case 1 and one other case (either case 2 or 3) were considered. **Choice D** is incorrect. This option overestimates the total number of combinations. **Choice E** is incorrect. This option over estimates the total number of combinations.

7 **Choice E is correct.** The formula for the perimeter of the square is given by *Perimeter* = 4*s*.

It is given that the perimeter is 20 meters, thus, $20 = 4s$. Dividing both sides by 4 yields $5 = s$. The area of the square is given by the formula $A = s^2$. Substituting the value of the side length into the formula yields $A = 5^2 = 25$ m^2.

Choice A is incorrect. This is the length of the side. **Choice B** is incorrect. This may result if the perimeter is 12. **Choice C** is incorrect. This may result if the perimeter is 16. **Choice D** is incorrect. This is the perimeter of the square.

8 **Choice D is correct.** The formula for the amount of water filled in 12 minutes is *water filled = rate × time*.

Substituting the given yields *water filled = 3 gallons per minute × 12 minutes = 36 gallons*.

36 gallons represents $\frac{3}{4}$ of the tank, thus the total capacity of the tank can be found by $\frac{3}{4} \times$ *Total capacity* = 36.

Dividing both sides by $\frac{3}{4}$ yields *Total capacity* = 48 *gallons*.

Choice A is incorrect. This is the given time. **Choice B** is incorrect. This is the amount of water filled in 8 minutes. **Choice C** is incorrect. This is the amount of water filled in 12 minutes. **Choice E** is incorrect. This is the amount of water filled in 20 minutes if the tank holds more than 60 gallons.

9 **Choice C is correct.** It is given that $x^2 - y^2$ is odd, where $x = 9$ and $y = m$.

Analyzing $x^2 - y^2$ being odd using the difference of square $x^2 - y^2 = (x - y)(x + y)$. For the product to be odd, both $x - y$ and $x + y$ must be odd since the product of two odd numbers is odd. Thus, both $x - y$ and $x + y$ must be odd.

Analyzing when this happens, then $x = 9$ is odd, and for $x - m$ and $x + m$ to be odd, m must be even. This is due to the sum or difference between an odd and an even number being odd, and the sum or difference between two odd numbers being even.

Thus, m must be even for $x^2 - y^2$ to be odd.

It is given that xy is divisible by 3. Since $x = 9$ is divisible by 3, it follows that for xy to be divisible by 3, m does not need to be divisible by 3, as x satisfies this condition.

Therefore, m can be any integer and still satisfies this condition.

Analyzing the two conditions, the correct answer is that m must be even.

Choice A is incorrect. This option contradicts, as m cannot be odd, as that would make $x^2 - y^2$ even. **Choice B** is incorrect. m does not need to be divisible by 3. **Choice D** is incorrect. This option is partially correct (divisible by 2) but unnecessarily restricts m from being divisible by 3. **Choice E** is incorrect. This option contradicts, as m cannot be odd.

10 **Choice B is correct.** Calculating the salary after the raise yields $1.12 \times 50{,}000 = \$56{,}000$.

Calculating the taxes that need to be paid yields $0.20 \times 56{,}000 = \$11{,}200$.

Thus, the take-home pay is $56{,}000 - 11{,}200 = \$44{,}800$.

Therefore, the correct answer is Choice B.

Choice A is incorrect. This is the taxes of his new salary. **Choice C** is incorrect. This is his salary last year. **Choice D** is incorrect. This is his salary after the raise. **Choice E** is incorrect. This is his salary if the raise is 20%.

11 **Choice B is correct.** Express the changes in terms of x. After a 20% increase, the value then becomes $1.2x$.

After a 25% decrease, the new value then becomes $0.75 \times 1.2x = 0.9x$.

The equation based on the given condition that the new value is 15 less than the original value of x is $0.9x = x - 15$. Subtracting x from both sides yields $-0.1x = -15$. Dividing both sides by -0.1 yields $x = 150$. Therefore, the original value of x is 150.

Choice A is incorrect. This is the value after a 25% decrease. **Choice C** is incorrect. This is the value after a

2 Quantitative Reasoning (Hard) Answers & Explanations   Section 5

20% increase. **Choice D** is incorrect. This is the value after a 30% increase. **Choice E** is incorrect. This is the value after a 40% increase.

12 **Choice A is correct.** Use the formula for the sum of the first n terms $S_n = \frac{n}{2}[2a + (n-1)d]$.

For $n = 7$, $119 = \frac{7}{2}[2a + 6d]$ or $2a + 6d = 34 \quad (1)$.

For $n = 10$, $230 = \frac{10}{2}[2a + 9d]$ or $2a + 9d = 46 \quad (2)$.

Solving the systems of equations by subtracting equation 1 from equation 2 yields $(2a + 6d) - (2a + 9d) = 34 - 46$ or $-3d = -12$.

Dividing both sides by -3 yields $d = 4$.

Choice B is incorrect. This may result if the sum of the first 10 terms is 260. **Choice C** is incorrect. This may result if the sum of the first 10 terms is 290. **Choice D** is incorrect. This may result if the sum of the first 10 terms is 320. **Choice E** is incorrect. This may result if the sum of the first 10 terms is 350.

13 **The correct answer is 3.** Solve each inequality to find the feasible region.

For $x + y \leq 10$, solve for y to get $y \leq 10 - x$.

For $x - y \geq 2$, solve for y to get $y \leq x - 2$.

Set $10 - x = x - 2$, to find the intersecting points.

This results in $2x = 12$. Divide both sides by 2 to get $x = 6$.

Substitute the value of x to solve for y which results in $y = 10 - 6 = 4$.

Check boundaries satisfying the constraints.

For $x = 3$, $y = 10 - 3 = 7$ and $y = 3 - 2 = 1$ (satisfy the constraint $y \geq 1$). Then $xy = 3(1) = 3$.

14 **Choice B is correct.** Calculate the average temperature for each city.

For City X, Average =
$\frac{5 + 6 + 9 + 12 + 17 + 20 + 23 + 22 + 19 + 14 + 10 + 6}{12}$

$= \frac{163}{12} = 13.58°C$.

For City Y, Average =
$\frac{8 + 9 + 12 + 15 + 20 + 23 + 26 + 25 + 22 + 17 + 12 + 9}{12}$

$= \frac{198}{12} = 16.50°C$.

Therefore, City Y has the greater average temperature for the year.

Choice A is incorrect. City Y has a greater average temperature. **Choice C** is incorrect. Both cities have different average temperatures. **Choice D** is incorrect. City Y has a greater average temperature. **Choice E** is incorrect. There is enough data to arrive at a conclusion.

15 **Choices B, D, and F are correct.** Substitute z from the first equation $2x - 3y = z$ into the second equation $4x + y = 2z$ to get $4x + y = 2(2x - 3y)$. Simplifying yields $4x + y = 4x - 6y$ or $y = 0$.

Substitute $y = 0$ into the first equation to get $2x - 3(0) = z$ or $z = 2x$.

Evaluating each statement:

For Choice A, $x = 2z - y$, substitute $z = 2x$ and $y = 0$ to get $x = 4x$, which is not valid.

For Choice B, $y = 2x - z$, substitute $z = 2x$ and $y = 0$ to get $0 = 0$, which is valid.

For Choice C, $x = \frac{3z + y}{2}$, substitute $z = 2x$ and $y = 0$ to get $x = 3x$, which is not valid.

For Choice D, $y = \frac{2z - 4x}{-1}$, substitute $z = 2x$ and $y = 0$ to get $0 = 0$, which is valid.

For Choice E, $x = -z - y$, substitute $z = 2x$ and $y = 0$ to get $x = -2x$, which is not valid.

For Choice F, $y = 4x - 2z$, substitute $z = 2x$ and $y = 0$ to get $0 = 0$, which is valid.

Therefore, from the evaluation, the correct answers are Choices B, D, and F.

Choice A is incorrect. From the explanation, this option is not valid. **Choice C** is incorrect. From the explanation, this option is not valid. **Choice E** is incorrect. From the explanation, this option is not valid.

This page is intentionally left blank

Chapter 4
Practice Test #3

IMPORTANT
READ THE INSTRUCTIONS BEFORE BEGINNING THE TEST

1. Take this test under real testing conditions. Put away any distractions and sit in a quiet place with no disturbances. Keep a rough paper, some pencils, and a calculator beside you.
2. Begin with **Section 1** of the test on page 110. Write your essay in 30 minutes.
3. Next, move to **Section 2 - Verbal Reasoning** on page 112.
   - ❏ Attempt all questions and note the number of correct answers using the answer key on page 132.
   - ❏ If you get fewer than 7 correct, proceed to **Section 4 - Verbal Reasoning (Easy)** on page 118.
   - ❏ If you get 7 or more correct, proceed to **Section 4 - Verbal Reasoning (Hard)** on page 122.
4. After that, take **Section 3 - Quantitative Reasoning** on page 115.
   - ❏ Complete the section, then check your score using the answer key on page 133.
   - ❏ If you get fewer than 7 correct, proceed to **Section 5 - Quantitative Reasoning (Easy)** on page 126.
   - ❏ If you get 7 or more correct, proceed to **Section 5 - Quantitative Reasoning (Hard)** on page 129.
5. Complete Section 4 and Section 5, respectively, and note down the number of correct answers you got right in each section.
6. Calculate your **Scaled Score** on page 317 for the test.
7. Review **detailed explanations** for all questions beginning on page 134.

Section 1 - Analytical Writing

Analyze an Issue
30 Minutes

The primary goal of technological advancement should be to increase people's efficiency so that they have more leisure time.

Write a response in which you discuss the extent to which you agree or disagree with the statement and explain your reasoning for the position you take. In developing and supporting your position, you should consider ways in which the statement might or might not hold true and explain how these considerations shape your position.

You may start writing your response here

Section 2 - Verbal Reasoning

18 Minutes | 12 Questions

For Questions 1 and 2, for each blank, select one entry from the corresponding column of choices. Fill all blanks in the way that best completes the text.

1. Petra's one-time importance as a key stop on a trade route is reflected in its unique and beautiful architecture; although the so-called "Great Temple" was almost certainly built by an Arab tribe known as the Nabataeans, its style reveals a _____ of cultural influences—its columns, for example, draw on both the Corinthian and Suleiman styles.

A	travesty
B	dearth
C	adulteration
D	plethora
E	imprecation

2. The sub–discipline of socio-cultural anthropology can best be understood by looking at its two (i) _____ topics. Cultural anthropology is the study of how the people of a culture make sense of the world around them. Conversely, social anthropology seeks to understand the relationship between the members of a culture. By understanding what (ii) _____ these two topics, it becomes much easier to understand the ways in which they work together.

Blank (i)	Blank (ii)
A constituent	D demarcates
B indistinct	E amalgamates
C aggregate	F denigrates

3. There are several key (i) _____ that are made by linguists. The most prominent is that spoken language is more (ii) _____ to the human psyche than written language. Most linguists feel justified in making this postulation for a variety of reasons: all cultures have spoken communication, but not all have written communication; vocal communication (iii) _____ written communication; developing humans learn to speak before they learn to write.

Blank (i)	Blank (ii)	Blank (iii)
A gaffes	D superfluous	G antecedes
B concessions	E fundamental	H succeeds
C presuppositions	F distressing	I ignores

For Questions 4 and 5, select one answer choice unless otherwise instructed.

Question 4 is based on this passage.

Prenatal genetic testing has become more and more common over the years. With testing technologies now being so easily accessed, women are increasingly choosing testing for the purpose of preparation. This reason is relatively unexamined in modern clinical research. Prenatal genetic testing is typically offered by healthcare providers and testing laboratories. The increase in a desire to have a fetus genetically screened reflects assumptions that the results can help families plan for having a child with a genetic condition, as long as those results are properly delivered and followed by clinical support. The preparation that genetic screening allows for can ultimately lead to better health and social outcomes for children and their families.

Section 2 - Verbal Reasoning

4. Based on the author's perspective, which of the following statements would the author most likely agree with?
   - A. Prenatal genetic screening helps families come to terms with their child's diagnosis more efficiently.
   - B. Coming to terms with a child's diagnosis earlier in pregnancy can make the transition into parenting a child with a disability easier emotionally.
   - C. Prenatal genetic testing is always beneficial, regardless of the diagnosis or subsequent steps taken.
   - D. Prenatal genetic testing is becoming more common solely because of new testing technologies becoming much more available.
   - E. While prenatal genetic testing can improve the lives of individuals born with genetic conditions, it does little to provide support to their caregivers.

5. Which of the following assumptions could be made based on the information in the passage?
   - A. Children with genetic conditions are likely to receive more support at a younger age when parents have undergone prenatal genetic screening.
   - B. Children with genetic conditions will likely be physically healthier than children without genetic conditions if prenatal genetic testing is completed.
   - C. Parents who undergo prenatal genetic testing will most likely have better relationships with their child's healthcare provider.
   - D. Mothers who undergo prenatal genetic testing are likely to have better birthing experiences.
   - E. Families of children with genetic conditions are less distraught when they find out about conditions before the birth.

For Questions 6 to 9, select the two answer choices that, when used to complete the sentence, fit the meaning of the sentence as a whole and produce complete sentences that are alike in meaning.

6. The wave phenomena can be observed travelling through solid media and the vacuum of space; it can also take the form of compression and rarefactions or be measured through the transfer of energy and momentum; this _____ often confuses and overwhelms students.
   - A. ubiquity
   - B. uniformity
   - C. pervasiveness
   - D. conformity
   - E. expressivity
   - F. petulance

7. Rapidly spreading diseases can cause a person to disproportionally weigh the _____ potentials of various New Age medicines over their metaphysical foundation, resulting in a susceptibility to scams.
   - A. prohibitive
   - B. palliative
   - C. luxurious
   - D. alleviative
   - E. intercalated
   - F. illegal

8. Aspiring business owners may wait until their government _____ that corporations are entities separate from their owners before they registering their businesses to ensure that they will not lose their personal wealth if their businesses are sued or undergo bankruptcy proceedings.
   - A. emends
   - B. palavers
   - C. gibes
   - D. promulgates
   - E. avers
   - F. inveighs

9. Understanding the mechanics of removing retinoblastomas via ocular surgery must be complimented with _____ in order to successfully complete such a technically demanding procedure.

- [A] tenacity
- [B] predilection
- [C] awareness
- [D] doggedness
- [E] contempt
- [F] sensitivity

For Questions 10 to 12, select one answer choice unless otherwise instructed.

Questions 10 to 12 are based on this passage.

The Eisenhower Executive Office Building, also known as the EEOB, sits right next door to the White House and has played an important role in the history of the United States. This building was designed by Supervising Architect of the Treasury, Alfred B. Mullett and it represents a rich architectural heritage. Built from 1871 to 1888, it is an outstanding example of architecture from the Second French Empire. It was crafted for the purpose of housing the growing staff of the War, State, and Navy Departments. Many buildings in the area showcase the somber classical revival style of architecture, but the EEOB embodies the hope and excitement prevalent in the post-Civil War period.

This building originally accommodated the three Executive Branch Departments that were most immediately involved in the formulation and implementation of the nation's foreign policy during the end of the nineteenth century and the beginning of the twentieth century. During this period, the United States grew into a strong international force. The EEOB has housed some of the nation's most important leaders and served as the setting of countless historic events.

10. Which of the following topics would the passage most likely discuss next?
- (A) The history of Dwight Eisenhower as a political leader
- (B) The design process of architect Alfred B. Mullett
- (C) Details of the nation's foreign policy during the early twentieth century
- (D) A physical description of the layout of the Eisenhower Executive Office Building
- (E) An analysis of the architectural design of the White House

11. Which of the following statements about the architectural design of the Eisenhower Executive Office Building can most accurately be inferred?
- (A) The design of the EEOB is like that of the White House.
- (B) The EEOB is a large building with multiple rooms.
- (C) The EEOB has a highly technical security system built in.
- (D) The design of the EEOB is dark and simple.
- (E) The design of the EEOB was a group effort from a multitude of American leaders.

12. What does the author most likely mean by, "the EEOB embodies the hope and excitement prevalent in the post-Civil War period"?
- (A) The design of the building is symbolic of the positive feelings in the country during this time.
- (B) The building housed countless historic events for optimistic Americans during this period.
- (C) Inspired by the Second French Empire, the building was brand new after the Civil War and, therefore, represents the newness of the state of the country.
- (D) The additional funding provided by the government due to rapidly growing departments showcases the overall excitement about the building and its design.
- (E) The EEOB was looked at as a representation of what Americans had gone through during the Civil War.

Section 3 - Quantitative Reasoning

18 Minutes | 12 Questions

1

$$x \leq 0.6\overline{16}$$
$$y \geq 0.6\overline{16}$$

Quantity A   **Quantity B**
x y

(A) Quantity A is greater.
(B) Quantity B is greater.
(C) The two quantities are equal.
(D) The relationship cannot be determined from the information given.

2

Line A : $3x + 3y + 5 = 0$
Line B: $8x + 4y + 2 = 0$

Quantity A   **Quantity B**
the slope of Line A   the slope of Line B

(A) Quantity A is greater.
(B) Quantity B is greater.
(C) The two quantities are equal.
(D) The relationship cannot be determined from the information given.

3

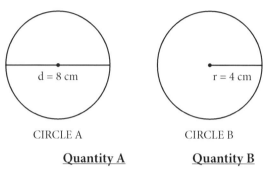

CIRCLE A   CIRCLE B

Quantity A   **Quantity B**
circumference of   circumference of
Circle A   Circle B

(A) Quantity A is greater.
(B) Quantity B is greater.
(C) The two quantities are equal.
(D) The relationship cannot be determined from the information given.

4

$$\frac{m}{3} + 10 \leq 12$$

Quantity A   **Quantity B**
m^2 50

(A) Quantity A is greater.
(B) Quantity B is greater.
(C) The two quantities are equal.
(D) The relationship cannot be determined from the information given.

Section 3 - Quantitative Reasoning

5

There are 350 students at Illinois High School in the graduating senior class. Of these students, $\frac{9}{10}$ are going to college. Of those going to college, $\frac{3}{5}$ are going to Illinois University. How many students are going to Illinois University?

- A) 95
- B) 189
- C) 210
- D) 315
- E) 525

Questions 6 to 8 are based on the following data.

The table gives the percentage of marks obtained by 8 students in six subjects in an examination.
Note: The numbers in brackets indicate the maximum marks in each subject.

Percentage of Marks						
Student	Math (120)	Physics (120)	Chemistry (110)	History (100)	Computer Science (60)	Geography (60)
Anne	80	75	90	75	70	80
Jessica	100	95	90	90	95	90
Amber	80	85	90	85	85	80
Gerald	95	90	85	80	85	90
Lee	90	85	90	85	90	85
Faith	90	95	90	85	90	85
Andrew	85	80	80	75	70	80
Dave	90	90	85	80	85	90

6

What is the average mark obtained by all the students in Math? (round off to the nearest whole number)

- A) 89
- B) 90
- C) 105
- D) 106
- E) 107

7

What was the total mark obtained by Andrew in all subjects?

- A) 450
- B) 451
- C) 465
- D) 470
- E) 475

8

In which subject/s is/are the overall percentage 85 or more?

- A) Math, Physics, History, Geography
- B) Math, Physics, Computer Science, Geography
- C) Math, History, Computer Science, Geography
- D) Math, Physics, Chemistry, Geography
- E) Computer Science, Physics, Chemistry, Geography

9

Simplify.
$$y^5x^3(y^2x^3 + y^3x^5 + y^{10} + x^{11})$$

- A) $y^7x^6 + y^8x^8 + y^{15} + x^{15}$
- B) $y^6x^7 + y^8x^8 + y^3x^5 + x^5y^{14}$
- C) $y^{10}x^9 + y^{15}x^{15} + y^{50}x^3 + x^{33}y^5$
- D) $y^9x^{10} + y^{15}x^{15} + y^3x^{50} + x^{53}y^{33}$
- E) $y^7x^6 + y^8x^8 + y^{15}x^3 + x^{14}y^5$

116 | *Practice Tests for the GRE*

Section 3 - Quantitative Reasoning

10

A bus travels at a constant speed of $\frac{3}{5}$ miles per minute. If the bus needs to cover a distance of $\frac{x}{2}$ miles, which of the following formulas to use to find the time it takes to cover x distance?

(A) $t = \frac{x}{6}$

(B) $t = 6(5x)$

(C) $t = \frac{6x}{5}$

(D) $t = \frac{x}{5}$

(E) $t = \frac{5x}{6}$

11

Two fair dice are rolled. Let x be the absolute value of the difference between the two numbers on the dice. Calculate the probability that $x < 4$.

(A) $\frac{1}{6}$

(B) $\frac{1}{3}$

(C) $\frac{1}{2}$

(D) $\frac{5}{6}$

(E) $\frac{6}{5}$

12

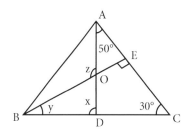

Find the value of z.

Section 4 - Verbal Reasoning (Easy)

23 Minutes | 15 Questions

For Questions 1 to 4, select one entry for each blank from the corresponding column of choices. Fill all the blanks in the way that best completes the text.

1. In order to _____ the hypothesized age of a given fossil, scientists rely on their knowledge of the radioactive decay rates of various isotopes.

(A) correlate
(B) discern
(C) substantiate
(D) gainsay
(E) palliate

2. In 1665, Robert Hooke discovered the cell and established the _____ for the development of cell theory, and based on his discoveries, other scientists were able to develop new theories.

(A) infrastructure
(B) innovation
(C) consequence
(D) foundation
(E) production

3. Modern botany has an extensive history. Dating back to the ancient Greeks, the discipline has been refined for centuries. Its study is of tremendous importance for a variety of reasons. All mammalian sources of food, regardless of how (i) _____ the route, inevitably come from plants. This (ii) _____ means that botany is an applicable field of study regardless of which group of animals you might be studying.

Blank (i)	Blank (ii)
(A) malevolent	(D) dilution
(B) circuitous	(E) prevalence
(C) fulminated	(F) mirth

4. There is an immense (i) _____ in the amount of worrying that parents do over violence in their children's movies. They (ii) _____ the use of explicit violence in modern cinema, yet never seem to turn a critical eye towards the movies of their day. The violence may have not been explicit, but it was still there. In many ways it was worse, because this violence was so (iii) _____ that it made cruel acts seem part of everyday life.

Blank (i)	Blank (ii)	Blank (iii)
(A) prosperity	(D) authenticate	(G) incisive
(B) irony	(E) theorize	(H) gracious
(C) singularity	(F) disparage	(I) blasé

Section 4 - Verbal Reasoning (Easy)

For Questions 5 to 7, select one answer choice unless otherwise instructed.

Questions 5 to 7 are based on this passage.

Starfish are a part of the phylum Echinodermata and are relatives of sand dollars, sea cucumbers, and sea urchins. Echinoderms can be found in most marine areas and there are nearly 2,000 species of starfish alive today. Astonishingly, most species of starfish have the unique capability of regenerating or regrowing damaged or missing arms. Similar to lizards that can detach their tails, starfish can willingly shed their arms as a way of defending themselves. If an arm is grabbed by a predatory animal, such as a crab, starfish can easily detach the arm and escape. Additionally, if an arm is resultantly damaged from an attack, a starfish can elect to lose the arm and grow a new, healthy one. This interesting skill has helped starfish remain prevalent in diverse marine habitats.

5. Which of the following statements best summarizes the passage?
   - A) Starfish are sea creatures of the phylum Echinodermata and the only known animals that can elect to detach and regrow limbs.
   - B) Starfish are an incredibly diverse species that is similar to sand dollars, sea cucumbers, and sea urchins and can be seen in almost all oceans.
   - C) Starfish face many predators in the wild and have little to no means of defending themselves.
   - D) Starfish are a group of echinoderms that can be found all over the world and come in a variety of shapes and sizes.
   - E) Starfish are a diverse group of echinoderms that display the unique skill of detaching and regenerating arms.

6. Which of the following would be the most appropriate title for this passage?
   - A) The Lifestyle of a Starfish
   - B) A Decline in the Starfish Population
   - C) Resilient Starfish
   - D) Creatures with Unique Skills
   - E) Thriving Echinoderms

7. Which of the following conclusions about starfish can be drawn from the passage?
   - A) Starfish are unable to move after they have shed a limb.
   - B) Starfish are most likely herbivores.
   - C) Starfish do not have a mechanism to injure their attackers.
   - D) Starfish enjoy living in rocky areas.
   - E) Starfish are easy prey for even small crabs.

For Questions 8 to 10, select the two answer choices that, when used to complete the sentence, fit the meaning of the sentence as a whole and produce complete sentences that are alike in meaning.

8. As he watched his inheritance pour into his bank account and the _____ urges begin pulsing through his veins, Stephen knew that he would have a difficult road ahead of him if he wanted to maintain his pre-wealth humility.
   - A) enlightened
   - B) supercilious
   - C) chic
   - D) vacuous
   - E) haughty
   - F) violent

9. In human physiology the _____ neural response takes care of precise, immediate action in direct response to pressure from the environment while the hormonal response utilizes slow, indirect action to coordinate the development and homeostasis of the body.
   - A) inglorious
   - B) instantaneous
   - C) violent
   - D) explosive
   - E) rapid
   - F) somatic

10. Although it ostensibly works just like any of the other Newtonian forces encountered in the laboratory environment, the application of friction often appears to be _____, and therefore challenging for students.

- [A] ironic
- [B] straightforward
- [C] inconsistent
- [D] deliberate
- [E] complaisant
- [F] unpredictable

For Questions 11 to 15, select one answer choice unless otherwise instructed.

Question 11 is based on this passage.

In comparison with the Western diet, many studies have found an extraordinary number of health benefits resulting from consuming a Mediterranean diet. The Mediterranean diet typically includes fruits, vegetables, grains, fish, poultry, and certain fats. This diet has been associated with a lower risk of heart disease and cancer, including breast cancer among women. Contrastingly, consuming a Western diet even with a baby in utero may lead to physiological dysfunctions of a child through epigenetic alterations.

11. Which of the following is the greatest strength in the author's argument for the consumption of a Mediterranean diet over a Western diet?

- (A) The author specifically outlines the foods that are included in a typical Mediterranean diet.
- (B) The author specifically describes which health conditions are less likely to occur when a Mediterranean diet is consumed.
- (C) The author suggests that consuming a Western diet when pregnant may lead to problems for children.
- (D) The author states that extraordinary health benefits can be reached when a Mediterranean diet is consumed.
- (E) The author explains the risks that come with consuming a Mediterranean diet.

Questions 12 and 13 are based on this passage.

The Federative Republic of Brazil is composed of twenty-six states and a federal district. The government of Brazil is similar to that of the United States, as it is run by an executive branch, legislative branch, and judiciary branch. In this democratic country, laws, statutes, and codes are passed by Congress thereafter courts uphold these rules when determining verdicts. The president acts as the Commander in Chief of the military, the head of state, and the government. Rather than using an electoral college system, the president is elected directly by the votes of the people. Then, a four-year term is served with one consecutive re-election permit.

12. Which of the following best summarizes the governmental structure of Brazil according to the passage?

- (A) Brazil is a representative democracy that operates under Separation of Powers.
- (B) Brazil is a representative democracy in which the elected president serves several important roles.
- (C) Brazil is a democratic nation in which Congress determines laws, statutes, and codes and the judicial branch upholds these rules.
- (D) Brazil is a direct democracy in which all eligible citizens get a say in all of the nation's decisions.
- (E) Brazil is a direct democracy composed of a judicial branch, legislative branch, and executive branch.

13. Besides educating the reader about the governmental structure of Brazil, what could this passage best be used for?

- (A) Providing background information in a prologue for a book about Brazilian culture.
- (B) Advertising to potential tourists who may wish to visit Brazil.
- (C) Making an argument against the electoral college system in the United States.
- (D) Comparing governmental structures of successful democratic countries for the purpose of planning a national reform.
- (E) Being included as a segment of a local Brazilian newspaper article.

Questions 14 and 15 are based on this passage.

The late nineteenth century brought about improvements in technology such as the invention of smaller, handheld cameras. This innovation made engaging in photography much more feasible to the general public. Middle-class citizens began snapping photographs of their family and friends in casual settings or at events. Others began using photographs as a means of facilitating political progress.

More serious photographers focused on the artistic merit of the medium. These "pictorialists" set out to show the world that photographs could be as thought-provoking and beautiful as paintings. They used various techniques to manipulate their works and set themselves apart from the trend of amateur photography.

For the following question, consider each of the choices separately and select all that apply.

14. How does the purpose of the first paragraph differ from the purpose of the second half?

   A. The first paragraph of the passage describes how handheld cameras became popular among the middle class while the second paragraph of the passage describes how painters switched to photography as a new artistic medium.

   B. The first paragraph of the passage describes how the invention of handheld cameras impacted the public while the second paragraph of the passage describes how serious photographers utilized handheld cameras for artistic purposes.

   C. The first paragraph of the passage describes how serious photographers set out to show the artistic merit of this medium while the second paragraph of the passage describes how photographs were used for commonplace purposes like political advertising.

15. Which of the following statements can be inferred about the history of photography based on the information provided in the passage?

   A. Prior to the late nineteenth century, professional photographers made comparable wages with professional painters.

   B. Prior to the late nineteenth century, photography was a well-appreciated artistic medium.

   C. Prior to the late nineteenth century, cameras were difficult to use and cumbersome to carry.

   D. Prior to the late nineteenth century, cameras were not considered valuable.

   E. Prior to the late nineteenth century, cameras were larger and not widely used by the public.

Section 4 - Verbal Reasoning (Hard)

23 Minutes | 15 Questions

For Questions 1 to 4, select one entry for each blank from the corresponding column of choices. Fill all the blanks in the way that best completes the text.

1. Robert Remark, a Polish embryologist, discovered that cells originated from the division of _____ cells and did not spontaneously appear.

   - Ⓐ inanimate
   - Ⓑ extant
   - Ⓒ living
   - Ⓓ surviving
   - Ⓔ mortal

2. Just the name "Biotechnology" evokes powerful images: the use of recombinant genes in genetic sequencing, applied immunology to fight diseases, and so on. But the lofty heading of "Biogerontology" includes many (i) _____ that one wouldn't typically associate with advanced medicine. Both the brewing of alcohol and the development of agriculture involve manipulating biological systems to make products. Therefore, even without the scientific (ii) _____ of medical techniques, these "rough-and-tumble" jobs also fall under the heading of "Biotechnology."

Blank (i)	Blank (ii)
Ⓐ verisimilitudes	Ⓓ exactitude
Ⓑ denigrations	Ⓔ unsophisticated
Ⓒ vocations	Ⓕ fallacy

3. The (i)_____ of the modern food industry in America is impressive. Only a small section of the country's population exists outside of its structure. Employing more than 16 million people (and providing more than 10% of American's GDP), changes in the food industry can be felt across the entire country. The (ii)_____ task of regulating such a dynamic and widespread industry falls to the Food and Drug Administration, or FDA.

Blank (i)	Blank (ii)
Ⓐ extensiveness	Ⓓ arduous
Ⓑ lethargy	Ⓔ ridiculous
Ⓒ bankruptcy	Ⓕ pernicious

4. A few of us watched in awe from the (i) _____ above town as the last of our makeshift barriers (ii) _____ and Cowtown, built on the shifting alluvial soils of the Temash Delta, crumbled and was swept away like so much (iii) _____ being sucked down a drain.

Blank (i)	Blank (ii)	Blank (iii)
Ⓐ estuary	Ⓓ capitulated	Ⓖ calumny
Ⓑ ravine	Ⓔ countenanced	Ⓗ aspersion
Ⓒ butte	Ⓕ assuaged	Ⓘ detritus

For Questions 5 to 9, select one answer choice unless otherwise instructed.

Questions 5 and 6 are based on this passage.

The human tongue can perceive a variety of tastes such as sweet, bitter, and salty. Sodium chloride is the typical salt molecule used in food, which elicits a pure salty flavor. The various sensory effects of salt in foods are not very well understood. For instance, salt increases the perceived thickness of liquids like soups, but the reason for this is unclear to scientists.

Sodium chloride is useful in cooking because of its ability to reduce the bitterness of other compounds found in food like caffeine, magnesium sulfate, and potassium chloride. The suppression of these bitter compounds can help bolden the pleasant taste of other ingredients. For example, adding sodium acetate, a mildly salty compound, to a mixture of sugar and urea enhances the perceived sweet taste.

5. Based on the information in the passage, which of the following recipes would benefit most from the addition of salt?

    (A) A recipe with sweet, salty, and bitter ingredients
    (B) A recipe with sweet and bitter ingredients
    (C) A recipe with sweet and salty ingredients
    (D) A recipe with no bitter or salty ingredients
    (E) A recipe with salty and bitter ingredients

For the following question, consider each of the choices separately and select all that apply.

6. How does the first paragraph contribute to the development of the passage?

    [A] The first paragraph introduces the main ideas of the passage: tastes and how salt impacts eating experiences.
    [B] The first paragraph provides a segue into the second paragraph by expressing the idea that salt has interesting capabilities of enhancing eating experiences.
    [C] The first paragraph discusses examples of the sensory effects of salt in foods before the second paragraph delves into one specific effect: suppressing bitter flavors.

Questions 7 to 9 are based on this passage.

Cultural heritage is an integral part of Singapore's history and national identity. Singapore is full of fascinating food, clothing, art, and traditions. Customary Singaporean dishes stem from global origins, which is representative of the diverse population of Singapore. One popular dish, rojak, is akin to a salad but utilizes distinctive ingredients depending on the Singaporean's ethnic background. For instance, Indian rojak includes squid, prawns, bean curd, and fried vegetables. On the other hand, Chinese rojak includes cucumber, pineapple, and fritters. Also, Malay rojak adds fermented soybeans to the compilation. A national attitude of togetherness, regardless of race, religion, or language, is often exhibited among Singaporeans. This is particularly evident during their myriads of unique festivals celebrating union and tradition.

Despite the value that many citizens place on cultural heritage, Singapore is still a burgeoning city. Not unlike other countries, Singapore must make a special effort to preserve its cultural identity while also appealing to the younger generation.

7. Based on the passage, how can the population of Singapore most accurately be described?

    (A) The population of Singapore is made up of mostly young people who the older citizens must appeal to in order for traditions to be passed on.
    (B) The population of Singapore is composed primarily of immigrants from other countries.
    (C) The population of Singapore includes families from a variety of ethnic origins, particularly those in and around Asia.
    (D) The population of Singapore is primarily composed of Indian, Chinese, and Malaysian citizens.
    (E) The population of Singapore is very diverse, but small, which makes an attitude of togetherness easy to maintain.

Section 4 - Verbal Reasoning (Hard)

8. Based on the first paragraph, which of the following would make the most appropriate slogan for Singapore?

    (A) The land of cultural festivities
    (B) The land where heritage and progressivity meet
    (C) The land of rich historical heritage
    (D) The land where different come together
    (E) The land of customization

9. Based on the information provided in the second paragraph, which of the following statements best represents a possible alternative explanation for Singaporeans needing to make a special effort to pass on traditions?

    (A) With the rise of new technologies, traditional cultural practices may not be viewed as necessary.
    (B) Singaporean festivals are becoming less riveting than they were previously.
    (C) The younger generation is looking to reconnect with their cultural roots.
    (D) Ingredients for commonly used Singaporean dishes are not as readily available as they once were.
    (E) Older Singaporeans display a disinclination to pass on cultural traditions.

For Questions 10 to 12, select the two answer choices that, when used to complete the sentence, fit the meaning of the sentence as a whole and produce complete sentences that are alike in meaning.

10. In accomplishing the seemingly impossible, the young woman was _____ by her desire to impress her parents.

    [A] inhibited
    [B] sedated
    [C] motivated
    [D] influenced
    [E] stymied
    [F] adjudicated

11. The rigid, often counter-intuitive machinations of science and the unassailable foundation on which it is built frequently chase away would-be practitioners of research and lead them to look for comfort in the _____ of the arts.

    [A] contradictions
    [B] flexibility
    [C] craftiness
    [D] mutability
    [E] expressivity
    [F] innovation

12. The pervasive institutionalization of the notion that beauty must be suffered for has crippled the didactic efficacy of modern media and _____ the self-confidence of a whole generation of children.

    [A] subverted
    [B] undermined
    [C] initiated
    [D] rectified
    [E] invigorated
    [F] objectified

Section 4 - Verbal Reasoning (Hard)

For Questions 13 to 15, select one answer choice unless otherwise instructed.

Question 13 is based on this passage.

Hunger is a critical issue worldwide, including in the United States. Many Americans receive some form of food assistance and make regular trips to a local food pantry. The Department of Agriculture defines food insecurity as, "multiple indications of disrupted eating patterns and reduced food intake." However, hunger is not the primary focus of most social service agencies. Thus, social workers must be mindful of the impacts of such serious problems and the interference with other obligations food insecurity may cause.

13. How does the sentence, "The Department of Agriculture defines food insecurity as, 'multiple indications of disrupted eating patterns and reduced food intake'" best support the author's argument?

   A. It provides a segue into the argument that hunger should be the primary focus of most social service agencies.
   B. It supports the idea that eating patterns should be regular in all healthy families.
   C. It elucidates an important term to clarify the concept being discussed.
   D. It introduces the department responsible for managing the issue discussed in the paragraph.
   E. It evokes sympathy from the reader for those who struggle with food insecurity.

Questions 14 and 15 are based on this passage.

Despite their undesirable reputation, swamps are one of the most important ecosystems on the planet. When floods occur due to heavy rain, swamps serve as giant sponges and absorb the excess water. This minimizes the negative effects that flooding has on other regions. Swamps also protect oceanside areas from storms that could otherwise deplete coastlines.

Furthermore, swamps act as water treatment plants by naturally purifying water and filtering waste. For instance, when too much nitrogen or other chemicals enter a swamp, plants absorb the chemicals. This excess of nitrogen can occur from human activities like agricultural practices that utilize nitrogen and phosphorus.

For the following question, consider each of the choices separately and select all that apply.

14. Based on the passage, which of the following are true statements about the nature of swamps?

   A. Swamps can positively impact other surrounding areas and ecosystems.
   B. Swamps can impact the environment by housing a variety of virulent chemicals.
   C. Swamps are more valuable than their unfavorable reputation suggests.

15. How does the first sentence of the second paragraph best contribute to the passage overall?

   A. This sentence transitions into a new topic relating to swamps by piquing the reader's interest.
   B. This sentence transitions into another reason that swamps are valuable and provides an example of how swamps can purify water.
   C. This sentence concludes the previous paragraph and explains a special capability of swamps.
   D. This sentence transitions into another reason that swamps are valuable and segues into the topic for the remainder of the second paragraph.
   E. This sentence transitions into a new topic relating to swamps and introduces the topic for the remainder of the second paragraph.

Section 5 - Quantitative Reasoning (Easy)

26 Minutes | 15 Questions

1

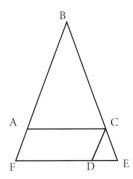

Triangles $\triangle ABC$, $\triangle FBE$ and $\triangle DCE$ are equilateral triangles. The ratio of DE and FE is 1:4.

Quantity A	Quantity B
Perimeter of $\triangle ABC$	Perimeter of parallelogram ACDF

- A) Quantity A is greater.
- B) Quantity B is greater.
- C) The two quantities are equal.
- D) The relationship cannot be determined from the information given.

2

I recorded the outside temperature at noon each day for one week. These were the results.

Day	Temperature (Fahrenheit)
Monday	82
Tuesday	84
Wednesday	80
Thursday	78
Friday	75
Saturday	79
Sunday	81

Quantity A	Quantity B
range of the temperatures	7

- A) Quantity A is greater.
- B) Quantity B is greater.
- C) The two quantities are equal.
- D) The relationship cannot be determined from the information given.

3

Quantity A	Quantity B
$|x|$	$\dfrac{x^3}{3}$

- A) Quantity A is greater.
- B) Quantity B is greater.
- C) The two quantities are equal.
- D) The relationship cannot be determined from the information given.

4

Refer to the given set: {1,2,3,4,5,6,7,8,9,10}

Quantity A	Quantity B
Common multiple of 2,3,6	10

- A) Quantity A is greater.
- B) Quantity B is greater.
- C) The two quantities are equal.
- D) The relationship cannot be determined from the information given.

5

Quantity A	Quantity B
The angle of a circle's sector has an arc length of 10π and a radius of 7.	The angle of a circle's sector has an area 24π of and a radius of 9.

A) Quantity A is greater.
B) Quantity B is greater.
C) The two quantities are equal.
D) The relationship cannot be determined from the information given.

6

Solve for x.
$$5x + 9 \geq -4x + 8$$

A) $x \geq -1/9$
B) $x \geq 17/9$
C) $x \geq -17$
D) $x \geq 1/9$
E) $x \geq -17/9$

7

A group of students conducted a survey on the number of hours per week that their peers in different Grade levels spend on extracurricular activity. The collected data are as follows.

6th Grade - 85, 90, 78, 92, 88
7th Grade - 79, 84, 91, 87, 85
8th Grade - 91, 89, 94, 87, 92
9th Grade - 95, 88, 85, 90, 95
10th Grade - 90, 90, 95, 88, 90

Which of the following options is true about the mean score of each grade level? Select all that apply.

A) 6th Grade has the highest mean score.
B) 8th Grade has the highest mean score.
C) 7th Grade has the highest mean score.
D) The mean scores of all five classes are the same.
D) $17500
E) The mean score of 6th Grade and 8th Grade are the same.
F) 9th Grade has the highest mean score.
G) 10th Grade has the highest mean score.

8

Solve for the Area of the given figure.

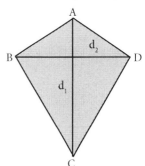

A) $A = \dfrac{d_1 + d_2}{2}$
B) $A = \dfrac{d_1(d_2)}{2}$
C) $A = \dfrac{2}{d_1 + d_2}$
D) $A = 2(d_1 + d_2)$
E) $A = 2(d_1 \times d_2)$

Section 5 - Quantitative Reasoning (Easy)

9

From a group of 5 managers (Jay, Kathlene, Trisha, Lee, Naomi), 2 people are randomly selected to attend a conference in New York. What is the probability Lee and Trisha are both selected?

- A) 10%
- B) 20%
- C) 40%
- D) 60%
- E) 100%

10

If Janice finished the work at a rate of $\dfrac{x-p}{r}$ and Rommel finished the same work at a rate $\dfrac{y}{pr}$, where $x, y, p, r > 0$. What is the value of x in terms of y, p & r?

- A) $x = \dfrac{y}{rp} - p$
- B) $x = -\dfrac{yr}{p} + p$
- C) $x = \dfrac{y}{p} + p$
- D) $x = \dfrac{y}{pr} + pr$
- E) $x = -\dfrac{yr}{p} + pr$

11

Alex walks 1 mile in 10 minutes. Cherry takes 12 minutes to walk 1 mile. If Alex & Cherry leave their homes at the same time. How far has Cherry walked when Alex has walked 1 mile?

- A) $\dfrac{1}{6}$
- B) $\dfrac{1}{3}$
- C) $\dfrac{1}{2}$
- D) $\dfrac{5}{6}$
- E) $\dfrac{6}{5}$

12

If $0 < y < x$, then which of the following is a possible value of $\dfrac{27x + 23y}{3x + 2y}$?

- A) 6.4
- B) 7.5
- C) 8.9
- D) 9.3
- E) 10.5

13

A purse contains 300 coins, 15 % are quarters, 10% are dimes and the rest are nickels. How much money is in the purse in nickels?

- A) $11.25
- B) $13.11
- C) $13.55
- D) $15.25
- E) $25.11

14

Let $f(x) = 2x^3 + 7x^2 - 4x$ and $g(x) = 4x - x^3$. If k is a positive number such that $f(k) = 0$, then what is $g(k)$?

[ ]

15

If $4x + 2y < n$ and $4y + 2x > m$, then $y - x$ must be?

- A) $< \dfrac{m-n}{2}$
- B) $\leq \dfrac{m-n}{2}$
- C) $> \dfrac{m-n}{2}$
- D) $\geq \dfrac{m-n}{2}$
- E) $\leq \dfrac{m+n}{2}$

128 | *Practice Tests for the GRE*

Section 5 - Quantitative Reasoning (Hard)

23 Minutes | 15 Questions

1

$$x < 0$$
$$y < 0$$

Quantity A	Quantity B
$x^2 + 4xy + y^2$	$(x + y)^2$

Ⓐ Quantity A is greater.
Ⓑ Quantity B is greater.
Ⓒ The two quantities are equal.
Ⓓ The relationship cannot be determined from the information given.

2

An arithmetic progression whose first term is –20 and the common difference is 4.

Quantity A	Quantity B
4th term	– 4

Ⓐ Quantity A is greater.
Ⓑ Quantity B is greater.
Ⓒ The two quantities are equal.
Ⓓ The relationship cannot be determined from the information given.

3

30 percent of 250 is p.
p percent of q is 80.

Quantity A	Quantity B
p	q

Ⓐ Quantity A is greater.
Ⓑ Quantity B is greater.
Ⓒ The two quantities are equal.
Ⓓ The relationship cannot be determined from the information given.

4

Triangle ABC has vertices $A(0, 0)$, $B(2, 0)$, $C(1, 2)$. Triangle DEF has vertices $D(0, 0)$, $E(4,0)$, $F(3, -y)$. Area of triangle ABC and triangle DEF is the same.

Quantity A	Quantity B
y	5

Ⓐ Quantity A is greater.
Ⓑ Quantity B is greater.
Ⓒ The two quantities are equal.
Ⓓ The relationship cannot be determined from the information given.

5

The length of rectangle B is 20 percent less than the length of rectangle A, and the width of rectangle B is 20 percent greater than the width of rectangle A.

Quantity A	Quantity B
The area of rectangle A	The area of rectangle B

Ⓐ Quantity A is greater.
Ⓑ Quantity B is greater.
Ⓒ The two quantities are equal.
Ⓓ The relationship cannot be determined from the information given.

Section 5 - Quantitative Reasoning (Hard)

6

Used Cars sold monthly at Car dealership Z

Price Range	# of cars sold
Under $7000	4
$7000 – $9999	15
$10000 – $12999	7
Over $13000	4

For the 30 used cars sold last month at car dealership Z, what could be the median price? Indicate all such price.

- [A] $3500
- [B] $7500
- [C] $8500
- [D] $9000
- [E] $9500
- [F] $15000
- [G] $17500

7

Which of the following integers has an even integer value for all positive integers x? Select all that apply.

- [A] $3x + 4$
- [B] $4x$
- [C] $x^2 + 3$
- [D] $x^2 - 2$

8

Which of the following is equivalent to $\dfrac{\frac{1}{a} - \frac{1}{b}}{b - a}$, with positive exponents? Indicate all that apply.

- [A] ab
- [B] $(ab)^{-1}$
- [C] $\dfrac{1}{ba}$
- [D] $\dfrac{1}{ab}$
- [E] $\dfrac{a}{b}$

9

If $x = \dfrac{1}{2}y$, x is what percent of y? Select all that apply.

- [A] 30 %
- [B] 40%
- [C] 50%
- [D] 75%

10

If $-1 < n < 1$, all of the following could be true except. Select all that apply.

- [A] $n^2 < n$
- [B] $n^2 < 2n$
- [C] $(n - 1)^2 > 0$
- [D] $16n^2 - 1 = 0$
- [E] $|n^2 - 1| > 1$

11

The figure shows a polygon with 9 sides. Find the value of the exterior angle x.

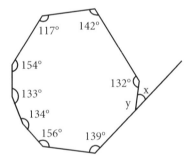

130 | *Practice Tests for the GRE*

Section 5 - Quantitative Reasoning (Hard)

12

Consider the data set $\{r, s, 32, 65, 89, 44, 90, 33\}$. For the set to have an arithmetic mean of less than equal to 50, what are the possible values of r and s, where $20 \leq r \leq s < 40$. Select all that apply.

- [A] $r = 21, s = 26$
- [B] $r = 21, s = 40$
- [C] $r = 20, s = 27$
- [D] $r = 22, s = 38$
- [E] $r = 23, s = 36$
- [F] $r = 23, s = 24$
- [G] $r = 24, s = 24$
- [H] $r = 24, s = 23$

13

A store offers two successive discounts on a product. The first discount is x% off the original price and the second discount is y% off the price after the first discount. After applying both discounts, the final price of the product is $36. If the original price of the product was $100, which of the following pairs (x, y) could be the possible discounts given? Select all that apply.

- [A] (25, 15)
- [B] (30, 20)
- [C] (40, 25)
- [D] (20, 10)
- [E] (15, 15)

14

Let $f(t) = 2t - 7$ and $g(t) = 4t + 1$.

Find t when $f(t) + g(t) = 30$.

- (A) 3
- (B) 6
- (C) 7
- (D) 8

15

A data set consists of 7 numbers: a, b, c, d, e, f and g. The mean of this data set is 25. If the value of a is increased by 5, the value of b is decreased by 4, the value of c is decreased by half, the value of d is increased by 5, the values of e, f, and g are the same.

What is the formula of the new mean of the data set? Select all that apply.

- [A] $\dfrac{(a+5)+(b-4)+(c-2)+(d-5)+e+f+g}{7}$
- [B] $\dfrac{(a+5)+(b-4)+\left(\dfrac{c}{2}\right)+(d-5)+e+f+g}{7}$
- [C] $\dfrac{(a+5)+(b+4)+\left(\dfrac{c}{2}\right)+(d-5)+e+f+g}{7}$
- [D] $\dfrac{a+b+\left(\dfrac{c}{2}\right)+d+e+f+g-5}{7}$
- [E] $\dfrac{a+b+c+d+e+f+g-2}{7}$
- [F] $\dfrac{a+b+\dfrac{c}{2}+d+e+f+g-4}{7}$
- [G] $\dfrac{a+b+c+d+e+f+g-6}{7}$

Answer Key

VERBAL REASONING

Section 2		
Q. No.	Correct Answer	Your Answer
1	D	
2	A, D	
3	C, E, G	
4	B	
5	A	
6	A, C	
7	B, D	
8	D, E	
9	A, D	
10	D	
11	B	
12	A	

Section 4 (Easy)		
Q. No.	Correct Answer	Your Answer
1	C	
2	D	
3	B, E	
4	B, F, I	
5	E	
6	C	
7	C	
8	B, E	
9	B, E	
10	C, F	
11	B	
12	A	
13	D	
14	B	
15	E	

Section 4 (Hard)		
Q. No.	Correct Answer	Your Answer
1	B	
2	C, D	
3	A, D	
4	C, D, I	
5	B	
6	A	
7	C	
8	D	
9	A	
10	C, D	
11	B, D	
12	A, B	
13	C	
14	A, C	
15	D	

Answer Key

QUANTITATIVE REASONING

Section 3		
Q. No.	Correct Answer	Your Answer
1	B	
2	A	
3	C	
4	B	
5	B	
6	E	
7	B	
8	D	
9	E	
10	E	
11	D	
12	140°	

Section 5 (Easy)		
Q. No.	Correct Answer	Your Answer
1	A	
2	A	
3	D	
4	B	
5	A	
6	A	
7	B, F, G	
8	A	
9	A	
10	C	
11	D	
12	D	
13	A	
14	15/8	
15	C	

Section 5 (Hard)		
Q. No.	Correct Answer	Your Answer
1	A	
2	B	
3	B	
4	B	
5	A	
6	B, C, D, E	
7	B	
8	B, C, D	
9	C	
10	E	
11	27°	
12	A, C, F	
13	D, E	
14	B	
15	B, F	

Analytical Writing — Answers & Explanations — Section 1

Analyze an Issue

The sample essay that follows was written in response to the prompt that appeared in the question.

To presume that technological advancements should serve the desires of humans for leisure is, at the very least, self-serving. Greater efficiency should make it possible for humans to accomplish more in a given period of time, However, advances in technology should improve not only the lives of humans in a variety of ways but also other life forms and the Earth itself. If any aspect of daily life on the planet is ignored by improvements in technology, some other aspect will suffer.

The advent of mechanization in the nineteenth century undoubtedly improved the efficiency of human activity. The cotton gin and the McCormack reaper changed agriculture forever by replacing backbreaking human labor with machine power. These advances enabled farmers to plant more crops and accomplish more work in less time. The steam engine enabled people to travel more quickly along the length of America's great rivers and across the country by train. Because more goods could move more efficiently, new factories arose and the demand for raw materials increased. Rather than creating more leisure time, mechanization created more jobs and a boost to the economies in countries that adopted it. In the twentieth century, mechanization entered the home, making it possible for housewives to complete household chores with greater efficiency. The vacuum cleaner eliminated the need to beat rugs hanging on a line in the backyard. The automatic washing machine replaced washboards and hand wringing of wet clothes. Eventually, the dishwasher and microwave would make short shrift of other kitchen chores. The upshot of these advances in technology had an effect contrary to creating more leisure time. Instead, women were able to enter the workforce. Greater efficiency in the home made possible the foray of housewives into the world of education, medicine, and business. Efficiency created by technological advances created time to complete more tasks rather than creating more leisure time.

Leisure time is not important when other aspects of life have not been improved by technological advances. The ability to spend leisure time traveling, for example, would have fewer benefits if all forms of travel had not been made safer. The frequency with which airliners crash and scores of people are killed has greatly diminished despite the fact that more planes and people take to the air every day. Going on vacation in the family car is safer because of air bags that make it more likely for passengers to survive a crash. Thanks to advances in communication technology, families can spend their leisure time enjoying any type of entertainment on their high-definition televisions.

More leisure time would be meaningless if technology had not made it possible to live longer, healthier lives. Implantable pacemakers and defibrillators enable people with heart disease to pursue active lifestyles. Those who previously were affected by debilitating osteoarthritis can have damaged joints replaced and enjoy their leisure time pain free. More children live to become healthy adults as a result of advances in vaccinations and treatment of childhood cancers. Advances in technology have allowed scientists to monitor the climate conditions on Earth. We know that human activity has contributed to the depletion of natural resources that affect the environment. The hole in the ozone layer caused by greenhouse gases has created an alarming increase in the incidence of skin cancer. Deforestation in the rain forests has led to the extinction of important plant and animal species. Climate change is melting the ice caps, imperiling the existence of polar bears and causing water levels to rise in coastal areas. Technological advances must address these conditions, or human leisure time will become meaningless.

1
Choice D is correct because the fact that Petra was located on a trade route, as well as the fact that its architecture apparently utilizes at least two column styles, suggests that it was probably influenced by a variety of cultures. The correct answer is plethora, which means abundance, or excess.

Choice A is incorrect because travesty (a debased likeness or imitation) implies that the architecture of Petra is merely a corruption of other cultural styles. **Choice B** is incorrect because dearth, which means scarcity or lack, does not align with the context of the passage. **Choice C** is incorrect because adulteration (debasement) implies that the architecture of Petra is merely a corruption of other cultural styles. **Choice E** is incorrect because imprecation is irrelevant in this context; it means a curse.

2
Choice A and D are correct because the rest of the passage talks of the two topics that compose sociocultural anthropology. "Constituent" means "component." If cultural anthropology and social anthropology are the two topics that make up sociocultural anthropology, then they must be its "constituent" topics. For the second blank, the passage is stressing on what differentiates cultural and social anthropology and thus, Choice D makes sense as "demarcates" means "differentiates."

Choice B is incorrect because "indistinct" means "unclear." The two topics are expounded on greatly, so they cannot be considered unclear. **Choice C** is incorrect because "aggregate" means "cumulative." The two main topics of sociocultural anthropology may very well be the cumulative results of other topics, but this is not implied anywhere in the passage. **Choice E** is incorrect because "amalgamates" means "combines." This is incorrect because the passage is trying to explain what differentiates the social and cultural anthropology, not what combines them. **Choice F** is incorrect because "denigrates" means "derides." The passage is not trying to deride the two fields of study.

3
Choice C, E, and G are correct. The first blank can be better understood by reading subsequent sentences. The first sentence talks of a key "something" that is made by linguists. The rest of the passage talks about a "postulation" that is made. We can infer that this is the general idea being alluded towards in the first sentence. "presuppositions" means assumptions or conjectures. The sentence introduces claims made by linguists, and "presuppositions" aligns with the idea of beliefs taken as true without definitive proof, which fits the context of linguistic theory. Choice E is correct because "fundamental" means essential or central. The passage discusses how spoken language is more basic or deeply rooted in human psychology than written language, making "fundamental" the most appropriate word. Choice G is correct because "antecedes" means "comes before." The passage lists reasons why spoken language is considered primary, one of which is that it comes before written language both developmentally and historically, so "antecedes" accurately captures this idea.

Choice A is incorrect because "gaffes" means mistakes. The passage isn't about errors made by linguists, but about foundational beliefs, so this word doesn't fit the context. **Choice B** is incorrect because "concessions" implies admitting defeat or yielding a point. The linguists are making confident claims, not reluctant admissions, so this term is inappropriate here. **Choice D** is incorrect because "superfluous" means unnecessary. The passage describes spoken language as essential and prevalent, not unneeded, making this choice illogical. **Choice F** is incorrect because "distressing" means upsetting or worrisome. There is no indication that the prevalence of spoken language causes worry or concern, so this word doesn't fit. **Choice H** is incorrect because "succeeds" means "comes after." The passage clearly indicates that vocal communication comes before written, so "succeeds" contradicts the intended meaning. **Choice I** is incorrect because "ignores" means disregards. The sentence focuses on chronological order, not on whether one form of communication is ignored, so this choice is not relevant.

4
Choice B is correct because the author believes that prenatal genetic screening allows parents to become aware of genetic conditions earlier and prepare for the parenting that will be needed. Therefore, the author would likely agree that prenatal genetic screening helps parents come to terms with a child's diagnosis ahead of time, leading to an easier transition.

Choice A is incorrect because the author does not claim that parents will come to terms with their child's condition more efficiently, or quicker, through a prenatal screening. Rather, the author expresses that parents can come to terms with the diagnosis earlier on (though likely at the same pace). This allows parents more time to prepare for the child's life after birth. **Choice C** is incorrect because the author states, "The results can help families plan for having a child with a genetic condition, as long as those results are properly delivered and followed by clinical support." In other words, if the results are not properly delivered and clinical support is not pursued subsequently, the results of genetic screening may not be as beneficial. **Choice D** is incorrect because the availability of new technologies is one reason that prenatal genetic screening is increasing, but is not necessarily the sole reason. The author does not claim that this is the only factor perpetuating the growth, and, based on the rest of the passage, it can be assumed that testing is increasing in popularity because of the desire to know about genetic conditions ahead of time as well. **Choice E** is incorrect because the passage states that prenatal genetic screening can ultimately lead to better health and social outcomes, not just for children, but also for their families.

5 **Choice A is correct** because the passage focuses on the idea that parents can better prepare for their child with a genetic condition. This would likely include setting up proper support as soon as the child is born.

Choice B is incorrect because the passage does say that genetic screening can lead to better health and social outcomes but implies that this is in comparison to other children with genetic conditions who were not screened. The author does not make any comparisons with the health outcomes of children who do not have genetic conditions. **Choice C** is incorrect because the passage does not discuss anything that alters the quality of a relationship with a healthcare provider. The only mention of healthcare providers is that they typically offer genetic testing. **Choice D** is incorrect because the passage discusses improved health and social outcomes but does not discuss the mother's birthing experience. **Choice E** is incorrect because the passage discusses families having the ability to prepare better but does not discuss the emotional state of families. Additionally, the passage states that there is not much clinical research in this area so something like this is unknown.

6 **Choice A and C are correct** because waves are described as existing anywhere and calculated in many ways, so the correct answer should reflect this diversity and range. "Ubiquity" and "Pervasiveness." These two words both mean extensiveness. The waves are obviously seen in an extensive array of mediums. Therefore, A and C are correct.

Choice B is incorrect because "Uniformity" means consistency, but the sentence implies that waves travel in different ways depending on the situation. **Choice D** is incorrect because "Conformity" means conventionalism. This doesn't work for the same reason that "Uniformity" doesn't work: the waves are different, not the same. **Choice E** is incorrect because "Expressivity" means articulateness, but wave don't express themselves in fluent speech. **Choice F** is incorrect because Petulance" is sullenness, which is a personality.

7 **Choice B and D are correct** because this sentence states that a person may become so desperate that he or she can only focus on one potential good of dangerous medicine rather than the many ills. A potential benefit that would cause someone to forget the problems must be the ability to lessen suffering. The words "Palliative" and "Alleviative" mean calming or soothing. It makes sense that someone desperate to be soothed from pain would only focus on a product's potential to provide that service rather than the plethora of problems that would come with it, including falling for a scam. Therefore, B and D are the correct answers.

Choice A is incorrect because "Prohibitive" means unaffordable, which would be a bad rather than good characteristic of New Age medicine. **Choice C** is incorrect because "Luxurious" means lavish, which doesn't fit the context of desperation. **Choice E** is incorrect because "Intercalated" means added or interposed, which doesn't make sense in the context of the question. **Choice F** is incorrect because "Illegal" means illicit, which would be considered negative, not the one possible benefit of the New Age medicine.

8 **Choice D and E are correct** because aspiring business owners might worry about registering their businesses, but do not because of a government action, so the correct answer must support the idea of the government taking action. The correct answers are Choice D, promulgates, because it means to widely advertise, and Choice, E, avers, which means to formally declare something to be true. These choices show that owners are more comfortable registering businesses once the information that the action is safe is spread to them by the government.

Choice A is incorrect because Choice A, emends, means to make improvements or corrections to something, but it is unclear whether the action taken was an improvement on an old law or if it is a completely new law. **Choice B is incorrect** because Choice B, palavers, means to talk unnecessarily at length, which is not a positive action from a government. **Choice C is incorrect** because Choice C, gibes, means to laugh with contempt and derision, so these are not positive actions for a government. **Choice F is incorrect** because Choice F, inveighs, meaning to rail against or protest strongly, is a possible government action, but the government is clearly in support of – not against – making corporations separate entities from their owners; if they were not, there would still be a reason for business owners to be worried

9 **Choice A and D are correct** because this sentence is saying that ocular surgery of the eye is a very difficult procedure, and that textbook knowledge needs to be coupled with something else in order to be successful in it. "Tenacity" and "Doggedness." both mean resolve and perseverance. These are the characteristics that would be indispensable in completing a difficult procedure.

Choice B is incorrect because "predilection" means taste or preference. Whether or not a doctor has preference does not change how the surgery will be performed. How "predilection" would be used in the sentence doesn't even specify what the doctor would have a preference for, so that answer choice is clearly wrong. **Choice C is incorrect** because "awareness" means mindfulness. While this answer choice technically makes sense both grammatically and logically, it can be assumed that all doctors have awareness. Furthermore, there is no matching answer choice for "awareness" making it wrong either way. **Choice E is incorrect** because "contempt" means dislike. There's no reason to believe that dislike for something (and that "something" wouldn't be specified if this answer was chosen) would cause a doctor to be better at their job. **Choice F is incorrect** because "sensitivity" means compassion. While compassion is a good trait for a doctor to have, there's no reason to believe that it will allow them to complete a technically demanding procedure. Furthermore, like "Awareness" there is no matching answer choice for "Sensitivity."

10 **Choice D is correct** because the passage focuses on the EEOB including its architectural style, purpose, and history. It highlights who built it when it was built, and why it was built. The passage is clearly going to continue discussing other aspects of the building.

Choice A is incorrect because only the Eisenhower building is discussed, not the person. It would be surprising for the passage to switch to discussing a person who has not even been mentioned. **Choice B is incorrect** because the first paragraph of the passage discusses the architect who designed the building. Only one sentence was provided, and it would be unlikely for the author to return to the topic again after writing another paragraph that is unrelated to the option. **Choice C is incorrect** because the passage is about a building. The fact that it housed leaders who worked on the nation's foreign policy is only included to provide additional information about the building, not to begin a discussion on foreign policy. **Choice E is incorrect** because this passage is about the Eisenhower building, not the White House or a variety of different buildings. The White House is only mentioned at the beginning of the passage because it helps to explain where the Eisenhower building is located.

11 **Choice B is correct** correct because the passage indicates that the building can accommodate multiple important leaders and be the site for several departments. It can be assumed that the building is spacious enough to meet the needs of these two tasks.

Choice A is incorrect because the passage does not compare the design of the EEOB to that of the White House at all and mentions that the EEOB looks different from other buildings in the area in the last sentence of the first paragraph. **Choice C is incorrect** because there is no mention of security measures. Also, it is an old and historic building, so it is unlikely that a highly technical security system would be included in the original design. **Choice D is incorrect** because the design is described as embodying hope and excitement rather than the somber design of other buildings in the area. Hope and excitement are more likely associated with light colors and lots of details rather than dark colors and simplicity. **Choice E is incorrect** because the passage explicitly states that Alfred B. Mullett designed the EEOB. It mentions other leaders that worked in the building, but no one else who was a part of the designing process.

12 **Choice A is correct** because the passage is focused on the design and creation of the EEOB. By saying it, "embodies" hope and excitement the author is using personification to explain the way the building looks. It is not somber-looking, like other buildings in the area, but is light and new just like the feelings of citizens across the nation.

Choice B is incorrect because the author is not saying the building literally encompassed anything such as specific events for optimistic Americans, but that it figuratively embodied an attitude of hope and excitement. In other words, this sentence does not say the building housed affairs but represents the feelings of many Americans during this time. **Choice C** is incorrect because the author does not state that the building was "brand new" after the war. Also, it is inaccurate to say that the country felt new after the war. It is more accurate to say that the country felt hopeful and positive about the future. **Choice D** is incorrect because the phrase in the question does not refer to the government increasing funding for the building. This is a large stretch from the actual meaning of the phrase, which simply talks about the general hope and excitement of the American population. **Choice E** is incorrect because the EEOB was a symbol of hope, not a representation of the trauma experienced by Americans previously.

3 Quantitative Reasoning — Answers & Explanations — Section 3

1 **Choice B is correct.**

Let's first analyze the recurring decimals for x and y.

$x \leq 0.6\overline{16}$ is equivalent to $x \leq 0.616161616$

$y \geq 0.61\overline{6}$ is equivalent to $y \geq 0.616666666$

From this, $0.61\overline{6} > 0.6\overline{16}$. Hence, $y > x$

Choice A is incorrect because Quantity A is less than Quantity B. **Choice C** is incorrect because Quantity A and B are not equal. **Choice D** is incorrect because a relation can be determined from the given equation.

2 **Choice A is correct** because the slope obtained for line A is greater than that of line B.

For line A, transform the equation to
$y = mx + b$.
Given:
$$3x + 3y + 5 = 0$$
Subtract $3x$ and 5 from both sides.
$$3x + 3y + 5 - 3x - 5 = 0 - 3x - 5$$
$$3y = -3x - 5$$
Divide both sides by 3.
$$\frac{3y}{3} = \frac{-3x}{3} - \frac{5}{3}$$
$$y = -x - \frac{5}{3}$$
Slope of line A : -1

For line B, transform the equation to $y = mx + b$.
Given:
$$8x + 4y + 2 = 0$$
Subtract $8x$ and 2 from both sides.
$$8x + 4y + 2 - 8x - 2 = 0 - 8x - 2$$
$$4y = -8x - 2$$
Divide both sides by 4.
$$\frac{4y}{4} = \frac{-8x}{4} - \frac{2}{4}$$
$$y = -2x - \frac{1}{2}$$
Slope of line B: -2

Choice B is incorrect because Quantity B is less than Quantity A. **Choice C** is incorrect because Quantity A is not equal to Quantity B. **Choice D** is incorrect because a relation can be determined from the given equation.

3 **Choice C is correct** because both Circle A and Circle B have the same circumference of 8π.

Find the circumference for both circles.

For Circle A: $d = 8$ cm

Circumference $= \pi d$
$= 8\pi$

For Circle B: $r = 4$ cm

Circumference $= 2\pi r = 2(4)\pi$
$= 8\pi$

Choice A is incorrect because Quantity A is not greater than Quantity B. **Choice B** is incorrect because Quantity B is not greater than Quantity A. **Choice D** is incorrect because a relation can be determined from the given equation.

4 **Choice B is correct** because the obtained value of m^2 is less than 50.

Find the value of m the given inequality.

Given. $\frac{m}{3} + 10 \leq 12$

Subtract 10 from both sides $\frac{m}{3} + 10 - 10 \leq 12 - 10$

$$\frac{m}{3} \leq 2$$

Multiply 3 to both sides $3\left(\frac{m}{3}\right) \leq 2(3)$

$$m \leq 6$$

Find the value of m^2.

When $m = 6$, $m^2 = 36$.

When $m = 5$, $m^2 = 25$.

When $m = 4$, $m^2 = 16$.

For every assigned value of m, m^2 is always less than 50.

Choice A is incorrect because Quantity A is always less than Quantity B. **Choice C** is incorrect because Quantity A will never be equal to Quantity B. **Choice D** is incorrect because a relation can be determined from the information given.

5 **Choice B is correct** because the number of students going to Illinois University is 189.

Find the number of students attending Illinois University.

Number of Students: 350

Number of Students going to college: $350\left(\frac{9}{10}\right) = 315$

For more practice, visit www.vibrantpublishers.com

Quantitative Reasoning — Answers & Explanations — Section 3

Number of Students going to college at Illinois University

$$315 \left(\frac{3}{5}\right) = 189$$

Choice A is incorrect because 95 is too few considering the first condition that $\frac{9}{10}$ of 350 are going to college. **Choice C** is incorrect because 210 is $\frac{2}{3}$ of the students going to college. **Choice D** is incorrect because 315 is the number of students going to college. **Choice E** is incorrect because 525 is greater than the number of students. The expected answer should be less than 350.

6 **Choice E is correct.**

Let's find the mark of each student from the given percentage of mark.

Let x be the mark for each student. Use the equation

$$x = n\left(\frac{\%}{100}\right)$$

Maximum mark for Math, $n = 120$

Anne: $x_1 = n\left(\frac{\%}{100}\right) = 120\left(\frac{80}{100}\right) = 96$

Jessica: $x_2 = n\left(\frac{\%}{100}\right) = 120\left(\frac{100}{100}\right) = 120$

Amber: $x_3 = n\left(\frac{\%}{100}\right) = 120\left(\frac{80}{100}\right) = 96$

Gerald: $x_4 = n\left(\frac{\%}{100}\right) = 120\left(\frac{95}{100}\right) = 114$

Lee: $x_5 = n\left(\frac{\%}{100}\right) = 120\left(\frac{90}{100}\right) = 108$

Faith: $x_6 = n\left(\frac{\%}{100}\right) = 120\left(\frac{90}{100}\right) = 108$

Andrew: $x_7 = n\left(\frac{\%}{100}\right) = 120\left(\frac{85}{100}\right) = 102$

Dave: $x_8 = n\left(\frac{\%}{100}\right) = 120\left(\frac{90}{100}\right) = 108$

The average mark of Math for all students is

$$\frac{96 + 120 + 96 + 114 + 108 + 108 + 102 + 108}{8} = 106.5$$

Choice E is correct because the obtained answer is 107.

Choice A is incorrect because 89 is obtained from the average of the percentage of the marks. **Choice B** is incorrect because 90 is too small for the average of the marks for Math. **Choice C** is incorrect because 105 is approximately close to the obtained answer but not accurate. **Choice D** is incorrect because 106 is not the correct rounded value of the obtained answer.

7 **Choice B is correct** because the obtained total mark of Andrew from all subjects is 451.

Find the mark of Andrew for each subject.

Mark for each subject = (Percentage obtained by Student) Maximum Mark

Total mark = mark for Math + mark for Physics + mark for Chemistry + mark for History + mark for Computer Science + mark for Geography

Total mark = (85% of 120) + (80% of 120) + (80% of 110) + (75% of 100) + (70% of 60) + (80% of 60)

= 102 + 96 + 88 + 75 + 42 + 48

= 451

Choice A is incorrect because 450 is close to the obtained answer but not accurate. **Choice C** is incorrect because 465 is more than the obtained total mark. **Choice D** is incorrect because 470 is obtained from taking Andrew's total percentage of the marks for each subject. **Choice E** is incorrect because 475 is more than the obtained total mark.

8 **Choice D is correct** because Math, Physics, Chemistry, and Geography has an average percentage mark of 85 or more.

Find the average percentage of students for each subject.

Use the formula:

Average = $x_1 + x_2 + x_3 + x_4 + x_5 + x_6 + x_7 + x_8 n$, where x_n percentage of each student.

$$\text{Average}_{Math} = \frac{80 + 100 + 80 + 95 + 90 + 90 + 85 + 90}{8}$$

$= 88.75$

$$\text{Average}_{Physics} = \frac{75 + 95 + 85 + 90 + 85 + 95 + 80 + 90}{8}$$

$= 86.88$

$$\text{Average}_{Chemistry} = \frac{90 + 90 + 90 + 85 + 90 + 90 + 80 + 85}{8}$$

$= 87.5$

$$\text{Average}_{History} = \frac{75 + 90 + 85 + 80 + 85 + 85 + 75 + 80}{8}$$

$= 81.88$

$$\text{Average}_{Computer\ Science} = \frac{70 + 95 + 85 + 85 + 90 + 90 + 70 + 85}{8}$$

$= 83.75$

Quantitative Reasoning — Answers & Explanations — Section 3

$$Average_{Geography} = \frac{80 + 90 + 80 + 90 + 85 + 85 + 80 + 90}{8}$$
$$= 85$$

Choice A is incorrect because History obtained an average of less than 85%. **Choice B** is incorrect because Computer Science obtained an average of less than 85%. **Choice C** is incorrect because both History and Computer Science obtained an average of less than 85%. **Choice E** is incorrect because Computer Science should not be on the list.

9 **Choice E is correct** because the given expression is equivalent to

$y^7x^6 + y^8x^{10} + y^{15}x^3 + x^{14}y^5$ when simplified.

To simplify the given expression, use the following properties:

Distributive Property of Multiplication : $x(a + b) = ax + ab$
Product of Exponents : $x^a(x^b) = x^{a+b}$
Simplify: $y^5x^3(y^2x^3 + y^3x^5 + y^{10} + x^{11})$
$= (y^{5+2}x^{3+3} + y^{5+3}x^{3+5} + y^{5+10}x^3 + y^5x^{3+11})$
$= y^7x^6 + y^8x^8 + y^{15}x^3 + x^{14}y^5$

Choice A is incorrect because the 3rd and 4th terms are incorrect. **Choice B** is incorrect because the exponents of x and y are interchanged. **Choice C** is incorrect because the exponents were multiplied instead of added. **Choice D** is incorrect because the exponents were multiplied instead of added and the x and y exponents were interchanged.

10 **Choice E is correct** because the equation to use to find the time is $t = \frac{5x}{6}$.

Given: $speed = \frac{3}{5}$ miles per minute

$distance = \frac{x}{2}$

From the speed formula, $speed = \frac{distance}{time}$, the formula for time is

$$time = \frac{distance}{speed}$$

Substitute values of speed and distance into the formula for time.

$$time = \frac{distance}{speed} = \frac{\frac{x}{2}}{\frac{3}{5}} = \frac{x}{2}(\frac{5}{3}) = \frac{5x}{6}$$

Choice A is incorrect because $t = \frac{x}{6}$ failed to use the speed formula. **Choice B** is incorrect because $t = 6(5x)$ is not a correct integration of an incorrect speed formula. **Choice C** is incorrect because $t = \frac{6x}{5}$ the coefficients of the numerator and denominator are interchanged. **Choice D** is incorrect because $t = \frac{x}{5}$ failed to use the speed formula.

11 **Choice D is correct** because the obtained probability $x < 4$ is $\frac{5}{6}$.

Find the total possible outcome of the two dice.

1st dice - 6 faces

2nd dice - 6 face

Total possible outcome of drawing two dice is $6 \times 6 = 36$.

Assign values to x.

x is the absolute value of the difference between the two numbers on the dice and x should be less than 4.

When $x = 0$, $|x| = |0| = 0$. The possible outcomes are (1,1), (2,2), (3,3), (4,4), (5,5), (6,6). **Outcomes: 6**

When $x = 1$, $|1| = |1| = 1$. The possible outcomes are (1,2), (2,3), (3,4), (4,5), (5,6),
(2,1), (3,2), (4,3), (5,4), (6,5),. **Outcomes: 10**

When $x = 2$, $|2| = |2| = 2$. The possible outcomes are (1,3),(3,1), (2,4), (4,2), (3,5), (5,3), (4,6), (6,4). **Outcomes: 8**

When $x = 3$, $|3| = |3| = 3$. The possible outcomes are (1,4), (4,1), (2,5), (5,2), (3,6),(6,3). **Outcomes: 6**

Find the total outcomes: $6 + 10 + 8 + 6 = 30$.

Solve for the probability when $x < 4$.

$$\frac{Total\ outcomes\ when\ x < 4}{Total\ possible\ outcomes\ of\ drawing\ two\ dice} = \frac{6 + 10 + 8 + 6}{6(6)}$$

$$= \frac{30}{36} = \frac{5}{6}$$

Choice A is incorrect because the probability $\frac{1}{6}$ is too low considering x is at an absolute value. **Choice B** is incorrect because the probability $\frac{1}{3}$ is too low considering x is at an absolute value. **Choice C** is incorrect because the probability should be greater than $\frac{1}{2}$ due to the absolute value of x. **Choice E** is incorrect because the probability should be less than 1.

12 **The correct answer is 140°.** In triangle ADC: Find the measure of angle using the angle sum property of triangles.

$$m\angle A + m\angle D + m\angle C = 180°$$
$$50° + m\angle D + 30° = 180°$$
$$m\angle D = 180° - 80°$$
$$m\angle D = 100°$$

In quadrilateral ODCE: Find $m\angle O$ using the angle sum property of quadrilaterals.

$$m\angle O + m\angle D + m\angle C + m\angle E = 360°$$
$$m\angle O + 100° + 30° + 90° = 360°$$
$$m\angle O = 360° - 220°$$
$$m\angle O = 140°$$

Looking at the figure, $m\angle O$ and $m\angle z$ are vertical angles. According to the vertical angle theorem, $m\angle z = m\angle O$. Hence, $m\angle z = 140°$.

Verbal Reasoning (Easy) — Answers & Explanations — Section 4

1 **Choice C is correct** because the sentence is discussing the hypothesized age rather than simply the age. This means that the scientists already have a guess, and are merely trying to confirm it. Substantiate, which means to establish by proof or evidence, achieves this end.

Choice A is incorrect because to correlate means to bring into mutual or reciprocal relation; it is hard to see what this could have to do with this sentence, particularly since there is no mention of anything the hypothesized age could be correlated with. **Choice B** is incorrect because discern means to perceive or recognize, which does not align with the context for the passage. **Choice D** is incorrect because It is unlikely that the scientists would be trying to gainsay - or dispute or contradict - their own hypothesis, so you can eliminate this. **Choice E** is incorrect because to palliate means to alleviate or to extenuate and is clearly out of place in this context.

2 **Choice D is correct** because Hooke's work was the basis for future theory, therefore, foundation is correct

Choice A is incorrect because infrastructure is not accurate, as he did not build all the necessary components for future study. **Choice B** is incorrect because Hooke's theory was innovative in that it was new, but innovative does not include the notion that Hooke created a starting point for other scientists. **Choice C** is incorrect because consequence suggests a cause and effect relationship. If one were to replace the blank with effect, the sentence would not make sense. **Choice E** is incorrect because production refers to something that is created or produced. Hooke himself did not produce the cell theories that were to follow his discovery.

3 **Choice B and E are correct** because the first blank is in a sentence that says how all food comes from plants. The sentence says that, regardless of a certain quality of the route the food takes, it still can be traced to plants. For the second blank, we want a word that stresses how plants provide food for all animals. Circuitous and prevalence, respectively, achieve these ends.

Choice A is incorrect because "malevolent" means "wicked." Obviously, the route cannot have personality traits, so this answer makes no sense. **Choice C** is incorrect because fulminated" means "raged." This answer does not make sense in the context of the question. **Choice D** is incorrect because "dilution" means "weakening." The passage does not imply that the widespread appearance of plants "weakens" them in any way. **Choice F** is incorrect because mirth means "happiness." This answer does not make sense in the context of the question.

4 **Choice B, F, and I are correct** because this passage is saying that parents who criticize the violence of their children's movies don't appreciate the level of violence in the films of their own generation. Irony is the incongruity of expected results versus actual results. It would be expected that parents would find violence in both their children's movies and their own to be offensive. Parents only finding offense in one group of films would be ironic. For the second blank, the passage is saying how parents do not like the use of violence in modern cinema. Disparage means "ridicule." The parents "worry" that their children have too much violence in their movies, so they must be disparaging the use of violence in cinema. For the third blank, the passage is stating that older movies do not use violence explicitly, but it is still present. Blasé means "nonchalant." If the violence in older movies was not done explicitly, but rather as "part of everyday life" then it must have been done nonchalantly.

Choice A is incorrect because prosperity means "wealth." Parents being offended by violence in their children's movies while not recognizing it in their own would not lead to wealth. **Choice C** is incorrect because singularity means "uniqueness." Parents criticizing violence in their children's movies while not recognizing it in their own would not lead to any type of uniqueness, either. **Choice D** is incorrect because authenticate means "endorse." The parents are not endorsing the violence of modern cinema, they are criticizing it. **Choice E** is incorrect because theorize means "conjecture." The parents are not theorizing anything about violence in modern cinema, they are openly criticizing it. **Choice G** is incorrect because incisive means "keen." The passage is saying that violence in older movies is done less explicitly, not that it is done "keenly." **Choice H** is incorrect because gracious means "kind." The passage is clearly not implying that there was something kind about violence in older movies.

5 **Choice E is correct** because it includes the key components of the passage: the diversity among starfish, their biological classification, and their unique ability to detach and regenerate arms. It summarizes the most important information in a concise and understandable format.

Choice A is incorrect because the passage compares starfish to lizards because both animals can willingly lose and regrow a body part. Therefore, starfish are not the only animals with this skill. **Choice B** is incorrect because it simply restates the first few sentences of the passage without including the critical information regarding arm regeneration. **Choice C** is incorrect because the passage only talks about one type of predator, crabs, and explains how starfish defend themselves by losing limbs. Thus, they do have a defense mechanism. **Choice D** is incorrect because it accurately summarizes only part of the passage and fails to mention the critical information regarding arm regeneration.

6 **Choice C is correct** because the passage only focuses on starfish, not other sea creatures. The passage thoroughly discusses the fact that starfish can regrow arms when needed. The word "resilient" means being able to recover quickly. Therefore, the word "resilient" can be applied to starfish that recover from attacks and continue to populate most marine areas with nearly 2,000 different species.

Choice A is incorrect because the passage does not talk about the lifestyle of a starfish beyond the defense mechanism used in the face of attacks. It does not talk about starfish's eating habits, sleeping, mating, or any other topics related to lifestyle. **Choice B** is incorrect because the passage does not discuss a decline in the starfish population. The only mention of the population is that there are nearly 2,000 different species across most marine areas. This title would not accurately represent the information expressed throughout the passage, such as the unique skill of arm regeneration. **Choice D** is incorrect because the passage only discusses one creature with a unique skill: starfish. The passage does not mention other creatures that have any unique abilities. The passage does state that lizards can also regenerate their tails, but only as a segue to introduce starfish. **Choice E** is incorrect because the focus of the passage is on starfish specifically, not all echinoderms. The only reason other echinoderms are mentioned is to provide additional background information on starfish.

7 **Choice C is correct** because the passage discusses the fact that starfish shed their limbs as a defense mechanism during attacks. It does not discuss any other defense mechanism that the starfish could use to injure an attacker. While it is not explicitly stated, it would likely be included if starfish used another method to defend themselves. In other words, if starfish could emit poison, sting, or bite their attackers there may not be a need to shed limbs at all, and this information would at least be discussed in the passage.

Choice A is incorrect because the passage states that starfish can shed a limb in order to escape from predators. To escape, starfish would need to be able to move even though they left behind a limb. **Choice B** is incorrect because the passage does not discuss starfish eating habits and it cannot be assumed that just because starfish serve as prey to some animals that they are not predators to other animals. It is possible that starfish may be both predator and prey in various cases. **Choice D** is incorrect because the passage does not provide any information regarding starfish habitats or preferences. There is not sufficient information provided to draw any conclusions about where starfish choose to live. **Choice E** is incorrect because although the passage does state that starfish are prey to crabs, it does not express that they are easy prey. In contrast, the passage discusses how starfish can get away after it has been captured by a crab, which suggests it may be difficult prey to kill.

8 **Choice B and E are correct** because this sentence talks of a person receiving a lot of money and feeling subsequent urges that drag him away from his previous disposition. This disposition is described as being a state of "composure." So we want words that stress how Steven might be giving in to the urges of the wealthy. Supercilious and haughty both mean snooty or self–important. It makes perfect sense that Steven would be afraid that wealth would make him self-important, and that it would cause him to lose his "pre–wealth composure.

Choice A is incorrect because enlightened means rational or tolerant. Steven was already like that, as the sentence explains, so he wouldn't be worried that wealth was making him more like that. **Choice C** is incorrect because chic means attractive or elegant. Steven may have very well been elegant and fashionable before he became wealthy, so this also does not work. **Choice D** is incorrect because vacuous means hollow or empty. "Hollow urges" doesn't make much sense unless you try to justify it with an incredibly figurative meaning, which makes this answer choice very weak. Moreover, there is no other term that matches it, so it can't be an answer. **Choice F** is incorrect because violent means vicious or forceful. It's doubtful that wealth would immediately make one violent, and once again, this answer choice has no partner in the answer tree.

9 **Choice B and E are correct** because In this sentence the neural response is being contrasted with the hormonal response. The hormonal response is being characterized as being slow and indirect; therefore, the correct answer should express the opposite meaning for the neural response. Instantaneous and rapid both mean quick or speedy. These words describe the contrast between the neural response and the hormonal response, which is described as slow and indirect. Therefore, B and E are the correct answers.

Choice A is incorrect because inglorious means shameful. This word does not describe the neural response in any capacity, least of all when compared to the hormonal response. **Choice C** is incorrect because violent means fierce or vehement. The neural response is also described as being precise and immediate. A violent action is not a precise one. **Choice D** is incorrect because explosive means volatile. This answer does not work for the same reason that "Violent" does not work: it contradicts the "precise" description given to the neural response. **Choice F** is incorrect because somatic means relating to the body. While the neural response is a component of the body the word "somatic" does not in any way distinguish the neural response from the hormonal response, which is also a part of the human body.

10 **Choice C and F are correct** because the passage implies that friction should be easy to understand. It "ostensibly works just like any of the other Newtonian forces" which means that friction should follow the same rules the other Newtonian forces do. But, as the passage insinuates, it ends up going against expectations and frustrating lab students. We want words that express the contradicting of expectations. The words inconsistent and unpredictable both achieve this end.

Choice A is incorrect because ironic means satirical or insincere, which makes no sense in the context of a scientific question. **Choice B** is incorrect because straightforward means direct and simple. If the application of friction was direct and simple then students would have no problem understanding it. **Choice D** is incorrect because deliberate means slow or cautious. The slow and cautious application of friction would, if anything, make it easier for students to understand.

Choice E is incorrect because complaisant means obliging or agreeable. This is a personality trait and makes no sense in the context of a scientific question.

11 **Choice B is correct** because the author supports the argument that the Mediterranean diet can improve health outcomes by giving concrete examples of lowering the risk of heart disease and cancer.

Choice A is incorrect because although the author does outline the foods included in a typical Mediterranean diet, this does not support the argument that the diet is healthier than a Western diet. It simply provides background information. **Choice C** is incorrect because although the author does use this statement to support the argument, it is not the strongest point of the argument. It is a suggestion by the author and states that there may be negative side effects for children. In contrast, the author claims that the risk of heart disease and cancer will be lowered, which is a much stronger argument. **Choice D** is incorrect because the author does make this claim, but then supports this claim with concrete examples. The claim alone is not a strength in the argument because it is simply the author's opinion. **Choice E** is incorrect because the author does not explain the risks of consuming the Mediterranean diet. This would be in sharp contrast with the author's argument that the Mediterranean diet should be consumed instead of the Western diet.

12 **Choice A is correct** because the passage explains that Brazil is a democratic country in which officials are elected to lead. In other words, Brazil is a representative democracy. Also, the passage explains Brazil's three branches of government, which is an example of Separation of Powers.

Choice B is incorrect because it includes important information about one branch of the government, but leaves out any information about the other two branches. Since this statement does not describe the legislative or judicial branches at all, it is not an accurate summary of the government as a whole. **Choice C** is incorrect because it includes important information about two branches of the government, but leaves out any information about the executive branch. Since this statement does not describe the president or the president's duties at all, it is not an accurate summary of the government as a whole. **Choice D** is incorrect because the passage explains Brazil's government as a representative democracy in which officials are elected into three branches. The passage does not state that the citizens directly vote on issues, as is the case in direct democracies. **Choice E is incorrect** because the passage explains Brazil's government as a representative democracy in which officials are elected into three branches. The passage does not state that the citizens directly vote on issues, as is the case in direct democracies.

13 **Choice D is correct** because the passage makes multiple points comparing the governmental structures of the United States and Brazil, such as having the same three branches of government, the roles of each branch, and the rules regarding presidential terms. Additionally, it points out a difference between the two nations by explaining that Brazil uses a direct voting system. This could serve as a part of a comparative piece if foreign leaders were looking to reform their system.

Choice A is incorrect because this passage is an informative piece specifically relating to the Brazilian government. If a book focused on Brazilian culture, such detailed information about how the government operates would not be necessary. **Choice B is incorrect** because this passage is not written as an advertisement and has no persuasive techniques or descriptive language. It does not discuss any potentially enjoyable experiences in Brazil, but only how the government is structured. **Choice C is incorrect** because the passage does not use any argumentative techniques or make any claims against the government of the United States. Rather, the passage is simply neutrally comparing two democracy-based governments. **Choice E is incorrect** because the purpose of local newspaper articles is to report on events happening in the area. A breakdown of the structure of the federal government would not be relevant in this context.

14 **Choice B is correct** because the first paragraph of the passage does describe how handheld cameras impacted the public by explaining that taking photographs was more feasible, people snapped photographs of their friends and family members, and photographs were used in politics. Then, the second paragraph of the passage describes how serious photographers were focused on the artistic medium by explaining the mission of pictorialists.

Choice A is incorrect because the first paragraph does not focus on the popularity of photography among the middle class, but the use of handheld cameras in a variety of ways. Then, the second paragraph of the passage does not discuss painters switching mediums, but photographers wanting to prove taking photographs was as artistically valuable as painting. **Choice C is incorrect** because it reverses the ideas presented in the first paragraph and second paragraph of the passage. The first paragraph of the passage describes how photographs were used for commonplace purposes like political advertising and the second paragraph of the passage describes how serious photographers set out to prove the artistic merit of photography.

15 **Choice E is correct** because the first sentence says the late nineteenth century brought the invention of, "smaller, handheld cameras." In other words, larger cameras had already been invented previously. Additionally, the passage discusses the fact that these smaller cameras became more widely used by the public, suggesting that prior to this time they were not.

Choice A is incorrect because the wages of both types of artists are not discussed in the passage. Additionally, the passage explains that pictorialists were striving to prove the artistic worth of cameras, suggesting that painters were more valued at the time. **Choice B is incorrect** because the passage explains that pictorialists were attempting to prove the artistic worth of cameras, suggesting that photographs as works of art were not originally appreciated. **Choice C is incorrect** because although it can be assumed that cameras were bigger prior to the late nineteenth century, the passage does not mention the ease of (or lack of ease) camera use for original cameras or handheld cameras. **Choice D is incorrect** because the passage does not discuss the value of cameras or how the value changed over time. It can be assumed that since the public did not have much access to them prior to the late nineteenth century, they were more valuable and rarer prior to that time.

Verbal Reasoning (Hard) — Answers & Explanations — Section 4

1 **Choice B is correct** because extant cells are cells that already exist. The distinction between new cells deriving from extant cells and those cells simply appearing is the main point of this sentence. This sentence clearly makes the comparison. The required word must be a contrast to the idea of cells that "spontaneously appear."

Choice A is incorrect because inanimate cells are non-moving cells; it is not clear if these cells exist or spontaneously appear. **Choice C** is incorrect because living does not make a specific contrast with "spontaneously appear". **Choice D** is incorrect because surviving does not make a specific contrast with "spontaneously appear". **Choice E** is incorrect because mortal does not make a specific contrast with "spontaneously appear".

2 **Choice C and D is correct** because the first blank talks about how there are "things" that fall under the heading of biotechnology that one wouldn't expect. We want a word that describes what these "things" might be. By reading further into the passage we see various jobs listed – brewers of alcohol and agricultural developers. Therefore, we want a word that describes a job. "Vocations" means "life's work." This describes the jobs that unexpectedly fall into the category of "biotechnology." The last sentence is comparing what you would expect to fall under the heading of "biotechnology" (medical procedures of a certain quality) with what you wouldn't expect ("rough-and-tumble" jobs). Therefore, we want a word that would contrast with the "rough-and-tumble" description given to the latter group of jobs. "Exactitude" means "precision." This word contrasts nicely with "rough-and-tumble."

Choice A is incorrect because "verisimilitudes" means "truths." This does not describe a field of work and therefore is incorrect. **Choice B** is incorrect because "denigrations" means "defamations." These are insults and not fields of work. **Choice E** is incorrect because "unsophistication" means "lack of refinement." This relates to "rough-and-tumble" and therefore is incorrect. **Choice F** is incorrect because "fallacy" means "misconception." This word does not contrast the scientific procedures with the "rough-and-tumble" jobs.

3 **Choices A and D are correct** because the passage is saying that the modern food industry in America is very large. "Extensiveness" means "comprehensiveness." This makes sense. An institution as large as the modern food industry would certainly be described as "extensive." Additionally, the passage talks of how this "dynamic and widespread" industry must be regulated. It can be inferred that "dynamic and widespread" must be difficult. Arduous means difficult, therefore, would be the other correct choice.

Choice B is incorrect because lethargy means tiredness, which does not align with the context of the passage. **Choice C** is incorrect because bankruptcy means insolvency, which does not align with the context of the passage. **Choice E** is incorrect because ridiculous means absurd. The passage makes no claim that regulating the food industry is an "absurd task." **Choice F** is incorrect because "pernicious" means "evil." The passage talks about the size of the food industry, but makes no comment as to its morality, or the morality of trying to regulate it.

4 **Choices C, D, and I is correct** because the butte means a hill, from which one could watch the flood, capitulated means to give way, which aligns with the word crumbled in the passage, and detritus, which means

Choice A is incorrect because the speaker cannot be watching his town wash away from an estuary or river, or he would have washed away as well. **Choice B** is incorrect because neither can he be watching from a ravine, as being in a narrow steep-walled canyon would not place him above the town or afford him a vista. **Choice E** is incorrect because the barriers did not countenance, meaning placate or pacify as this would make no sense in the context of the sentence. **Choice F** is incorrect because the barriers did not assuage, that is, soothe the flood waters. **Choice G** is incorrect because calumny does not make sense in the context of the sentence. It refers to verbal attacks meant to destroy reputations or friendships (calumny). **Choice H** is incorrect because aspersions does not make sense in the context of the sentence. It refers to disparaging remarks (aspersions) that cast doubt

3 Verbal Reasoning (Hard) — Answers & Explanations — Section 4

5 **Choice B is correct** because the passage explains that salt can suppress bitter tastes and enhance other enjoyable flavors, such as sweetness. Therefore, salt would best serve a recipe that needed to minimize bitter flavors and maximize sweet flavors.

Choice A is incorrect because the addition of salt would best serve a recipe with sweet and bitter ingredients so that the sweetness can be enhanced, and the bitterness can be suppressed. The presence of salty ingredients is not necessary. **Choice C** is incorrect because the addition of salt would best serve a recipe with sweet and bitter ingredients so that the sweetness can be enhanced, and the bitterness can be suppressed. If there are no bitter ingredients, salt may not be needed. **Choice D** is incorrect because the passage explains that salt lessens bitter flavors and enhances pleasant ones. Therefore, if a recipe had no bitter flavors the salt would have nothing to suppress. **Choice E** is incorrect because although salt can suppress bitter flavors, this recipe does not have any sweet flavors to enhance. Also, there are already salty ingredients present in the recipe so the addition of salt may not be necessary.

6 **Choice A is correct** because the first paragraph introduces the two main ideas. The idea of taste is introduced as the author states "The human tongue can perceive a variety of tastes such as sweet, bitter, and salty." The idea of how salt impacts eating experiences is introduced as the author expresses that salt has various sensory effects including altering perceived thickness of liquids. **Choice B is correct** because the author suggests salt has interesting capabilities of enhancing eating experiences by referring to the sensory effects salt has in food then providing an example of how salt increases perceived thickness. The second paragraph delves deeper into salt's unique capabilities.

Choice C is incorrect because the first paragraph only discusses one single example of a sensory effect that salt has on food, which is increasing perceived thickness. Otherwise, the first paragraph only states that salt does indeed have sensory effects on foods.

7 **Choice C is correct** because the passage describes the population as diverse before explaining that some Singaporeans have Indian, Chinese, or Malaysian ethnic roots.

Choice A is incorrect because the passage does not state that Singapore is made up of more younger people than older people. It only states that it is an evolving city that must try to appeal to a younger generation. **Choice B** is incorrect because although the passage does discuss the population having a variety of different ethnic origins, the passage does not suggest that the people have immigrated from other countries rather than being born in Singapore. **Choice D** is incorrect because the passage does not suggest that these three people groups make up the majority of the population. The passage does provide three examples of how a traditional Singaporean dish can be altered based on those three ethnic backgrounds. However, there is no reason to assume that other ethnic groups are not widely present in Singapore. **Choice E** is incorrect because although the passage does express that Singaporeans have an attitude of togetherness, it does not express that this is easy to maintain or that the population is small. Oppositely, the passage states that special effort must be made to preserve this cultural ideal of togetherness.

8 **Choice D is correct** because it reflects the overall message of the first paragraph, which is the fact that Singaporeans have both unity and diversity. Their population includes many ethnic backgrounds, but they strive to stick together as one nation.

Choice A is incorrect because it only includes information about the festivals and does not recognize the overall message of having unity among diverse individuals. The information provided in the passage about food and festivals is only there to support the idea that Singaporeans celebrate together and value cultural heritage despite having different backgrounds. **Choice B** is incorrect because it reflects information provided in the second paragraph, not the first paragraph. **Choice C** is incorrect because the first paragraph focuses on how cultural identity in Singapore is carried out today, rather than historically. The only mention of Singapore's history is in the first sentence of the passage. **Choice E** is incorrect because it does not reflect the overall message of the paragraph. The message is more than information about customizing specific dishes. It is the fact that there is unity among a diverse population. The information about adapting dishes to unique groups' preferences is only intended to support the idea that Singaporeans have a sense of togetherness despite having different backgrounds.

Practice Tests for the GRE

Verbal Reasoning (Hard) — Answers & Explanations — Section 4

9 **Choice A is correct** because this is a possible reason that people might have to make an additional effort to pass on cultural traditions. As the second paragraph states, the city is rapidly growing and must appeal to a younger generation, but also cultural practices may take additional time and effort that is not viewed as necessary.

Choice B is incorrect because there is no reason to believe that Singaporean festivals have become any less interesting. If they were interesting historically, they are likely to continue being interesting as they are passed down to the younger generation, especially if older citizens are putting in special effort. **Choice C** is incorrect because the passage does not suggest that the younger generation is looking to reconnect with cultural roots. Oppositely, the passage states that the older generation must make a special effort to pass on traditions. **Choice D** is incorrect because there is no reason to believe that ingredients for Singaporean dishes are not as readily available. Nothing in the passage relates to this topic. **Choice E** is incorrect because the passage states that older Singaporeans are making a special effort to pass on traditions, not that they have little desire.

10 **Choice C and D are correct** because motivated and influenced convey that the "young woman" was inspired by "her desire to impress her parents."

Choice A is incorrect because inhibited suggests a level of negative influence and does not fit well with sentence. **Choice B** is incorrect because sedated suggests different levels of negative influence and does not fit well with the sentence. **Choice E** is incorrect because stymied suggests different levels of negative influence and does not fit well with the sentence. **Choice F** is incorrect because adjudicated has no other similar words among the options.

11 **Choice B and D are correct** because the sentence is saying that people flock away from science because it is too strict. Therefore, the characteristic that we want in art must be the opposite of this. "Flexibility" and "Mutability." both express a changeableness that contrasts the "rigid mechanisms" of science and are close synonyms.

Choice A is incorrect because contradictions means inconsistencies. While contradictions definitely aren't strict, that quality would not attract a person who has already left science specifically because it was "counter–intuitive." **Choice C** is incorrect because craftiness means cunningness or slyness. which breaks away from rigidity of science but not in the fluid manner implied by the passage. **Choice E** is incorrect because expressivity means eloquence. This might look like a good answer but the sciences can be expressive as well. It's fluidity we're concerned with, and this answer does not provide that. **Choice F** is incorrect because "innovation" means novelty. Innovation is shared with both art and science, so a person would not leave one for the other while citing "innovation" as the reason.

12 **Choice A and B are correct** because this sentence is saying that modern superficial standards have damaged the media, and done something to children. If it damaged all of modern media then it can be safely assumed that it damaged children, too. Therefore, "Subverted" and "Undermined" are the correct answers. They both mean damaged or weakened. Modern superficiality is damaging the self-confidence of young children. This makes perfect sense. So, a and b are correct.

Choice C is incorrect because "Initiated" means began. If superficiality-initiated confidence then it would be helping children, so that answer must be wrong. **Choice D** is incorrect because "Rectified" means fixed. Again, since superficiality is described as doing damage then this answer cannot be correct. **Choice E** is incorrect because "Invigorated" means strengthened. Again, this sentiment is the opposite of what the sentence wants to convey. **Choice F** is incorrect because To invigorate confidence would be a good thing, "Objectified" means portrayed, often with negative connotations. But it is beauty that is being objectified, not the self-confidence of children.

13 **Choice C is correct** because the purpose of the sentence is to provide a definition for food insecurity so that the reader can better understand the issue being faced and the author's argument.

Choice A is incorrect because the author does not make an argument that hunger should be the primary focus of agencies. The author does say that hunger is not the primary focus, but only claims that social workers must be aware of the impacts of this issue. **Choice B** is incorrect because the author does not argue that eating patterns must be regular in all healthy families. Such an absolute cannot be assumed. The author does state that disrupted eating patterns are one component of what characterizes food insecurity. **Choice D** is incorrect because although the sentence does introduce the department, this does not serve the author's argument in any way. **Choice E** is incorrect because the reader may or may not feel

Verbal Reasoning (Hard)   Answers & Explanations   Section 4

sympathetic, and the purpose of the statement is not to evoke sympathy but to provide a factual definition of a term.

14 **Choice A is correct** because the passage expresses the positive impacts that swamps have on other areas such as absorbing water to minimize flooding problems, protecting coastlines, and absorbing excess chemicals. **Choice C is correct** because the passage describes many reasons swamps are valuable such as absorbing water to minimize flooding problems, protecting coastlines, and absorbing excess chemicals. However, as stated in the passage, swamps have undesirable reputations.

Choice B is incorrect because the passage states that an excess of chemicals sometimes occurs, but swamps can naturally purify the water. Therefore, the passage does not indicate that hazardous chemicals are often in swamps.

15 **Choice D is correct** because this sentence transitions into another reason that swamps are valuable. The first paragraph talks about absorbing floods and protecting coastlines, but this sentence uses the word "also" to add a third reason to the list: purifying water. Then, this sentence introduces the topic for the remainder of the second paragraph, which discusses how swamps complete the purification process.

Choice A is incorrect because the sentence does not introduce a new topic about swamps, but rather continues discussing the reasons that swamps are valuable. **Choice B** is incorrect because although the sentence does transition into another reason that swamps are valuable, it does not provide an example of how swamps can purify water. It simply states that swamps can purify water and the examples are included in the following sentences. **Choice C** is incorrect because this sentence does not conclude the previous paragraph which discusses coastline protection and flood absorption. Instead, it introduces a third reason that swamps are valuable. **Choice E** is incorrect because the sentence does not introduce a new topic about swamps, but rather continues discussing the reasons that swamps are valuable.

Quantitative Reasoning (Easy)   Answers & Explanations   Section 5

1 **Choice A is correct** because Quantity A is greater than Quantity B.

Let $DE = 1$ unit and $FE = 4$ units because the ratio of DE to FE is 1:4

We obtained the following measurements of the sides of triangles $\triangle ABC$ and $\triangle DCE$.

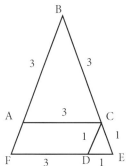

Find the perimeter of $\triangle ABC$.

Perimeter $= \overline{AC} + \overline{AB} + \overline{BC}$

Perimeter $= 3 + 3 + 3$

Perimeter $= 9$

Find the perimeter of of parallelogram ACDF

Perimeter $= \overline{AC} + \overline{CD} + \overline{FD} + \overline{AF}$

Perimeter $= 3 + 1 + 3 + 1$

Perimeter $= 8$

Choice B is incorrect because Quantity B is not greater than Quantity B. **Choice C** is incorrect because Quantity A and Quantity B are not equal. **Choice D** is incorrect because a relation can be determined from the given information.

2 **Choice A is correct** because the range of the given data is 9 which is greater than 7.

Range = highest value − lowest value = 84 − 75 = 9

Choice B is incorrect because Quantity B is less than Quantity A. **Choice C** is incorrect because Quantity A and Quantity B are not equal. **Choice D** is incorrect because a relation can be determined from the given data

3 **Choice D is correct.** Assign values to x and find the Quantity A and Quantity B.

x	$\lvert x \rvert$	$\dfrac{x^3}{3}$
−3	3	−9
−2	2	$-\dfrac{8}{3}$ or −2.67
−1	1	$-\dfrac{1}{3}$ or −0.33
0	0	0
1	1	$\dfrac{1}{3}$ or 0.33
2	2	$\dfrac{8}{3}$ or 2.67
3	3	$\dfrac{27}{3}$ or 9

From the obtained values,

- if x is a negative number, Quantity A is greater than Quantity B.
- if x is 0, Quantity A is equal to Quantity B.
- if x is 1, Quantity A is greater than Quantity B.
- if x is greater than 1, Quantity B is greater than Quantity A.

Hence, Choice D is correct because the given quantities cannot determine any relation.

Choice A is incorrect because Quantity A is sometimes greater than Quantity B. **Choice B** is incorrect because Quantity B is equal to Quantity A. **Choice C** is incorrect because Quantity A and Quantity B are equal only when $x = 0$.

4 **Choice B is correct** because the common multiple of 2,3 and 6 from the given set is 6 which is less than 10.

Choice A is incorrect because Quantity A is less than Quantity B. **Choice C** is incorrect because Quantity A and Quantity B are not equal. **Choice D** is incorrect because a relation can be determined from the given information.

5 **Choice A is correct** because the obtained angle for Quantity A is $\dfrac{10}{7}\pi$ which is greater than the obtained angle for Quantity B, $\dfrac{16}{27}\pi$.

Solve for the angle in radians for Quantity A using the Arc Length formula, $L = \theta r$.

3 Quantitative Reasoning (Easy) Answers & Explanations   Section 5

Given: *Arc Length* = 10π, *radius* = 7

$$L = \theta r$$
$$10\pi = \theta(7)$$
$$\frac{10}{7}\pi = \theta$$

Solve for the angle in radians for Quantity B using the Area of the Sector formula, $A = \frac{1}{2}r^2\theta$.

Given: *Area of the Sector* = 24π, *radius* = 9

$$A = \frac{1}{2}r^2\theta.$$
$$24\pi = \frac{1}{2}(9)^2\theta.$$
$$\theta = \frac{16}{27}\pi.$$
$$\frac{10}{7}\pi > \frac{16}{27}\pi$$

Choice B is incorrect because Quantity B is less than Quantity A. **Choice C** is incorrect because Quantity A and Quantity B are not equal. **Choice D** is incorrect because a relation can be determined from the given information.

6 **Choice A is correct** because the obtained value of *x* is $x \geq -1/9$.

Solve the given inequality.

$$5x + 9 \geq -4x + 8$$
$$5x + 4x \geq 8 - 9$$
$$9x \geq -1$$
$$x \geq -1/9$$

Choice B is incorrect because the RHS should have been negative. **Choice C** is incorrect because the 9 should have been subtracted from both sides. **Choice D** is incorrect because the RHS should have been negative. **Choice E** is incorrect because the RHS was not correctly evaluated.

7 **Choice B, Choice F and Choice G are correct** because the obtained mean of 8th Grade, 9th Grade and 10th Grade have the greatest value among the other Grade levels.

Solve for the mean of each Grade level using the Mean Formula, $m = \frac{sum\ of\ the\ terms}{number\ of\ terms}$

6th Grade:
$$m = \frac{sum\ of\ the\ terms}{number\ of\ terms} = \frac{85 + 90 + 78 + 92 + 88}{5} = 86.6$$

7th Grade:
$$m = \frac{sum\ of\ the\ terms}{number\ of\ terms} = \frac{79 + 84 + 91 + 87 + 85}{5} = 85.2$$

8th Grade:
$$m = \frac{sum\ of\ the\ terms}{number\ of\ terms} = \frac{91 + 89 + 94 + 87 + 92}{5} = 90.6$$

9th Grade:
$$m = \frac{sum\ of\ the\ terms}{number\ of\ terms} = \frac{95 + 88 + 85 + 90 + 95}{5} = 90.6$$

10th Grade:
$$m = \frac{sum\ of\ the\ terms}{number\ of\ terms} = \frac{90 + 90 + 95 + 88 + 90}{5} = 90.6$$

Choice A is incorrect because 6th Grade is not the highest mean. **Choice C** is incorrect because 7th Grade has the lowest mean. **Choice D** is incorrect because the means of the 3 Grade levels are not equal. **Choice E** is incorrect because 6th Grade and 8th Grade means are not equal.

8 **Choice A is correct** because the area of a Kite given its diagonals is $A = \frac{d_1 + d_2}{2}$

Choice B is incorrect because it does not represent the formula for the Area of a kite. **Choice C** is incorrect because it does not represent the formula for the Area of a kite. **Choice D** is incorrect because it does not represent the formula for the Area of a kite. **Choice E** is incorrect because it does not represent the formula for the Area of a kite.

9 **Choice A is correct** because the probability that both Lee and Trisha will be selected is 10%.

Find the number of ways to choose 2 people from the 5 managers using the combination formula $\binom{n}{k}$, where *n* is the total number of items to choose from and *k* is the number of items to choose.

Given: $n = 5, k = 2$

$$\binom{n}{k} = \frac{5!}{2!(5-2)!} = \frac{5(4)(3)(2)(1)}{2(1)(3)(2)(1)} = \frac{20}{2} = 10$$

Therefore, there are 10 possible ways to select 2 persons from the 5 managers.

3 Quantitative Reasoning (Easy)   Answers & Explanations   Section 5

If Lee and Trisha are to be selected, there is exactly 1 favorable outcome for this.

Find the probability that both Lee and Trisha are selected.

$$Probability = \frac{Number\ of\ favorable\ outcomes}{Total\ number\ of\ outcomes} = \frac{1}{10}$$

To express the probability as a percentage: $\frac{1}{10}(100) = 10\%$

Choice B is incorrect because 20% is 1 out of 5. **Choice C** is incorrect because 40% is 3 out of 5. **Choice D** is incorrect because 60% is 4 out of 5. **Choice E** is incorrect because 100% is 5 out of 5.

10 **Choice C is correct** because $x = \frac{y}{p} + p$ is obtained when solving for x.

Given: Janice' rate $= \frac{x - p}{r}$

Rommel's rate $= \frac{y}{pr}$

Both did the same work, hence $\frac{x - p}{r} = \frac{y}{pr}$.

Solve for x in terms of y, p and r.

$$\frac{x - p}{r} = \frac{y}{pr}$$
$$yr = pr(x - p)$$
$$\frac{yr}{pr} = (x - p)$$
$$\frac{yr}{pr} + p = x$$
$$\frac{y}{p} + p = x$$

Choice A is incorrect because the operation between the terms in the RHS is subtraction and not addition. **Choice B** is incorrect because the sign of each term is interchanged. **Choice D** is incorrect because r is misplaced to the second term. **Choice E** is incorrect because r is misplaced and signs are interchanged.

11 **Choice D is correct** because Cherry has walked a distance of $\frac{5}{6}$ when Alex has walked 1 mile.

Find the speed of each person. Dividing both sides by 3

Alex : $speed = \frac{distance}{time} = \frac{1\ mile}{10\ minutes}$

Cherry : $speed = \frac{distance}{time} = \frac{1\ mile}{12\ minutes}$

They walked together and Alex walked 1 mile with a time of 10 minutes, find the distance that Cherry walked for 10 minutes.

Cherry : $distance = speed\ (time) = \frac{1\ mile}{12\ minutes}(10\ minutes)$

$$= \frac{10}{12}\ or\ \frac{5}{6}$$

Choice A is incorrect because Cherry walked more than a distance of $\frac{1}{6}$ mile after Alex has walked 1 mile in 10 seconds. **Choice B** is incorrect because Cherry walked more than a distance of $\frac{1}{3}$ mile after Alex has walked 1 mile in 10 seconds. **Choice C** is incorrect because Cherry walked more than a distance of $\frac{1}{2}$ mile after Alex has walked 1 mile in 10 seconds. **Choice E** is incorrect because Cherry did not walk more than Alex after 10 seconds.

12 **Choice D is correct.** Simplify the given expression.

$$\frac{27x + 23y}{3x + 2y} = \frac{27x + 18y + 5y}{3x + 2y}$$
$$= \frac{27x + 18y}{3x + 2y} + \frac{5y}{3x + 2y}$$
$$= \frac{9(3x + 2y)}{3x + 2y} + \frac{5y}{3x + 2y}$$
$$= 9 + \frac{5y}{3x + 2y}$$

From the given condition $0 < y < x$, x and y are positive values. Hence, $\frac{5y}{3x + 2y}$ is also positive.

Also, take note that $\frac{5y}{3x + 2y} < 1$.

For the possible values of $\frac{27x + 23y}{3x + 2y}$ we obtained the simplified form $9 + \frac{5y}{3x + 2y}$.

The possible values should be greater than 9 but less than 10.

Choice A is incorrect because the value should have been greater than 9 but less than 10. **Choice B** is incorrect because 7.5 is less than 9. **Choice C** is incorrect because 8.9 is less than 9. **Choice E** is incorrect because 10.5 is greater than 10.

3 Quantitative Reasoning (Easy) Answers & Explanations   Section 5 3

13 **Choice A is correct** because the obtained value of 225 nickel coins is $11.25.

Find the number of nickel coins from the purse.

Given : $n = 300$ coins , 15 % are quarters, 10% are dimes

Percentage of nickel coins: 100% – 15% quarters – 10% dimes
$$=75\% \text{ or } 0.75$$

Number of nickel coins from the purse = 300(0.75)
$$=225 \text{ nickel coins}$$

Find the value of the nickel coins.

A nickel coin is equivalent to $0.05. Therefore, 225($0.05)=$11.25.

Choice B is incorrect because the value of the nickel coins is not $13.11. **Choice C** is incorrect because the value of the nickel coins is not $13.55. **Choice D** is incorrect because the value of the nickel coins is not $15.25. **Choice E** is incorrect because the value of the nickel coins is not $25.11.

14 **The correct answer is 15/8.** Given: $f(x) = 2x^3 + 7x^2 - 4x$ and $g(x) = 4x - x^3$

Find k when $f(k)=0$.

$$2k^3 + 7k^2 - 4k = 0$$

Common term $\quad k(2k^2 + 7k - 4) = 0$

Break the expression into groups $k((2k^2 - k)+ (8k - 4)) = 0$

Factor out k from $(2k^2 - k)$ $k(k(2k - 1) + (8k - 4))=0$

Factor out 4 from $(8k - 4)$ $k(k(2k - 1) +4(2k - 1))=0$

Factor out common term $(2k - 1)$ $k(2k - 1)(k + 4)=0$

Roots are: $k = 0, k = 1/2, k = -4$

We take the positive value of k which is $k = 1/2$.

Find $g(k) = 4x - x^3$.

$g(1/2) = 4(1/2) - (1/2)^3$

$g(1/2) = 15/8$

15 **Choice C is correct** because the obtained value is equivalent to $(y - x) > \dfrac{m - n}{2}$.

Multiply the 2nd inequality by –1.

$(-1)(4y + 2x > m)$

$-4y - 2x < - m$

$-2x - 4y < - m$

Add both inequalities.

$\quad 4x + 2y < n$

$+\quad -2x - 4y < - m$

$\quad 2x - 2y < n - m$

$\quad 2(x - y) < n - m$

$\quad (x - y) < \dfrac{n - m}{2}$

To find $(y - x)$ multiply both sides by (-1).

$(-1)(x - y) < \dfrac{n - m}{2}(-1)$

$(-x + y) > \dfrac{-n + m}{2}$

$(y - x) > \dfrac{m - n}{2}$

Choice A is incorrect because the inequality symbol used is the opposite of the obtained inequality. **Choice B** is incorrect because the inequality symbol is incorrect. **Choice D** is incorrect because the inequality symbol should have been > only and not ≥. **Choice E** is incorrect because obtained expression and the inequality symbol are incorrect.

3 Quantitative Reasoning (Hard) Answers & Explanations — Section 5

1 **Choice A is correct** because when we assign values for x, Quantity A is always greater.

Assign values of x and y find the value of Quantity A and Quantity B.

x	y	Quantity A	Quantity B
−1	−1	$(-1)^2 + 4(-1)(-1) + (-1)^2 = 6$	$(-1-1)^2 = 4$
−2	−2	$(-2)^2 + 4(-2)(-2) + (-2)^2 = 24$	$(-2-2)^2 = 16$
−3	−3	$(-3)^2 + 4(-3)(-3) + (-3)^2 = 54$	$(-3-3)^2 = 36$

From the table, Quantity A is always greater than Quantity B.

Choice B is incorrect because Quantity B is always less than Quantity A for any value of x and y. **Choice C** is incorrect because Quantity A and Quantity B are not equal for any value of x and y. **Choice D** is incorrect because a relation can be determined from the given information.

2 **Choice B is correct** because Quantity B is greater than the obtained value of the 4th term of the arithmetic progression.

Given: $a_1 = -20$, $d = 4$

Find a_4.

Use the formula $a_n = a_1 + (n-1)d$

$a_4 = -20 + (4-1)4$

$a_4 = -20 + (3)4$

$a_4 = -20 + 12$

$a_4 = -8$

$-4 > -8$, hence, Quantity B is greater than Quantity A.

Choice A is incorrect because Quantity A is less than Quantity B. **Choice C** is incorrect because Quantity A is not equal to Quantity B. **Choice D** is incorrect because a relation can be determined from the given information.

3 **Choice B is correct** because the obtained value of q is greater than the obtained value of p.

Solve for p.

$p = 250(0.3) = 75$

Solve for q.

$\dfrac{p\%}{100}(q) = 80$

$\left(\dfrac{75}{100}\right)(q) = 80$

$q = 80\left(\dfrac{100}{75}\right)$

$q = \dfrac{8000}{75}$

$q = 106\dfrac{2}{3}$

Hence, $q > p$.

Choice A is incorrect because Quantity A is less than Quantity B. **Choice C** is incorrect because Quantity A and Quantity B are not equal. **Choice D** is incorrect because a relation can be determined from the given information.

4 **Choice B is correct** because the obtained value of y is 1 which is less than 5.

Find the area of Triangle ABC.

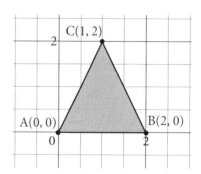

$A = \dfrac{1}{2}bh$

$A = \dfrac{1}{2}(2)(2)$

$A = 2$

Find y if the area of Triangle DEF is 2.

Vertices of DEF : $D(0, 0)$, $E(4, 0)$, $F(3, -y)$

Base: from $(0, 0)$ to $(4, 0)$ has 4 units along the x-axis.

Height: from $(3, -y)$ to the base has y units along the negative y-axis.

$A = \dfrac{1}{2}(4)(y)$

$2 = 2(y)$

$2 = 2y$

$1 = y$

Choice A is incorrect because Quantity A is less than Quantity B. **Choice C** is incorrect because Quantity A and Quantity B are not equal. **Choice D** is incorrect because the relations can be determined from the information given.

Quantitative Reasoning (Hard)   Answers & Explanations   Section 5

5 **Choice A is correct** because the obtained Area of rectangle A is greater than the obtained value of the Area of rectangle B.

Solve for the area of rectangle A:

Let x be the width and y be the length of rectangle A.

$$A = width\ (length)$$
$$A = xy$$

Solve for the area of rectangle B:

$$A = width\ (length)$$
$$A = 1.2x\ (0.8y)$$
$$A = 0.96xy$$

Hence, the area of rectangle A is greater than the area of rectangle B.

Choice B is incorrect because Quantity B is less than Quantity A. **Choice C** is incorrect because Quantity A is not equal to Quantity B. **Choice D** is incorrect because the relations can be determined from the information given.

6 **Choice B, Choice C, Choice D, Choice E are correct** because these values are within the median price $7000-$9999.

There are 30 cars, the median price is at 15th and 16th car.

Car 1 - 4 falls to the price below $7000.

Car 5- 19 falls to the price range below $7000 – $9999.

Car 20 - 26 falls to the price range below $10000 – $12999.

Car 27-20 falls to the price above $13000.

Hence, median price are between $7000 – $9999.

Choice A is incorrect because $3500 is below the obtained median price. **Choice F** is incorrect because $15000 is above the obtained median price. **Choice G** is incorrect because $17500 is above the obtained median price.

7 **Choice B is correct** because $4x$ is always even. Any number multiplied to an even number 4 is always an even number.

Choice A is incorrect because $3x$ is odd when x is odd and $3x$ is even when x is even. Adding 4 will result in either odd or even depending on the value of x. **Choice C** is incorrect because $x^2 + 3$ can be odd or even depending on the value of x. **Choice D** is incorrect because $x^2 - 2$ can be odd or even depending on the value of x.

8 **Choice B, Choice C and Choice D** because $\frac{1}{ba}$ and $\frac{1}{ab}$ are equivalent to the simplified form of $\dfrac{\frac{1}{a} - \frac{1}{b}}{b - a}$.

Simplify $\dfrac{\frac{1}{a} - \frac{1}{b}}{b - a}$.

$$= \dfrac{\frac{b-a}{ab}}{b-a}$$

$$= \frac{b-a}{ab}\left(\frac{1}{b-a}\right)$$

$$= \frac{1}{ab}$$

Choice B is correct because $(ab)^{-1} = \frac{1}{ab}$

Choice A is incorrect because ab is not equivalent to the simplified form of the given expression. **Choice E** is incorrect because $\frac{a}{b}$ is not equivalent to the simplified form of the given expression.

9 **Choice C is correct** because the obtained value of x is 50% of y.

Given: $x = \frac{1}{2}y$

Let $y = 100$, then $x = \frac{1}{2}100 = 50$.

x is what percent of y? % $= \frac{x}{y}(100) = \frac{50}{100}(100) = 50\%$.

Choice A is incorrect because the obtained percentage is less than 50%. **Choice B** is incorrect because the obtained percentage is less than 50%. **Choice D** is incorrect because the obtained percentage is greater than 50%

10 **Choice E is correct** because the solution of when n within the given range $-1 < n < 1$ does not satisfy $|n - 1| > 1$, making it impossible for this inequality to be true.

Choice A is incorrect because $n^2 < n$ could be true for some values of $-1 < n < 1$. **Choice B** is incorrect because $n^2 < 2n$ could be true for some values of $-1 < n < 1$. **Choice C** is incorrect because $(n - 1)^2 > 0$ could be true for some values of $-1 < n < 1$. **Choice D** is incorrect because $16n^2 - 1 = 0$ could be true for some values of $-1 < n < 1$.

3 Quantitative Reasoning (Hard) Answers & Explanations   Section 5

11 The correct answer is 27°.

Find the missing interior angle y of the 9-sided polygon using the formula for sum of the interior angles of a polygon.

Sum of interior angles $= (n - 2)180°$
$= (9 - 2)180°$
$= 1260°$

$1260° = 132° + 142° + 117° + 154° + 133° + 134° + 156° + 139° + y$
$1260° = 1107° + y$
$1260° - 1107° = y$
$153° = y$

Find the exterior angle x.

Angle x and angle y are supplementary angles. Hence, $m\angle y + m\angle x = 180°$.

$153° + m\angle x = 180°$
$m\angle x = 180° - 153°$
$m\angle x = 27°$.

12 **Choice A, Choice C, and Choice F are correct** because the given values of r and s satisfied the given conditions and its obtained minimum values.

Given: $r, s, 32, 65, 89, 44, 90, 33$

Arithmetic mean $= \dfrac{r + s + 32 + 65 + 89 + 44 + 90 + 33}{8}$

$50 \geq \dfrac{r + s + 353}{8}$

$400 \geq r + s + 353$

$400 - 353 \geq r + s$

$47 \geq r + s$

Consider the given conditions:
$47 \geq r + s$ and $20 \leq r < s < 40$.
Let's assign values to r and s that satisfies both conditions.

r	s	
20	27	true
21	26	true
22	25	true
23	24	true
24	23	False because $r < s$
25	22	False because $r < s$

Choice B is incorrect because it failed to satisfy the condition $47 \geq r + s$ and $s < 40$. **Choice D** is incorrect because it failed to satisfy the condition $47 \geq r + s$. **Choice E** is incorrect because it r should not be equal to s. **Choice G** is incorrect because it failed to satisfy the condition $r < s$. **Choice H** is incorrect because it fails to satisfy the condition $r < s$.

13 **Choice D and Choice E are correct** because it obtained an initial price of $72.

Use the formula for successive discounts
$P(1 - \dfrac{x}{100})(1 - \dfrac{y}{100})$, where P is the original price, x is the first discount and y is the second discount.

Solve for each pair.

1. For $(x, y) = (25, 15)$:
$P(1 - \dfrac{x}{100})(1 - \dfrac{y}{100}) = 100(1 - \dfrac{25}{100})(1 - \dfrac{15}{100})$
$= 100(0.75)(0.85)$
$= 63.75$
≈ 64

2. For $(x, y) = (30, 20)$:
$P(1 - \dfrac{x}{100})(1 - \dfrac{y}{100}) = 100(1 - \dfrac{30}{100})(1 - \dfrac{20}{100})$
$= 100(0.70)(0.80)$
$= 56$

3. For $(x, y) = (40, 25)$:
$P(1 - \dfrac{x}{100})(1 - \dfrac{y}{100}) = 100(1 - \dfrac{40}{100})(1 - \dfrac{25}{100})$
$= 100(0.60)(0.75)$
$= 45$

4. For $(x, y) = (20, 10)$:
$P(1 - \dfrac{x}{100})(1 - \dfrac{y}{100}) = 100(1 - \dfrac{20}{100})(1 - \dfrac{10}{100})$
$= 100(0.80)(0.90)$
$= 72$

5. For $(x, y) = (15, 15)$:
$P(1 - \dfrac{x}{100})(1 - \dfrac{y}{100}) = 100(1 - \dfrac{15}{100})(1 - \dfrac{15}{100})$
$= 100(0.85)(0.85)$

Quantitative Reasoning (Hard) Answers & Explanations — Section 5

= 72.25

≈ 72

Choice A is incorrect because the combined discounts did not obtained an initial price of $72. **Choice B is incorrect** because the combined discounts obtained an initial price lower than $72. **Choice C is incorrect** because the combined discounts obtained an initial price lower than $72.

14 **Choice B is correct** because 6 is the obtained value of t when $f(t) + g(t) = 30$.

Given: $f(t) = 2t - 7$ and $g(t) = 4t + 1$.

Find $f(t) + g(t) = 30$.

$(2t - 7) + (4t + 1) = 30$

$2t + 4t - 7 + 1 = 30$

$6t - 6 = 30$

$6t = 30 + 6$

$6t = 36$

$t = 6$

Choice A is incorrect because 3 is not the obtained value of t when $f(t) + g(t) = 30$. **Choice C is incorrect** because 7 is not the obtained value of t when $f(t) + g(t) = 30$. **Choice D is incorrect** because 8 is not the obtained value of t when $f(t) + g(t) = 30$.

15 **Choice B and Choice F are correct** because it represents the formula for the new mean.

Let's find the formula for the old mean.

$$\overline{x}_{old} = \frac{a+b+c+d+e+f+g}{7}$$

Let's consider the given conditions.

Old data set	New data set
a	a + 5
b	b − 4
c	$\frac{c}{2}$
d	d − 5
e	e
f	f
g	g

Let's find the formula for the new mean using the given conditions.

$$\overline{x}_{new} = \frac{(a+5)+(b-4)+\left(\frac{c}{2}\right)+(d-5)+e+f+g}{7}$$

Simplify the numerator of the new mean.

$$\overline{x}_{new} = \frac{(a+5)+(b-4)+\left(\frac{c}{2}\right)+(d-5)+e+f+g}{7}$$

$$\overline{x}_{new} = \frac{a+5+b-4+\frac{c}{2}+d-5+e+f+g}{7}$$

$$\overline{x}_{new} = \frac{a+b+\frac{c}{2}+d+e+f+g+5-4-5}{7}$$

$$\overline{x}_{new} = \frac{a+b+\frac{c}{2}+d+e+f+g-4}{7}$$

Choice A is incorrect because the new data set for c is decreased by 2 instead of half. **Choice C is incorrect** because the new data set for b is increased by 4 instead of decreased by 4. **Choice D is incorrect** because the numerator is incorrectly simplified. **Choice E is incorrect** because the new data set for c and the numerators are incorrect. **Choice G is incorrect** because the numerator is incorrectly simplified.

Chapter 5
Practice Test #4

IMPORTANT
READ THE INSTRUCTIONS BEFORE BEGINNING THE TEST

1. Take this test under real testing conditions. Put away any distractions and sit in a quiet place with no disturbances. Keep a rough paper, some pencils, and a calculator beside you.
2. Begin with **Section 1** of the test on page 160. Write your essay in 30 minutes.
3. Next, move to **Section 2 - Verbal Reasoning** on page 162.
   - ❏ Attempt all questions and note the number of correct answers using the answer key on page 182.
   - ❏ If you get fewer than 7 correct, proceed to **Section 4 - Verbal Reasoning (Easy)** on page 168.
   - ❏ If you get 7 or more correct, proceed to **Section 4 - Verbal Reasoning (Hard)** on page 172.
4. After that, take **Section 3 - Quantitative Reasoning** on page 165.
   - ❏ Complete the section, then check your score using the answer key on page 183.
   - ❏ If you get fewer than 7 correct, proceed to **Section 5 - Quantitative Reasoning (Easy)** on page 176.
   - ❏ If you get 7 or more correct, proceed to **Section 5 - Quantitative Reasoning (Hard)** on page 199.
5. Complete Section 4 and Section 5, respectively, and note down the number of correct answers you got right in each section.
6. Calculate your **Scaled Score** on page 317 for the test.
7. Review **detailed explanations** for all questions beginning on page 184.

For more practice, visit www.vibrantpublishers.com

Analyze an Issue
30 Minutes

In order to become well-rounded individuals, all college students should be required to take courses in which they read poetry, novels, mythology, and other types of imaginative literature. Write a response in which you discuss the extent to which you agree or disagree with the recommendation and explain your reasoning for the position you take. In developing and supporting your position, describe specific circumstances in which adopting the recommendation would or would not be advantageous and explain how these examples shape your position.

You may start writing your response here

Section 2 - Verbal Reasoning

18 Minutes | 12 Questions

For Questions 1 and 2, for each blank, select one entry from the corresponding column of choices. Fill all blanks in the way that best completes the text.

1. The unit of time known as a second is a scientific measurement of the time it takes for a cesium atom to _____ 9,192,631,770 times between two radiation states.

A persist
B forge
C feign
D oscillate
E antedate

2. Music has been (i) _____ component of cultural life since antiquity. Choruses and instruments often accompanied Greek tragedies, and boys learned both singing and music theory from a young age. Much of the musical theory that these young Greeks learned is still (ii) _____. The theory can be seen, sometimes completely intact, in both religious and classical Western music.

Blank (i)	Blank (ii)
A a contested	D gamut
B an integral	E partition
C an invidious	F extant

3. For more than a generation, the United States was the (i) _____ force in automobile production. Shortly before the Great Depression, for instance, more than 90% of all automobiles on Earth had been manufactured in America. This dominance (ii) _____ over many decades, and in 1980, Japan became the world's top automobile producer. This victory was (iii) _____, however, as China surged to the front of the pack in 2009, leaving the United States and Japan competing for a distant second.

Blank (i)	Blank (ii)	Blank (iii)
A debatable	D waned	G tenacious
B preponderant	E illuminated	H ephemeral
C superfluous	F proliferated	I condescending

For Questions 4 and 5, select one answer choice unless otherwise instructed.

Question 4 is based on this passage.

Alhambra in Granada, Spain, was the seat of the last Muslim kingdom on the Iberian Peninsula for about three hundred years. The elegant fortress built at the orders of the sultan was originally adorned with intricate mosaics and Arabic inscriptions covering many of the walls, columns, floors, and other surfaces. Later, Christian rulers made major modifications such as adding the enclosed Lindaraja Courtyard, but possibly because the calligraphy was unintelligible, they, fortunately, did not destroy all of the Muslim ornamentation and poetry which is now considered among the finest examples extant from the period.

Section 2 - Verbal Reasoning

For the following question, consider each of the choices separately and select all that apply.

4. According to the passage, which of the following statements are true?

   A. The Alhambra was extremely ornamented because it was only used as a residence for the sultan.
   B. The Muslim kingdom lasted about three hundred years on the Iberian Peninsula.
   C. Christians left artwork in the Alhambra because they were not cognizant that it included texts.

Question 5 is based on this passage.

At about the size of a domestic cat, a newly discovered feline, *Leopardus pardinoides*, resides in the cloud forests of Costa Rica and Panama at elevations between 2,000 and 3,000 meters. One of the major threats to the survival of this rare feline—called a clouded tiger cat—is disease transferred from domestic animals via insects, so a wildlife conservationist from State University of Maranhao in Brazil, Tadeu de Oliveira, has initiated a vaccination program for local pets to help preserve the species.

5. Which of the following most undermines Tadeau de Oliveira's proposal?

   A. Most habitations in Panama and Costa Rica are at elevations below 1,500 meters.
   B. Habitat loss due to ranching is another large threat to clouded tiger cats.
   C. Clouded tiger cats typically bear only one kitten at a time, after a gestation of 75 days.
   D. Many pets are kept in cages at night, but clouded tiger cats are nocturnal.
   E. More domestic animals are kept for food than as pets in Costa Rica and Panama.

For Questions 6 to 9, select the two answer choices that, when used to complete the sentence, fit the meaning of the sentence as a whole and produce complete sentences that are alike in meaning.

6. In order to ensure their own survival fitness, organic molecules must establish _____ between their propensities to grow via chemical reaction and their need to maintain the geometric simplicity that is essential for life.

   A. a synthesis
   B. an algorithm
   C. an equation
   D. a deduction
   E. a fission
   F. a unity

7. Many advocates for prison reform point to the penal system's disproportionately harsh sentences for African-American as an example of _____ racism.

   A. laissez-faire
   B. institutionalized
   C. infrequent
   D. accidental
   E. entrenched
   F. progressive

8. The two defendants decided to reconceive and re-synthesize their respective stories in light of a growing feeling that their two _____ explanations of what happened the night of the crime would arouse the suspicions of the jury.

   A. hilarious
   B. harmonious
   C. discordant
   D. incongruous
   E. syphoned
   F. dastardly

9. The financial volatility of the massive banking institutions means that even the most innocuous of corporate action needs to be thoroughly _____ by a team of lawyers who specialize in everything from international finance to political organization.

- [A] vetted
- [B] delineated
- [C] prioritized
- [D] extemporized
- [E] assessed
- [F] rewritten

For Questions 10 to 12, select one answer choice unless otherwise instructed.

Questions 10 to 12 are based on this passage.

Humor can be a very successful advertising tool in many media such as television or SNS, but there were no formal studies of how effective it is for two-sided advertising—advertising that provides at least one negative comment about the product—until Martin Eisend conducted a series of experiments on students enrolled in a marketing class in a German university in 2021.

Eisend divided the students and presented four conditions: one-sided or two-sided print advertising about retirement plans, either with or without a visual humorous element. The results of the study indicated that humor greatly increased the perception of one-sided advertisements that were all positive and contained humor, but had a slight negative effect on the perception of two-sided humor.

A follow-up study using different students began by questioning whether the students felt high or low involvement with the product and topic. These students were shown a two-sided advertisement either with or without visual humor, then asked to rate their level of surprise, distraction, and brand attitude, which refers to interest in purchasing the product. The high involvement students rated higher levels of surprise and distraction, and lower levels of brand attitude than the students who had low involvement.

10. The author would likely agree with which of the following claims about Eisend's experiments?

- [A] The visual humor Eisend used was such that most average viewers would find it humorous.
- [B] People who have high involvement in an advertisement tend to have a low sense of humor.
- [C] It is more difficult to incorporate humor into certain types of advertising than others.
- [D] Eisend's results cannot be extrapolated from print to other forms of advertisements.
- [E] It establishes that one-sided advertisements are more successful than two-sided advertisements.

11. Which of the following best describes the function of the second paragraph of the passage?

- [A] It provides an introduction to the various types of advertising and humor Eisend tested.
- [B] It discusses the methodology that Eisend employed to establish a point of reference.
- [C] It points out the mechanisms which make humor successful for one-sided advertising.
- [D] It defends the use of humor to appeal to consumers in one-sided advertising.
- [E] It presents a hypothesis which Eisend intended to disprove through his experiments.

12. It can be inferred that humor in advertising is likely to

- [A] persuade the consumer to feel more positive about the product if the humor is visual rather than textual in nature
- [B] influence people to pay more attention to the negative aspects of the product in two-sided advertising
- [C] work most effectively when the person is less engaged in comparing the pros and cons of making a purchase
- [D] increase over time because more consumers are engaged in using visual media like television and SNS
- [E] decrease the brand attitude for the majority of consumers who are exposed to a two-sided advertisement

Section 3 - Quantitative Reasoning

18 Minutes | 12 Questions

1.

$$x^2 < y^2$$

Quantity A	Quantity B
x	y

Ⓐ Quantity A is greater.
Ⓑ Quantity B is greater.
Ⓒ The two quantities are equal.
Ⓓ The relationship cannot be determined from the information given.

2.

A random sample of tire pressures for a tire manufacturing company was normally distributed. The mean tire pressure was found to be 33 psi and the sample set had a standard deviation of 2.

Quantity A	Quantity B
The fraction of tires with a tire pressure greater than 36.	$\frac{1}{5}$

Ⓐ Quantity A is greater.
Ⓑ Quantity B is greater.
Ⓒ The two quantities are equal.
Ⓓ The relationship cannot be determined from the information given.

3.

$$(x-1)^2 + (y+3)^2 = 25$$
$$x - y = 3$$

Quantity A	Quantity B
$x + y$	5

Ⓐ Quantity A is greater.
Ⓑ Quantity B is greater.
Ⓒ The two quantities are equal.
Ⓓ The relationship cannot be determined from the information given.

4.

$$y^2 + 6y = -9$$
$$\frac{z}{y} + \frac{z}{x} = 0$$

Quantity A	Quantity B
x	1

Ⓐ Quantity A is greater.
Ⓑ Quantity B is greater.
Ⓒ The two quantities are equal.
Ⓓ The relationship cannot be determined from the information given.

5.

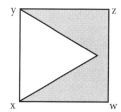

In the figure, XYZW is a square and XAY is an equilateral triangle. If XY = 6, what is the area of the shaded region?

Ⓐ $9\sqrt{3}$
Ⓑ $36 - 18\sqrt{3}$
Ⓒ $36 - 9\sqrt{3}$
Ⓓ $18\sqrt{3}$
Ⓔ 36

Section 3 - Quantitative Reasoning

6

Using the digits 1, 2, 3, and 4 to create a 4-digit number with no repeated digits, what is the probability of all possible combinations that the number is divisible by 7?

- A) $\frac{1}{24}$
- B) $\frac{1}{12}$
- C) $\frac{1}{8}$
- D) $\frac{1}{6}$
- E) $\frac{1}{3}$

7

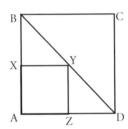

If ABCD and AXYZ are both squares and BY = DY, what is the ratio of the area of triangle BXY to the area of square ABCD?

Questions 8 to 10 are based on the following data.

Year	Trash Produced in US (Million Tons)
1990	180
1995	210
2000	230
2005	250
2010	250
2015	260
2020	290

Trash Categories 2005

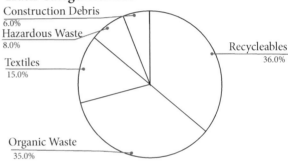

Construction Debris 6.0%
Hazardous Waste 8.0%
Textiles 15.0%
Recycleables 36.0%
Organic Waste 35.0%

Trash Categories 2015

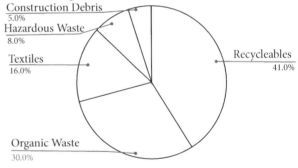

Construction Debris 5.0%
Hazardous Waste 8.0%
Textiles 16.0%
Recycleables 41.0%
Organic Waste 30.0%

8

Of every 100 million tons of trash produced in the US in 2005, approximately how many tons of that trash was hazardous waste?

- A) 8
- B) 15
- C) 20
- D) 35
- E) 80

9

Which of the following statements must be true? Indicate all that apply.

- [A] There were more tons of construction debris and textiles combined in 2015 compared to 2005.
- [B] The percentage of trash in 2005 to 2015 decreased for all categories except recyclables.
- [C] The ratio of organic waste in 2005 to the ratio of organic waste in 2015 is 6:7.
- [D] There were more textiles thrown away in 2005 compared to 2015.
- [E] The greatest increase in trash production occurred from 2015 to 2020.

10

How many more millions of tons of trash was recyclables in 2015 compared to 2005?

- (A) 12.5
- (B) 13
- (C) 16.6
- (D) 18
- (E) 21.3

11

A printer prints 57 pages every 45 minutes. If the printer starts printing at 1:00 p.m. and prints non-stop until a time between 5:00 p.m. to 6:00 p.m., which of the following could be the amount of pages printed during this period?

Indicate all such values.

- [A] 300
- [B] 305
- [C] 320
- [D] 374
- [E] 400

12

A manufacturing company discounts its product by 20% and then later discounts it again by 10%. The new discounted price would have to be increased by approximately what percentage to get back to the original price?

[ ] %

Section 4 - Verbal Reasoning (Easy)

23 Minutes | 15 Questions

For Questions 1 to 4, select one entry for each blank from the corresponding column of choices. Fill all the blanks in the way that best completes the text.

1. By carefully comparing the sounds of musical scales performed by an opera singer and several violinists playing Stradivarius violins, researcher Joseph Nagyvary has shown that the Italian master–violin makers, including Antonio Stradavari, were able to _____ the vowel and consonant sounds of speech into their instruments.

   - (A) disclose
   - (B) yield
   - (C) impart
   - (D) output
   - (E) relinquish

2. The wide variety of complicated physical phenomena in the observable universe can, ironically, be explained in terms of four _____ forces and their interactions: the gravitational force, electromagnetic force, strong nuclear force, and weak nuclear force.

   - (A) fundamental
   - (B) superfluous
   - (C) regressive
   - (D) excessive
   - (E) intricate

3. Improvisational theater has a long history. The first attempt at improvisation in theater is believed to have been in the sixteenth century. The rules for improvisation were more stricter back then, but over time artists became comfortable (i) _____ their approach. Improvisational theater has now featured Nobel Prize winning writers and stand-up comedians. The new-found (ii) _____ with which improvisational theater is allowed to proceed has opened up actors to attempt styles they never would have otherwise.

Blank (i)	Blank (ii)
(A) diversifying	(D) fluidity
(B) conflating	(E) perniciousness
(C) truncating	(F) maleficence

4. The film industry exemplifies (i) _____ club: six movie studios receive more than 90% of all the revenue generated from the American box office. This model is thought to stifle growth, both creatively and financially. The (ii) _____ is evident: few new studios mean few new ideas. And financially speaking, the lack of competition hurts the studios in the long run. No competition means no (iii) _____ to evolve their business strategy, which leave studios unprepared when dramatic shifts occur in the state of the economy.

Blank (i)	Blank (ii)	Blank (iii)
(A) a communal	(D) encumbrance	(G) dissuasion
(B) an indiscriminate	(E) alleviation	(H) inducement
(C) an elitist	(F) opacity	(I) ingratitude

Section 4 - Verbal Reasoning (Easy)

For Questions 5 to 9, select one answer choice unless otherwise instructed.

Questions 5 and 6 are based on this passage.

Argentine-Italian Leonor Fini was the most prominent female artist associated with the Surrealist movement. Though not officially a member, she participated in their group shows, and her broad oeuvre—including drawings, paintings, costume and set designs for plays and movies, furniture, accessories, and even a perfume bottle—explored Surrealist themes of fantasy and dreams. Fini had no formal art training before moving to Paris and fraternizing with Salvador Dali, Man Ray, Max Ernst, and other members of the movement, though she disliked the founder, Andre Breton. Her motivation for creating eccentric artwork was just as distinctive as theirs: rheumatic conjunctivitis compelled her to spend two months with both eyes swathed in bandages. That experience allowed her to explore her mind's images without the interference of regular visual input and she strove to capture those fleeting ideas in her art.

5. Which of the following characterizes the relationship of Fini with the other members of the Surrealist movement?

   (A) Though she did artwork in the Surrealist style, Fini did not maintain connections with most of the Surrealists.
   (B) She was congenial with certain members and did not refrain from involvement in their various activities.
   (C) Andre Breton would not admit Fini into the official Surrealist circle, but she still was active in some of their events.
   (D) Despite not being an official Surrealist, Fini became romantically involved and spent time with some of the members.
   (E) Fini explored a wide variety of art media because she was not restricted by the limitations of the Surrealist movement.

6. The author uses the word "distinctive" to refer to Fini's motivation in order to do which of the following?

   (A) To show that very few people suffered from rheumatic conjunctivitis at the time
   (B) To highlight the extent of the misfortune that Fini suffered before doing her art
   (C) To emphasize Fini's talent at painting despite her inability to see
   (D) To stress that the other artists studied art before joining the Surrealist movement
   (E) To point out the reason that Fini is considered to be among the Surrealist artists

Questions 7 to 9 are based on this passage.

Bats are the only extant mammals that have evolved the ability of sustained flight, a transformation that began about 52 million years ago. Although they look like birds, they employ entirely different patterns of wing motions for locomotion, as their wings have significantly more joints and there are complex muscles embedded in the skin. By manipulating their intricate wings, bats make the membranous structures billow in complex patterns to catch the air, enabling them to maneuver rapidly through confined areas. Sensitive hairs on the wings expedite flight by conveying information to the nervous system about details such as wind speed and pressure so they can maneuver and catch prey, even in the dark.

Northeastern University assistant professor of engineering Alireza Remezani is now trying to replicate the mechanisms of bat locomotion in flying robots that could be used to inspect enclosed or potentially unstable spaces such as sewer lines and caves, as such efforts could assist in paleological research and surveys for mining companies. However, the challenge involves more than making wings that replicate the complex flapping: the navigational controls must be able to rapidly process input and adapt to evade obstacles in flight.

Section 4 - Verbal Reasoning (Easy)

7. It can be inferred from the passage that bat wings evolved complex muscles embedded in the skin in order to
   - A facilitate navigation around obstacles by making rapid changes to the wing shape
   - B allow the bats to catch prey in situations in which there is no light
   - C fly in enclosed spaces where birds are unable to navigate
   - D eliminate reliance on feathers and other structures found in bird wings
   - E there would be no other method for manipulating the multiple joints in the wings

8. According to the passage, birds and bats have which of the following in common?
   - A They developed flight in order to catch prey.
   - B They flap their wings in a variety of ways.
   - C They evolved wings during approximately the same period.
   - D They are being used as prototypes for flying robots.
   - E They have similar superficial body structures.

9. It can be inferred that Alireza Remezani's research into bat locomotion is based in part on
   - A an interest in determining ways in which bat wings differ from bird wings
   - B the desire to create a robot that is able to advance research on bat flight
   - C the hopes of developing a robot that can repair sewer lines and other enclosed spaces
   - D the potential of reducing injuries to human workers in a market with particular requirements
   - E the possibility of better understanding how bat wings evolved their complex structures

For Questions 10 to 12, select the two answer choices that, when used to complete the sentence, fit the meaning of the sentence as a whole and produce complete sentences that are alike in meaning.

10. The main property differentiating frosted window glass from regular glass is that it is _____ and blurs or softens the light that is transmitted through it.
    - A translucent
    - B obscured
    - C crystalline
    - D semi-opaque
    - E undiluted
    - F diaphanous

11. Viscosity is the _____ between neigh boring parcels of liquid that are moving at different velocities.
    - A attribute
    - B resistance
    - C conductivity
    - D agreement
    - E friction
    - F altercation

12. While thematic construction and dense intellectual interpolations characterize modern art, many still find refuge in the _____ of primitive works, in some cases tracing this interest all the way back to prehistoric cave paintings.
    - A innocence
    - B inexperience
    - C precision
    - D professionalism
    - E imperviousness
    - F effervescence

For Questions 13 to 15, select one answer choice unless otherwise instructed.

Question 13 is based on this passage.

Coercion is the most basic of all leadership techniques: the leader gives direct orders and requires that they are followed. This method tends to be ineffective over extended periods because followers tend to feel pressured and underappreciated. However, there is a notable exception, as there is one situation in which coercion is the most effective style of evoking a response; namely, emergency situations where lives are at stake, benefit from a strong leader who is barking commands, as followers do not take time to assess the various ramifications and alternatives under such conditions.

13. Which of the following, if true, would most seriously undermine the claim about the benefits of coercive leadership?

    A) Employees who do repetitive tasks, such as manufacturing, sustain fewer injuries in environments where coercion is used.
    B) Leaders who are trained in other techniques, including transformative or democratic methods, can often successfully use coercion.
    C) Workplaces that utilize coercion tend to have a higher turnover rate than comparable workplaces that use a coaching leadership style.
    D) Workers who are adequately trained in emergency response drills can effectively deal with emergency situations without any leader.
    E) Most business management programs teach a variety of leadership styles to supplement coercive methods.

Questions 14 and 15 are based on this passage.

According to University of Massachusetts Amherst professor of classics Eric Poehler, archaeologists can increase their knowledge of Pompeii, a Roman city buried under 20 feet of ash when Mount Vesuvius erupted in 79 A.D., even though the Italian government has placed an indefinite moratorium on excavation. Poehler emphasizes that earlier studies often disregarded graffiti, incomplete frescos, and broken pottery; even the first systematic excavations of the site that were carried out under the command of Don Carlos, King of Naples, between 1750 and 1764, were conducted by laborers who were untrained in scientific techniques or were blatant treasure hunters. Since modern technology can facilitate the reconstruction of larger objects by extrapolating from existing fragments, careful analyses of discarded objects can enhance the understanding of everyday life from that period.

14. In the passage, the author is primarily concerned with

    A) summarizing the potential benefits of analyzing incomplete artwork from Pompeii
    B) comparing the excavation techniques used by archaeologists in the past and present
    C) resolving a misunderstanding about an earlier method of conducting excavations
    D) refuting the claim that there is a moratorium on the potential discoveries in Pompeii
    E) presenting an approach for continued research in a place where excavation is forbidden

15. The author implies which of the following about the excavation techniques used under the command of Don Carlos?

    A) The excavation focused on previously ignored graffiti, but it was interpreted incorrectly.
    B) The work was terminated because there were not enough skilled laborers in the project.
    C) Many of the workers stole objects, but the overall plan was a methodical investigation.
    D) Poehler feels that the focus should have been on studying graffiti rather than excavating.
    E) Due to poor techniques, workers could not extrapolate facts about everyday life in Pompeii.

Section 4 - Verbal Reasoning (Hard)

23 Minutes | 15 Questions

For Questions 1 to 4, select one entry for each blank from the corresponding column of choices. Fill all the blanks in the way that best completes the text.

1. It's hard to believe that a field of study as _____ as inorganic bond angles is so essential for the comprehension and manipulation of chemical compounds.

   - (A) pedestrian
   - (B) prevalent
   - (C) torpid
   - (D) applicable
   - (E) parsimonious

2. Atheism and agnosticism are not as (i) _____ opposed to religion as people often think. In reality, there is a spectrum that runs from religious to irreligious, with many gray areas in between. There is no hard and fast line distinguishing any two groups that fall between "religious" and "irreligious." For instance, some religions (such as Buddhism) actually describe their followers as being atheistic. Instances like this disprove the existence of a strict (ii) _____ between religious affiliations.

Blank (i)	Blank (ii)
(A) frugally	(D) gamut
(B) diametrically	(E) partition
(C) judiciously	(F) accord

3. Even the most (i) _____ of glances at one of Vincent van Gogh's paintings will give the viewer some idea of his highly distinctive style. His use of bold brushstrokes and (ii) _____ colors give his art an unusual emotional intensity—an intensity that can be somewhat disconcerting when one remembers his (iii) _____ struggle with mental illness.

Blank (i)	Blank (ii)	Blank (iii)
(A) cursory	(D) incarnadine	(G) iniquitous
(B) jaundiced	(E) funereal	(H) harrowing
(C) perspicacious	(F) dynamic	(I) affected

4. If there's one good thing that can be said about the (i) _____ of the construction industry, it's that it makes it a good (ii) _____ for economic health. The construction industry is usually one of the first industries to come to a halt during a recession, and one of the first to regain capital during a recovery. As a result, trends for the overall economy can be (iii) _____ from the trends of the construction industry.

Blank (i)	Blank (ii)	Blank (iii)
(A) affectability	(D) benchmark	(G) ameliorated
(B) frugality	(E) complication	(H) extrapolated
(C) insignificance	(F) impediment	(I) enervated

Section 4 - Verbal Reasoning (Hard)

For Questions 5 and 9, select one answer choice unless otherwise instructed.

Questions 5 and 6 are based on this passage.

Solar and wind power usually gain the most public attention in discussions of renewable energy sources, but geothermal energy is a more effective alternative to those because it has the additional benefit of not being reliant on weather conditions; the heat generated inside the earth is consistent and can be used in many ways. At present, geothermal energy primarily comes from naturally heated reservoirs of water, though future technology may use artificial subterranean lakes.

At its most basic, geothermal energy involves drilling into these bodies of water and siphoning off steam. As might be expected, that steam can be used for heating purposes, and it can also drive turbines to produce electricity. Less intuitively, geothermal energy can be used for cooling as well, since groundwater can absorb excess heat.

For the following question, consider each of the choices separately and select all that apply.

5. Which of the following, if true, would most significantly weaken the conclusion that geothermal energy is more effective than other renewable energy sources?

   A. Ocean wave energy has the highest energy density of all renewable resources and could produce up to 66 percent of the current energy used in the US.
   B. One megawatt hour of energy can be produced using between 1,700 and 4,000 gallons of water, though not all of that water is returned to the original reservoir.
   C. Natural reservoirs are only found in certain regions of the world, typically areas with extensive volcanic activity.

6. The passage suggests that the cooling of homes using geothermal energy

   A. requires simpler technology than cooling homes using solar or wind power.
   B. is conducted using a different process than heating homes using geothermal energy.
   C. is currently a theoretical option that has not yet been put into practice.
   D. necessitates separate facilities from those used to generate heat.
   E. is more expensive to implement than generating electricity using geothermal energy.

Questions 7 to 9 are based on this passage.

One of the few women to earn a career as a painter in the Baroque period, Artemisia Gentileschi (1593-c. 1656) was respected by contemporaries as a court painter who dramatically depicted the allegorical and mythological scenes popular at the time using bold lighting in the *chiaroscuro* style exemplified by the famous Caravaggio, who might have taught the technique in person as he was a frequent visitor to the Gentileschi home. Despite her popularity at the time, after her death, most art historians overlooked her works, possibly because of her gender. In the twentieth century, feminists revived interest in Gentileschi, claiming that she fit the stereotype of women painters who adeptly used the period's conventions to capture the strength and defiance of their female subjects.

A show curated by Ann Sutherland Harris and Linda Nochlin in 1976 triggered a reevaluation of the artist's work. Showing a large number of the pictures together, it was clear that Gentileschi was a master of composition and detail. Her women are not stereotyped, but reveal a sensitivity to the human form that could only be achieved through using live models. The drama of her paintings is not stylistic, but rather based on observing the natural folds of skin as her subjects make authentic gestures in response to the situations they are in.

Section 4 - Verbal Reasoning (Hard)

7. In the passage, the author is primarily concerned with

   A. criticizing a limited view of Gentileschi's painting as being overly influenced by the work of a famous male artist
   B. evaluating Gentileschi's status and reputation as a female painter during the Baroque period
   C. reassessing whether Gentileschi's subject matter was restricted to certain stereotypical topics.
   D. establishing that there is a different aspect to Gentileschi's work that had mostly been overlooked.
   E. explaining the challenges that Gentileschi overcame in order to become one of the few women painters of the Baroque period.

8. Which of the following, if true, would most clearly strengthen Harris and Nochlin's argument about Gentileschi's paintings?

   A. One of Gentileschi's most famous paintings is the allegorical Judith and her Maidservant, painted at the height of her career in 1625.
   B. After 1630, Gentileschi was known to collaborate with other painters in Naples on both panel paintings and murals.
   C. Virginia Vezzi was another successful female artist at the time, and she was known to be friends with Gentileschi.
   D. Art historian Griselda Pollock claims that the subjects of Gentileschi's paintings were often chosen by the client who paid for the paintings.
   E. Caravaggio was unusual at the time for using live models, a practice which gave his work a lifelike depth to his subject's skin.

9. In the context of the passage as a whole, the highlighted sentence serves primarily to

   A. establish a perspective that is disproved in the following paragraph
   B. offer a transition in the way Gentileschi was viewed by the artistic community
   C. present the reason for creating a show in 1976 dedicated only to Gentileschi
   D. show why few serious analyses were made of Gentileschi's artwork in the past
   E. argue that Gentileschi abandoned contemporary trends in favor of painting strong women

For Questions 10 to 12, select the two answer choices that, when used to complete the sentence, fit the meaning of the sentence as a whole and produce complete sentences that are alike in meaning.

10. The pace of the game had slowed to a crawl so when the _____ of an intercepted pass unexpectedly broke the monotony, the lethargic crowd, even those cheering for the losing team, burst into raucous applause.

    A. frisson
    B. immediacy
    C. thrill
    D. folly
    E. rapidity
    F. arrogance

11. The _____ of using quantum physics to discover new universes is not yet known.

    A. transfusion
    B. broadcast
    C. ramifications
    D. ratifications
    E. strident
    F. consequences

12. The newly patented polymer attracts other chemicals in the water, including dissolved metals, and _____ them for easy removal.

    A. rainfall
    B. accelerates
    C. consolidates
    D. precipitation
    E. impels
    F. precipitates

Section 4 - Verbal Reasoning (Hard)

For Questions 13 and 15, select one answer choice unless otherwise instructed.

Question 13 is based on this passage.

Chronic inflammation can contribute to serious conditions such as Alzheimer's disease and cardiovascular disease. A German study from 2013 compared the number of inflammatory molecules in 20 men who ran downhill on a ten percent grade for forty minutes. After the workout, men who sat in an ice bath that was 4 degrees Celsius (40 degrees Fahrenheit) showed a lower amount of inflammatory molecules than the control group. Though the differences in the results were statistically not extremely large, the study supports the assertion that cold therapy is beneficial in alleviating the adverse effects of inflammation.

13. Which of the following, if true, would most seriously weaken the conclusion that cold therapy alleviates the effects of inflammation?

    A) There are dozens of inflammatory molecules that were not measured in the German study, though the ones measured are considered indicative of adverse effects.

    B) Persistent chronic inflammation is also associated with gout, but none of the participants in the German study had gout at the beginning of the experiment.

    C) A follow-up study that included men walking uphill on a five percent grade for two minutes generated results after the ice bath that were considered not statistically significant.

    D) A 2015 study showed that 20 women who sat in an ice bath that was 2 degrees Celsius after exercising had a higher number of inflammatory molecules than women who did not.

    E) A similar study compared the inflammatory molecules after 40 men and women did a series of aerobic exercises, and the men had fewer inflammatory molecules than the women did.

Questions 14 and 15 are based on this passage.

Textile arts such as knitting, crochet, embroidery, tatting, and applique have long been crafts that have fallen into gender stereotypes d. The roots of that perspective date back to the Middle Ages, when formal arts such as painting and sculpture were dominated by guilds exclusive to men, and only after undergoing a long apprenticeship. Women running their households made functional textiles for home use, and the skills were typically passed down from mother to daughter rather than taught formally.

That partitioning was—and to a degree, still is—persistent, as wealthy women in the Victorian Era of the 1800s often did needlework to pass time. During the World Wars and Great Depression, women made or mended garments and other household items out of thrift, further reinforcing the belief that textiles were for the provenance of domestic utility.

For the following questions, consider each of the choices separately and select all that apply.

14. According to the passage, textile arts in the Middle Ages and the period of the World Wars had which of the following in common?

    A) They were primarily produced by women of leisure.

    B) They were not considered occupations for men.

    C) They were viewed as beneath the status of true art.

15. The author of the passage implies which of the following about the common view of textile arts?

    A) It was believed that practical items could not have artistic value.

    B) There continues to be a bias suggesting that women are most suited to make it.

    C) Prior to the Middle Ages, men also participated in the making of textiles.

Section 5 - Quantitative Reasoning (Easy)

26 Minutes | 15 Questions

1

In a balloon pack, there are green and white balloons. The white balloons constitute $\frac{5}{8}$ of the balloons.

Quantity A
The fraction of green balloons.

Quantity B
The ratio of green balloons to white balloons.

Ⓐ Quantity A is greater.
Ⓑ Quantity B is greater.
Ⓒ The two quantities are equal.
Ⓓ The relationship cannot be determined from the information given.

2

A box has side lengths 3, 5, and 9.

Quantity A
The surface area of the box

Quantity B
The volume of the box

Ⓐ Quantity A is greater.
Ⓑ Quantity B is greater.
Ⓒ The two quantities are equal.
Ⓓ The relationship cannot be determined from the information given.

3

$$3^8 = \frac{3^8}{3^x}$$

Quantity A
x

Quantity B
0

Ⓐ Quantity A is greater.
Ⓑ Quantity B is greater.
Ⓒ The two quantities are equal.
Ⓓ The relationship cannot be determined from the information given.

4

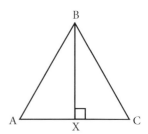

The perimeter of the equilateral triangle ABC is 24.

Quantity A
The perimeter of triangle BCX

Quantity B
The area of triangle BCX

Ⓐ Quantity A is greater.
Ⓑ Quantity B is greater.
Ⓒ The two quantities are equal.
Ⓓ The relationship cannot be determined from the information given.

5

The distance from $(a, 5)$ to $(4, 8)$ is 5.

Quantity A
a

Quantity B
8

Ⓐ Quantity A is greater.
Ⓑ Quantity B is greater.
Ⓒ The two quantities are equal.
Ⓓ The relationship cannot be determined from the information given.

Section 5 - Quantitative Reasoning (Easy)

6

The numbers x, y, and z form a sequence where y is 4 more than x and z is 16 more than y.
Also $\frac{x}{y} = \frac{y}{z}$

Quantity A	Quantity B
y	$\frac{17}{3}$

Ⓐ Quantity A is greater.
Ⓑ Quantity B is greater.
Ⓒ The two quantities are equal.
Ⓓ The relationship cannot be determined from the information given.

7

A store priced a jar of pasta sauce at $4.55. The next year they raised the price of the pasta sauce to $5.15. Each year after this they increased the price of the pasta sauce by this same amount. After 5 years, what would be the percent increase from the original pasta sauce price?

Ⓐ 13%
Ⓑ 40%
Ⓒ 66%
Ⓓ 75%
Ⓔ 110%

8

Car A is traveling at 60 $\frac{km}{hr}$. Car B is traveling at 45 $\frac{miles}{hour}$. What is the approximate positive difference in the two cars' speed in $\frac{miles}{hour}$? (Use the approximation that 1 mile equals 1.6 kilometers).

Ⓐ 2.0
Ⓑ 4.5
Ⓒ 7.5
Ⓓ 13.5
Ⓔ 15.0

9

If $-6 \leq x \leq 10$ and $-2 \leq y \leq 1$, then what is the greatest possible value of $x - y$?

10

A student takes out a simple interest loan to pay for one year of college. The loan amount was $11,500 and the student was able to pay it back along with $2,070 in interest after 3 years. What was the interest rate on the loan?

Ⓐ 3%
Ⓑ 6%
Ⓒ 12%
Ⓓ 15%
Ⓔ 18%

11

In how many different ways can the letters of the word 'REMIT' be arranged in such a way that 'M' comes before 'R'?

Ⓐ 30
Ⓑ 40
Ⓒ 60
Ⓓ 80
Ⓔ 120

12

If n is the unit digits of the expression $15^8 \times 24^4$, what is the value of n?

Ⓐ 0
Ⓑ 3
Ⓒ 4
Ⓓ 5
Ⓔ 6

Section 5 - Quantitative Reasoning (Easy)

13

List L has a median that is greater than the average (arithmetic mean). Which of the following could be List L?

Indicate all such answers.

- [A] 1, 7, 8, 9, 9
- [B] 1, 2, 7, 8, 9
- [C] 1, 2, 3, 4, 5
- [D] 3, 3, 3, 3, 3
- [E] 1, 2, 3, 4, 9

14

Which of the following sets of numbers has the greatest standard deviation?

- (A) 1.1, 1.2, 1.3
- (B) 0, 1, 2
- (C) −1, 0, 1
- (D) 1, 3, 5
- (E) 1, 3, 7

15

The points P(10, t) and R(19, 2) are in the xy-plane. Which of the following statements alone gives sufficient additional information to determine the value of t?

Indicate all such statements.

- [A] The slope of the line going through the points P(10, t) and R(19, 2) is $-\frac{1}{3}$.
- [B] The distance between the points P(10, t) and R(19, 2) is $\sqrt{106}$
- [C] The point T$\left(\frac{29}{2}, \frac{7}{2}\right)$ is the midpoint of the line segment whose endpoints are P(10, t) and R(19, 2).

178 | Practice Tests for the GRE

Section 5 - Quantitative Reasoning (Hard)

23 Minutes | 15 Questions

1

Set A = {5, 4, 7, 9, 20}

Set B = {0, 5, 4, 7, 9}

Quantity A
The mean of Set A

Quantity B
The mean of Set B

(A) Quantity A is greater.
(B) Quantity B is greater.
(C) The two quantities are equal.
(D) The relationship cannot be determined from the information given.

2

$$-3 < x \leq 3$$

Quantity A
$\frac{1}{2}|4 - x|$

Quantity B
$2|x|$

(A) Quantity A is greater.
(B) Quantity B is greater.
(C) The two quantities are equal.
(D) The relationship cannot be determined from the information given.

3

$$a > 1 \text{ and } b > 1$$

Quantity A
$1 + \dfrac{a^b}{a^{b+1}}$

Quantity B
$1 + \dfrac{a^{b+1}}{a^b}$

(A) Quantity A is greater.
(B) Quantity B is greater.
(C) The two quantities are equal.
(D) The relationship cannot be determined from the information given.

4

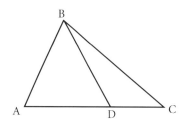

AB = DB and ∠BDC = 115°

Quantity A
∠A

Quantity B
∠C

(A) Quantity A is greater.
(B) Quantity B is greater.
(C) The two quantities are equal.
(D) The relationship cannot be determined from the information given.

5

A regular polygon has interior angles that measure 1080° and sides of length 3.

Quantity A
The numerical value of the measure of each exterior angle of the polygon

Quantity B
The area of the polygon

(A) Quantity A is greater.
(B) Quantity B is greater.
(C) The two quantities are equal.
(D) The relationship cannot be determined from the information given.

Section 5 - Quantitative Reasoning (Hard)

6

A school board committee can be formed from the 10 members of the school board which include Lee and Paula. Four people will be selected at random for the committee. What is the probability that Lee will be on the committee, but not Paula?

A) $\frac{7}{30} - \frac{4}{15}$
B) $\frac{1}{4}$
C) $\frac{4}{15}$
D) $\frac{1}{3}$
E) $\frac{5}{12}$

7

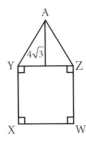

In the figure above, triangle YAZ is an equilateral triangle. What is the area of square XYZW?

A) 4
B) 8
C) 16
D) 48
E) 64

8

Packing Machine A can package 20 boxes every minute. Packing Machine B can package 14 boxes every minute. After how many hours will Packing Machine A package 900 more boxes than Packing Machine B?

A) 1
B) 1.5
C) 2
D) 2.5
E) 3

9

If x and y are integers and $\frac{y^2}{x}$ is even, which of the following must be true?

A) y and x are both even
B) $y = x$
C) $x > y$
D) y is divisible by x
E) $x - y$ is odd

10

A company has 150 employees, 60% of which are remote workers. The company does not lay off any employees and adds another 30 employees of which 40% are remote workers. What is the approximate percentage of the company's total employee workforce that are remote workers?

A) 58%
B) 60%
C) 65%
D) 74%
E) 82%

Section 5 - Quantitative Reasoning (Hard)

11

If x is $18\frac{1}{2}\%$ of 600, which of the following expressions could be equivalent to x?

Indicate all such answers.

- [A] 37% of 300
- [B] 9% of 1200
- [C] $13\frac{7}{8}\%$ of 800
- [D] 111% of 100
- [E] 0.1% of 1000
- [F] $\frac{1}{4}\%$ of 2400

12

The sequence 2, 6, 10, 2, 6, 10, 2, 6, 10 repeats in the pattern 2, 6, 10 indefinitely. What is the sum of the values from the 20th term to the 50th term?

- (A) 120
- (B) 180
- (C) 200
- (D) 240
- (E) 300

13

$$-14 \leq x \leq 5$$
$$-3 \leq y \leq 15$$

If x and y are integers, what is the maximum possible value of $\frac{x-y}{xy}$?

[   ]

14

Advertising Expenditure (in thousands)	Sales Revenue (in thousands)
1.5	12
3.2	22
4.5	30
4.8	38
5.5	40
6.0	51

The table above shows the sales revenue based on advertising expenditures. Which of the following best describes the line of best fit for the data set?

- (A) $y = 0.12x + 12$
- (B) $y = 8.2x - 2.5$
- (C) $y = 3.8x + 4$
- (D) $y = -5x + 12$
- (E) $y = -1.4x - 9.1$

15

If $x^2 y^3 z^4 < 0$, which of the following statements must be true?

Indicate all such statements.

- [A] xyz is negative
- [B] xz is positive
- [C] $x^2 y$ is negative
- [D] x is positive
- [E] y is negative

Answer Key

VERBAL REASONING

Section 2

Q. No.	Correct Answer	Your Answer
1	C	
2	B, F	
3	B, D, H	
4	C	
5	E	
6	A, F	
7	B, E	
8	C, D	
9	A, E	
10	A	
11	B	
12	C	

Section 4 (Easy)

Q. No.	Correct Answer	Your Answer
1	C	
2	A	
3	A, D	
4	C, D, H	
5	B	
6	D	
7	A	
8	E	
9	D	
10	A, D	
11	B, E	
12	A, B	
13	A	
14	E	
15	C	

Section 4 (Hard)

Q. No.	Correct Answer	Your Answer
1	A	
2	B, E	
3	A, F, H	
4	A, D, H	
5	B, C	
6	B	
7	D	
8	E	
9	B	
10	A, C	
11	C, F	
12	C, F	
13	D	
14	B, C	
15	A, B, C	

Practice Tests for the GRE

Answer Key

QUANTITATIVE REASONING

Section 3		
Q. No.	Correct Answer	Your Answer
1	D	
2	B	
3	D	
4	A	
5	C	
6	A	
7	1/8	
8	A	
9	A	
10	C	
11	B, C, D	
12	38.89	

Section 5 (Easy)		
Q. No.	Correct Answer	Your Answer
1	B	
2	A	
3	C	
4	A	
5	D	
6	B	
7	C	
8	C	
9	12	
10	B	
11	C	
12	A	
13	A, B	
14	E	
15	A, C	

Section 5 (Hard)		
Q. No.	Correct Answer	Your Answer
1	A	
2	D	
3	B	
4	A	
5	A	
6	C	
7	E	
8	D	
9	D	
10	A	
11	A, C, D	
12	B	
13	2	
14	B	
15	C, E	

Analytical Writing — Answers & Explanations — Section 1

Analyze an Issue

The sample essay that follows was written in response to the prompt that appeared in the question.

It is impossible to identify well-rounded individuals on the street, in the workplace, or at the gym. It is unlikely that anyone is choosing his or her friends based on their being well-rounded. It is probably impossible to define well-rounded; everyone would have a point of view. It is true that in the early days of higher education, one aimed to become a "man of letters", knowledgeable to some degree in a variety of subjects. That luxury is not longer desirable or practical. University students are entering a different world.

I like to think of myself as well-rounded. I am interested in a variety of topics, and I participate in a variety of activities. I carry on conversations easily with my friends and family as well as people I meet in the grocery store or at an airport. My seatmates on trains and planes find me engaging. I answer most of the questions on Jeopardy! correctly, and I can complete the New York Times crossword puzzle. I like and can cook food from a variety of cuisines. I can order correctly from a menu written in French. I like HGTV, the Food Network, and action movies. My friends think I'm funny, and I cry over sappy commercials on TV. None of my self-perceived well-roundedness is a result of courses that I either did or did not take in college.

My mother taught me to knit and sew. I got my love of gardening from my father. I think I taught myself to read. My sister taught me how to see different perspectives on an issue. I learned to swim during lessons on cold mornings at the local pool. I learned to play the piano from an older lady who tapped out the measures with a plastic knitting needle on the top of the piano. I learned to drive from a kind and patient man who did not use deodorant and wouldn't let his students roll down the car windows in the heat of the summer. My friends taught me about friendship. I obtained all of these skills before I went to college.

So, what did college teach me? College taught me how to live in close quarters with hundreds of other girls from different states and backgrounds. College taught me to understand football, to party on the weekends, and how to join the best sorority on campus. College taught me to sign up for classes that ended by 1:00 pm and met on Mondays, Wednesdays, and Fridays, so I'd have two full days off from classes. College eventually taught me how to manage my time. It taught me the classes I would need to get a degree in my major.

High school seniors plan to enter colleges and universities with the goal of getting a job after graduation, and that is what college should do. When today's high-school seniors graduate from college, they will have enormous debt. While in college, they must focus on courses that serve practical purposes. They will need immediate employment in order to meet their financial obligations. They will become well-rounded by living their lives after college.

Verbal Reasoning — Answers & Explanations — Section 2

1 **Choice D is correct** because "oscillate" means to move or swing back and forth at a regular speed. Since the sentence expresses that something is happening a certain number of times "between" two states, it implies that there is a back-and-forth movement and thus, this word would fit with the context provided.

Choice A is incorrect because "persist" means to continue firmly and for a prolonged period. This word would not apply because we are discussing a specific time period, which is that of a second. Also, something does not persist a certain number of times. Rather, something could rise and fall a certain number of times, making Choice D the better option. **Choice B** is incorrect because "forge" means to produce something, oftentimes with difficulty. In this sentence, the atom is not producing anything but is fluctuating between two radiation states. Nothing is generated from the atom. So, Choice D is the better option. **Choice C** is incorrect because "feign" means pretending to be affected. This word would not make sense in the sentence because an atom does not pretend to be affected by two radiation states. Rather, an atom could rise up and down between two radiation states, making Choice D the better option. **Choice E** is incorrect because "antedate" means preceding in time or happening before. This word does not fit in the context of the sentence because it does not accurately describe the action of the atom between two radiation states. It does not precede the radiation states but alternates between them. Therefore, Choice D is the best option.

2 **Choice B is correct** because "integral" means necessary or essential to make complete. Saying that music has been an essential part of the culture makes sense and aligns with the message of the rest of the passage. **Choice F is correct** because "extant" means still in existence or surviving. The sentence is saying that the musical theory learned by the Greeks is still surviving today, as seen by its presence in Western music.

Choice A is incorrect because "contested" means to oppose something as wrong. It would not make sense for this word to be used because music has not been opposed in cultures, as evidenced by the remainder of the passage discussing the cultural importance of music. **Choice C** is incorrect because "invidious" means causing discontent or animosity. It would not make sense for this word to be used because music has not caused any turmoil in cultures. **Choice D** is incorrect because "gamut" means the complete range or scope of something. This word is a noun, so it would not fit in the blank, which requires an adjective. Additionally, the meaning of the word does not fit because the sentence is describing the relevance of Greek musical theories today, not the vastness. **Choice E** is incorrect because "partition" means the action of dividing into parts. This word is a verb, so it would not fit the blank, which requires an adjective. Additionally, the meaning of the word does not fit because the sentence is describing the relevance of Greek musical theories today, not its division.

3 **Choice B is correct** because "preponderant" means predominant in influence or importance. This word fits in the blank because the sentence is describing the type of force the United States had in automobile production. Because the passage goes on to explain that Japan and China later took hold of the industry, it can be assumed that the first sentence is expressing that the United States was once on top. **Choice D is correct** because "waned" means to become progressively smaller or decrease over time. This word fits in the blank because prior to this sentence the passage is describing the dominance that the United States had over the automobile industry. After this sentence the passage discusses Japan and China gaining dominance. Therefore, the power of the United States in the industry became smaller. **Choice H is correct** because "ephemeral" means lasting for a very short time. This word fits in the blank because the sentence is describing Japan's dominance in the industry for only a few decades before China overtook the industry.

Choice A is incorrect because "debatable" means open to argument. Since the United States manufactured more than 90% of the world's automobiles during that time, its powerful influence over the industry is not debatable. Therefore, Choice B is the better option. **Choice C** is incorrect because "superfluous" means more than enough. This word would not fit in the blank because it does not describe the strong position of the United States over the automobile industry. The United States was powerful, but not more than enough to the point of being unnecessary. Therefore, Choice B is the better option. **Choice E** is incorrect because "illuminated" means lit with bright lights or shining. This word does not fit in the blank because it would not make sense for the dominance of the United States to be lit with bright lights. Also, it would not align with the second clause of the sentence, which discusses Japan gaining dominance over the industry. **Choice F** is incorrect because "proliferated" means to increase and multiply rapidly. However, this is the opposite of what the sentence is trying to say. The sentence expresses that something happened to the dominance of the United States in the industry before Japan became the world's top producer. It would not make sense for the dominance of the United States to grow and then Japan to take over. Rather, the dominance of the United States waned, making Choice D the better option. **Choice G is incorrect** because "tenacious" means keeping a firm hold and not relinquishing a position. This word would not fit in the blank because the sentence is explaining how Japan lost its hold on the industry and China readily took over. Therefore, Choice H is the better option. **Choice I is incorrect** because "condescending" means showing patronizing superiority. This word would not accurately describe the position of the nation of Japan over the automobile industry. Rather, Japan's control was, "ephemeral" or, "short-lived" before China took over.

4 **Choice C is correct** because the last sentence states that the Christian rulers "did not destroy all of the Muslim ornamentation and poetry" so they left the artwork. The reason is "possibly because the calligraphy was unintelligible" meaning they could not read the elegant writing. In other words, they likely were not even "cognizant" or "aware" that the images were "texts" or "written matter."

Choice A is incorrect because the passage states that the sultan built "the elegant fortress." Therefore, it can be assumed that the Alhambra served a purpose greater than just a "residence" or "home" for the sultan. It likely was also a strategic place for protection or defense. **Choice B is incorrect** because the passage states that the Alhambra was "the seat of the last Muslim kingdom on the Iberian Peninsula for about three hundred years." This suggests that the kingdom existed for longer than that and that earlier Muslim kingdoms—or the earlier part of the last Muslim kingdom—had their "seat" or headquarters elsewhere.

5 **Choice E is correct** because it shows that a vaccination program for pets may not be sufficient to reduce the number of domestic animals with transmittable diseases. If only pets are vaccinated, then the tiger cats might still get sick from diseases from the food animals.

Choice A is incorrect because even if habitations are not close to the tiger cats, the vaccination program could limit the diseases. Then there would be fewer diseases to transfer via insects to the cats, and the program might be effective for saving the cats. **Choice B is incorrect**

because it shows a second problem affecting the tiger cats, but the vaccination program could still work. If so, then the species would have one less problem reducing the numbers. **Choice C is incorrect** because it could show that the vaccination program is essential because the population does not grow quickly. If even one or two tiger cats are saved because they do not get disease, the population might have a better chance of survival. **Choice D is incorrect** because the text specifies that the diseases are transferred via insects, so even if the cats are nocturnal and not in direct contact with domestic animals, they could still catch the diseases. Therefore, a program that reduces the diseases also reduces the chances of the tiger cats succumbing.

6 **Choice A is correct** because "synthesis" means a combination of things to form a system. The sentence is discussing two tendencies of behavior among molecules, which are growing and maintaining simple shapes. Therefore, molecules must establish a system that combines these two behaviors in order to survive. **Choice F is correct** because "unity" means the state of being united and joined. The sentence is discussing two tendencies of behavior among molecules, which are growing and maintaining simple shapes. Therefore, molecules must establish a joined network that combines these two behaviors in order to survive.

Choice B is incorrect because "algorithm" means a set of rules to be followed in calculations. This word does not accurately describe the balanced relationship that must be formed between the two propensities of the molecule in order for it to survive. **Choice C is incorrect** because "equation" means the processing of equating one thing with another. This word does not accurately describe the balanced relationship that must be formed between the two propensities of the molecule in order for it to survive. The two propensities of the molecule are very dissimilar and not presented as the same thing. **Choice D is incorrect** because "deduction" is the action of subtracting something. This word does not accurately describe the balanced relationship that must be formed between the two propensities of the molecule in order for it to survive. Neither of the processes is being subtracted or eliminated in any way. **Choice E is incorrect** because "fission" is the action of splitting something into parts. This word does not accurately describe the balanced relationship that must be formed between the two propensities of the molecule in order for it to survive. Neither of the processes is being split or divided in any way.

Verbal Reasoning — Answers & Explanations — Section 2

7 **Choice B is correct** because "institutionalized" means a custom is established as part of an official organization. In this sentence, the penal system is the official organization being discussed. Harsher sentences for a particular group would qualify as racism by an institution. **Choice E is correct** because "entrenched" means a practice that is firmly established and ingrained. The practice of delivering harsher sentences to African-Americans could be considered an ingrained practice by the long-established penal system.

Choice A is incorrect because "laissez-faire" means an attitude of letting things take their course or allowing the people to choose. This does not accurately describe the way the sentence is portraying the penal system's tendency to deliver harsher punishments to African-Americans. Rather, the penal system is portrayed as unjust or overly harsh. **Choice C** is incorrect because "infrequent" means not occurring regularly. This does not accurately describe the way the sentence is portraying the penal system's tendency to deliver harsher punishments to African-Americans. The sentence makes no mention of the frequency by which these sentences are given and is simply trying to express the unjustness of the situation as it is occurring. **Choice D** is incorrect because "accidental" means happening unintentionally or by chance. This does not accurately describe the way the sentence is portraying the penal system's tendency to deliver harsher punishments to African-Americans. The sentence is trying to express that there is consistently harsher treatment according to skin color, not that African-Americans have coincidentally received harsher treatment. Therefore, Choices B and E are better options. **Choice F** is incorrect because "progressive" means happening gradually in stages or advocating for social reform. Neither of these definitions accurately describe the way the sentence is portraying the penal system's tendency to deliver harsher punishments to African-Americans.

8 **Choice C is correct** because "discordant" means disagreeing. In other words, the sentence is saying that the two defendants originally presented stories to the court that were not aligned which led to the need to re-synthesize their stories so they would match. **Choice D is correct** because "incongruous" means not in harmony or agreement. In other words, the sentence is saying that the two defendants originally presented stories to the court that were not aligned, which led to the need to re-synthesize their stories so they would match.

Choice A is incorrect because "hilarious" means extremely amusing. This word would not fit in the blank because there is no reason to believe that presenting amusing stories to the jury would arouse suspicions. **Choice B** is incorrect because "harmonious" means consistent and free from disagreement. This is the opposite of what the sentence is expressing. It would not make sense for two agreeing stories to arouse suspicions among the jury. Rather, if the two stories were incongruous or discordant the stories would need to be revised to match. **Choice E** is incorrect because "syphoned" means to draw or transfer a liquid or other resources. This word is a verb, which does not fit in the blank that requires an adjective. Additionally, this word does not make sense in the sentence because stories cannot be syphoned and this word does not explain why the stories would need to be revised. **Choice F** is incorrect because "dastardly" means wicked and cruel. This word would not fit in the blank because there is no reason to believe that presenting cruel stories to the jury would arouse suspicions. It does not express why the stories need to be revised to match.

9 **Choice A is correct** because "vetted" means something was critically examined by a trustworthy individual. This word fits in the blank because the job being described involves finances and politics of corporate banking institutions. Corporate actions would need to be examined by a worthy professional like a specialty lawyer. **Choice E is correct** because "assessed" means the evaluation of something. This word fits in the blank because it is describing a high stakes job involving finances and politics of corporate banking institutions. The sentence is saying that all corporate actions need to first be assessed by professionals who are competent in the relevant areas.

Choice B is incorrect because "delineated" means portraying a precise position. This word would not fit in the blank because it requires a word that is describing a process that experienced lawyers go through to evaluate corporate actions. Portraying a precise position does not relate to the analysis of a decision, so Choices A and E are better options. **Choice C** is incorrect because "prioritized" means designated as more important than other things. This word would not fit in the blank because the lawyers described in the sentence are evaluating the corporate actions, not prioritizing them. There is no indication that certain actions are being placed ahead of others. **Choice D** is incorrect because "extemporized" means composed without preparation or improvised. This word would not fit in the blank because lawyers are examining high-stakes corporate actions. It is unlikely that improvisation would be a part of this process. Rather, the massive banking institutions are looking to have actions critically analyzed. **Choice F** is incorrect because "rewritten" means to write again with alterations. This word would not fit in the blank because corporate actions are being analyzed, but not necessarily rewritten. The sentence does not indicate the lawyers making revisions or changing the actions, but simply assessing them.

10 **Choice A is correct** because if the humor was only appealing to a few people, then it would not be effective in determining how people react when they see something funny in advertising. The students would not respond uniformly to the presence of humor, but rather to whether they enjoyed that particular type. Therefore, the humor was most likely designed to be appealing to the "average" or "most" viewers.

Choice B is incorrect because the fact that people with high involvement saw the humor as surprising and distracting did not necessarily dislike it. Rather, they thought it drew their attention from the focus of the advertisement. **Choice C** is incorrect because the text does not focus on the way that the advertisements are created. It is impossible to determine from the information given whether some advertisements are harder to make than others. **Choice D** is incorrect because the author refers to humor in advertisements of all sorts in the first paragraph. Even though Eisend's study focused on print advertisements, it is implied that other humorous two-sided advertising would likely have similar results based on whether the people are engaged or not. **Choice E** is incorrect because while humor is more successful in one-sided advertisements, there is no indication about whether one-sided advertisements in general are more successful. It is possible that two-sided, non-humorous advertising generates the greatest results.

11 **Choice B is correct** because the second paragraph shows that Eisend divided the students into four conditions to determine whether humor was effective in two-sided advertising, and found that it was not, even though it was effective for the one-sided advertising. His second experiment delved into the reasons for that finding.

Choice A is incorrect because while the paragraph mentions that the advertising was print and referred to retirement plans, there is no discussion of "various" or "different" types of advertisements. There is also no description of what the humorous element was other than "visual." **Choice C** is incorrect because there are not "mechanisms" or "reasons" for why the advertising is effective, just a claim that humor works for one-sided advertising. **Choice D** is incorrect because while the paragraph does say that humor was effective in one-sided advertising, the purpose of the paragraph is not to "defend" or "establish that point." The passage is establishing whether humor is effective in two-sided advertising, so there is no need to emphasize the point in one-sided advertising except to establish that the humor used was indeed considered humorous. **Choice E** is incorrect because Eisend did not try to "disprove" or "show the results were wrong." Rather, he was trying to determine why people preferred humor in one-sided advertising but not in two-sided advertising.

12 **Choice C is correct** because the second paragraph states that humor had "a slight negative effect on the perception of two-sided humor" meaning that it could hinder the way a person received advertising that had positive and negative points about the product. The third paragraph shows that people with "high involvement" or "who were more interested in making a purchase" felt that the humor was more surprising and distracting. They also had "lower levels of brand attitude" implying that they were not as favorably impressed with the brand. Therefore, the implication is that people who have lower involvement are more likely to find the humor appealing.

Choice A is incorrect because the text refers to a study done using visual humor, but there is no comparison with textual humor. Therefore, it is impossible to determine from the material given which is more appealing. **Choice B** is incorrect because while the high-engagement audience had a lower brand attitude, there is no indication about what aspect of the advertisement affected the decision. The mention of a high level of distraction indicates that they did not pay as close attention to the content, so they may, for example, have ignored the negative points. **Choice D** is incorrect because the text does not refer to trends in media use over time. If anything, Eisend's research may indicate that humor will be used less in two-sided advertisements because it does not engage part of the intended audience well. **Choice E** is incorrect because the text states that "high involvement" students had lower brand attitude for humor in two-sided advertising, but there is no discussion about whether most people who see the advertisement are highly involved. The "majority" or "most" viewers could be uninterested in the product one way or another.

4 Quantitative Reasoning   Answers & Explanations   Section 3

1 **Choice D is correct** because for integer values y would always be greater than x, but this may not be the case for any combinations of negatives and positives. For example, if $x^2 = 4$ and $y^2 = 16$, it could be found that x is 2 or -2 and
y is 4 or -4. If x were 2 and y was -4, x would be greater than y.

Choice A is incorrect because only in some circumstances is x greater than y. **Choice B** is incorrect because y is greater than x in some circumstances only. **Choice C** is incorrect because x does not equal y.

2 **Choice B is correct** because using rules of normal distributions Quantity A can be found to be under 16%.

To find this, first, identify that a tire pressure greater than 36 would put you above one standard deviation above the mean since one standard deviation would be 35 (33 psi + standard deviation of 2).

Apply the rule that 68% of data is found within one standard deviation of the mean in both directions. That means 34% lies one standard deviation above the mean. That 34% plus the 50% of the data below the mean adds to 84% of the data being within 1 standard deviation. That would leave 100% − 84% = 16% of the data.

36 is just slightly above 35 meaning even a smaller percent of the sample would be accounted for with this number. Quantity A, therefore could be concluded to be under 16%. Quantity B as a percent would be 20% making it larger than Quantity A.

Choice A is incorrect because Quantity A is under 16% and Quantity B is 20% so Quantity A is not larger. **Choice C** is incorrect because the two quantities are not equal. **Choice D** is incorrect because it is possible to compare the quantities.

3 **Choice D is correct** because there are two solutions to the system of equations (4, 1) and (−3, −6). Therefore, it is not possible to determine the exact comparison between Quantity A and Quantity B since Quantity A could be 5 (4 + 1) or −9 (−3 + −6). In the first instance, Quantity A would equal Quantity B, but in the second instance, Quantity B would be bigger.

To find the solutions, rewrite the linear expression in terms of y to get $y = x − 3$.

Then substitute for $y = x − 3$ for y in the top equation to get $(x − 1)^2 + (x − 3 + 3)^2 = 25$. Simplifying this expression would get you the new statement. $(x − 1)^2 + x^2 = 25$

Expand the equation to get $x^2 − 2x + 1 + x^2 = 25$. Then combine like terms to get $2x^2 − 2x + 1 = 25$. Subtract 25 on both sides to get $2x^2 − 2x − 24 = 0$. Factor out a 2 and then factor the remaining $2(x^2 − x − 12)$ to get $2(x + 3)(x − 4) = 0$.

Setting each factor equal to zero would get you $x + 3 = 0$ and $x − 4 = 0$ which gives you the two solutions, $x = −3$ and $x = 4$.

Plug both solutions in to solve for y. Using the second equation $x − y = 3$, you would get $y = 1$ (4 − y = 3) and $y = −6$ (−3 − y = 3).

Plugging these solution pairs into the equation for Quantity A would give you 4 + 1 = 5 and −3 + −6 = −9.

Choice A is incorrect because Quantity A could only equal 5 or -9, both of which are not greater than Quantity B. **Choice B** is incorrect because while Quantity B would be greater than Quantity A if it equaled −9, there is another solution for Quantity A that is equal to Quantity B. **Choice C** is incorrect because while there is one occurrence where Quantity A equals Quantity B, it is not always the case.

4 **Choice A is correct** because x can be found to equal 3 which makes Quantity A larger than Quantity B.

First, solve the first expression for y, by rearranging it and setting it equal to 0. Add over 9 to get $y^2 + 6y + 9 = 0$. Factoring this expression will give you $(y + 3)^2 = 0$. Set the statement $y + 3$ equal to 0 to get $y = −3$.

Plug in $y = −3$ into the second expression to identify x. To make the expression $\dfrac{z}{-3} + \dfrac{z}{x} = 0$ true, you can rearrange and cross multiply. Subtract $\dfrac{z}{x}$ to get $\dfrac{z}{-3} = \dfrac{-z}{x}$. Cross multiply to get $xz = 3z$. Divide by z to find $x = 3$.

Choice B is incorrect because 1 is not greater than 3. **Choice C** is incorrect because x does not equal 1. **Choice D** is incorrect because it is possible to determine the value of both quantities and compare them.

5 **Choice C is correct** because if you subtract the area of the triangle from the area of the square you will get $36 − 9\sqrt{3}$. This area is also the same as the area of the shaded region.

To find the area of the square, multiply base times height to get $6 \times 6 = 36$.

To find the area of the triangle, use the formula $A = \dfrac{\sqrt{3}}{4} a^2$.

Quantitative Reasoning — Answers & Explanations — Section 3

Plugging in the side length of 6 you would get $A = \frac{\sqrt{3}}{4}(6)^2$ which gives you $\frac{36\sqrt{3}}{4}$ which simplifies to be $9\sqrt{3}$.

The area of the shaded region can be found by subtracting the area of the triangle from the area of the square. This gives us $36 - 9\sqrt{3}$.

Choice A is incorrect because this is the area of the triangle, not the shaded region. **Choice B** is incorrect because this answer results from not solving for the area of the triangle correctly. **Choice D** is incorrect because this answer results from a calculation error. **Choice E** is incorrect because this is the entire area of the square.

6 **Choice A is correct** because there is a total possible combination of 24 options for the 4-digit numbers possible using the numbers 1, 2, 3, and 4. This is found using 4!. Of those 24 options, you have to find which are divisible by 7.

The rules to determine if a number is divisible by 7 is to remove the last digit, double it, and then subtract it from the remaining number until you get something that is divisible by 7. For example, the number 1234 would be $123 - (4 \times 2) = 115$. You can go again to get the statement $11 - (5 \times 2) = 1$. So this number is not divisible by 7.

Continuing this method and looking for patterns to shorten your search, it can be concluded quickly that none of the 1000s, 2000s, or 3000s work with 7. Only one number, 4123 is divisible by 7. This is seen by using $412 - (3 \times 2) = 406$ which then becomes the statement of $40 - (6 \times 2) = 28$. The number 28 is divisible by 7.

Choice B is incorrect because there is only one option out of the 24 that is divisible by 7. **Choice C** is incorrect because there is only one option out of the 24 that is divisible by 7. **Choice D** is incorrect because there is only one option out of the 24 that is divisible by 7. **Choice E** is incorrect because there is only one option out of the 24 that is divisible by 7.

7 **The correct answer is $\frac{1}{8}$.** because it can be concluded that triangle ABD is one half the area of square ABCD. It can also be concluded that triangle BXY is one fourth of the area of triangle ABD since you can divide the square AXYZ into two triangles that would be congruent to triangle BXY and triangle YZD. Triangle BXY would be one of four triangles that make up the triangle that makes half of the larger square. Relating these ideas together, you can conclude $\frac{1}{4}$ of $\frac{1}{2}$ of the total area would be equal to $\frac{1}{8}$.

8 **Choice A is correct** because according to the pie chart labeled "Trash Categories 2005", 8% of all trash was hazardous waste. The phrase "of every 100" means percentage so this matches to answer A.

Choice B is incorrect because this would result from a calculation error. **Choice C** is incorrect because this would result from a calculation error. **Choice D** is incorrect because this would result from a calculation error. **Choice E** is incorrect because this would result from a calculation error.

9 **Choice A is correct** because the amount of construction debris and textiles accounts for 21% of all trash in 2005 and 2015, but there was more trash produced in 2015.

Choice B is incorrect because textiles also increased in percentage between 2005 and 2015. **Choice C** is incorrect because it compares the percentages, not the actual values of organic waste. **Choice D** is incorrect because the amount of trash and the percent of textiles making up the composition of the trash both increased. **Choice E** is incorrect because the greatest increase in trash production was a tied between 1990 to 1995 and 2015 to 2020 with both periods seeing an increase of 30 million tons.

10 **Choice C is correct** because the recyclables in 2015 were 106.6 million tons (260×0.41) and the recyclables in 2005 were 90 million tons (250×0.41). The difference between these two numbers is 16.6 million tons.

Choice A is incorrect because this would result from finding the amount of recyclables each year using the millions of tons from 2005. **Choice B** is incorrect because this would result from finding the amount of recyclables each year using the millions of tons from 2015. **Choice D** is incorrect because this would result from a calculation error. **Choice E** is incorrect because this would result from a calculation error.

11 **Choices B, C, and D are correct.** The printing rate per hour can be calculated to be 76 pages per hour. To find this, turn 57 pages per 45 minutes into a rate per 60 minutes by setting up the ratio $\frac{57}{45} = \frac{x}{60}$. Cross multiplying will get you $45x = 3420$. Dividing by 45 will result in $x = 76$ pages per hour. If the printer started at 1:00 p.m. and ran until 5:00 p.m., the least amount of pages printed would be

76 pages per hour times 4 hours which yields 304 pages. If the printer started at 1:00 p.m. and ran until 6:00 p.m., the most amount of pages printed would be 76 pages per hour times 5 hours which is 380 pages. Any answers that fall within the range of 304 and 380 would work. Choice B is correct because it is within the range of 304 to 380. Choice C is correct because it is within the range of 304 to 380. Choice D is correct because it is within the range of 304 to 380.

Choice A is incorrect because it falls outside the range of 304 to 380. **Choice E** is incorrect because it falls outside the range of 304 to 380.

12 **The correct answer is 38.89** because you can write an algebraic expression to solve the relationship between the original price and the new price with both discounts.

Let x be the original price. You can denote 20% off by indicating x to be 80% of its original value with the expression $0.80x$.

Another 10% off would be indicated by multiplying the first discounted price by 90% of its value or $(0.90)(0.80)x$. This would then yield the new price which we will call y.

Set the expressions equal to each other to get the equation $(0.90)(0.80)x = y$. To determine what y must be multiplied by to yield x, divide both sides by 0.90 and 0.80. You will get $x = \dfrac{y}{(0.90)(0.80)}$.

Simplifying this expression will get you $x = \dfrac{25y}{18}$. This means the discounted price can be multiplied by approximately 1.3889 to get the original price.

Therefore, the percent increase will be 1.3889 − 1 to get 0.3889 which is equal to 38.89%.

Verbal Reasoning (Easy) — Answers & Explanations — Section 4

1 **Choice C is correct** because "impart" means to communicate or bestow a quality. This sentence is expressing the fact that violin makers have the ability to converse the sounds of speech in their musical production. In other words, aspects of speech are imparted in violin music.

Choice A is incorrect because "disclose" means making secret information known. This word does not fit in the blank because vowel and consonant sounds are not secret information. Rather, they are simply aspects of language that have been crafted into violin music, making Choice C the better option. **Choice B** is incorrect because "yield" means to produce or provide, such as in a harvest. This word does not fit in the blank because nothing physical is being provided from violin music. Rather, aspects of language are conveyed, which makes Choice C the better option. **Choice D** is incorrect because "output" refers to the amount of something produced. Although the sentence describes vowel and consonant sounds being included in the production of music, this word does not fit in the blank because the sentence does not discuss the specific number of sounds being delivered. Rather, the sentence is discussing the inclusion of language sounds within music, making Choice C the better option. **Choice E** is incorrect because "relinquish" means voluntarily giving up. This word does not fit in the blank because nothing is being given up by anyone else. Rather, the vowel and consonant sounds are simply being included in the production of violin music, making choice C the better option.

2 **Choice A is correct** because "fundamental" means something is of central importance. Because the sentence is explaining the four forces that are responsible for the wide variety of phenomena in the observable universe, these forces are undoubtedly important.

Choice B is incorrect because "superfluous" means unnecessary and more than enough. This word does not fit in the blank because the four forces responsible for phenomena in the observable universe are undoubtedly important and not at all unnecessary. **Choice C** is incorrect because "regressive" means gradually decreasing. This word does not fit in the blank because the sentence makes no indication that anything is decreasing. Rather, the sentence is stating that there are four important forces responsible for physical phenomena. Therefore, Choice A is the better option. **Choice D** is incorrect because "excessive" means more than necessary. This word does not fit in the blank because the four forces responsible for phenomena in the observable universe are undoubtedly necessary and not at all unwarranted. **Choice E** is incorrect because "intricate" means very complicated or detailed. The sentence begins by stating that the variety of complicated physical phenomena are ironically explained in some way. The word, "ironically" suggests that the second part of the sentence will act in opposition to the first part. Since the first part discussed complicated phenomena, the second part will likely discuss the opposite. So, Choice A is the better option.

3 **Choice A is correct** because "diversifying" means becoming varied. This word fits in the blank because the sentence is expressing that improvisation was originally more stringent, but that as it progressed actors became more comfortable behaving in wide-ranging forms. **Choice D is correct** because "fluidity" means moving along with elegance or grace. This word fits in the blank because the sentence is expressing that improvisational theater was not as comfortable as scripted theater at first, but that over time a flow was established that allowed actors to branch out from their usual styles.

Choice B is incorrect because "conflating" means combining two or more things into one. This word does not fit in the blank because the actors were not combining anything. Rather, they were changing their approaches to acting. Therefore, choice A is the better option. **Choice C** is incorrect because "truncating" means making something shorter or quicker by removing the end of it. This word does not fit in the blank because actors were not removing any aspect of their performance and the passage does not indicate that performances were shorter in any way. Rather, they were altering their approaches to acting. Therefore, choice A is the better option. **Choice E** is incorrect because "perniciousness" means grave harmfulness or deadliness. This word does not fit in the blank because the sentence is not describing theater as being harmful or dangerous in any way. Rather, the sentence is describing theater as becoming more natural. Therefore, choice A is the better option. **Choice F** is incorrect because "maleficence" means an act of committing harm or evil. This word does not fit in the blank because the sentence is not describing theater as being harmful or evil in any way. Rather, the sentence is describing theater as becoming more natural. Therefore, choice A is the better option.

4 Choice C is correct because "elitist" refers to an attitude that favors a social elite class. This word fits in the blank because only six movie studios in the nation monopolize more than 90% of profits. In other words, only a select number of individuals actually have much influence over the industry. **Choice D is correct** because "encumbrance" means a burden or impediment. This word fits in the blank because the sentence states that this model of operating is actually hurting, or hindering, those six movie studios. **Choice H is correct** because "inducement" refers to a persuasive influence to do something. This word fits in the blank because the sentence describes that the lack of competition means there is no motivation or persuasion to make changes.

Choice A is incorrect because "communal" means something shared by all members for common use. This word does not fit in the blank because the sentence is describing the movie industry's elitist setup—stating that only six movie studios receive more than 90% of the nation's movie revenue. This is the opposite of a communal structure, so Choice C is the better option. **Choice B** is incorrect because "indiscriminate" means done at random without careful judgment. This word does not fit in the blank because nothing in the sentence indicates that the movie studios are doing anything randomly. Therefore, Choice C is the better option. **Choice E** is incorrect because "alleviation" refers to the action of making suffering less severe. This word does not fit in the blank because the sentence doesn't suggest that the movie studios are suffering or in need of relief. Therefore, Choice D is the better option. **Choice F** is incorrect because "opacity" means obscurity or a lack of transparency. This is the opposite of what the sentence is saying, which is that something is evident or very clear. Therefore, Choice D is the better option. **Choice G** is incorrect because "dissuasion" means persuading someone not to take a particular course of action. This word doesn't fit because the passage explains that, in the absence of competition, there is no persuasion or influence on movie studios to act or change. Therefore, Choice H is the better option. **Choice I** is incorrect because "ingratitude" means a lack of thankfulness. This word doesn't fit in the blank because the sentence says nothing about studios being thankful. Therefore, Choice H is the better option.

5 Choice B is correct because the passage states that Fini "fraternized with" or "was friendly with" members such as Dali, Man Ray, and Ernst. Therefore, she was "congenial" or "pleasant" with them. In addition, she participated in group shows, so she was involved rather than "refraining" or "staying out of" such activities.

Choice A is incorrect because the passage explicitly states that Fini fraternized "with Salvador Dali, Man Ray, Max Ernst, and other members of the movement." Since "fraternized" refers to "spending time with someone" Fini had connections with at least a few of the members. It is unclear from the passage whether she avoids contact with "most" only that she did not like the founder, Breton. **Choice C** is incorrect because while Fini did participate in some group events like shows, there is no indication that Breton forbade her from joining. It is possible that Fini chose not to join because she did not like him. **Choice D** is incorrect because the passage does not refer to "romantic" relationships between Fini or any of the other Surrealists, even though she spent time with them. **Choice E** is incorrect because there is no indication that Surrealists were "restricted" or "not allowed" to explore a variety of media; the fact that Fini did a range of art styles could be representative of the group's pattern as a whole.

6 Choice D is correct because "distinctive" refers to something that is unique or one-of-a-kind. The word "likewise" emphasizes the fact that the motivation was not the only thing that was unique. Therefore, the earlier claim that Fini had "no formal art training" is compared here. In other words, the others had different motivations and education.

Choice A is incorrect because it is unclear whether rheumatic conjunctivitis was common or not; the passage only implies that the other Surrealist artists did not have their eyes covered for two months due to it. **Choice B** is incorrect because "distinctive" means "unique" and it does not contain any element of tragedy. Therefore, the word does not stress Fini's suffering or misfortune but only highlights the difference from other Surrealist artists. **Choice C** is incorrect because there is no indication that Fini painted while suffering from rheumatic conjunctivitis, only that she was inspired by the images she saw in her mind as a result of that experience. **Choice E** is incorrect because Fini's different motivation for painting was not a reason to be classified as a Surrealist; if anything, the difference would highlight the fact that she was not a standard group member.

7 **Choice A is correct** because the text states that manipulating the wings allows bats to "maneuver rapidly through confined areas" so presumably, the muscles are part of what help move the wings into the necessary "complex patterns" so the bats can "catch the air." Since Remezani is concerned about controlling the robots to "evade obstacles in flight" part of the maneuvering is around obstacles. Therefore, "navigation" or "control" is "facilitated" or "made easier."

Choice B is incorrect because the "sensitive hairs on the wings" not the muscles, are what "expedite" or "assist" flight "so they can maneuver and catch prey, even in the dark." **Choice C** is incorrect because while bats are described as having different wing shapes and features than birds, the text does not say that birds are "unable" or "cannot" navigate in the enclosed spaces. Presumably, they could still enter, but not move as fast or easily. **Choice D** is incorrect because while the text implies that bats do not have feathers because they have wing hairs instead, the evolution of muscles in the skin was not necessarily to "eliminate" or "stop" using such features. **Choice E** is incorrect because while the bats have wings with many joints, they could presumably have evolved to move the wings using regular muscles under the skin rather than develop specialized muscles within the skin itself. In fact, it is possible based on the information given that the bats have both kinds of muscles in their wings.

8 **Choice E is correct** because the second sentence states that bats "look like birds." In other words, they appear "superficially" or "on the surface" to have the same body shape or structure.

Choice A is incorrect because there is no discussion in the text about why birds evolved sustained flight. **Choice B** is incorrect because the passage states that bats have "complex flapping" but there is no discussion about how birds fly. It is possible that they manipulate their wings in only one way because they have fewer joints to make adjustments. **Choice C** is incorrect because the text states that bats evolved flight about 52 million years ago, but does not mention when birds evolved flight. **Choice D** is incorrect because there is no discussion about using birds as prototypes for robots, only bats.

9 **Choice D is correct** because the goal of creating a flying robot is "to inspect enclosed or potentially unstable spaces" which means that the robot could conduct a survey in an area that could be too small for a human to enter or collapse. It is logical to assume that Remezani therefore is envisioning that the robot could enter dangerous areas for paleological research and mining surveys instead of a human, reducing the chances of injuries to a human in such places.

Choice A is incorrect because there is no indication that Remezani is interested in studying bird wings at all. He is not concerned about differences in the wings; he is concerned about how to make a robot that flies like a bat does. **Choice B** is incorrect because while the research will indeed advance the knowledge of bat flight, Remezani wants to use the knowledge to make robots for mining companies and paleological research, not more research on bats. **Choice C** is incorrect because the passage only refers to the desire to "inspect" enclosed spaces. In other words, the robot would probably be used to analyze or survey the place, but other equipment would do any actual repairs. **Choice E** is incorrect because while Remezani may be curious how the evolution occurred, the text indicates that he is more interested in determining how to copy the flight for use in a robot.

10 **Choice A is correct** because "translucent" means allowing light to pass through without showing detailed shapes. This word fits in the blank because the sentence describes how frosted window glass blurs and softens light, but still allows it to pass through. **Choice D is correct** because "semi-opaque" means not fully clear. This word fits in the blank because the sentence explains that the frosted window blurs and softens light, allowing it through without revealing detailed shapes.

Choice B is incorrect because "obscure" means concealed or hidden from view. This word does not fit in the blank because the sentence indicates that some light passes through, so the view is not completely blocked. **Choice C** is incorrect because "crystalline" means having the structure or form of a crystal. This word does not fit because the sentence discusses the amount of light passing through the window, not its physical structure. **Choice E** is incorrect because "undiluted" means not weakened or moderated in any way. This word does not fit in the blank because the sentence describes the blurry view through a frosted window. If the window were undiluted, the view would not be softened or blurred. Therefore, Choices A and D are better options. **Choice F** is incorrect because "diaphanous" refers to a light, delicate texture, typically of fabric. Since the sentence is describing the appearance of the frosted window rather than its texture, Choices A and D are more appropriate.

4 Verbal Reasoning (Easy) — Answers & Explanations — Section 4

11 **Choice B is correct** because "resistance" means the refusal to comply with something or the act of preventing an action. This word fits in the blank because the sentence describes portions of liquid interacting with one another. Two liquids could resist or hinder each other's movement. **Choice E is correct** because "friction" refers to a force that opposes motion. This word fits in the blank because the sentence describes how portions of liquid interact. Two liquids could oppose or slow each other's movement through friction.

Choice A is incorrect because "attribute" means a quality or characteristic of something. This word does not fit in the blank because the sentence is describing the relationship and interaction between two parcels of liquid, requiring a word that reflects motion or physical force. Therefore, Choices B and E are better options. **Choice C is incorrect** because "conductivity" is the measure of how well a substance conducts electricity. This word does not fit in the blank because the sentence is not about electricity, and conductivity is not relevant to the interaction between parcels of liquid in this context. Therefore, Choices B and E are better options. **Choice D is incorrect** because "agreement" means harmony or accordance in opinion. This word does not fit in the blank because the sentence is about parcels of liquid, which cannot form opinions or reach agreements. Therefore, Choices B and E are better options. **Choice F is incorrect** because "altercation" means a noisy argument. This word does not fit in the blank because the sentence is referring to parcels of liquid, which cannot engage in arguments. Therefore, Choices B and E are better options.

12 **Choice A is correct** because "innocence" means a sense of purity and lack of corruption. This word fits in the blank because the sentence begins by discussing complex and polarizing modern works of art, then contrasts them with primitive works. Artwork that appears innocent would represent the opposite of the modern pieces described. **Choice B is correct** because "inexperience" means a lack of knowledge or skill. This word fits in the blank because the sentence contrasts sophisticated modern art with primitive works. Artwork that appears inexperienced would stand in opposition to the complex nature of modern art.

Choice C is incorrect because "precision" means being exact and accurate. This word does not fit in the blank because the sentence is describing ancient, simpler art. The reference to cave paintings suggests simplicity rather than exactness or technical precision. **Choice D is incorrect** because "professionalism" means the competence or skill expected of a professional. This word does not fit because it does not accurately describe primitive artwork. The sentence is emphasizing simplicity and contrast, not skill or formal standards. **Choice E is incorrect** because "imperviousness" means being impenetrable or unaffected by external influences. This word does not fit in the blank because the sentence focuses on the contrast between the emotional or conceptual weight of modern art and the simplicity of primitive art, not on how artwork responds to influence. **Choice F is incorrect** because "effervescence" means vivacity or liveliness. This word does not fit in the blank because the sentence is describing primitive works as simpler and potentially more subdued, not vibrant or energetic. Therefore, Choices A and B are the better options.

13 **Choice A is correct** because the conclusion about coercive leadership is that it is not beneficial or effective in the long term except in emergency situations. However, Choice A indicates that even in some long-term situations, there can be benefits, since there are fewer injuries even when there is no emergency.

Choice B is incorrect because even if a leader can switch between different leadership styles, coercive leadership may be ineffective except in emergency situations. **Choice C is incorrect** because it supports the claim that coercive leadership does not work well in the long run; another form has better results as far as employee turnover. Presumably, the reason is that the "followers tend to feel pressured and underappreciated" so they move to different jobs. **Choice D is incorrect** because it does not show that coercive leadership does not work in emergency situations; it only identifies a situation in which leadership is not needed. **Choice E is incorrect** because it only suggests that it is better to have a wide range of leadership styles than just use coercion, which supports the claim that coercion is only effective in emergency situations.

14 **Choice E is correct** because the passage begins by describing Pompeii and the fact that there is a "moratorium" or "ban" on excavation. In other words, digging is not allowed in Pompeii. However, Poehler suggests studying fragments and graffiti, since those things were "disregarded" or "ignored" in the past. Since modern technology can "facilitate" or "help" reconstruct what the larger objects look like, it is possible to learn more using this approach even though digging is no longer allowed.

Choice A is incorrect because while the passage does say that studying the fragments can "enhance modern understanding of everyday life from that period" that is the only benefit discussed. There is no "summary" or "list" of different benefits, nor is there an in-depth discussion of one benefit. **Choice B** is incorrect because the excavation techniques in the time of Don Carlos are mentioned, as is the fact that "modern techniques" are used, but the main point of the passage is not to contrast how these methods worked. The concern is how to continue research even though there is a moratorium on digging. **Choice C** is incorrect because there is no indication of a "misunderstanding" about how earlier methods were conducted. Though earlier methods were incomplete, that problem is correctly identified. **Choice D** is incorrect because the passage does not "refute" or "disprove" the claim that there is a "moratorium" or "ban" on all research, only on digging. Rather, the passage shows what can be done despite the ban.

15 **Choice C is correct** because the passage states that many of the workers were "blatant treasure hunters" meaning that they were deliberately working to get things they felt were valuable. If that is true, it is likely that these people stole items that they wanted. On the other hand, the overall plan was "methodical" or "conducted in an orderly way" since the passage points out that Don Carlos led the "first systematic excavations of the site."

Choice A is incorrect because the passage indicates that "even" Don Carlos did not focus on graffiti, since the workers were interested in stealing things or did not know what to study as they were "untrained." Therefore, today it is possible to learn from these things that had been ignored earlier. **Choice B** is incorrect because there is no indication why Don Carlos "terminated" or "ended" the excavations. It could have stopped after the king's death. **Choice D** is incorrect because while Poehler feels that studying graffiti is important, he does not indicate that earlier research should not have done any excavation. He is just suggesting a fuller investigation which involves the study of graffiti and fragments when excavation is done. **Choice E** is incorrect because there is no indication that Don Carlos was unable to find any facts about Pompeii at all. The passage only indicates that there is a possibility to expand on what is already known since it refers to the fact that fragments and graffiti can "enhance understanding." In other words, the earlier archaeologists found some facts, and now it is possible to expand on those facts.

Verbal Reasoning (Hard) — Answers & Explanations — Section 4

1 **Choice A is correct** because "pedestrian", in this context, means dull or lacking excitement. This word fits in the blank because it is describing a field that may seem dry or uninteresting but is actually critical to the application of chemistry.

Choice B is incorrect because "prevalent" means widespread in a particular area or time. The sentence is not discussing how common or widespread the study of inorganic bond angles is; rather, it is describing the perceived quality of the field. Since the sentence suggests the field seems boring, Choice A is the best fit. **Choice C is incorrect** because "torpid" means inactive or lethargic. The sentence does not comment on the level of activity in the field of inorganic bond angles. Instead, it contrasts the field's perceived dullness with its actual importance, making Choice A the better option. **Choice D is incorrect** because "applicable" means relevant or appropriate to a situation. This word does not convey the dullness or dryness implied in the sentence. The sentence suggests the field appears boring despite its critical value, so a more negative descriptor like "pedestrian" fits better. **Choice E is incorrect** because "parsimonious" means stingy or frugal. The sentence does not address anything related to frugality or spending. Since it's discussing the field's perceived lack of excitement, Choice A is the most appropriate choice.

2 **Choice B is correct** because "diametrically" means completely and directly. This word fits in the blank because the passage is explaining that atheists and agnostics may not be as fully opposed to religion as commonly believed. In other words, they are not necessarily diametrically against religion. **Choice E is correct** because "partition" means a division into parts. This word fits in the blank because the sentence expresses that there is not necessarily a firm line between religious and irreligious people. In other words, there is no definite partition separating the two groups.

Choice A is incorrect because "frugally" means done in an economical way without waste. This word does not fit in the blank because it does not describe the degree of opposition to religion. It is unrelated to the meaning conveyed in the sentence. Therefore, Choice B is the better option. **Choice C is incorrect** because "judiciously" means with good judgment or sense. This word does not fit because the sentence is not discussing the wisdom or reasoning of atheists and agnostics—it is discussing how strongly they oppose religion. Therefore, Choice B is the better option. **Choice D is incorrect** because "gamut" means the complete range or scope of something. The sentence is not describing a wide range of views or experiences, but rather the lack of a dividing line between religious and irreligious people. Therefore, Choice E is the better option. **Choice F is incorrect** because "accord" means an official agreement or treaty. The passage does not mention any formal agreement between religious and irreligious people. Instead, it refers to a perceived division between the groups, making Choice E the more appropriate word.

3 **Choice A is correct** because "cursory" means hasty to the point of lacking detail. This word fits in the blank because the sentence is describing that the most insignificant glance at a painting can still reveal much about the artist. **Choice F is correct** because "dynamic" means characterized by constant change, energy, or progress. This word fits in the blank because the sentence describes the unique colors that give the artist's work exceptional emotional intensity. **Choice H is correct** because "harrowing" means acutely distressing. This word fits in the blank because the sentence discusses the emotional pain and severity of the artist's struggle with mental illness.

Choice B is incorrect because "jaundiced" means affected by bitterness or envy. This does not describe how a viewer might glance at a painting. A better fit is Choice A, which reflects a brief or superficial look. **Choice C is incorrect** because "perspicacious" means having a keen understanding or insight. This does not fit the context of a quick glance at a painting. Again, Choice A is more appropriate. **Choice D is incorrect** because "incarnadine" refers to a bright crimson color. Since the sentence discusses a range of colors creating emotional intensity—not one specific color—Choice F is more suitable. **Choice E is incorrect** because "funereal" means having a mournful or somber tone appropriate for a funeral. This does not match the description of the bold and emotionally powerful use of color in the artist's work. Choice F better captures the intended meaning. **Choice G is incorrect** because "iniquitous" means morally wrong or unjust. While mental illness can be tragic, it is not appropriately described using moral terms like "iniquitous." Choice H is more accurate. **Choice I is incorrect** because "affected" means influenced by an external factor. This word does not express the emotional intensity or severity of the artist's mental illness, making Choice H the better option.

Verbal Reasoning (Hard) — Answers & Explanations — Section 4

4 **Choice A is correct** because "affectability" means the ability to be influenced by something. This word fits in the blank because the sentence expresses that the construction industry is seriously impacted by the condition of the economy. **Choice D is correct** because "benchmark" means a point of reference against which things can be assessed. This word fits in the blank because the passage explains that the condition of the construction industry can reflect the overall health of the economy. Therefore, the construction industry can serve as a benchmark for economic performance. **Choice H is correct** because "extrapolated" means extending known information to predict unknown outcomes. This word fits in the blank because the passage describes how the status of the construction industry can be used to predict economic trends. In other words, changes in construction can be extrapolated to infer the condition of the broader economy.

Choice B is incorrect because "frugality" means being economical or thrifty. This word does not fit in the blank because the sentence is not discussing spending habits within the construction industry. Instead, it emphasizes how the industry is influenced by economic conditions. **Choice C is incorrect** because "insignificance" means being too small or unimportant to matter. This word does not fit in the blank because the passage presents the construction industry as a meaningful and telling indicator of the economy, not something unimportant. **Choice E is incorrect** because "complication" refers to a difficulty or problem. This word does not fit in the blank because the passage is not suggesting that the construction industry hinders or complicates economic understanding. Instead, it helps reflect it, making Choice D the better option. **Choice F is incorrect** because "impediment" means an obstacle or hindrance. This does not fit in the blank because the construction industry is not obstructing economic assessment—it is actually serving as a reference point, which makes Choice D a more appropriate fit. **Choice G is incorrect** because "ameliorated" means made better or improved. This word does not fit in the blank because the construction industry is not improving the economy directly; rather, it serves as an indicator of its current state. **Choice I is incorrect** because "enervated" means weakened or drained of vitality. This does not fit in the blank because the construction industry is not depleting the economy's energy—it is being used to signal trends in economic activity.

5 **Choice B is correct** because the goal is to "weaken" the claim that geothermal energy is better than solar and wind. Choice B shows that a large amount of water is needed and some is not returned to the reservoir. If that is true, then it is possible that the reservoir will be depleted over time and there will be no more water. **Choice C is correct** because it shows that geothermal energy is only possible to use in certain areas. Technology will change, but for now, there is a reliance on natural reservoirs. Though geothermal energy may be effective in those places, it is not the best alternative in every situation.

Choice A is incorrect because it only shows that a third alternative may be even more effective than geothermal, wind, and solar energy. However, the conclusion in the passage is that geothermal energy is better than solar and wind. Choice A introduces an unrelated variable.

6 **Choice B is correct** because the passage indicates that cooling is possible because "groundwater can absorb excess heat" but that steam is used for heating purposes. Presumably, piping steam off for heat occurs in a different way than returning heat to water.

Choice A is incorrect because there is no discussion about the technology used in solar or wind power, so it is unclear from the information given which is more complex. **Choice C is incorrect** because the passage states that "future technology may use artificial subterranean lakes" but there is no other discussion about which technology has been used or not. Since geothermal energy "is used for cooling" it appears that the process is already being done. **Choice D is incorrect** because there is no discussion about whether different geothermal energy processes have to be done in different locations. The "facilities" or "buildings" might be the same, with one section using the heat and one putting heat back into the water to cool. **Choice E is incorrect** because there is no discussion about the price of any process in the passage. Cooling may be a little surprising to think about with heated water, but it may be cheaper than making electricity and then cooling the water using that electricity.

7 **Choice D is correct** because the first paragraph gives the standard view of Gentileschi's work as just capturing the strength and defiance of women. However, the second paragraph "establishes" or "shows" that the view is too limited since she drew models in a lifelike way that did not follow conventional patterns. Therefore, most people had "overlooked" or "did not pay attention" to that view until it was introduced by Harris and Nochlin in 1976. **Choice A** is incorrect because while the passage states that Caravaggio influenced Gentileschi's work, there is no evidence that it was "overly" or "too" influential. **Choice B** is incorrect because the passage mentions that Gentileschi was a respected female painter, but the main idea of the passage is not to show her "status and reputation" or "how famous she was." Instead, the passage is questioning whether her paintings were overly stereotyped. **Choice C** is incorrect because the passage does not change the view that the subjects of the paintings were stereotyped; it accepts that Gentileschi mostly painted "allegorical and mythological scenes popular at the time." Rather, the passage assesses whether she used stereotypical painting treatments in rendering skin. **Choice E** is incorrect because while the passage says it was unusual for a woman to be a painter, there is no other discussion of "obstacles" or "barriers" to her painting.

8 **Choice E is correct** because it shows that even though it was unusual to use live models, Gentileschi was aware of the practice, since she knew Caravaggio, a person who used models. She may even have learned to use live models from him. Since Harris and Nochlin's claim is that Gentileschi was a master of detail and probably used live models to achieve that level of detail, this choice supports the idea that she did indeed do so.

Choice A is incorrect because it stresses the allegorical or stylistic nature of Gentileschi's work by citing a painting that is allegorical rather than supporting the claim that her work was not stylized. **Choice B** is incorrect because Harris and Nochlin say that Gentileschi used live models, but if she worked with other artists, they may have added the natural details. Therefore, this choice does not strengthen the claim that she used models. **Choice C** is incorrect because it only shows that another woman was a painter and a friend of Gentileschi, which does not strengthen the idea that Gentileschi had a naturalistic style. **Choice D** is incorrect because it talks about the subject of the paintings, but does not say whether the paintings were naturalistic or not.

9 **Choice B is correct** because the highlighted sentence refers to how Gentileschi was viewed by feminists in the twentieth century. That is a contrast to the previous situation, where she was ignored by art historians because she was a woman. The highlighted sentence also sets up a contrast with the following paragraph, in which a more rounded view of Gentileschi is presented.

Choice A is incorrect because the perspective that Gentileschi painted strong and defiant women is not "disproved" or "shown to be wrong." Rather, the following paragraph shows that the artist used subtle details to convey strength and defiance. **Choice C** is incorrect because there is no discussion about why Harris and Nochlin decided to feature Gentileschi's work in the show. It is possible that they put the exhibit together in order to disprove the common stereotype. **Choice D** is incorrect because the preceding sentence talks about why few analyses were made of Gentileschi's work as she was a woman. The fact that her art was viewed as strong and defiant shows why the feminists chose to analyze her work. **Choice E** is incorrect because the sentence states that she painted strong women, but there is no indication that she "abandoned" or "did not use" the contemporary trends. Rather, the sentence shows that she "adeptly used the period's conventions" or "followed the styles of the day."

10 **Choice A is correct** because "frisson" means a sudden strong feeling of excitement. This word fits in the blank because the sentence describes the reaction of the crowd when something significant happened during an otherwise uneventful game. **Choice C is correct** because "thrill" also means a sudden feeling of excitement or pleasure. Like "frisson" this word matches the context of the crowd's reaction to the intercepted pass in a slow-paced game.

Choice B is incorrect because "immediacy" means urgency or instant relevance. This word does not fit in the blank because the game is described as having slowed to a crawl, implying that the intercepted pass came after a long lull, not with urgency. **Choice D** is incorrect because "folly" means foolishness or a lack of good sense. This does not accurately describe the intercepted pass or the crowd's reaction—it was a moment of excitement, not senselessness. **Choice E** is incorrect because "rapidity" means speed or swiftness. This word does not fit the context, as the game had slowed significantly, and the sentence does not suggest a fast pace. **Choice F** is incorrect because "arrogance" means excessive pride or self-importance. This word has no relevance to the context of an intercepted pass creating excitement among spectators and does not logically fit the sentence.

Verbal Reasoning (Hard) — Answers & Explanations — Section 4

11 **Choice C is correct** because "ramifications" means the consequences of an action. This word fits the blank because the sentence is describing the act of using quantum physics to discover new universes while noting that the resulting effects of such an action are unknown. **Choice F is correct** because "consequences" means the result or effect of an action. This word fits the blank because the sentence explains that although quantum physics may help discover new universes, the effects of such a discovery remain uncertain.

Choice A is incorrect because "transfusion" refers to the act of transferring something—usually blood—into another being. This term does not relate to the subject of the sentence. Quantum physics is not giving or receiving anything in a way that fits this definition. **Choice B** is incorrect because "broadcast" refers to transmitting information by radio or television. This word does not relate to the scientific exploration described in the sentence. Quantum physics is not being transmitted in this context. **Choice D** is incorrect because "ratifications" means the formal approval of an agreement or treaty. There is no mention of treaties or official agreements in the sentence, so this word does not logically fit. **Choice E** is incorrect because "strident" is an adjective meaning loud and harsh. Since the blank requires a noun and the sentence has no indication of anything being loud or harsh, this word is both grammatically and contextually inappropriate.

12 **Choice C is correct** because "consolidates" means combining a number of things into a solid whole. This word fits the context of the sentence, which discusses dissolved chemicals being made easier to remove. Rather than removing many small particles, the polymer attracts them and turns them into a solid whole. **Choice F is correct** because in chemistry, "precipitates" means a dissolved substance is deposited in solid form. This accurately fits the context, which involves removing dissolved chemicals by turning them into a solid.

Choice A is incorrect because "rainfall" is a noun that does not fit in the blank, which requires a verb. Also, the fall of rain is irrelevant in the context of the sentence, which discusses using polymer to remove chemicals from water. **Choice B** is incorrect because "accelerates" means to begin to move more quickly. This word does not fit the sentence because the sentence does not mention anything about the speed of chemicals dissolving, consolidating, or being removed from the water. **Choice D** is incorrect because "precipitation" is a noun that does not fit in the blank, which requires a verb. Therefore, Choice F is the better option. **Choice E** is incorrect because "impels" means to drive forward or propel. This word does not fit the context of the sentence, which discusses making the removal of dissolved chemicals from water easier—not speed or force. Therefore, Choices C and F are the better options.

13 **Choice D is correct** because the goal is to weaken the claim that cold therapy "alleviates" or "reduces" the effects of inflammation, but women in a colder bath had more inflammatory molecules than a group that did not have a cold bath after exercising. If that is true, then the women experienced a negative or worse effect, since they had more inflammation.

Choice A is incorrect because if the molecules measured are considered adequate to show adverse effects, then more molecules do not need to be measured. **Choice B** is incorrect because it strengthens rather than weakens the results of the experiment by showing that one possible problem that might interfere with the results was eliminated: people with chronic inflammation from a different source were not included. **Choice C** is incorrect because it shows that a situation in which men did not experience a large amount of exercise did not result in a "statistically significant" or "valid" difference. However, these men may not have done enough exercise to provoke an inflammatory response. **Choice E** is incorrect because even though men and women had different responses, ice might have reduced the inflammation in both cases.

14 **Choice B is correct** because the first paragraph states that "women made functional textiles for home use" because textile arts "fall into gender stereotypes" starting in the Middle Ages. In the World Wars, that "partitioning was persistent" because textiles "were the provenance of domestic utility." In other words, women and not men did textile arts during those periods. **Choice C is correct** because the first paragraph states that textile arts were crafts, showing that they were considered beneath "true" arts like painting and sculpture, which men studied for a long time to produce. In addition, the second paragraph shows that the textile arts were used for "garments and other household items" and were made out of "thrift" or "the need to save money." Therefore, they were not thought of as manifestations of artistic expression.

Choice A is incorrect because the passage points out that in the Victorian Era, "wealthy woman" would "pass time" by doing needlework, but this view is not necessarily true for the Middle Ages or the World Wars. In the Middle Ages, "women running their households" made textiles for use in the home, and during the World Wars, women did textiles for thrift, so they may have been doing other things to save money and run their homes other than relaxing idly.

15 **Choice A is correct** because the passage indicates that women were associated with making textiles and that these items were functional for home use or garments, so it is reasonable to assume that one reason for that view is that they were practical rather than ornamental like sculpture or painting. **Choice B is correct** because the passage states that "That partitioning was—and to a degree, still is—persistent." In other words, though the perception is less strong, it still exists. Thus, the belief is that women, not men, should make textile art. **Choice C is correct** because the passage states that the stereotype of textile arts "dates back to the Middle Ages." If the roots went farther back in time, then the passage would say that the roots started in an earlier period. Therefore, "prior to" or "before" that period, textile arts were not thought to be women's arts. If so, then men probably made them as well.

Quantitative Reasoning (Easy)   Answers & Explanations   Section 5

1 **Choice B is correct** because the fraction of green balloons would be $\frac{3}{8}$ and the ratio of green balloons to white balloons would be $\frac{3}{5}$. Therefore, Quantity B is larger since $\frac{3}{5} > \frac{3}{8}$.

Choice A is incorrect because $\frac{3}{8}$ is not larger than $\frac{3}{5}$. **Choice C** is incorrect because $\frac{3}{8}$ does not equal $\frac{3}{5}$. **Choice D** is incorrect because it is possible to determine a relationship between the values.

2 **Choice A is correct** because the surface area of the box is 174 while the volume of the box is 135.

- To find surface area use the formula $S = 2lw + 2lh + 2wh$. Plugging into this formula with the given dimensions would get you $S = 2(5)(3) + 2(5)(9) + 2(3)(9)$ which equals 174.
- To find volume, use the formula $V = lwh$. Plugging into this will get you $V = (5)(3)(9)$ which equals 135.

Choice B is incorrect because the volume is not greater than the surface area. **Choice C** is incorrect because the surface area is not equal to the volume. **Choice D** is incorrect because it is possible to solve for the surface area and volume.

3 **Choice C is correct** because to make the two sides of the equation match, you would only be able to divide by 1. Setting 3^x equal to 1 would mean the exponent would have to be 0. This makes $x = 0$ which means both Quantity A and Quantity B are the same.

Choice A is incorrect because Quantity A is not greater than Quantity B. **Choice B** is incorrect because Quantity B is not greater than Quantity A. **Choice D** is incorrect because it is possible to determine a relationship.

4 **Choice A is correct** because the perimeter of triangle BCX can be determined to be $12 + 4\sqrt{3}$ which is approximately 18.9 and this is greater than the area of triangle BCX which would be $8\sqrt{3}$ which is approximately 13.9.

To find the perimeter of triangle BCX, you first need to find its side lengths. Since you know that triangle ABC has a perimeter of 24 and is an equilateral triangle, you know all three side lengths are equal. Dividing 24 by 3 would give a side length of 8.

Triangle BCX can be determined to be a 30-60-90 triangle and follows the ratio of side lengths of x, $x\sqrt{3}$, and $2x$. Knowing the hypotenuse of the triangle is 8, that would make its shortest leg 4 and its longest leg $4\sqrt{3}$. The perimeter of the triangle is therefore $8 + 4 + 4\sqrt{3}$ which equals $12 + 4\sqrt{3}$.

To find the area of triangle BCX, use the formula $A = \frac{1}{2}bh$. Plugging into this formula you would get $A = \frac{1}{2}(4)(4\sqrt{3})$ which can be simplified to be $8\sqrt{3}$.

Choice B is incorrect because the perimeter is greater than the area. **Choice C** is incorrect because the perimeter and area are not equal. **Choice D** is incorrect because it is possible to determine a relationship between the perimeter and area.

5 **Choice D is correct** because using the distance formula it can be found that a equals either 0 or 8 which makes it not possible to identify a relationship.

- Plug in your known values into the distance formula to solve for a.
  $d = \sqrt{(x_2 - x_1)^2 + (y_2 - y_1)^2}$.
- Set equal to the known distance to get
  $5 = \sqrt{(4 - a)^2 + (8 - 5)^2}$.
- Simplify $5 = \sqrt{(4 - a)^2 + 9}$ and then square both sides to get $25 = (4 - a)^2 + 9$.
- Subtract 9 from both sides to get $16 = (4 - a)^2$.
- Take the square root of both sides and make sure to account for both solutions. The square root of 16 will give you both 4 and −4 so your two equations will be $4 = 4 - a$ and $-4 = 4 - a$.
- Solve both equations to get $a = 8$ and $a = 0$.

Choice A is incorrect because a would not be greater than 8 in any instance. **Choice B** is incorrect because a could equal 8. **Choice C** is incorrect because a could equal 0.

6 **Choice B is correct** because y can be found to equal $\frac{16}{3}$ which is less than $\frac{17}{3}$.

To solve for y, first, write out all the given information into mathematical formulas. The statement y is 4 more than x would give us the equation $y - 4 = x$. The statement z is 16 more than y would give us the equation $z = y + 16$.

202 | *Practice Tests for the GRE*

4 Quantitative Reasoning (Easy) Answers & Explanations   Section 5 4

Cross multiply the given statement $\frac{x}{y} = \frac{y}{z}$ to get $y^2 = xz$. Then plug in the formulas from the last step to get $y^2 = (y - 4)(y + 16)$.

Distribute and simplify the expression to get $y^2 = y^2 + 12y - 64$. Now solve for y by canceling the y^2 on both sides and then subtracting over the $12y$ to get $-12y = -64$. Divide both sides by -12 and you will get $y = \frac{16}{3}$.

Choice A is incorrect because y is less than $\frac{17}{3}$. **Choice C** is incorrect because y does not equal $\frac{17}{3}$. **Choice D** is incorrect because it is possible to solve for a relationship between the two values.

7 **Choice C is correct** because using a linear relationship you can determine the percent increase to be

- Each year the price of the pasta sauce went up $0.60. After 5 years, this would put the price of the pasta sauce at $7.55 ($4.55 + (0.6 \times 5)$).
- To find the percent increase from the original plug into the formula $\left|\frac{initial - final}{initial}\right| \times 100$. Plugging in would get you $\left|\frac{4.55 - 7.55}{4.55}\right| \times 100$ which equals about 66%.

Choice A is incorrect because this is just the percent increase for one year. **Choice B** is incorrect because this is the answer if you incorrectly solved with 7.55 as the initial value in the formula. **Choice D** is incorrect because this would result from a calculation error. **Choice E** is incorrect because this would result from a calculation error.

8 **Choice C is correct** because if you convert Car A's speed to $\frac{miles}{hour}$ by dividing by 1.6 you will get $\frac{60}{1.6} = 37.5$. Subtracting $45 - 37.5$ would give you 7.5 as the positive difference between the two speeds in $\frac{miles}{hour}$.

Choice A is incorrect because this answer results from a calculation error. **Choice B** is incorrect because this answer results from a calculation error. **Choice D** is incorrect because this answer results from a calculation error. **Choice E** is incorrect because this is the difference between the two speeds if you do not convert.

9 **The correct answer is 12** because to get the greatest possible value of $x - y$ you would want to to plug in the greatest possible value of x and the most negative value of y. The greatest possible value of x is 10 and the most negative value of y is -2. Plugging these in will give you $10 - (-2)$ which equals 12.

10 **Choice B is correct** because using the formula for simple interest, $S = Prt$, you would get an interest rate of 6%. Setting the equation equal to the interest earned and plugging in the principal balance and time would give you $2,070 = (11,500)(r)(3)$. Multiply and then divide to get $r = 0.06$ which would be 6%.

Choice A is incorrect because this is the result of a calculation error. **Choice C** is incorrect because this is the result of a calculation error. **Choice D** is incorrect because this is the result of a calculation error. **Choice E** is incorrect because this is not accounting for 3 years.

11 **Choice C is correct** because it can be concluded that half of all possible arrangements puts 'M' before 'R'. Think of if we just had two letters RM, the possible arrangements would be RM and MR. Half of these arrangements put 'M' before 'R'. This will occur on any scale. To find all arrangements use 5! to get 120. Then divide 120 in half to get 60 possible occurrences.

Choice A is incorrect because this does not account for all possible options. **Choice B** is incorrect because this does not account for all possible options. **Choice D** is incorrect because this is more than the possible occurrences. **Choice E** is incorrect because this is just the total way to rearrange the letters and not instances where 'M' comes before 'R'.

12 **Choice A is correct** because you can use the repeated units digits of both numbers and their powers to solve.

Any digit that ends in a 5 always has a unit digit of 5 when raised to any power. For example, $5^2 = 25$ and $15^3 = 3375$. Therefore, the unit digit of 15^8 would give us a 5.

Any digit that ends in a 4 goes through a cycle when raised to a power. Unit digits will end in a 4 for odd powers and a 6 for even powers. Therefore, the unit digit of 24^4 would give us a 6.

Multiplying 5 by 6 would give us 30 which has a units digit of 0.

Choice B is incorrect because this is the result of a calculation error. **Choice C** is incorrect because this is the

4 Quantitative Reasoning (Easy) Answers & Explanations   Section 5

result of a calculation error. **Choice D** is incorrect because this is the unit digit just for 15^8. **Choice E** is incorrect because this is the unit digit just for 24^4.

13 **Choice A and B are correct.** A data set that has a median greater than the average would have one or two numbers that are much smaller than the rest. Choice A is correct because it has one number that is smaller than the rest so the average is less than the median. Choice B is correct because it has two numbers that are smaller than the rest so the average will be less than the median.

Choice C is incorrect because it has an even distribution of numbers so its median and average would be the same. **Choice D** is incorrect because any data set that consists of the same repeated number has the same median and average. **Choice E** is incorrect because there is one larger number that makes the mean greater than the median.

14 **Choice E is correct** because the data set with the greatest standard deviation can be found quickly by evaluating the spread of the numbers. All of the other data sets are spread out by 0.1 to 2. Answer E has the highest range of 6 which is often indicative of high standard deviation as well.

Choice A is incorrect because this set's standard deviation is less than Choice E's. **Choice B** is incorrect because this set's standard deviation is less than Choice E's. **Choice C** is incorrect because this set's standard deviation is less than Choice E's. **Choice D** is incorrect because this set's standard deviation is less than Choice E's.

15 **Choices A and C are correct.** Choice A is correct because you can use the slope formula $\frac{y_2 - y_1}{x_2 - x_1}$ to evaluate the missing y value of point P. Plugging into this formula you would get $-\frac{1}{3} = \frac{2 - t}{19 - 10}$.

Simplify to get the statement $-\frac{1}{3} = \frac{2 - t}{9}$. Cross multiply to get $-9 = 6 - 3t$. Subtract 6 and divide by -3 to solve for $t = 5$. Choice C is correct because you can use the midpoint formula $m = \frac{y_1 + y_2}{2}$ to find point P. Plugging into the midpoint formula you would get $\frac{7}{2} = \frac{t + 2}{2}$ which would give you $t = 5$.

Choice B is incorrect because the distance formula will result in two possible values for the y coordinate for point P.

4 Quantitative Reasoning (Hard) Answers & Explanations — Section 5

1 **Choice A is correct** because to find the mean you will add all the numbers together and divide by the amount of numbers in the set. Set A's mean would equal $\frac{5+4+7+9+20}{5}$ which simplifies to be 9. Set B's mean would equal $\frac{0+5+4+7+9}{5}$ which simplifies to be 5. This makes Quantity A greater than Quantity B.

Choice B is incorrect because Set B's mean is less than Set A's mean. **Choice C** is incorrect because the two means are not equal. **Choice D** is incorrect because it is possible to solve for both means.

2 **Choice D is correct** because it is possible to get values where Quantity A is greater and less than Quantity B.

For example, if you plug in −3 into Quantity A, you would get the statement $\frac{1}{2}|4-(-3)|$ which equals $\frac{7}{2}$. For Quantity B, if $x = -3$, then you would get $2|-3|$ which equals 6. In this situation, Quantity B is greater than Quantity A.

If you plug in the value 0, Quantity A would be $\frac{1}{2}|4-0|$ which equals 2. Quantity B would be $2|0|$ which equals 0. This would mean Quantity A is greater than Quantity B.

Choice A is incorrect because only sometimes is Quantity A greater. **Choice B** is incorrect because only sometimes is Quantity B greater. **Choice C** is incorrect because Quantity A and Quantity B do not always equal each other.

3 **Choice B is correct** because the equations can be simplified to determine the exponent value of Quantity B will be greater.

Use the properties of exponents and the rule that when you divide terms with the same base, you can divide exponents to simplify the equation $\frac{a^b}{a^{b+1}}$ to get $\frac{1}{a}$ since $b - (b+1)$ would leave you with −1.

Apply the same idea to $\frac{a^{b+1}}{a^b}$ to get a^1 by subtracting $b + 1 - b = 1$.

This means Quantity A equals $1 + \frac{1}{a}$ and Quantity B equals $1 + a$. If $a > 1$ then a will be greater than $\frac{1}{a}$ making Quantity B greater than Quantity A.

Choice A is incorrect because the exponent value of Quantity A is less than the exponent value of Quantity B. **Choice C** is incorrect because the two simplified quantities do not equal each other. **Choice D** is incorrect because it is possible to compare the quantities.

4 **Choice A is correct** because ∠A can be found to be 65° and you can deduce Symbol C to be less than 65.

If ∠BDC = 115° then you can use 180 − 115 to find that ∠BDA = 65° since these angles are supplementary. Using the fact AB = DB, you can also conclude ∠A = 65° since congruent sides of angles have equal angle measures.

If ∠A = 65° and ∠D = 65° then ∠ABD must 50° be since 180 − (65 + 65) = 50. This means ∠DBC plus ∠C must be equal to 180 minus 115 which is 65°. Therefore, it is not possible for ∠C ≥ 65° since ∠DBC + ∠C = 65°.

Choice B is incorrect because ∠C is less than 65°. **Choice C** is incorrect because the two values cannot be equal. **Choice D** is incorrect because it is possible to determine a relationship.

5 **Choice A is correct** because the polygon is an octagon with exterior angles each measuring 45° and an area of approximately 43.46. This would make Quantity A larger than Quantity B.

To determine that the shape is an octagon use the idea that the sum of interior angles is equal to 180 times the number of sides minus 2. This would mean $1080 = 180(n − 2)$. Solve for n by dividing by 180 to get $6 = n − 2$. Then add 2 to get $n = 8$.

Now use the relationship that exterior angles of polygons must always add up to 360 and divide 360 by 8 to get the value of each exterior angle to be 45.

To find the area of an octagon, you can use the formula $A = 2(1 + \sqrt{2})a^2$ where a is your side length. Plugging in 3 to get $A = 2(1 + \sqrt{2})3^2$ which will simplify to be about 43.46.

Choice B is incorrect because the area is not greater than the numerical value of each exterior angle. **Choice C** is incorrect because the two quantities are not equal. **Choice D** is incorrect because it is possible to determine a relationship between the two quantities.

6 **Choice C is correct** because you will first need to determine the number of possible combinations by using $_{10}C_4$ since there are 10 possible options for 4 spots. This will give you 210 total options.

If you place Lee on the committees you will have 3 spots to fill with 8 possible options (10 members minus Lee and Paula). This will give you the combination $_8C_3$ which equals 56.

4 Quantitative Reasoning (Hard) Answers & Explanations Section 5

This means of all possible options, 56 of the possible committees would include Lee and not Paula which would be a probability of $\frac{56}{210}$ which simplifies to $\frac{4}{15}$.

Choice A is incorrect because this would be the result if you used $_8C_2$. **Choice B** is incorrect because this would result from not using combinations. **Choice D** is incorrect because this would be the result if you used $_8C_4$. **Choice E** is incorrect because this would result from a calculation error.

7 **Choice E is correct** because since YAZ is an equilateral triangle, it can be determined that side length YZ is 8 based on 30-60-90 ratios of x, $x\sqrt{3}$, and $2x$. The longest leg is $x\sqrt{3}$ which is $4\sqrt{3}$ so the hypotenuse must be 8 since it is $2x$. Since YZ is 8, that means the area of the square is 64 since $A = s^2$ which would be $A = 8^2 = 64$.

Choice A is incorrect because this would result from a calculation error. **Choice B** is incorrect because this is the side length, not the area of the square. **Choice C** is incorrect because this would be the area if the side length was incorrectly determined to be 4. **Choice D** is incorrect because this would result from a calculation error.

8 **Choice D is correct** because you can create the equation $20t - 14t = 900$ from the given information, where t is the time in minutes. Simplifying this expression would get you $6t = 900$. Divide both sides by 6 to get $t = 150$. Divide this by 60 to get 2.5 hours.

Choice A is incorrect because Machine A has only packaged 360 more boxes at this point. **Choice B** is incorrect because Machine A has only packaged 540 more boxes at this point. **Choice C** is incorrect because Machine A has only packaged 720 more boxes at this point. **Choice E** is incorrect because Machine A packaged over 900 boxes more at this point.

9 **Choice D is correct** because by process of elimination, all other answers can be ruled out, and testing numerous options will confirm that y is always divisible by x. For example, if $y = 4$ and $x = 2$, then $\frac{4^2}{2} = 2$ would satisfy the statement that $\frac{y^2}{x}$ is even. This then shows y is divisible by x because $\frac{4}{2}$ equals 2.

Choice A is incorrect because you can divide an even number by an odd number to get an even number, for example, if $y = 6$ and $x = 3$ the statements still hold. **Choice B** is incorrect because x does not have to equal y. **Choice C** is incorrect because there are instances where x can be less than y, for example, $x = 2$ and $y = 4$ hold the statements true. **Choice E** is incorrect because x and y could both be even integers and an even minus an even is not an odd.

10 **Choice A is correct** because of the original 150 employees, 60% were remote workers which can be found using the expression $150 \times 0.60 = 90$ and of the 30 new employees, 40% of them are remote workers which can be found using the expression $30 \times 0.40 = 12$. Adding these numbers together gets you 102 workers. Divide 102 by the total workforce of 180 employees to get approximately 58%.

Choice B is incorrect because this is the percentage of just the original workers who are remote. **Choice C** is incorrect because this would result from a calculation error. **Choice D** is incorrect because this would result from a calculation error. **Choice E** is incorrect because this would result from a calculation error.

11 **Choices A, C and D are correct** because from the given information you can solve for x by multiplying 600 by 0.185 to get 111 for x. This will give you 111. (37% will be 0.37 when converted to a demical and $300 \times 0.37 = 111$). Choice C is correct because this will give you 111. ($13\frac{7}{8}$% equals 13.875% which is 0.1385 when converted to a decimal so $0.13875 \times 800 = 111$). Choice D is correct because this will give you 111. (111% is 1.11 when converted to a decimal and $1.11 \times 100 = 111$).

Choice B is incorrect because this will not give you 111. (9% is 0.09 when converted to a decimal so $0.09 \times 1200 = 108$). **Choice E** is incorrect because this will not give you 111. (0.1% is 0.001 when converted to a decimal and $0.001 \times 1000 = 1$). **Choice F** is incorrect because this will not give you 111. ($\frac{1}{4}$% is 0.25% which is 0.0025 as a decimal so $0.0025 \times 2400 = 6$)

12 **Choice B is correct** because to find the 20th and 50th term, divide both by 3 since the sequence repeats every 2. 20 divided by 3 yields a remainder of 2 which means the 20th term is the 2nd term or 6. Dividing 50 by 3 gives a remainder of 2 as well which means the 50th term is also 6.

4 Quantitative Reasoning (Hard) Answers & Explanations — Section 5

Start the pattern as 6, 10, 2 to account for this, and evaluate how many of these three terms you will have between 20 and 50. 50 - 20 gives us 30 numbers which divided by 3 means we would get 10 sets. Adding together 6 + 10 + 2 yields 18 and multiplying 18 by 10 gives us 180.

Choice A is incorrect because this would result from a calculation error. **Choice C** is incorrect because this would result from a calculation error. **Choice D** is incorrect because this would result from a calculation error. **Choice E** is incorrect because this is the sum of all terms from the 1st to the 50th.

13 **The correct answer is 2** because it is important to first simplify the expression to understand if we are looking for the largest or smallest x and y. The equation can be simplified to be $\frac{1}{x} - \frac{1}{y}$ by first splitting the expression into $\frac{x}{xy} - \frac{y}{xy}$ and canceling like terms. To get the maximum possible value of this new expression, you would want the lowest possible positive value of x and the smallest possible negative value of y since they are in the denominator of the expressions. The lowest possible positive value of x is 1 which would make the first statement equal 1. If you plug in the lowest negative value of y you would get $1 - (-1)$ which is 2.

14 **Choice B is correct** because you can approximate the slope of the line using any two points. If you plug (1.5, 12) and (3.2, 22) into the slope formula $\frac{y_2 - y_1}{x_2 - x_1}$ you would get $\frac{22 - 12}{3.2 - 1.5}$ which equals 5.8 so you should look for a slope that is fairly large and positive. This would eliminate all answers except for Choice B and Choice C. Now plug into both equations one of the points and see which one is most accurate. Using the point (4.5, 30), Choice B gets closest with a value of 34.4 ($y = 8.2(4.5) - 2.5 = 34.4$) whereas Choice C outputs 21.2 ($y = 3.8(4.5) + 4 = 21.1$).

Choice A is incorrect because its slope does not match the slope of the data set. **Choice C** is incorrect because it does not accurately represent the values in the graph. **Choice D** is incorrect because it has a negative slope. **Choice E** is incorrect because it has a negative slope.

15 **Choices C and E are correct.** It is only possible to determine that y is negative since the other two numbers being raised to an even power would make them positive. If $x^2y^3z^4 < 0$ then it must be y making the entire statement negative. Choice C is correct because it does not matter what x is because any number squared would be positive. Since y is negative, x^2y has to be negative as well. Choice E is correct because y must be negative for the given statement to be negative.

Choice A is incorrect because x or z could be negative and even though y is negative xyz could be positive or negative. **Choice B** is incorrect because x or z could be negative so xz could be positive or negative. **Choice D** is incorrect because x could be positive or negative.

This page is intentionally left blank

Chapter 6
Practice Test #5

IMPORTANT
READ THE INSTRUCTIONS BEFORE BEGINNING THE TEST

1. Take this test under real testing conditions. Put away any distractions and sit in a quiet place with no disturbances. Keep a rough paper, some pencils, and a calculator beside you.

2. Begin with **Section 1** of the test on page 210. Write your essay in 30 minutes.

3. Next, move to **Section 2 - Verbal Reasoning** on page 212.
   - ❏ Attempt all questions and note the number of correct answers using the answer key on page 232.
   - ❏ If you get fewer than 7 correct, proceed to **Section 4 - Verbal Reasoning (Easy)** on page 218.
   - ❏ If you get 7 or more correct, proceed to **Section 4 - Verbal Reasoning (Hard)** on page 222.

4. After that, take **Section 3 - Quantitative Reasoning** on page 215.
   - ❏ Complete the section, then check your score using the answer key on page 233.
   - ❏ If you get fewer than 7 correct, proceed to **Section 5 - Quantitative Reasoning (Easy)** on page 226.
   - ❏ If you get 7 or more correct, proceed to **Section 5 - Quantitative Reasoning (Hard)** on page 229.

5. Complete Section 4 and Section 5, respectively, and note down the number of correct answers you got right in each section.

6. Calculate your **Scaled Score** on page 317 for the test.

7. Review **detailed explanations** for all questions beginning on page 234.

Section 1 - Analytical Writing

Analyze an Issue
30 Minutes

People should undertake risky action only after they have carefully considered its consequences. Write a response in which you discuss the extent to which you agree or disagree with the recommendation and explain your reasoning for the position you take. In developing and supporting your position, describe specific circumstances in which adopting the recommendation would or would not be advantageous and explain how these examples shape your position.

You may start writing your response here

Section 2 - Verbal Reasoning

18 Minutes | 12 Questions

For Questions 1 and 2, for each blank, select one entry from the corresponding column of choices. Fill all blanks in the way that best completes the text.

1. Our group worked _____ on the account; for months many of us got to work early and left late, and some even took work home.

A ambiguously
B exultantly
C formidably
D imperturbably
E assiduously

2. The (i) _____ nature of paleontology is as exciting as it is frustrating. A team of paleontologists can spend months on one site, digging meticulously through layers of topsoil, only to come home empty-handed. And after this entire painstaking process is over, it is entirely possible that the team will be (ii) _____ to discover that a rainstorm uncovered in an hour what they couldn't in an entire summer.

Blank (i)	Blank (ii)
A capricious	D disillusioned
B intractable	E rapt
C pensive	F debilitated

3. The Hundred Schools of Thought was a profoundly (i) _____ period in the history of philosophy. From roughly 800 BCE to 200 BCE, philosophers and teachers enjoyed unprecedented development and influence in Chinese politics. Unfortunately, many of these influences were (ii) _____ from history when the Qin Dynasty launched a campaign of bloody retribution against those it felt promoted dissent. Still, the (iii) _____ ideas from the Hundred Schools of Thought have had lasting influences in our modern world.

Blank (i)	Blank (ii)	Blank (iii)
A inane	D liberated	G lamented
B vibrant	E expunged	H defunct
C avaricious	F inoculated	I extant

For Questions 4 and 5, select one answer choice unless otherwise instructed.

Question 4 is based on this passage.

Recent studies conducted in Australia indicate that one of the sources of superbugs - antibiotic-resistant bacteria - that have posed significant health risks to the public may be the feces of certain seagulls. Although only one out of every ten seagulls examined was carrying a strain that was resistant to an antibiotic, hand-washing after coming into contact with any droppings is recommended to reduce the risk of infection. Findings are still preliminary, but stronger precautions and more effective waste management practices have been advised.

Section 2 - Verbal Reasoning

For the following question, consider each of the choices separately and select all that apply.

4. According to the passage, what actions may need to be taken in response to the threat seagulls pose to public health?

   A. Since contact with droppings is necessary for infection and washing one's hands is effective at eliminating the risk of contamination, no action needs to be taken.

   B. Since washing hands only reduces the risk and antibiotic-resistant infections are very hard to treat, preventive measures are recommended.

   C. Immediate action by governments globally is needed to issue severe warnings and prevent any possible contact.

Question 5 is based on this passage.

Candy's Chocolate Shoppe has stores in several malls throughout the state. Sales have increased every year. Her best-selling item is a chocolate-covered cream flavored with locally produced maple syrup. Candy has recently contracted to open stores in two malls in another state next year. She plans to feature the chocolate-covered maple cream and has placed a large order for future delivery to her new stores. She predicts that the popular candy will generate significant sales and profits in these stores.

5. Which of the following conditions could undermine Candy's prediction of sales and profits in her new stores?

   A. Her lease agreement requires her to pay a percentage of her sales to the mall management.

   B. These malls have other candy stores that feature their own locally-sourced specialty items.

   C. The new malls have 20 more stores than the malls where she currently has shops.

   D. The weather conditions this past spring were not favorable for sap production in the maple trees.

   E. The unemployment rate in the state where her new stores will be located is lower than the national average.

For Questions 6 to 9, select the two answer choices that, when used to complete the sentence, fit the meaning of the sentence as a whole and produce complete sentences that are alike in meaning.

6. The legendary teacher possessed unparalleled learning but nobody could ask him to elucidate any of his theories because in spite of the communal nature of his works, his _____ outmatched even his brilliance.

   A. superciliousness
   B. popularity
   C. reclusiveness
   D. obtuseness
   E. unimportance
   F. solitariness

7. The new _____ of the skin cell left cancer researchers perplexed as it did not appear to be like any other cell that had been radiated.

   A. structure
   B. edifice
   C. department
   D. morphology
   E. genus
   F. tabulation

8. He made his words as _____ and neutral as humanly possible, but he knew in the back of his mind that human nature would cause his audience to only take away from his speech what they wanted to hear.

   A. fungible
   B. optional
   C. objective
   D. subjective
   E. figurative
   F. impartial

Section 2 - Verbal Reasoning

9. In response to overwhelming physiological damage from the environment, the human body will go to amazing lengths to protect its vital organs, even to the point of sacrificing _____ appendages.

   - [A] mandatory
   - [B] inessential
   - [C] identical
   - [D] dispensable
   - [E] asymmetrical
   - [F] embryological

For Questions 10 to 12, select one answer choice unless otherwise instructed.

Questions 10 to 12 are based on this passage.

By the 1890s Social Darwinist ideas were popular and were making themselves felt, influencing social policies in the United States and elsewhere. Social Darwinism saw human society as based on a struggle for survival, in which the superior, the fittest, would triumph and the inferior would be swept to the wayside. It was more or less the ancient "predator ethic"—the idea that might makes right, that the strong are entitled to oppress the weak—dressed up in pseudoscientific clothes. If the struggle for survival was the way of the world, then it was only natural that human society should operate in the same way. Social Darwinism also dovetailed with racist thinking: American segregationists used the idea to promote the second-class status of black folk as a positive good. In Germany, Ernst Haeckel took the idea even farther, using it as a framework to propose Aryan race-supremacy notions and German militarism.

10. Select the sentence that explains how humans justified the tenets of Social Darwinism.

For the following question, consider each of the choices separately and select all that apply.

11. According to the passage, which of the following are examples of "predator ethic"?

    - [A] Cyber-bullying
    - [B] Involuntary commitment to a mental institution
    - [C] Incarcerating people based on their race

12. The use of the word "dovetailed" in the context of this passage most closely matches which of the following definitions?

    - (A) Coincided with
    - (B) Deviated from
    - (C) Fit together
    - (D) Having a series of indentations suggesting dovetails
    - (E) Split apart

Section 3 - Quantitative Reasoning

18 Minutes | 12 Questions

1

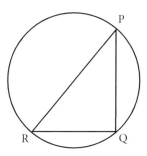

In the figure above, PQR is inscribed in a circle. The measure of angle RQP is greater than 90°, and the area of the circle is 36π.

Quantity A	Quantity B
The length of line segment RP	12

- Ⓐ Quantity A is greater.
- Ⓑ Quantity B is greater.
- Ⓒ The two quantities are equal.
- Ⓓ The relationship cannot be determined from the information given.

2

Quantity A	Quantity B
The area of a rectangle with a perimeter of 40	The area of a square with a perimeter of 40

- Ⓐ Quantity A is greater.
- Ⓑ Quantity B is greater.
- Ⓒ The two quantities are equal.
- Ⓓ The relationship cannot be determined from the information given.

3

$|z| \leq 1$

Quantity A	Quantity B
z^2	$1 - z$

- Ⓐ Quantity A is greater.
- Ⓑ Quantity B is greater.
- Ⓒ The two quantities are equal.
- Ⓓ The relationship cannot be determined from the information given.

4

R = {5, 10, 3, x, 12, 23, 4, 18}

The range of set R is 21.

Quantity A	Quantity B
x	2

- Ⓐ Quantity A is greater.
- Ⓑ Quantity B is greater.
- Ⓒ The two quantities are equal.
- Ⓓ The relationship cannot be determined from the information given.

5

When the positive number a is divided by 54, the remainder is 30. Which of the following must be a divisor of a?

- Ⓐ 6
- Ⓑ 7
- Ⓒ 8
- Ⓓ 10
- Ⓔ 11

Section 3 - Quantitative Reasoning

Questions 6 to 8 are based on the following data.

Store Sales from 2000-2020

Year	Store A Sales	Store B Sales
2000	$1,453,140	$932,121
2010	$1,536,834	$1,231,034
2020	$2,103,431	$1,694,145

Percentages of Sold Products in 2010 in Store A

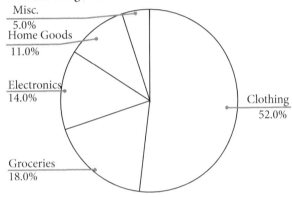

6

What was the percent increase in sales for Store A from 2000 to 2020? (round to the nearest percent)

[ ] %

7

What was the approximate total value of the Home Goods products sold in Store A in 2010?

- A) $159,845
- B) $169,052
- C) $173,245
- D) $215,156
- E) $261,565

8

What was the average rate of change in sales per year for Store B in the years 2000 to 2010?

- A) $29,891.30
- B) $46,311.10
- C) $55,321.25
- D) $152,123.30$
- E) $298,913.00

9

If $\frac{x}{8} + \frac{x}{3} + 13 = x$, then $x = ?$

- A) 16
- B) 24
- C) 32
- D) 48
- E) 72

10

If the diameter of a circle is tripled, what is the ratio of the area of the original circle to the area of half of the new circle?

[ ]

11

Angelo sold $\frac{2}{5}$ more cars than Beth and each person sold an integer number of cars. Which of the following could be the number of cars sold by Angelo and Beth combined?

Indicate all such answers.

- [A] 36
- [B] 44
- [C] 48
- [D] 0

12

If $\frac{3x + 4y}{4y - 3x} = 3$, then $x = ?$

- (A) $\frac{2y}{3}$
- (B) $\frac{3y}{4}$
- (C) $\frac{4y}{3}$
- (D) $2y$
- (E) y

Section 4 - Verbal Reasoning (Easy)

23 Minutes | 15 Questions

For Questions 1 to 4, select one entry for each blank from the corresponding column of choices. Fill all the blanks in the way that best completes the text.

1. Psychologists refer to the ability to determine what information is important and what is background noise as signal detection, as it is the act of detecting what signals require or deserve focus and which can be _____.

A unheeded
B rejected
C considered
D abandoned
E underestimated

2. The subtlety that goes into the construction of poems makes them difficult to (i) _____. Without strict use of genre conventions, every poem seems to be completely unique. Therefore, unlike prose writing, one rarely sees works of poetry divided (ii) _____ into genres. While everybody can identify a science fiction novel, or a romance novel, such distinctions are difficult to make in the field of poetry.

Blank (i)	Blank (ii)
A inoculate	D incontrovertibly
B inculcate	E libidinously
C catalog	F debatably

3. Pediatric heart surgeons are an elite group. They go through more than ten years of training in their field before becoming fully qualified. The stress alone can (i) _____ even the best. They are responsible for correcting defects in hearts that are oftentimes barely a month old. The (ii) _____ of these surgeons creates a massive demand for their services; oftentimes patients are flown in from great distances, the risk of travel (iii) _____ by necessity.

Blank (i)	Blank (ii)	Blank (iii)
A debilitate	D paucity	G superseded
B buttress	E opalescence	H delineated
C assuage	F ubiquity	I critiqued

4. The concept of social stratification has been the focus of sociological studies; its (i) _____ in Western societies has been of particular focus. The (ii) _____ of this topic can be appreciated with even a cursory glance at textbooks—writers of history, economics, and civil rights continuously point to social stratification as the source of various communal ills. However, some sociologists argue that this ubiquity actually (iii) _____ social stratification. They claim that the prevalence of social stratification means that it is a natural component of any society.

Blank (i)	Blank (ii)	Blank (iii)
A manifestation	D reticence	G substantiates
B contradiction	E contradistinction	H fissures
C ambiguousness	F pervasiveness	I fractures

Section 4 - Verbal Reasoning (Easy)

For Questions 5 to 7, select one answer choice unless otherwise instructed.

Questions 5 to 7 are based on this passage.

Now, of all the various responsibilities, expressed, implied, or assumed by the United States in Haiti, it would naturally be supposed that the financial obligation would be foremost. Indeed, the sister republic of Santo Domingo was taken over by the United States Navy for no other reason than failure to pay its internal debt. But Haiti for over one hundred years scrupulously paid its external and internal debt—a fact worth remembering when one hears of "anarchy and disorder" in that land—until five years ago when under the financial guardianship of the United States interest on both the internal and, with one exception, external debt was defaulted; and this in spite of the fact that specified revenues were pledged for the payment of this interest. Apart from the distinct injury to the honor and reputation of the country, the hardship on individuals has been great.

5. This passage discusses which of the following issues regarding the United States' policies toward Haiti?

   A) The unfairness of the U.S.'s treatment of Haiti in comparison to its actions toward Santo Domingo.
   B) The comparative importance of internal vs. external debt to Haiti's financial infrastructure.
   C) The reasons that the United States assumed financial guardianship in Haiti.
   D) The role of the United States in regard to Haiti's financial crisis.
   E) The reasons that designated revenues were not used to pay Haiti's debts.

6. Based on the passage, with which of the following statements would the author probably agree?

   A) Haiti's default on its debts can be attributed to anarchy and disorder in the country.
   B) Haiti defaulted on its debts despite the best efforts of the United States.
   C) Haiti does not fully deserve its reputation for "anarchy and disorder".
   D) Revenues set aside for interest payments should have instead been used to pay down internal debt.
   E) While the United States was primarily concerned with the issue of internal debt, Haiti erred by attempting to pay down internal and external debts simultaneously.

For the following question, consider each of the choices separately and select all that apply.

7. The passage implies which of the following about the country of Haiti?

   A) Many people assume that Haiti's economic crisis is its own fault.
   B) Financial insolvency is not typical of Haiti.
   C) Haitian citizens have suffered in tangible ways from the default.

For Questions 8 to 10, select the two answer choices that, when used to complete the sentence, fit the meaning of the sentence as a whole and produce complete sentences that are alike in meaning.

8. Even comparing such extremes as residents of mountains of Tenochtitlan with the aborigines of Australia, it is notable how even in spite of _____ appearances and customs, people all over the world have tremendous similarities.

   A) disparate
   B) concurrent
   C) idyllic
   D) dissimilar
   E) uniform
   F) familiar

Section 4 - Verbal Reasoning (Easy)

9. That tree blooms at the end of summer, when many others are becoming _____ and no longer producing fruit.

   - [A] stagnant
   - [B] quiescent
   - [C] inertia
   - [D] indolence
   - [E] dormant
   - [F] sloth

10. The poet Rumi wrote volumes of _____ poems describing the intricacies of love in thirteenth century Persia; though written hundreds of years ago, the poems described the multi-faceted nature of love with evocative, mellifluous language so enduring that they are still read and quoted throughout the world in the present day.

    - [A] odoriferous
    - [B] desultory
    - [C] redolent
    - [D] fecund
    - [E] restive
    - [F] nostalgic

For Questions 11 to 15, select one answer choice unless otherwise instructed.

Question 11 is based on this passage.

The Way became the Pilgrims' Way in 1174, four years after Thomas à Becket was murdered in Canterbury Cathedral. His tomb in the Cathedral became the second shrine in Christendom, and pilgrims came to it along the old trackway through Surrey, from Farnham, east of the Hog's Back along the hills to Canterbury in Kent. Henry the Second, one of the earliest pilgrims of all, made his act of repentance a few days after landing at Southampton from France, on February 8, 1174. Or so legend relates, and adds that he swore to walk barefoot; history is less precise. After Henry, the stream of devotees multiplied.

11. Which of the following would, if true, most effectively strengthen the passage's argument?

    - (A) A detailed definition of the term "pilgrim" from the relevant period.
    - (B) A document showing that Henry the Second was not related to Thomas à Becket's murder.
    - (C) Receipts showing that Henry the Second stayed at an inn near Farnham.
    - (D) A description of a newspaper article that recorded Henry the Second's journey with a reference to the name Pilgrim's Way.
    - (E) A private journal which explains Henry the Second's alleged refusal to wear shoes.

Questions 12 and 13 are based on this passage.

Located in northern Spain, the earliest cave paintings of the Paleolithic era remain a testament to the ingenuity of our distant ancestors. Archaeologists currently believe these works of art developed in stages over long periods of time, deemed to have appeared, by some estimates, as far back as 36,000 years ago. Depicting both animals and anthropomorphic creatures, this rock art also sheds light on the spiritual aspects of the early *homo sapiens*.

Perhaps most striking of all, the techniques of both engraving and painting reveal tremendous skill and nuance. For instance, the exploitation of the contours in the stone walls shows an adept appreciation of natural material, resulting in a 3D quality. Undoubtedly, the creative vision and execution of the artwork continue to speak volumes over the millennia.

12. According to the passage, what does rock art reveal about early human expression?

    (A) Cave paintings focused on the wildlife that surrounded and likely posed a threat to early cave dwellers.
    (B) Rock art reflects a depth of artistic vision that deserves appreciation.
    (C) Early cave artists used natural resources in their work without significant regard for its environmental impact.
    (D) Cave paintings were created by several artists over time who collaborated on a unified vision.
    (E) Developed primarily for educational purposes, cave paintings evolved gradually into forms of religious expression.

13. According to the passage, what is the best meaning of the word "deemed"?

    (A) Concluded definitively, based on rigorous research
    (B) Hypothesized, before exploring the archaeological data
    (C) Estimated, based on available evidence
    (D) Proposed, refuting previously conceived estimates
    (E) Negated, claiming the current estimate is incorrect

Questions 14 and 15 are based on this passage.

The staggering wealth gap in the US tends to be examined through modern-day inequalities in socioeconomic conditions. However, a new study links at least some of the disproportionate distribution to the generational wealth passed on since the times of slavery. It was discovered that up to 28% of Congress have inherited fortunes amassed by enslaving people for labor, accounting for a higher net worth on average than non-descendants of slave-holders.

This refutes the commonly held notion that slavery was an institution of the past with no bearing on modern socioeconomic dynamics. In addition, it challenges the underpinnings of the American Dream, based on a level playing field where equality reigns. These findings warrant a deeper look into the vestiges of slave-begotten wealth and its impact on society today.

14. What is the central idea of the passage?

    (A) Fortunes amassed under slavery eclipse those acquired since its abolition and cannot be disregarded as a pivotal factor in modern socioeconomic disparities.
    (B) The profits accrued under the defunct labor system of slavery have precipitated a disproportionate distribution of wealth, whose repercussions are seen in legislation.
    (C) Inherited wealth remains a determinant in socioeconomic success, despite 'American Dream' optimism, as evidenced by the opportunities afforded to descendants of slaveholders.
    (D) Wealth inherited from slave-holding ancestors remains a propitious factor of ascension in US society, and its influence on the modern wealth gap deserves further scrutiny.
    (E) Inherited wealth facilitates the pursuit of public office by descendants of slaveholders more so than by non-descendants on account of social connections among elected officials.

15. Select a sentence that expresses the opinion that these findings may dislodge previously-held perceptions about personal, modern-day benefits from slavery.

Section 4 - Verbal Reasoning (Hard)

23 Minutes | 15 Questions

For Questions 1 to 4, select one entry for each blank from the corresponding column of choices. Fill all the blanks in the way that best completes the text.

1. Particle physicists continue to wrestle with the _____ problem of why the universe is made of matter and not antimatter, as logic would prescribe.

   - A) wayward
   - B) intractable
   - C) resolute
   - D) perverse
   - E) pliant

2. Until recently, nobody expected to find (i) _____ in the field of hydrology. But as population numbers keep soaring and water supplies keep drying up, the study of water distribution across planet Earth suddenly becomes essential. Countries that once (ii) _____ the notion of monitoring their water supply are now actively seeking out the top hydrologists in the field. The once obscure profession has exploded into the mainstream seemingly overnight.

Blank (i)	Blank (ii)
A) prominence	D) recalculated
B) ignominy	E) denigrated
C) extravagance	F) co-opted

3. The music industry saw tremendous innovations in both technology and artistry during the 20th century. The invention of the radio (i) _____ many of the stylistic changes. Because of the radio, music was no longer (ii) _____ to concert houses and clubs. As a result, it became possible for all citizens to hear music and contribute to its development. This explains the massive (iii) _____ of musical genres in the 20th century. From psychedelic to rockabilly, popular music no longer followed the strict rules of the previous centuries.

Blank (i)	Blank (ii)	Blank (iii)
A) circumvented	D) sardonic	G) guileless
B) facilitated	E) schematized	H) portly
C) barred	F) quiescent	I) tumultuous

4. He couldn't get any work done in the heat. It (i) _____ every attempt he made at finishing his report. No position was comfortable to sit in, and he was upset to find that no fan was powerful enough to (ii) _____ the thick waves of humidity. And for the first time he wasn't looking forward to sleeping, either. He knew that he was going to wake up (iii) _____ throughout the night, each time drenched with sweat and desperately thirsty.

Blank (i)	Blank (ii)	Blank (iii)
A) subverted	D) augment	G) exquisitely
B) subsisted	E) penetrate	H) volubly
C) sanctioned	F) succor	I) sporadically

Section 4 - Verbal Reasoning (Hard)

For Questions 5 and 6, select one answer choice unless otherwise instructed.

Questions 5 and 6 are based on this passage.

Bottled water has come under a new wave of scrutiny in a recent study that discovered about a quarter million microplastic particles suspended in a single liter. Much of the microplastics discovered are suspected to have leached out from the plastic bottles themselves; however, it is not certain at which point the microplastics appear in the water in its journey from source to glass.

With over 430 million tonnes of plastic produced annually, microplastics have concerned oncologists, particularly because the additives found in the chemicals have been shown to cross cell membranes and reside in body tissue. While the effects of these chemicals over time have not been ascertained, scientists involved in the study express caution against the purchase of bottled water.

For the following question, consider each of the choices separately and select all that apply.

5. Which of the following could be an alternative explanation for the presence of microplastics in bottled water?

   A. Discarded plastics could be affecting the sources where the water is collected.
   B. Microplastics that are airborne may land in the bottles after being opened.
   C. Microplastics may contaminate bottles during the production process.

6. Select a sentence which states the reason for bottled water becoming more of a concern than before.

Questions 7 to 9 are based on this passage.

In the perennial debate about whether meaning and social impact are requisites for value in art, one particular work of Picasso, *Guernica*, serves to bridge the divide. Picasso, with his trailblazing approach to form and avant-garde techniques, was known to have pushed the limits of Cubist and Surrealist movements. To the degree that, while grappling with deeper human themes, the unforgettable quality of Picasso's oeuvre resides mostly in its audacious aesthetic visuals.

In the work, *Guernica*, however, produced on a true-to-life size canvas and portraying the horrid reality of the 1937 air attack on the Basque town of *Guernica*, Picasso ventured far beyond the aesthetic value of his work. Using his seasoned paint strokes, he engaged the global community with a clear and stark message against war.

The unmistakably Picasso-esque figures in *Guernica* are depicted in their reaction to the destruction around them, from an inconsolable mother holding her child to the bone-chilling fear in even the horse's countenance. It's a visually stunning tableau reflecting the helplessness of the most vulnerable as the often-forgotten consequence of warfare. Even today, the piece continues to resonate with an anti-war message that transcends art circles. Far surpassing the notion of "art for art's sake" it has left an indelible mark on viewers for both form and substance.

7. Which of the following is the most significant point concerning the impact of Guernica as a work of art?

   A. *Guernica*'s value is in its humanitarian message, which brings to bear a subjective perspective on the evaluation of the work of art for more than its aesthetic value.
   B. While straying from the ethos of his other pieces, *Guernica* transmits its message by virtue of Picasso's mastery of an inimitable artistic style that continues to impress viewers.
   C. *Guernica* escapes the reductive nature of conventional assessment as it employs revolutionary and iconoclastic art techniques to convey a timeless theme.
   D. The impact of *Guernica* remains relevant today as a result of its real-life context and subsequent role in cultural production, with broader implications on society itself.
   E. The striking imagery and unusual size of *Guernica* make it stand out in Picasso's body of work, enabling it to be the vehicle of a humanitarian message.

Section 4 - Verbal Reasoning (Hard)

8. Which of the following most strongly supports the author's claim?

   A. The fact that Picasso traveled extensively to display the piece in several major cities around the globe.
   B. The fact that *Guernica* has been replicated on household items and commercialized by museum gift shops.
   C. The fact that tourists traveling in northern Spain often have been drawn to visit the Basque town of *Guernica* as a result of having seen or heard of the painting.
   D. The fact that the Museum of Peace in *Guernica* features an exploration of the meaning of peace, a retrospective with survivors' testimonies, and an exhibit dedicated to the painting's history.
   E. The fact that *Guernica* was later used to raise awareness of the war and fundraise for reconstruction efforts.

9. The function of the third paragraph is:

   A. To highlight the contrast of subject matter chosen by Picasso, in comparison to his earlier work.
   B. To provide the reader with an idea of how *Guernica* conveyed its anti-war message, explaining why it would have an impact on viewers today.
   C. To impress upon readers the effects that warfare invariably has on vulnerable populations.
   D. To critique Picasso's use of emotionally charged imagery that crowds out any perceivable message.
   E. To examine how the piece engaged in deeper themes while still having value for its aesthetics.

For Questions 10 to 12, select the two answer choices that, when used to complete the sentence, fit the meaning of the sentence as a whole and produce complete sentences that are alike in meaning.

10. It is quite remarkable to see a book in such _____ condition; I've never seen a 17th-century first edition of that high standard before.

    A. sanitary
    B. untarnished
    C. purified
    D. pristine
    E. immaculate
    F. adulterated

11. In all respects, the designs were unpopular with the masses, they were both _____ and impractical.

    A. sophisticated
    B. ill-bred
    C. clumsy
    D. gauche
    E. butterfingered
    F. couth

12. Even though the other members of the board saw the future of the corporation being predicated on raw sales, he knew that the sales themselves were predicated on more human intra–office endeavors such as a quality working _____ between employees.

    A. turbidity
    B. condescension
    C. relationship
    D. rapport
    E. despair
    F. synecdoche

Section 4 - Verbal Reasoning (Hard)

For Questions 13 to 15, select one answer choice unless otherwise instructed.

Question 13 is based on this passage.

In the jungles of India, which preserve a state of things which has existed for immemorial years, lives the tiger, his stripes simulating jungle reeds, his noiseless approach learnt from nature in countless millions of lessons of success and failure, his perfectly powerful claws and execution methods; and, living in the same jungle, and with him as one of the conditions of life, are small deer, alert, swift, light of build, inconspicuous of color, sharp of hearing, keen-eyed, keen-scented—because any downward variation from these attributes means swift and certain death. To capture the deer is a condition, of the tiger's life, to escape the tiger a condition of the deer's; and they play a great contest under these conditions, with life as the stake. The most alert deer almost always escape.

13. Which of the following events would cause the greatest decline in the number of tigers in the jungles of India?

    Ⓐ An increase in rain that causes jungle reeds to flourish
    Ⓑ Destruction of the food source for the deer
    Ⓒ A mutation increasing the deer's ability to see colors
    Ⓓ An increase in eco-tourism attracting more people to watch the animals
    Ⓔ The addition of an invasive new species of deer

Questions 14 and 15 are based on this passage.

As a force that facilitates the course of events, language exerts unquestionable impact. However, the extent to which it affects physical reality remains debatable. According to ancient Japanese beliefs, expressed in the term kotodama meaning "word spirit" words have an almost magical capacity to transform the tangible. But how literal is this transformation?

Modern research, availing itself of imaging tools such as fMRI, is now able to corroborate this mystical claim. A systematic review of over 100 studies indicated ways by which language acquisition and use physically affected neuronal structures. Exposure to multilingual speech, in particular, correlated with perceptible increases in gray and white matter in the auditory cortex. Language altering our neuronal reality perhaps lends credence to the claim that external reality is also susceptible to its effects.

For the following question, consider each of the choices separately and select all that apply.

14. According to the passage, which of the following positions is the author likely to defend?

    A. Language is a vehicle of communication that transcends descriptive and reactive qualities.
    B. The use of language can potentially have material effects on physical surroundings.
    C. Language manifests as physical neuronal alterations through intangible forces yet unexplainable by science.

15. Select a sentence that reflects the author's position that the neurological evidence is not entirely sufficient to prove the concept of *kotodama* correct.

Section 5 - Quantitative Reasoning (Easy)

26 Minutes | 15 Questions

1

Quantity A	Quantity B
The standard deviation of the data set 13, 14, 15	The standard deviation of the dataset 13, 14, 14, 14, 14, 15

- Ⓐ Quantity A is greater.
- Ⓑ Quantity B is greater.
- Ⓒ The two quantities are equal.
- Ⓓ The relationship cannot be determined from the information given.

2

The values x and y are both integers greater than 1.

Quantity A	Quantity B
$6(\frac{1}{x} + 3y)$	$5x + 3y$

- Ⓐ Quantity A is greater.
- Ⓑ Quantity B is greater.
- Ⓒ The two quantities are equal.
- Ⓓ The relationship cannot be determined from the information given.

3

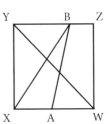

In the figure, XYZW is a square, the diagonal YW is equal to 16 and A is the midpoint of segment XW.

Quantity A	Quantity B
The area of ABZW	64

- Ⓐ Quantity A is greater.
- Ⓑ Quantity B is greater.
- Ⓒ The two quantities are equal.
- Ⓓ The relationship cannot be determined from the information given.

4

Line k has a y-intercept at 6 and a slope of $-\frac{3}{4}$. The point $(x, 9)$ exists on the line.

Quantity A	Quantity B
x	0

- Ⓐ Quantity A is greater.
- Ⓑ Quantity B is greater.
- Ⓒ The two quantities are equal.
- Ⓓ The relationship cannot be determined from the information given.

Section 5 - Quantitative Reasoning (Easy)

5

A certain jar contains x amount of red, green, and yellow jelly beans. The probability of drawing a red jellybean is $\frac{4}{7}$. There are more green than yellow jelly beans.

Quantity A	Quantity B
The probability of drawing a yellow jelly bean	$\frac{1}{7}$

(A) Quantity A is greater.
(B) Quantity B is greater.
(C) The two quantities are equal.
(D) The relationship cannot be determined from the information given.

6

An MBA student must take five more courses to complete their coursework. They can take the classes in any order, but one of the classes is a prerequisite for the other meaning it must be taken first. How many different combinations of class orders are possible with these final five courses?

(A) 15
(B) 24
(C) 25
(D) 120
(E) 3125

7

If a is increased by 5% to get b and b is decreased by 20% to get c, what percent of c is a?

(A) 25%
(B) 84%
(C) 96%
(D) 120%
(E) 180%

8

In triangle ABC, the measure of angle A is 35° and the measure of angle C is between 15° and 45°. Which could be the measure of angle B?

Indicate all such measures.

[A] 90°
[B] 100°
[C] 110°
[D] 120°
[E] 130°
[F] 140°

9

If the ratio of x to y is 4 to 13 and the ratio of y to z is 3 to 10, then what is the ratio of x to z?

(A) $\frac{6}{65}$
(B) $\frac{12}{65}$
(C) $\frac{1}{4}$
(D) $\frac{2}{5}$
(E) $\frac{10}{13}$

10

A three-digit number with the same hundreds and units digit is also a prime number. How many such numbers are there?

(A) 1
(B) 4
(C) 10
(D) 14
(E) 20

Section 5 - Quantitative Reasoning (Easy)

11

The mean of a data set of 9 integers is 45 and the median is 28. What is the least value possible for the greatest number in this data set that works within these measures?

[   ]

12

A cleaning solution contains 15% of chemical A. Robert wants a cleaning solution with a 35% concentration of chemical A. He has 10 fluid ounces of another cleaning solution that contains a 50% concentration of chemical A. How many fluid ounces of the 15% cleaning solution does he need to add to the 50% cleaning solution to reach the 35% concentration?

- A) 1.25
- B) 2.5
- C) 3.5
- D) 7.5
- E) 10

13

If x and y are integers, and $(x^{-2})(y^{-5}) = 512^{-1}$, then what is the value of $x + y$?

- A) 2
- B) 3
- C) 4
- D) 5
- E) 6

14

If x and y are integers, then $\dfrac{x(x+1)(x+3)}{2^y + 1}$ must be an integer if which of the following is true?

- A) x is even
- B) x is odd
- C) x is divisible by two
- D) y is even
- E) y is equal to 0

15

Eleanor made between $\dfrac{1}{8}$ and $\dfrac{1}{3}$ of her total income from freelancing last month. If she made $650 freelancing, which of the following could have been her net income last month?

Indicate all such answers.

- [A] $1000
- [B] $1350
- [C] $1900
- [D] $2400
- [E] $5000

Section 5 - Quantitative Reasoning (Hard)

23 Minutes | 15 Questions

1

$$0 < a < b < 1$$

Quantity A	Quantity B
$66\frac{2}{3}\%$ of a	50% of b

- Ⓐ Quantity A is greater.
- Ⓑ Quantity B is greater.
- Ⓒ The two quantities are equal.
- Ⓓ The relationship cannot be determined from the information given.

2

$a_1, a_2, 18, 54, 162,..4374$ is a geometric sequence.

Quantity A	Quantity B
The number of terms in the sequence	$a_1 + a_2$

- Ⓐ Quantity A is greater.
- Ⓑ Quantity B is greater.
- Ⓒ The two quantities are equal.
- Ⓓ The relationship cannot be determined from the information given.

3

$$x < 0$$

Quantity A	Quantity B
$\dfrac{-x}{x-1}$	$\dfrac{x-1}{-x}$

- Ⓐ Quantity A is greater.
- Ⓑ Quantity B is greater.
- Ⓒ The two quantities are equal.
- Ⓓ The relationship cannot be determined from the information given.

4

Triangle ABC is scalene and angle B is a right angle. Point D lies on AC and connects to B to form an altitude of the triangle. Triangle BDC is isosceles.

$AB = 4\sqrt{7}$ and $BC = 4\sqrt{2}$

Quantity A	Quantity B
The length of AD	8

- Ⓐ Quantity A is greater.
- Ⓑ Quantity B is greater.
- Ⓒ The two quantities are equal.
- Ⓓ The relationship cannot be determined from the information given.

5

The area of Rectangle A is 340. The side lengths of Rectangle B are 3 times as long as the sides of Rectangle A. What is the area of rectangle B?

- Ⓐ 1020
- Ⓑ 2040
- Ⓒ 3060
- Ⓓ 4080
- Ⓔ 5020

6

If the range of the price of the computers sold at a store on Monday is $950 and the list of the price of computers sold on Monday consists of $1000, $550, $1200, $1420, $750, and x. Which of the following could be the median price?

Indicate all possible answers.

- ☐ A $875
- ☐ B $950
- ☐ C $1100

Section 5 - Quantitative Reasoning (Hard)

7

If *a* and *b* are odd integers and *b* < *a*, which of the following equals the number of odd integers that are greater than *b*, but less than *a*?

- A) $\dfrac{(a-b-2)}{2}$
- B) $\dfrac{(a-b+2)}{2}$
- C) $\dfrac{(a-b)}{2}$
- D) $a-b$
- E) $a-b-2$

8

For which of the following functions is $f(a+b) = f(a)f(b)$ for all positive numbers *a* and *b*?

- A) $f(x) = \dfrac{3}{x}$
- B) $f(x) = \sqrt{x}$
- C) $f(x) = x^2$
- D) $f(x) = 2^x$
- E) $f(x) = x + 4$

9

A warehouse worker takes 6 hours to unload a shipment. Working with an autonomous robot, the shipment only takes 2 hours to unload. How much time would the autonomous robot take to unload the shipment on its own?

- A) 1 hour
- B) 3 hours
- C) 4 hours
- D) 5 hours
- E) 6 hours

10

If n is an integer and $|-n + 3| < |n|$, which of the following must be positive?

- A) $-n$
- B) $n - 3$
- C) $-n + 3$
- D) $(-n)(n + 3)$
- E) $(n)(n + 3)$

11

The sum of the interior angles of a regular polygon equals 1800°. What is the measure of each exterior angle of the polygon?

☐

12

If the average of 45, 65, *x*, and *x* is less than 80, what is the largest possible value of integer *x*?

- A) 75
- B) 80
- C) 100
- D) 104
- E) 105

13

If *a* and *b* are positive numbers and $x = a^2 b$, a 10% increase in *a* and a 45% decrease in *b* would result in which of the following changes to *x*?

- A) An increase of 55%
- B) An increase of 66.55%
- C) A decrease of 33.45%
- D) A decrease of 49.5%
- E) A decrease of 166%

14

If $2.1x + 1.2y = -0.3x + 1.5y$ and $y^2 = 16$, what is the value of x?

Indicate all such values.

- [A] -0.5
- [B] $-0.2.5$
- [C] 0.25
- [D] 0.5

15

If the average of a, b, and 12 is equal to the average of a, b, 12, and 36, what is the average of a and b?

(A) 12
(B) 20
(C) 26
(D) 48
(E) 64

Answer Key

VERBAL REASONING

Section 2		
Q. No.	Correct Answer	Your Answer
1	E	
2	A, D	
3	B, E, I	
4	B	
5	D	
6	C, F	
7	A, D	
8	C, F	
9	B, D	
10	If the...same way.	
11	A, C	
12	C	

Section 4 (Easy)		
Q. No.	Correct Answer	Your Answer
1	A	
2	C, D	
3	A, D, G	
4	A, F, G	
5	D	
6	C	
7	A, B, C	
8	A, D	
9	B, E	
10	B, C	
11	D	
12	B	
13	C	
14	D	
15	This refutes... dynamics.	

Section 4 (Hard)		
Q. No.	Correct Answer	Your Answer
1	B	
2	A, E	
3	B, D, I	
4	A, E, I	
5	A, B, C	
6	Bottled... single liter.	
7	D	
8	E	
9	B	
10	D, E	
11	C, D	
12	C, D	
13	B	
14	A, B	
15	Language...its effects.	

Answer Key

QUANTITATIVE REASONING

Section 3		
Q. No.	Correct Answer	Your Answer
1	B	
2	D	
3	D	
4	D	
5	A	
6	45	
7	B	
8	A	
9	B	
10	$\frac{2}{9}$	
11	A, C	
12	A	

Section 5 (Easy)		
Q. No.	Correct Answer	Your Answer
1	A	
2	D	
3	B	
4	B	
5	C	
6	B	
7	B	
8	B, C, D, E	
9	A	
10	D	
11	67	
12	D	
13	E	
14	E	
15	D, E	

Section 5 (Hard)		
Q. No.	Correct Answer	Your Answer
1	D	
2	C	
3	A	
4	C	
5	C	
6	A, C	
7	A	
8	D	
9	B	
10	E	
11	30	
12	D	
13	C	
14	A, D	
15	D	

Analytical Writing — Answers & Explanations — Section 1

Analyze an Issue

The sample essay that follows was written in response to the prompt that appeared in the question.

Some people are born risk takers. Psychologists will tell you that it is component of one's personality, and those who take risks sometimes exhibit negative behavior while others take risks that ultimately benefit themselves and others. The names of risk takers can be found in various halls of fame as well as on Wanted Posters. Famous risk takers range from the infamous like Al Capone and Bernie Maidoff to the innovators like Bill Gates, Mark Zuckerberg, and Frank Lloyd Wright. Even though these and others knew the possible consequences of their actions, they were not deterred from reaching their goals. Those who do not take risks will not suffer the possible negative consequences, but neither will they experience the rewards.

Where would we be without those who took great risks with general disregard for the consequences? Marie and Pierre Curie literally risked their lives to experiment with radioactivity. The medical progress that resulted from their work not only earned the Curies the Noble Prize but made possible early treatment of some cancers. Other scientists followed in their footsteps, and the benefits to mankind have been enormous. Other medical pioneers include Jonas Salk who saved countless children from death or paralysis when he tested his new polio vaccine on himself, his wife and his own children. Risking his and his family's lives led to mass administration of the vaccine to school children all over America, and virtually made the iron lung obsolete.

Early explorers risked traveling to areas marked on maps with the foreboding phrase, "Here there be dragons", and expanded the known world. In efforts to find a shorter route to India, sailors like Christopher Columbus set off with his crew in three small boats and bumped into the Western Hemisphere. Charles Lindbergh flew solo across the Atlantic in a small plane in hopes of reaching the European continent. Since that time, man has used flight to reach the moon and establish space stations. If these adventurers had spent too much time thinking about the consequences, they may very well have just stayed home.

In the later years of the twentieth century pioneers in technology arose. Bill Gates, founder of Microsoft and one of the richest men in the world, dropped out of prestigious Harvard University to pursue computing. Steve Jobs, the brains behind Apple computers, also dropped out of college. These men defied the popular wisdom that one needs a college education to get anywhere in this world and created a universe of communication on a level never before seen.

Great political leaders have taken great risks for the sake of reform or revolution. Martin Luther King, Jr and Mohandas Gandhi (after whom King modeled his protests), risked everything and, ultimately, lost their lives for the sake of equality and independence. Both men certainly considered the consequences of their actions, but deemed that the potential rewards made the risks acceptable. All minorities and repressed populations in the United States lead lives of greater opportunity thanks to the leadership of Martin Luther King, Jr, and India exists as an independent country as a result of Gandhi's actions.

Just as there are consequences for taking risks, there are consequences for failing to take risks. Those who fear the unknown are doomed to live meager lives. It may be trite but nonetheless true to say that if you do what you've always done, you'll get what you've always had.

Verbal Reasoning — Answers & Explanations — Section 2

1 **Choice E is correct** because "assiduously" means working with great care, dedication, and persistence. This fits the sentence perfectly, as it describes how the group worked long hours—arriving early, staying late, and even taking work home—all of which point to sustained, diligent effort.

Choice A is incorrect because "ambiguously" means unclearly or having more than one meaning. This does not describe a way of working and does not align with the clear, purposeful effort described in the sentence. **Choice B is incorrect** because "exultantly" means with great joy or triumph. While it suggests enthusiasm, it doesn't match the tone of hard, tireless work implied by the description of long hours and extra effort. **Choice C is incorrect** because "formidably" means impressively powerful or capable in a way that might inspire fear or respect. It describes someone's capabilities, not how they work, and is too vague in this context. **Choice D is incorrect** because "imperturbably" means calm and unshaken, even under pressure. While this might describe emotional composure, it does not convey the sense of effort and industriousness required by the sentence.

2 **Choice A is correct** because "capricious" means subject to sudden changes in mood. This fits the sentence well, as it describes the contrasting emotions that arise when practicing paleontology. The field can be both exhilarating and frustrating, suggesting a constantly shifting emotional landscape that aligns with the definition of "capricious." **Choice D is correct** because "disillusioned" means being disappointed in something that turned out to be less good than originally thought, or defeated in expectations. This word fits the sentence because it describes the way paleontologists would be disheartened that their arduous efforts went to waste while a natural phenomenon completed the task easily.

Choice B is incorrect because "intractable" means hard to control or deal with. This word does not apply to the sentence because the text does not suggest that paleontology is difficult to deal with in a practical sense. Rather, the passage expresses that practicing paleontology can be a bit of an emotional rollercoaster, making Choice A the better option. **Choice C is incorrect** because "pensive" means engaged in deep or serious thought. This word does not fit the context of the sentence because the sentence describes the field of paleontology using two other emotions: exciting and frustrating. The remainder of the passage does not suggest that paleontologists must remain stoic or solemn. Therefore, Choice A is the better option. **Choice E is incorrect** because "rapt" means completely fascinated. This word does not fit in the blank because it does not accurately describe the feeling paleontologists would likely experience upon discovering that their arduous efforts went to waste while a natural phenomenon completed the task easily. Rather, they would feel annoyed or disheartened, making Choice D the better option. **Choice F is incorrect** because "debilitated" means in a weakened or infirm state. This word does not fit in the blank because it does not accurately describe the feeling paleontologists would likely experience upon discovering that their arduous efforts went to waste while a natural phenomenon completed the task easily. Nothing in the passage suggests paleontologists are weak or can be in a weakened state as a result of their work. Therefore, Choice D is the better option.

3 **Choice B is correct** because "vibrant" means full of energy and enthusiasm. This word fits the context of the sentence because it accurately describes the period of history according to the following sentences. **Choice E is correct** because "expunged" means erased. This word fits the context of the sentence because it accurately describes the way the influence over Chinese politics from the Hundred Schools of Thought era was removed by the Qin Dynasty. **Choice I is correct** because "extant" means surviving. This word fits the context of the sentence because it accurately describes how ideas from the Hundred Schools of Thought era remained alive and continued to influence the modern world, despite the Qin Dynasty's attempt to expunge them.

Choice A is incorrect because "inane" means silly or stupid. This word does not fit the context of the sentence because it does not accurately describe the period of history as portrayed in the passage. The period is described as enjoyable and influential, so calling it silly does not align with that tone. **Choice C is incorrect** because "avaricious" means showing extreme greed for wealth. This word does not fit the context of the sentence because it does not accurately describe the period of history. The passage emphasizes enjoyment and long-lasting influence, with no mention of greed or material desire. **Choice D is incorrect** because "liberated" means freed from imprisonment or traditional ideas. This word does not fit the context of the sentence because the ideas from the Hundred Schools of Thought were not being set free. Rather, the Qin Dynasty was attempting to eliminate them from history, making Choice E the better

Verbal Reasoning — Answers & Explanations — Section 2

option. **Choice F is incorrect** because "inoculated" means immunized against a disease. This word does not fit the context of the sentence because there is no mention of disease or prevention. The topic is based on political and philosophical influence, not health, so Choice E is more appropriate. **Choice G is incorrect** because "lamented" means mourned or grieved over something that no longer exists. This is the opposite of what the sentence conveys, as it describes ideas that continue to influence the modern world. Therefore, Choice I is the better option. **Choice H is incorrect** because "defunct" means no longer existing. This also contradicts the sentence, which emphasizes the survival and ongoing influence of ideas. Therefore, Choice I is the better option.

4 **Choice B is correct** because the passage states that hand-washing only "reduces the risk of infection" and that resultant infections may cause significant health problems, advising further action to be taken to alert the general public and take better care of waste management.

Choice A is incorrect because the passage refers to health risks and advises precautions to be taken. Therefore, it cannot be said that seagulls pose no threat to public health. **Choice C is incorrect** because the precautions are "advised" rather than required. Only one out of ten seagulls' feces were infected with superbugs, and these findings are "preliminary." Moreover, the study was conducted in Australia, and therefore, it is not clear what implications the findings may have on seagull populations worldwide.

5 **Choice D is correct** because Candy is predicting that sales of the maple–flavored creams will ensure significant sales and profits in her new stores. If she cannot get enough maple syrup to provide sufficient inventory, her sales will fail to live up to expectations.

Choice A is incorrect because she may be paying a percentage of her sales to the management of the malls where she currently has stores, but this would only affect her expected profits if the percentage is too high. **Choice B is incorrect** because the sales of candy in other stores will have no direct bearing on her sales. Customers at the mall may even be drawn to Candy's maple creams as something new. **Choice C is incorrect** because the fact that the new malls have more stores than the malls where Candy currently operates should help her business succeed, as there are likely to be more customers daily. **Choice E is incorrect** because although the lower unemployment rate might affect Candy's ability to hire salespeople, we don't know how many employees she needs. Moreover, a lower unemployment rate generally means more people have discretionary income to spend.

6 **Choice C is correct** because "reclusiveness" means preferring isolation or seclusion from others. This word fits the context of the sentence because it explains why no one could ask him to expand on his brilliant theories. In other words, people rarely had access to him because he remained isolated. **Choice F is correct** because "solitariness" means the state of being alone. This word fits the context of the sentence because it explains why others could not question him about his ideas—he was always by himself.

Choice A is incorrect because "superciliousness" means having an exaggerated sense of one's own importance. This word does not fit the sentence, as there is no mention of the man being arrogant or selfish. His pride would not explain why others couldn't ask him questions, whereas being reclusive or solitary would. Therefore, Choices C and F are better options. **Choice B is incorrect** because "popularity" refers to being liked and admired by others. While he may have been well known due to his brilliant theories, popularity would not prevent others from asking him questions. By contrast, if he were reclusive or solitary, that would offer a logical reason. Thus, Choices C and F are more appropriate. **Choice D is incorrect** because "obtuseness" means being slow to understand. This contradicts the description of the man as a brilliant teacher with legendary theories. Therefore, this word does not fit the sentence, making Choices C and F the better selections. **Choice E is incorrect** because "unimportance" means lacking significance. This directly contradicts the sentence, which describes the man as a legend with brilliant theories. Hence, this word does not logically explain why others could not question him. Choices C and F are better suited.

7 **Choice A is correct** because "structure" refers to the arrangement of parts within something complex. This word fits the context of the sentence because it accurately describes a skin cell that was intricate enough to confuse researchers. **Choice D is correct** because "morphology" refers to the study of the forms and structure of things. This word fits the context of the sentence because it reflects how researchers would examine an unusual or complex cell.

Choice B is incorrect because "edifice" typically means a large, complex system or structure, often metaphorically used to describe systems of beliefs. This does not fit the context of cancer cell research, where physical structure—not ideological systems—is being discussed. Therefore, Choices A and D are better options. **Choice C is incorrect** because "department" refers to a division within a larger organization. Since the sentence is about a skin cell, not an organizational structure, "department" is contextually inappropriate. Thus, Choices A and D are more suitable. **Choice E is incorrect** because "genus" refers to a group of biologically related organisms. The sentence discusses a single, specific cell, not a classification group. Therefore, this word does not fit, making Choices A and D the better answers. **Choice F is incorrect** because "tabulation" refers to the organization of data in tables (rows and columns). The researchers are not categorizing or tabulating data in this sentence—they are examining the physical characteristics of a complex cell. Hence, Choices A and D are more accurate.

8 **Choice C is correct** because "objective" means representing facts without being influenced by personal feelings or opinions. This word fits the context of the sentence because it aligns with the idea that the speaker was attempting to speak neutrally, even though listeners might still distort the meaning of his words. **Choice F is correct** because "impartial" means treating all viewpoints equally and fairly. This word fits the context of the sentence because it supports the idea that the speaker was trying to remain neutral in his speech to prevent misinterpretation.

Choice A is incorrect because "fungible" means replaceable by another identical item. This word does not fit the context of the sentence because it refers to objects or resources, not styles of speaking. One cannot speak in a "fungible" way. Therefore, Choices C and F are better options. **Choice B is incorrect** because "optional" means not required or obligatory. This word does not make sense in the context of speech style. One cannot speak in an "optional" way, and nothing in the passage suggests a choice or offer is being made. Thus, Choices C and F are more appropriate. **Choice D is incorrect** because "subjective" means based on or influenced by personal feelings or opinions. This is the opposite of the intended meaning of the sentence. The speaker is described as trying to remain neutral, not personal, in his communication. Therefore, Choices C and F are more accurate. **Choice E is incorrect** because "figurative" means using metaphorical language rather than literal. This does not align with the sentence, which suggests the speaker is trying to be clear and neutral to avoid misinterpretation. Speaking figuratively would increase the chance of being misunderstood, so Choices C and F are better choices.

9 **Choice B is correct** because "inessential" means not absolutely necessary. This word fits the context of the sentence, which explains that the body will sacrifice certain parts to protect more important ones (i.e., "vital organs"). Thus, it implies that whatever is being sacrificed is not critical for survival. **Choice D is correct** because "dispensable" means something that can be done without. This word also fits the context because the sentence discusses the body's ability to give up less important parts to preserve vital organs, suggesting those sacrificed parts are not essential for life.

Choice A is incorrect because "mandatory" means required or obligatory. This contradicts the sentence's idea that the body sacrifices something of lesser importance. If a part were mandatory, it could not be given up to protect vital organs. **Choice C is incorrect** because "identical" means exactly alike. The sentence is not making any comparison of sameness between body parts. Instead, it focuses on the concept of relative importance and what can be sacrificed, making this word irrelevant in context. **Choice E is incorrect** because "asymmetrical" means lacking symmetry or balance in form. The sentence does not address appearance or structure, but rather the necessity or dispensability of certain body parts. Thus, this word does not fit. **Choice F is incorrect** because "embryological" refers to prenatal development. The sentence discusses the body's reaction to protect vital organs, which applies to fully developed humans, not fetuses. Therefore, this word does not fit the context.

10 "If the struggle for survival was the way of the world, then it was only natural that human society should operate in the same way."

This sentence is an example of conditional logic. Social Darwinists assumed that if this condition exists in the animal world, then it must also exist in the human world.

Verbal Reasoning — Answers & Explanations — Section 2

11 **Choice A is correct** because bullies adopt the role of predator when they select those who are weak in some way as targets of rumors or harmful insults. **Choice C is correct** because it involves using power to target innocent people based on something they cannot control.

Choice B is incorrect because involuntary commitment could be the result of a court proceeding that relies on expert testimony and is not necessarily a predatory action.

12 **Choice C is correct** because "dovetailed" in this context means that Social Darwinism and racist thinking fit together smoothly and naturally. The passage discusses how these ideologies reinforced one another, just as dovetail joints interlock securely in woodworking. The metaphor emphasizes the alignment and mutual reinforcement of the ideas.

Choice A is incorrect because "coincided with" implies simply happening at the same time, but does not convey the idea of integration or mutual support that "dovetailed" does. **Choice B** is incorrect because "deviated from" means to differ or go in another direction, which is the opposite of the intended meaning. **Choice D** is incorrect because it describes the physical shape of a dovetail joint, which is not relevant in this metaphorical usage referring to the fitting together of ideas. **Choice E** is incorrect because "split apart" suggests separation or disconnection, which contradicts the passage's implication that Social Darwinism and racist thinking were aligned.

5 Quantitative Reasoning   Answers & Explanations   Section 3

1 **Choice B is correct** because the diameter of the circle can be found to be 12 by using the area formula $A = \Pi r^2$. Plugging in the $36 = r^2$ gives you 6 for the radius. The length of line segment RP would be equal to the diameter if angle RQP was equal to 90° and the length of line segment RP would be less than the diameter if the angle was not equal to 90°. Since the angle is greater than 90° the length of RP can't be greater than the diameter or equal to the diameter.

Choice A is incorrect because a line segment inside a circle can't be greater than the diameter since the diameter would be the greatest length of a segment. **Choice C** is incorrect because the two quantities cannot be equal since the angle is not equal 90°. **Choice D** is incorrect because it is possible to identify a relationship between the two quantities.

2 **Choice D is correct** because a rectangle can have multiple different options for the length and width based on the area which would impact the perimeter of the quadrilateral.

The area of a square with a perimeter of 40 would be 100 because all sides in a square are equal. If you divide the perimeter by the number of sides, you would get the side length. 40 divided by 4 equals 10 for each side. To find the area of a square, just square the side length.

10^2 equals an area of 100.

The area of the rectangle would have many additional options. To find the combination of options, you would use the perimeter equation for a rectangle $P = 2l + 2w$. Plugging in a perimeter of 40 would give you endless combinations of numbers.

Hypothetically rectangles are squares so there is one combination of side lengths that would make Quantity A and B equal, but there are other options that would result in different relationships.

Choice A is incorrect because there are only some instances where Quantity A is greater than Quantity B. **Choice B** is incorrect because there are only some instances where Quantity B is greater than Quantity A. **Choice C** is incorrect because Quantity A can equal Quantity B, but this is not always the case.

3 **Choice D is correct** because if $|z| \leq 1$ it would stand to reason that z is a fraction or decimal. If you square a fraction or decimal you would end up with a number less than the original value. If you subtract a fraction or decimal from 1, you could end up with a number that is greater or less than the original value squared. Any value of z that is greater than $\frac{1}{2}$ would make Quantity A greater. Any value less than or equal to $\frac{1}{2}$ would make Quantity B greater.

Choice A is incorrect because only some values of z would make this greater. **Choice B** is incorrect because only some value of z would make this greater. **Choice C** is incorrect because only a certain value of z would make the quantities equal.

4 **Choice D is correct** because the range can be found by subtracting the greatest number of the data set from the lowest number of the data set and there are two possible options for x based on this. Since 23 is the greatest value and the range is 21, this means one possible option is that the lowest number is 2. Since there is no 2 in the data set, x must equal 2.

Alternatively, x could be the maximum so using the current minimum of 3, x would equal the range plus the minimum 21 + 3 which would be 24.

Choice A is incorrect because Quantity A is not greater than Quantity B when $x = 2$. **Choice B** is incorrect because Quantity B is not greater than Quantity A. **Choice C** is incorrect because Quantity A and Quantity B are not equal when $x = 24$.

5 **Choice A is correct** because you can write out the mathematical statement $a = 54x + 30$ based on the idea that a is 30 more than any multiple x of 54. You can factor this statement to be equal to $a = 6(9x + 5)$. This means a must be divisible by 6.

Choice B is incorrect because 7 is not a divisor. **Choice C** is incorrect because 8 is not a divisor. **Choice D** is incorrect because 10 is not a divisor. **Choice E** is incorrect because 11 is not a divisor.

Quantitative Reasoning — Answers & Explanations — Section 3

6 The correct answer is **45** because to find the percent increase use the formula $\frac{initial - final}{initial} \times 100$. Plugging in the values from the table for the Store A sales in 2000 and 2020, you would get $\left|\frac{\$1,453,140 - \$2,103,431}{\$1,453,140}\right| \times 100$ which is equal to 44.75% when rounded off to the nearest percentage is 45%.

7 **Choice B is correct** because to solve you need to find 11% of the 2010 sales for Store A. This would be found by multiplying 1,536,834 by 0.11 to get approximately $169,052.
Choice A is incorrect because this answer would result from a calculation error. **Choice C** is incorrect because this answer would result from a calculation error. **Choice D** is incorrect because this answer would result from a calculation error. **Choice E** is incorrect because this answer would result from a calculation error.

8 **Choice A is correct** because to find the average rate of change in sales per year you would use the rate of change formula $\frac{Sales\ in\ 2010 - Sales\ in\ 2000}{Change\ in\ Years}$. Filling this in you would get $\frac{1,231,034 - 932,121}{2010 - 2000}$ which equals $\frac{298913}{10}$. This simplifies to be $29,891.30.
Choice B is incorrect because this is the average rate of change for 2010 to 2020. **Choice C** is incorrect because this answer would result from a calculation error. **Choice D** is incorrect because this answer would result from a calculation error. **Choice E** is incorrect because this would be the answer if you did not divide by the number of years.

9 **Choice B is correct** because to solve for x first eliminate the fractions by multiplying by the least common multiple of 8 and 3, 24. You would then get $3x + 8x + 312 = 24x$. Combine like terms and collect all of the x values on one side to get $11x + 312 = 24x$ and then $312 = 13x$. Divide both sides by 13 to get $x = 24$.
Choice A is incorrect because 16 does not go evenly into 3 so it would not result in a whole number. **Choice C** is incorrect because 32 does not go evenly into 3 so it would not result in a whole number. **Choice D** is incorrect because you would get the false statement 35 = 48 when you plug in 48. **Choice E** is incorrect because you would get the false statement 46 = 72 when you plug in 72.

10 The correct answer is $\frac{2}{9}$ because if the diameter of a circle is tripled that means the radius is tripled as well. Plugging this change into the area formula of $A = \pi r^2$ would give us a new area of $\pi(3r)^2$ or $9\pi r^2$. Now set up the ratio of the area of the original circle over half of the new circle to get $\frac{\pi r^2}{4.5\pi r^2}$. This would simplify to $\frac{1}{4.5}$ which is the same as $\frac{2}{9}$.

11 **Choices A and C are correct.** Choice A is correct because 36 is divisible by 2.4 with no remainder. Choice C is correct because 48 is divisible by 2.4 with no remainder. To find the total number of cars sold by both Angelo and Beth, start with x to represent the number of cars Beth sold. The amount of cards Angelo sold can then be represented as $x + \frac{2}{5}x$. Adding this to the number of cars Beth sold would get you the equation $x + x + \frac{2}{5}x$ which simplifies to $2.4x$. Any number that is divisible by 2.4 would work.
Choice B is incorrect because 44 is not divisible by 2.4. **Choice D** is incorrect because 50 is not divisible by 2.4.

12 **Choice A is correct** because you can cross-multiply the fraction to solve and isolate x. Start by multiplying both sides by $4y - 3x$ to get $3x + 4y = 3(4y - 3x)$. Then distribute to get $3x + 4y = 12y - 9x$. Collect all of the x values on one side and all of the y values on the other to get the statement $12x = 8y$. Divide both sides by 12 and simplify to get $\frac{2y}{3}$.
Choice B is incorrect because this would result from an error when rearranging terms. **Choice C** is incorrect because this would result from an error when rearranging terms. **Choice D** is incorrect because this would result from an error when rearranging terms. **Choice E** is incorrect because this would result from an error when rearranging terms.

Verbal Reasoning (Easy) — Answers & Explanations — Section 4

1 **Choice A is correct** because "unheeded" means heard or noticed, but disregarded. This word fits the context of the sentence because it accurately describes what can be done with information that does not deserve focus.

Choice B is incorrect because "rejected" means to dismiss as inadequate or nonpreferred. This word does not fit the context of the sentence because it implies an active dismissal based on inadequacy or preference. The sentence refers to irrelevant information being disregarded without necessarily undergoing evaluation. Therefore, Choice A is the better answer. **Choice C** is incorrect because "considered" means having been thought about carefully. This word does not fit the context of the sentence because irrelevant information should not be carefully thought about—it should be ignored. Therefore, Choice A is the better option. **Choice D** is incorrect because "abandoned" means deserted or left behind. This word does not fully fit the context of the sentence because it implies that the information was once valued or included, which is not the case here. The sentence is about information that was never deserving of attention in the first place. Therefore, Choice A is the better option. **Choice E** is incorrect because "underestimated" means to regard something as smaller or less important than it is. This word does not fit the context because it implies a misjudgment of value. The sentence refers to information that is correctly identified as unimportant and therefore ignored. Thus, Choice A is the best option.

2 **Choice C is correct** because "catalog" means making a systemized list of items of the same type. This word fits the context of the sentence because it describes the action of categorizing poetry, which the rest of the passage goes on to explain is quite challenging compared to other types of writing. **Choice D is correct** because "incontrovertibly" means undeniably true. This word fits the context of the passage because it accurately describes the way other genres, like romance and science fiction, are easily separated. Poetry, however, is only divided in debatable ways because of its complexity.

Choice A is incorrect because "inoculate" means to immunize against a disease. This word does not fit the context of the sentence because poems cannot be inoculated. In addition, the concepts of disease and disease prevention are unrelated to the topic being discussed in the passage. **Choice B** is incorrect because "inculcate" means to instill through persistent instruction. This word does not fit the context of the sentence because poems cannot be inculcated, as inanimate objects cannot hold beliefs or practice habits. Additionally, this topic is unrelated to the focus of the passage, which is categorizing genres of poetry. **Choice E** is incorrect because "libidinously" means marked by lustful desires. This word does not fit the context of the sentence because it does not accurately describe the way poems would be categorized into genres. Rather than being divided in a sexual or sensual way, it would make more sense for written works to be divided incontrovertibly, making Choice D the better option. **Choice F** is incorrect because "debatably" means a matter that is uncertain because people have different opinions. This word does not fit the context of the sentence because it is the opposite of what the sentence is trying to express. The sentence conveys that poetry is rarely easy to categorize, unlike other forms of writing, because it can be interpreted differently by people. Therefore, Choice D is the better option.

3 **Choice A is correct** because "debilitate" means making someone weak and infirm. This word fits the context of the sentence because it accurately describes what the stress of such a high-stakes job can do to even the best doctors. The following sentences provide more information about the heaviness of the occupation, which makes clear that "debilitate" is the correct word. **Choice D is correct** because "paucity" means the presence of something in a scarce quantity. This word fits the context of the sentence because it accurately describes the lack of trained pediatric surgeons that creates such a strong demand among children with heart conditions. **Choice G is correct** because "superseded" means one thing is replaced with something that is better or more important. This word fits the context of the sentence because it describes how the less important risk of travel is outweighed by the benefit of receiving pediatric heart surgical services in the face of such serious issues.

Choice B is incorrect because "buttress" means a source of defense or support, particularly in buildings. This word does not fit the context of the sentence because it does not accurately describe the effect that stress would have on "even the best" surgeons. Rather than supporting the surgeons, stress would burden them, making Choice A the best option. **Choice C** is incorrect because "assuage" means to satisfy or make an unpleasant feeling less intense. This word does not fit the context of the sentence because it does not accurately describe the effect that stress would have on "even the best" surgeons. Rather than satisfying or helping the surgeons, stress would burden them, making Choice A the best option. **Choice E** is incorrect because "opalescence" means the visual property of reflecting an iridescent light. This word does not fit the context of the sentence because it does not accurately describe the factor that creates massive demand for these surgeons. The visual appearance of the surgeons would not necessarily create a greater need for their services. In addition, it is unlikely that people would be described as opalescent. Therefore, Choice D is the best option. **Choice F** is incorrect because "ubiquity" means being very common and appearing everywhere. This word does not fit the context of the sentence because it does not accurately describe the factor that creates massive demand for these surgeons. This word expresses the opposite of what the sentence conveys. Rather than being common, pediatric heart surgeons are rare. So, people must travel great lengths to access their care. Thus, Choice D is the best option. **Choice H** is incorrect because "delineated" means to describe or portray precisely. This word does not fit the context of the sentence because it does not accurately describe the role that the risk of travel plays in comparison with medical necessity. The risk of travel is not being portrayed precisely; rather, it is being overshadowed. This makes Choice G the best option. **Choice I** is incorrect because "critiqued" means evaluated in an analytical way. This word does not fit the context of the sentence because it does not accurately describe the role that the risk of travel plays in comparison with medical necessity. The risk of travel is not being assessed; rather, it is being overshadowed. This makes Choice G the best option.

4 **Choice A is correct** because "manifestation" means the embodiment or display of an abstract idea. This word fits in the context of the sentence because social stratification is an idea that is being clearly exhibited or embodied in Western societies. **Choice F is correct** because "pervasiveness" means widespread presence. This word fits the context because it accurately describes how social stratification is prevalent across various societies, making it evident even from a quick glance at a textbook. **Choice G is correct** because "substantiates" means to provide evidence that supports a claim. This word fits the sentence because it explains how the ubiquity of social stratification is seen as evidence for its natural role in any society.

Choice B is incorrect because "contradiction" means an opposition between two things. The sentence discusses a single idea—social stratification—not two opposing concepts. **Choice C** is incorrect because "ambiguousness" means being unclear or open to interpretation. Social stratification in Western societies is not presented as unclear, but rather as a clear example of the concept. **Choice D** is incorrect because "reticence" refers to restraint or reserve. The passage is highlighting how widespread social stratification is—not how restrained or hidden it is. **Choice E** is incorrect because "contradistinction" means drawing contrast between two things. Since the sentence does not involve comparison or contrasting elements, this word does not fit. **Choice H** is incorrect because "fissures" means splits or cracks. The sentence does not suggest that the commonness of social stratification divides or weakens it. **Choice I** is incorrect because "fractures" means breaks or cracks in something solid. Again, the sentence argues that the ubiquity of stratification supports its naturalness, not that it breaks it apart.

5 **Choice D is correct** because the first sentence mentions the responsibility of the United States in regard to Haiti, while a later sentence asserts that Haiti was under the U.S.'s financial guardianship, implying that the U.S. shares some responsibility.

Choice A is incorrect because the passage does compare the treatment of the two countries but does not imply that one policy was fairer than the other. **Choice B** is incorrect because the passage discusses internal and external debt but does not explain how they operate in Haiti's infrastructure. **Choice C** is incorrect because the passage states that the United States had guardianship at a certain point, but does not explain its reasons for doing so. **Choice E** is incorrect because the passage makes a pointed reference to the fact that designated funds were set aside but does not explore why they were not used.

6 **Choice C is correct** because the purpose of the passage is to point out the culpability of the United States for Haiti's financial condition. Haiti's reputation is mentioned so that the author can rebut it with a counter-example, the country's previous fiscal responsibility.

Choice A is incorrect because the author downplays Haiti's chaotic reputation by noting its history of financial responsibility. **Choice B** is incorrect because the author strongly implies that the United States did not live up to its responsibilities to Haiti by continually reminding the reader that the U.S. was in charge when problems occurred. **Choice D** is incorrect because the author mentions the designated revenues but does not suggest an

5 Verbal Reasoning (Easy) Answers & Explanations Section 4

alternate way to use them. **Choice E is incorrect** because the author does not draw this conclusion or suggest that Haiti diverged from the U.S.'s wishes.

7 **Choice A is correct** because the entire point of the passage is to disabuse the reader of this notion and point out the culpability of the United States in the matter. **Choice B is correct** because it is covered when the author points out Haiti's history of successful debt management. **Choice C is correct** because it is found in the last sentence when the author notes the hardships that individuals have suffered.

8 **Choice A is correct** because "disparate" means very different in kind. This word fits the context of the sentence because it accurately describes the vast differences in appearance and customs between the two referenced groups. The sentence explains that, although groups can be extremely different, humans across the globe still have much in common. **Choice D is correct** because "dissimilar" means not alike. This word fits the context of the sentence because it accurately describes the vast differences in appearance and customs between the two referenced groups. The sentence explains that, although groups can be extremely different, humans across the globe still have much in common.

Choice B is incorrect because "concurrent" means occurring or existing at the same time. This word does not fit the context of the sentence because it does not describe the appearances and customs of various groups. Although they might exist at the same time, the sentence emphasizes that these things are different from one another. **Choice C is incorrect** because "idyllic" means happy, peaceful, or picturesque. This word does not fit the context of the sentence because it does not describe the appearances and customs of various groups. The sentence is not focused on idealizing the customs, but on highlighting their differences. **Choice E is incorrect** because "uniform" means unchanging or the same throughout. This word does not fit the context of the sentence because it is the opposite of what the sentence conveys. The sentence emphasizes cultural differences, not sameness. **Choice F is incorrect** because "familiar" means well known from previous experience or association. This word does not fit the context of the sentence because it does not accurately describe the appearances and customs of various groups. The sentence focuses on how these customs differ, not on how recognizable they are.

9 **Choice B is correct** because "quiescent" means in a state of inactivity or dormancy. This word fits the context of the sentence because it describes what other trees are doing at the end of summer. Rather than producing fruit, they are entering a period of rest. In contrast, the tree that is the subject of the sentence is blooming. **Choice E is correct** because "dormant" means temporarily inactive. This word fits the context of the sentence because it accurately describes the state of most trees at the end of summer. While they prepare for a period of inactivity, the subject tree does the opposite by blooming.

Choice A is incorrect because "stagnant" means having no movement or current, typically referring to water or air. This word does not fit the context of the sentence because trees do not move or flow. Their inactivity is better described as "dormant" or "quiescent." **Choice C is incorrect** because "inertia" refers to the tendency to remain unchanged, often in a physical or mechanical sense. This word does not fit the context, as the trees are not remaining in a single state but are transitioning into dormancy. **Choice D is incorrect** because "indolence" means avoidance of activity or laziness. This word implies a conscious choice, which does not apply to trees. The inactivity of trees is natural and seasonal, making "dormant" or "quiescent" more accurate descriptions. **Choice F is incorrect** because "sloth" means a reluctance to work or make an effort. Like "indolence" it implies intentional laziness, which is not appropriate when describing trees. Therefore, "dormant" and "quiescent" are the more suitable choices.

10 **Choice B is correct** because "dulcet" means sweet and soothing. This word fits the context of the sentence because it accurately describes poems that focus on the topic of love. The poems are later described as evocative and mellifluous, which supports the idea that they were sweet and pleasant to the ear. **Choice C is correct** because "redolent" means strongly reminiscent. This word fits the context because it describes poems written long ago that continue to be cherished today. The author, Rumi, was reflecting on love in a way that evokes strong memories and emotions.

Choice A is incorrect because "odoriferous" means giving off a smell, usually an unpleasant one. This word does not fit the context because poems are not physical objects that emit odors. Additionally, the sentence describes the poems as beautiful and romantic, making this word

Verbal Reasoning (Easy) — Answers & Explanations — Section 4

inappropriate. **Choice D** is incorrect because "fecund" means fertile or capable of producing an abundance of offspring or growth. This word does not describe poems, which are inanimate and cannot reproduce or grow in a literal sense. **Choice E** is incorrect because "restive" means unable to remain still or silent, typically due to impatience or boredom. Since poems are inanimate, they cannot exhibit such behavior. Moreover, the tone of the sentence is calm and reflective, not agitated. **Choice F** is incorrect because "nostalgic" means reflecting fondly on the past. While the poems were written long ago, the sentence focuses on their content—love—not on reminiscing about a past time or era. Therefore, "dulcet" and "redolent" are more accurate choices.

11 **Choice D is correct** because the first sentence of this passage introduces the argument that needs strengthening: when the Pilgrim's Way was created. Choice D effectively supports the idea by showing that the term was used at the date suggested in the passage, as it was printed in a newspaper.

Choice A is incorrect because the meaning of "pilgrim" is not essential, as long as the name was used at the time. **Choice B** is incorrect because it is not related to the topic of the Way, only Henry the Second, so it can be eliminated. **Choice C** is incorrect because it establishes that Henry the Second used the Way, but does not show what it was called at the time. **Choice E** is incorrect because it is also unrelated to the name, only to details of one person who walked there.

12 **Choice B is correct** because the passage refers to rock art as a "testament to the ingenuity" of early humans, depicting not only surrounding creatures but also a spiritual dimension. It describes the use of varied techniques as "striking" and the art itself showing "creative vision." This all implies the work is impressive in artistic depth and, therefore, deserving of appreciation.

Choice A is incorrect because the passage states that the artwork "depict[ed] both animals and anthropomorphic creatures" which means that wildlife alone was not the focus. Also, there is no indication that the animals depicted were predators and likely posed a threat. **Choice C** is incorrect because there was no mention of a disregard for resources in the passage. The term "exploitation" here means the artists incorporated the forms of the stone rather than misusing or wasting any material. **Choice D** is incorrect because the passage states that rock art is thought to have "developed in stages over long periods of time" which implies that many generations were involved. In addition, it cannot be concluded that they were working towards a unified vision. **Choice E** is incorrect because the passage states the artwork "sheds light on the spiritual aspects" of the early humans, which suggests they may have had a religious meaning. There is no mention of the artwork being used for educational purposes.

13 **Choice C is correct** because a concrete year is not given, but only an approximation to the nearest millennium. This amounts to an educated guess "by some estimates" based on certain findings. The estimation is further underlined by the previous phrase that reads, archaeologists "currently believe…" which implies a lack of certainty.

Choice A is incorrect because "concluded" is a very strong assertion that leaves no room for doubt, whereas the sentence, using the phrase "by some estimates" suggests this is one estimation out of several, and it might be reconsidered in the future. **Choice B** is incorrect because a hypothesis is made before experimenting or testing data. However, the passage suggests that the time periods, using the expression "by some estimates" were arrived at after some consideration. **Choice D** is incorrect because the passage makes no reference to a previously considered time period for the artwork. The phrase, "currently believe" implies that there has been a change in thinking, but in reference to the fact that the artwork was made in stages instead of in a single period, not to how far back the paintings date. **Choice E** is incorrect because there is no mention of a previously considered starting date for the artwork. So, there is no opposition to a previous claim, only the statement that the art is considered to have been started as early as 36,000 years ago.

14 **Choice D is correct** because the central idea is that wealth produced by slavery plays a role in the wealth gap, as can be seen in the composition of modern social hierarchy. This is supported by the fact that the wealth of 28% of congress members (positions of high social status) can be traced to ancestors who enslaved people for labor. Additionally, the author states that such "vestiges of slave-begotten wealth" deserve a "deeper look."

Choice A is incorrect because the passage does not state that fortunes produced under slavery are greater than ("eclipse") those made since its abolition. Also, it makes the point that slavery-produced wealth accounts for "at least some" of the disproportion, rather than claiming it is a "pivotal" factor in modern-day inequalities. **Choice B** is incorrect because the passage does not state that slavery profits have led suddenly ("precipitated") in the wealth gap, but rather that they are a significant factor out of many to be considered. It also does not make the direct link between slaveholder descendants in congress and legislation. **Choice C** is incorrect because the passage does not analyze the privileges that come along with inherited wealth in general but focuses on wealth passed down from slaveholding ancestors. Also, it suggests that these findings challenge the basis of the American Dream as a secondary point ("In addition…"). It is not the central idea, which is the socioeconomic influence of slavery on the wealth gap and modern US society. **Choice E** is incorrect because while it might be the case that connections in public office help facilitate entry, it is not the main idea, which centers on wealth inherited from slave-holders being an influential factor in the wealth gap.

15 **"These findings may refute the commonly held notion that slavery was an institution of the past with no bearing on modern socio-economic dynamics."**

This sentence is correct because it states that the findings about generational wealth being linked to slavery may "refute the commonly held notion" which means it may change the perception on the topic of "slavery [having] no bearing on modern socioeconomic dynamics." In other words, the findings suggest that certain people still benefit from the profits made under slavery and to a larger extent than previously believed.

Verbal Reasoning (Hard) — Answers & Explanations — Section 4

1 **Choice B is correct** because "intractable" means hard to control or deal with. This word fits the context of the sentence because it accurately describes the nature of the problem the physicists deal with. They cannot understand this important question about the basis of the universe, and the problem is hard to handle.

Choice A is incorrect because "wayward" means difficult to predict because of unusual behavior. This word does not fit the context of the sentence because the physicists are not trying to predict anything about the universe, but rather to understand something that occurred previously. **Choice C** is incorrect because "resolute" means admirably purposeful and unwavering. This word does not fit the context of the sentence because it does not accurately describe the nature of the problem physicists are facing. This problem has been burdensome, not admirable. Therefore, Choice B is the better option. **Choice D** is incorrect because "perverse" means showing a deliberate desire to behave in an unacceptable way. This word does not fit the context of the sentence because it does not accurately describe the nature of the problem physicists are facing. The physicists are not challenged by the current behavior of the universe, but by a phenomenon that occurred previously. **Choice E** is incorrect because "pliant" means flexible, adaptable, and easily influenced. This word does not fit the context of the sentence because it does not accurately describe the nature of the problem physicists are facing. The physicists are not challenged by the flexibility of the universe, but by its past creation.

2 **Choice A is correct** because "prominence" means the state of being important or famous. This word fits the context of the sentence because it expresses the fact that, although hydrologists were not idolized previously, they may be rising in social importance with the increasing need to understand and monitor water usage. **Choice E is correct** because "denigrated" means criticized unfairly. This word fits the context of the sentence because it describes the way that countries once looked down upon monitoring water supplies, although they are now seeking out top hydrologists.

Choice B is incorrect because "ignominy" means public shame or disgrace. This word does not fit the context of the sentence because it is unlikely that anyone would seek this out. Rather, people would seek fame and importance. Also, it does not align with the message the passage is trying to convey about the increasing need for hydrologists and their corresponding rise in prominence.

Choice C is incorrect because "extravagance" means a lack of restraint in spending money. This word does not fit the context of the sentence because it does not relate to the discussion about hydrologists and their recent rise in social importance. The passage is not discussing money or belongings, but rather explaining the change in the field of hydrology. **Choice D** is incorrect because "recalculated" means to calculate again, usually using different data. This word does not fit the context of the sentence because a notion cannot be calculated or recalculated. In addition, the topic being discussed does not have anything to do with numbers or data. Rather, the notion of monitoring water was criticized, or denigrated. **Choice F** is incorrect because "co-opted" means choosing to elect or invite someone into membership. This word does not fit the context of the sentence because it does not relate to the topic being discussed. In this passage, there are no committees or other groups that include formal members. It does not make sense for a notion to be co-opted.

3 **Choice B is correct** because "facilitated" means to make something easier. This word fits in the context of the sentence because it explains how the invention of the radio led to changes in the music industry. This invention was the catalyst that led to many stylistic changes or made it easier for them to come about. **Choice D is correct** because "shackled" means chained and restrained. This word fits in the context of the sentence in a metaphorical way because it describes how music was previously stuck in concert houses and clubs before the invention of the radio made music more available. **Choice I is correct** because "proliferation" means a rapid increase in numbers. This word fits the context of the sentence because it describes the way musical genres grew and expanded in the 20th century after the invention of the radio. The rapid increase in numbers refers to the rapid increase of musical genres and styles.

Choice A is incorrect because "circumvented" means to find a way around something. This word does not fit in the context of the sentence because the radio did not go around stylistic changes. This would not make sense and does not describe the way that the invention of the radio impacted the music industry. As opposed to going around the stylistic changes, the invention of the radio facilitated changes. **Choice C** is incorrect because "barred" means marked off or closed by a rod. This word does not fit in the context of the sentence because the invention of the radio facilitated stylistic changes. It did not block them off. Therefore, Choice B is the better option. **Choice**

Verbal Reasoning (Hard) — Answers & Explanations — Section 4

E is incorrect because "schematized" means to form into a systematic arrangement. This word does not fit in the context of the sentence because music was not previously sorted in a systematic way in concert houses and pubs. Rather, it was confined to those locations before the invention of the radio allowed music to be played in a variety of settings. **Choice F is incorrect because** "quiescent" means a state of inactivity or dormancy. This word does not fit in the context of the sentence because music was not being described as inactive, but simply confined to particular locations. Therefore, Choice D is the best option. **Choice G is incorrect because** "guileless" means innocent, naïve, and without deception. This word is incorrect because it is an adjective, and the blank requires a noun. Also, it does not fit the context of the sentence because music is not being described as naïve in the 20th century. Rather, it was rapidly growing and changing. This makes Choice I the best option. **Choice H is incorrect because** "portly" means having a stout body. This word is incorrect because it is an adjective, and the blank requires a noun. Also, it does not fit the context of the sentence because music is not being described as fat in the 20th century. Rather, it was rapidly growing and changing. This makes Choice I the best option.

4 **Choice A is correct** because "subverted" means undermining power and authority. This word fits in the context of the sentence because it describes the way the heat interfered with the person's efforts to finish his report. Although the person was determined, the heat gained dominance over him. **Choice E is correct** because "penetrate" means forcing a way into or through something. This word fits in the context of the sentence because it accurately describes the fans' inability to make it through the thick waves of humidity. In other words, the air was so humid that wind could not be felt through it. **Choice I is correct** because "sporadically" means at irregular intervals. This word fits in the context of the sentence because it accurately describes the way one would wake up throughout the night due to the heat. In other words, the person will wake up at irregular intervals due to the discomfort of being sweaty and thirsty.

Choice B is incorrect because "subsisted" means to maintain or support oneself. This word does not fit in the context of the sentence because the heat is not supporting itself, and this does not relate to the person's attempts at finishing his report. Rather, the heat is undermining his attempts, making Choice A the better option. **Choice C is incorrect because** "sanctioned" means giving an official approval or penalty. This word does not fit in the context of the sentence because the heat is not sanctioning anything, nor does it relate to the person's efforts to finish the report. The heat is interfering with his efforts, making Choice A the better option. **Choice D is incorrect because** "augment" means making something greater by adding to it. This word does not fit in the context of the sentence because the fans are not trying to add to the thick waves of humidity. Rather, the sentence expresses that no fan could produce wind strong enough to get through the humidity, making Choice E the best option. **Choice F** is incorrect because "succor" means to give assistance to. This word does not fit in the context of the sentence because the fans are not trying to assist the thick waves of humidity. Rather, the sentence expresses that no fan could create wind powerful enough to cut through the humidity, making Choice E the best option. **Choice G** is incorrect because "exquisitely" means in an extremely beautiful manner. This word does not fit in the context of the sentence because it does not describe how the person is going to wake up throughout the night. The passage implies discomfort and irritation, not beauty. The person is going to wake up at irregular intervals, making Choice I the best option. **Choice H is incorrect because** "volubly" means to speak in a way that is confident and forceful. This word does not fit in the context of the sentence because waking up has no connection to speaking. The sentence is about the frequency of waking, not how someone talks, making Choice I the best option.

5 **Choice A is correct** because the passage mentions 430 million tonnes of plastic produced, much of which gets discarded and runs the risk of contaminating water sources. **Choice B is correct** because the passage states that it is not certain at which point the particles appear, therefore, it cannot be ruled out that microplastics that travel by air can settle into an open bottle of water. **Choice C is correct** because the handling and bottling of water may expose the contents to microplastics present at the bottling plant.

Verbal Reasoning (Hard) — Answers & Explanations — Section 4

6 "Bottled water has come under a new wave of scrutiny in a recent study that discovered about a quarter million microplastic particles suspended in a single liter."

This sentence is correct because it presents the recent finding of "a quarter million microplastic particles suspended in a single liter." This has led to a "new wave of scrutiny" indicating that the quantity of microplastic particles is higher than previously expected, making plastic bottles even more of a concern than previously thought.

7 **Choice D is correct** because the passage discusses *Guernica* in the context of real events and in terms of its ability to "engage the global community" with a "message against war." Given that it "transcends art circles" and leaves an "indelible mark on viewers" the work is shown to be not only a response to the attack but also an enduring cultural statement with "social impact."

Choice A is incorrect because *Guernica* is discussed within the context of real events, and how it has impressed viewers. This is not a subjective perspective of the work, but rather a more objective look at its value and impact. **Choice B** is incorrect because even though Picasso's style and mastery were evident, the discussion centers more on the impact of the subject of the painting than the art techniques used in its execution. **Choice C** is incorrect because *Guernica* is not discussed for its artistic techniques, but rather as a work of art that has more than "aesthetic value." Although the piece is described as "visually stunning" the main idea is that it carried a humanitarian message and that "Picasso ventured far beyond the aesthetic value of his work." **Choice E** is incorrect because the main point of the passage is about the power of the subject matter. The "true-to-life" canvas and stark imagery of the piece were the means by which the message was transmitted, but they were not the most significant point made about its impact.

8 **Choice E is correct** because the passage claims that *Guernica* is an example of art having meaning beyond its subjective value. The painting, serving as a catalyst for raising awareness and funds, strengthens the argument that it played a role beyond the art world, reaching the sphere of social perceptions and having a tangible impact.

Choice A is incorrect because although Picasso exhibited the piece around the world, one cannot infer that it had any social or political impact from the exhibitions alone. **Choice B** is incorrect because although it is true, the argument that this piece transmits an impactful message would not be strengthened by the fact that it has been commercialized as a popular museum souvenir, as many works of art become souvenirs regardless of their social impact. **Choice C** is incorrect because the effect of the painting on local tourism is not relevant to convey a humanitarian message. **Choice D** is incorrect because the Museum of Peace is a dedication to the memory of the attack, and although it features the painting, it is not a strong argument for the impact of the painting's message.

9 **Choice B is correct** because the passage previously stated that *Guernica* was painted with a message that distinguished it from other works of art centered on aesthetics and form. This paragraph reinforces the claim that *Guernica* presented more universal themes by providing examples of the poignant imagery used to denounce the war.

Choice A is incorrect because the third paragraph does not make any reference to Picasso's earlier work, which would be necessary to make a comparison. Instead, it presents examples of how the subject matter in *Guernica* was able to carry a message, while still being "visually stunning." **Choice C** is incorrect because although this is the message of the artwork, the paragraph itself provides examples in the painting that demonstrate the timelessness of the subject matter for the larger debate on art and its value. **Choice D** is incorrect because the paragraph does not suggest that the visuals take away from the message, but rather that they are the vehicles for transmitting it. **Choice E** is incorrect because the paragraph focuses on the subject matter and its depiction rather than the techniques or aesthetics used in its execution.

10 **Choice D is correct** because "pristine" means in its original, unspoiled condition. This fits the context of the sentence, which emphasizes how unusual it is to see a centuries-old book so well-preserved. The use of "remarkable" and "high standard" aligns with the idea that the book appears untouched by time. **Choice E is correct** because "immaculate" means perfectly clean or free from any blemish or flaw. This fits well in the context of an antique book being described as exceptionally well-maintained, reinforcing the speaker's astonishment at its quality.

Verbal Reasoning (Hard) — Answers & Explanations

Choice A is incorrect because "sanitary" refers to cleanliness in a hygienic sense, often related to health or sterilization. This word doesn't fit the context of describing the condition of a rare book—it implies germ-free rather than well-preserved. **Choice B is incorrect** because "untarnished" can mean not damaged or not spoiled, but it is more often used metaphorically (e.g., "untarnished reputation"). It lacks the precise implication of physical perfection needed in this sentence about an old book's condition. **Choice C is incorrect** because "purified" means cleansed of impurities, typically in a chemical, religious, or spiritual sense. It does not appropriately describe a book's physical condition or its preservation. **Choice F is incorrect** because "adulterated" means made worse by the addition of inferior substances. This clearly contradicts the positive tone of the sentence, which describes the book as remarkably high in quality.

11 **Choice C is correct** because "clumsy" means done awkwardly or without elegance. This word fits the context of the sentence because it describes designs that were displeasing to people, and it pairs logically with the word "impractical." **Choice D is correct** because "gauche" means unsophisticated and lacking grace. This word fits the context of the sentence because it also describes designs that were displeasing to people and aligns well with the word "impractical."

Choice A is incorrect because "sophisticated" means highly developed and cultured. This word does not fit the context of the sentence because it suggests a positive quality, which contradicts the description of the designs as "impractical" and displeasing. **Choice B is incorrect** because "ill-bred" means badly brought up or rude. This word does not fit the context of the sentence because it typically describes a person, not a design. Since designs are inanimate objects, they cannot be rude or poorly raised. **Choice E is incorrect** because "butterfingered" refers to a person who lacks coordination with their hands. This word is inappropriate here because a design cannot have hand coordination or be described using traits reserved for people. **Choice F is incorrect** because "couth" means well-mannered. This word does not fit the context of the sentence because it refers to behavior or manners, which cannot be attributed to designs, as they are inanimate objects.

12 **Choice C is correct** because "relationship" refers to the way in which people are connected. This word fits the context of the sentence because it describes how employees worked well together, which resulted in adequate sales. **Choice D is correct** because "rapport" means a harmonious relationship among people. This word fits the context of the sentence because it describes the positive connection between employees that led to good sales for the company.

Choice A is incorrect because "turbidity" refers to the cloudiness or clarity of a fluid. This word does not fit the context of the sentence, which discusses human interactions, not measurements of liquids. **Choice B is incorrect** because "condescension" means a patronizing attitude of superiority. This word suggests negative, uncooperative behavior, which contradicts the sentence's positive tone about employee interactions and successful sales. **Choice E is incorrect** because "despair" means a complete loss of hope. This word implies sadness and helplessness, which does not align with the sentence's emphasis on positive collaboration and good sales. **Choice F is incorrect** because "synecdoche" is a figure of speech in which a part represents the whole or vice versa. This term relates to language and literary devices, not to workplace relationships or employee interactions..

13 **Choice B is correct** because if the deer do not have an adequate food supply, they will die. If there are fewer deer reproducing, there will be a decline in successive generations. A smaller deer population means a reduction in the food supply for the tigers, and they will not survive in traditional numbers.

Choice A is incorrect because the tigers hide in the reeds. If there are more reeds, then they can hide from the deer better. **Choice C is incorrect** because if the deer can see the tigers better, they will be able to flee. The tigers will weaken without a food source. **Choice D** is unrelated to the problem; ecotourism, if anything, may include management methods to ensure that animal populations remain high for visitors to see. **Choice E is incorrect** because the tigers have a new food source that has not adapted to avoid them, so they can potentially eat more food.

Verbal Reasoning (Hard) — Answers & Explanations

14 **Choice A is correct** because the passage is mainly about whether language can influence physical reality, rather than just describe or react to it. After the author introduces the concept of *kotodama*, which claims that words have tangible effects on reality, they refer to modern research in neuroscience. They conclude with the position that language transcends mere description and reaction, given the fact that brains undergo physical changes as a result of language use. **Choice B is correct** because the passage reads that modern research "corroborates" this claim, which means that it provides evidence of its legitimacy. The author ends in the last line by suggesting that the link between physical brain changes and environmental changes may be established in the future. **Choice C is incorrect** because the passage bases its points on the results of modern research and scientific tools, such as fMRI. Although it may not have been established how these neuronal structures change on a molecular level, the tone of the passage, with its emphasis on "perceptible" changes, does not suggest that the author would think that brain changes come about mysteriously.

15 **"Language altering our neuronal reality perhaps lends credence to the claim that external reality is also susceptible to its effects."**

This sentence is correct because it states that language alters our "neuronal reality." However, about physical changes in external reality, the author writes that the findings "perhaps" bolster the claim that language transforms physical reality, which means the case can be made for it while conceding that the evidence is not overwhelming. In addition, it states that reality may be "susceptible" to the effects of language, indicating a possible, though not certain, outcome.

5 Quantitative Reasoning (Easy) — Answers & Explanations — Section 5

1 **Choice A is correct** because the standard deviation of Quantity A would be higher than that of the standard deviation of Quantity B. This can be concluded based on Quantity B's data set having more values central to the mean while Quantity A has more spread. If you were to calculate the standard deviation of the data set in Quantity A it would be approximately 0.816 and the standard deviation of the data set in Quantity B would be approximately 0.577.

Choice B is incorrect because the standard deviation of the data set in Quantity B is lower. **Choice C** is incorrect because the standard deviations are not the same. **Choice D** is incorrect because it is possible to solve for both standard deviations.

2 **Choice D is correct** because if you distribute and compare the equations there are instances where Quantity A will be greater and there are other instances where Quantity B will be greater. Quantity A can be simplified to be $\frac{6}{x} + 18y$.

An example of Quantity B being greater is when $x = 12$ and $y = 2$. This would make $\frac{6}{x} + 18y$ equal to $\frac{6}{12} + 18(2)$ which equals $\frac{73}{2}$. For Quantity B, $x = 12$ and $y = 2$ would be $5(12) + 3(2)$ which is 66. Since $66 > \frac{73}{2}$ it is possible for Quantity B to be greater than Quantity A.

Quantity A can be greater than Quantity B for some situations such as when $x = 2$ and $y = 3$. In this case, Quantity A would be $\frac{6}{2} + 18(3)$ which equals 57. For Quantity B, when you input the values $x = 2$ and $y = 3$ you would get $5(2) + 3(3)$ which equals 19. Since $57 > 19$, Quantity A can be greater than Quantity B.

Choice A is incorrect because Quantity A is only greater in some cases. **Choice B** is incorrect because Quantity B is only greater in some cases. **Choice C** is incorrect because the two values would never be equal.

3 **Choice B is correct** because since A is the midpoint of XW, B is likely a little less than the midpoint of YZ. That means the area of ABZW is likely less than half the entirety of square XYZW's area.

To find the area of square XYZW, use the length of the diagonal YW to find the side length of the square. Applying the 45-45-90 rules with the ratios x, x, and $x\sqrt{2}$ would show that the hypotenuse of 16 equals $x\sqrt{2}$. Divide both sides by $\sqrt{2}$ and rationalize to get x equals $8\sqrt{2}$.

If each side of the square equals $8\sqrt{2}$, use the area formula of $A = s^2$ to get an area of 128.

Half of the square's area would therefore be 64 so since ABZW is less than half of the square, it must be less than 64.

Choice A is incorrect because the area of ABZW is less than half the area of XYZW. **Choice C** is incorrect because the area of ABZW does not equal 64. **Choice D** is incorrect because it is possible to compare the two quantities.

4 **Choice B is correct** because the equation of the line can be found to be $y = -\frac{3}{4}x + 6$ based on the formula $y = mx + b$ where m is the slope and b is the y-intercept.

Setting y equal to 9 would give us −4 for x. To solve $9 = -\frac{3}{4}x + 6$, subtract 6 first to get $3 = -\frac{3}{4}x$. Multiply both sides by $-\frac{4}{3}$ and you will get $x = -4$.

Choice A is incorrect because x is less than 0. **Choice C** is incorrect because x does not equal 0. **Choice D** is incorrect because it is possible to determine the relationship between the values.

5 **Choice C is correct** because if the probability of choosing a red jelly bean is $\frac{4}{7}$, that means the probability of choosing a yellow or green jelly bean would be $\frac{3}{7}$. If there were 7 jelly beans in the jar, 4 would have to be red and then 2 would have to be green and 1 would be yellow since there are more green than yellow. This means the probability of drawing a yellow jellybean would be $\frac{1}{7}$.

Choice A is incorrect because Quantity A equals Quantity B. **Choice B** is incorrect because Quantity A equals Quantity B. **Choice D** is incorrect because Quantity A equals Quantity B.

5 Quantitative Reasoning (Easy)   Answers & Explanations   Section 5

6 **Choice B is correct** because if the order of the five classes did not matter you would use 5! To show 5 classes with 5 spots, no replacement. In this case, since two of the courses must go together, drop one of the classes and one of the spots to treat these two courses as one. This would mean you would now use 4! which would equal 24.

Choice A is incorrect because this would be if you added the classes 5 + 4 + 3 + 2 + 1 which is not how to find the number of possibilities. **Choice C is incorrect** because this would be the result if you just multiplied 5 times 5. **Choice D is incorrect** because this is 5! which does not account for the prerequisite course requirement. **Choice E is incorrect** because this would assume replacement, but this is not the case in this scenario.

7 **Choice B is correct** because a can be found to equal $0.84c$ which means a is 84% of c. To find this, create equations based on the statements given.

The statement a is increased by 5% to get b can be written as $1.05a = b$.

The statement b is decreased by 20% to get c can be written as $0.8b = c$.

Substituting the first statement into the second would get you $0.8(1.05a) = c$ which simplifies to $0.84a = c$.

Choice A is incorrect because this is just adding the percentages which is not the correct way to solve. **Choice C is incorrect** because this would result from a calculation error. **Choice D is incorrect** because this is what percent a is of c. **Choice E is incorrect** because this would be the result if you did a percent increase instead of a percent decrease for the relationship between b and c.

8 **Choices B, C, D and E are correct** because it falls in the range of 100 to 130. To find the range of possible values for the measure of angle B, use the possible measures of angle C. If angle C was 45°, you would have 80° of the triangle for angles A and C which would leave 100° for angle B (180 − 80 = 100). If angle C was 15°, you would have 50° of the triangle for angles A and C which would leave 130° for angle B (180 − 50 = 130). Any value that lies between 100 and 130 inclusive would work for the degrees of angle B.

Choice A is incorrect because it falls outside the range of 100 to 130. **Choice F is incorrect** because it falls outside the range of 100 to 130.

9 **Choice A is correct** because it is helpful to find a common multiple of 13 and 3 to compare the ratios. The least common multiple of 13 and 3 is 39. If y equals 39 you can adjust the ratios accordingly to compare.

If x to y is 4 to 13, then x would be 12 if y was 39.

$(\frac{4}{13} = \frac{x}{39})$

If y to z is 3 to 10 then z would be 130 if y was 39.

$(\frac{3}{10} = \frac{39}{z})$

Now you can do a direct comparison of $x:y:z$ as 12:39:130. This would give the ratio of x to z as 12 to 130 which simplifies to 6 to 65.

Choice B is incorrect because this results from a computation error when comparing ratios. **Choice C is incorrect** because this results from a computation error when comparing ratios. **Choice D is incorrect because** this results from a computation error when comparing ratios. **Choice E is incorrect** because this results from a computation error when comparing ratios.

10 **Choice D is correct** because there are 14 prime three-digit numbers that have the same hundreds and units digit.

To shortcut finding this, you can automatically rule out any values in the 200s, 400s, 600s, and 800s because they will always be divisible by 2 which would not make them prime. The 500s can also be ruled out because they would end in 5s which would make all the numbers non-prime.

In the 100s, 300s, 700s, and 900s certain patterns will repeat. For the 100s, the prime values with the same hundreds and one's digits will be 101, 131, 151, 181, and 191.

For the 300s, the values will be 313, 353, 373, and 383. For the 700s, 727, 757, 787, and 797. For the 900s, just 929.

Choice A is incorrect because there is more than 1 three-digit prime number with the same hundreds and units digit. **Choice B is incorrect** because there are more than 4 three-digit prime numbers with the same hundreds and units digit. **Choice C is incorrect** because there are more than 10 three-digit prime numbers with the same hundreds and units digit. **Choice E is incorrect** because there are less than 20 three-digit prime numbers with the same hundreds and units digit.

Quantitative Reasoning (Easy) Answers & Explanations   Section 5

11 **The correct answer is 67** because you can use the distribution of the data set to figure out the greatest value.

Use the given mean to evaluate the sum of the numbers. Since you can find the mean by using the formula average = $\frac{sum\ of\ the\ numbers}{total\ amount\ of\ numbers}$, you can plug in $45 = \frac{x}{9}$ and then multiply both sides by 9 to get 405.

Use this to figure out the number distribution further. If you are aiming for the lowest value for the greatest number, all numbers below the median should be the greatest value possible which would be 28. This would make the first five numbers of the data set 28 for a total sum of 140.

There are four numbers left to determine with one of them being the greatest number. The lowest value of the greatest number will occur when the numbers to the right of the median are evenly distributed. Subtract 405 by 140 to find that you still have a sum of 265 to distribute amongst 4 numbers. Dividing 265 by 4 yields 66.25. Since the numbers have to be integers the last 4 numbers will be 66, 66, 66, and 67.

12 **Choice D is correct** because 2.5 fluid ounces of the 15% concentration would allow for 35% as the final concentration.

Let x be the unknown number of fluid ounces. Use the idea that volume times percent would get you the amount of chemical A and set up the relationship of the information as $0.15x + 0.50(10) = 0.35(x + 10)$.

Distribute to get $0.15x + 5 = 0.35x + 3.5$. Then simplify by subtracting $0.15x$ and 3.5 from both sides. You will now have $2.5 = 0.2x$. Dividing by 0.2 will yield 1.25.

Choice A is incorrect because this would not result in the correct concentration. **Choice B** is incorrect because this would not result in the correct concentration. **Choice C** is incorrect because this would not result in the correct concentration. **Choice E** is incorrect because this would not result in the correct concentration.

13 **Choice E is correct** because $x + y$ can be found to equal 6. Rewrite the negative exponents as positives to get $\left(\frac{1}{x^2}\right)\left(\frac{1}{y^5}\right) = \left(\frac{1}{512}\right)$. Since x and y are both in the denominator you can assume $x^2 y^5$ must equal 512. To find multiples of 512 create a prime factorization tree like this:

$$512$$
$$64 \qquad 8$$
$$8 \quad 8 \qquad 2 \quad 4$$
$$2\ 4 \quad 2\ 4 \qquad\qquad 2\ 2$$
$$2\ 2 \quad\ 2\ 2$$

You are looking for numbers that repeat twice and five times. There are multiple 2s in the prime factorization so it would make sense to write the factorization as 2^9 which can then be split into 2^5 and 2^4. Another way to write 2^4 would be 4^2. This means y equals 2 and x equals 4. Adding $2 + 4$ would give us 6.

Choice A is incorrect because $x + y$ does not equal 2.
Choice B is incorrect because $x + y$ does not equal 3.
Choice C is incorrect because $x + y$ does not equal 4.
Choice D is incorrect because $x + y$ does not equal 5.

14 **Choice E is correct** because the numerator will always be an even number which means dividing by the denominator would always result in an integer if the denominator is 2. If $y = 0$ then the denominator would be $2^0 + 1$ which simplifies to $1 + 1 = 2$. You can test the numerator always being an even number by plugging in an odd number like 3 to get $3(4)(6)$ which gives you an even number, 72. Plugging in an even number like 2 gets you $2(3)(5)$ which gives you an even number, 30.

Choice A is incorrect because x being even does not always guarantee an integer. **Choice B** is incorrect because x being odd does not always guarantee an integer. **Choice C** is incorrect because x being divisible by 2 does not always guarantee an integer. **Choice D** is incorrect because y being even does not always guarantee an integer.

5 Quantitative Reasoning (Easy) Answers & Explanations   Section 5

15 **Choices D and E are correct** because this number is between $1950 and $5200. If $650 was the total amount made freelancing, you can find the range of the next income by setting up a proportion. If $\frac{1}{8}$ of the net income was freelancing you would set up the equation as $\frac{1}{8} = \frac{650}{x}$. Cross-multiplying will give you $5200. The lower bounds for total net income will be found using the expression $\frac{1}{3} = \frac{650}{x}$ which would give you $1950. Therefore any number between $1950 and $5200 can be the net income.

Choice A is incorrect because this number is not between $1950 and $5200. **Choice B** is incorrect because this number is not between $1950 and $5200. **Choice C** is incorrect because this number is not between $1950 and $5200.

5 Quantitative Reasoning (Hard) Answers & Explanations Section 5

1 **Choice D is correct** because there are some scenarios where Quantity A is larger than Quantity B and there are some situations where Quantity B is greater than Quantity A.

For example, if $a = \frac{1}{3}$ and $b = \frac{1}{2}$ then Quantity A would be $0.\overline{22}$ and Quantity B would be 0.25. To find these numbers, first convert the percentages into decimals and then multiply by the value of a and b. $66\frac{2}{3}\%$ would become $0.\overline{66}$ times $\frac{1}{3}$ (or $0.\overline{33}$ as a decimal) which equals $0.\overline{22}$. 50% would become 0.50 times $\frac{1}{2}$ (or 0.50 as a decimal) which equals 0.25. In this scenario, Quantity B would be greater since $0.25 > 0.\overline{22}$.

Alternatively, if $a = \frac{2}{3}$ and $b = \frac{17}{25}$ then Quantity A would be $0.\overline{44}$ and Quantity B would be 0.34. To find these numbers, first convert the percentages into decimals and then multiply by the value of a and b. $66\frac{2}{3}\%$ would become $0.\overline{66}$ times $\frac{2}{3}$ (or $0.\overline{66}$ as a decimal) which equals $0.\overline{44}$. 50% would become 0.50 times $\frac{17}{25}$ (or 0.68 as a decimal) which equals 0.34. In this scenario Quantity A would be greater since $0.\overline{44} > 0.34$.

Choice A is incorrect because Quantity A is not always greater than Quantity B. **Choice B** is incorrect because Quantity B is not always greater than Quantity A. **Choice C** is incorrect because Quantity A does not always equal Quantity B.

2 **Choice C is correct** because there are 8 terms in the sequence and $a_1 + a_2$ also equals 8.

To determine the value of a_1 and a_2, first find the common ratio by dividing one term by another. Dividing 54 by 18 would give the common ratio of 3. Now use the recursive formula of $a_n = ra_{n-1}$ to find the a_1 and a_2. For a_2, fill in the expression as $a_3 = ra_2$ which would get you $18 = 3a_2$. Divide both sides by 3 to get $a_2 = 6$. Use this value to get a_1 which would be $a_2 = ra_1$. Filled in you would get $6 = 3a_1$ and dividing both sides by 3 would get you $a_1 = 2$. Therefore, $a_1 + a_2 = 2 + 6 = 8$.

To find the number of terms in the sequence, you can use the explicit formula $a_n = a_1 r^{n-1}$. Plugging in the final term would get you $4374 = 2(3)^{n-1}$. Divide both sides by 2 to get $2187 = (3)^{n-1}$. Using a log, rearrange to get $\log_3 2187 = n - 1$. Simplify to get $7 = n - 1$. Add 1 and you will get $n = 8$ which means there are 8 terms in the sequence.

Choice A is incorrect because the two quantities are equal. **Choice B** is incorrect because the two quantities are equal. **Choice D** is incorrect because it is possible to solve for a relationship between Quantity A and Quantity B.

3 **Choice A is correct** because since $x < 0$, the value of Quantity A will always be greater than Quantity B. For example, if you plug in $x = -2$ then Quantity A would be $\frac{-(-2)}{(-2)-1}$ which simplifies to be $\frac{2}{-3}$ or $-\frac{2}{3}$. Quantity B would be $\frac{-2-1}{-(-2)}$ which would equal $\frac{-3}{2}$. Quantity A is less negative and therefore the greater number.

Choice B is incorrect because Quantity B would be less than Quantity A. **Choice C** is incorrect because the two quantities cannot be equal. **Choice D** is incorrect because it is possible to compare the two quantities.

4 **Choice C is correct** because the length of AD can be found to equal 8 using the properties of triangles.

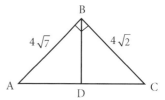

Draw a diagram representing the triangle ABC with the altitude DB drawn in. Labeling the side lengths, you will see that you can solve for the hypotenuse AC with the Pythagorean theorem $a^2 + b^2 = c^2$. Filling this in with the two values known would get you $(4\sqrt{7})^2 + (4\sqrt{2})^2 = c^2$. Simplify to get $112 + 32 = c^2$ and $144 = c^2$. Take the square root to find $c = 12$ meaning AC is length 12.

Since triangle BDC is isosceles, you can use the 45-45-90 ratio of x, x, and $x\sqrt{2}$ to find the length of DC. Using BC as $x\sqrt{2}$ would get you $x\sqrt{2} = 4\sqrt{2}$. Dividing both sides by $\sqrt{2}$ gives you $x = 4$ meaning side DC is length 4.

Subtracting DC from AC will get you the length of AD. Therefore, $12 - 4 = 8$ so side AD equals 8 and Quantity A equals Quantity B.

Choice A is incorrect because the quantities are equal. **Choice B** is incorrect because the quantities are equal. **Choice D** is incorrect because it is possible to determine the relationship from the given information.

For more practice, visit www.vibrantpublishers.com

5 Quantitative Reasoning (Hard) Answers & Explanations Section 5

5 **Choice C is correct** because if each side length is 3 times as large, then the area formula would change from $A = lw$ to $A = (3l)(3w)$. This means the new area will be 9 times as large. Multiplying 340 by 9 equals 3060.

Choice A is incorrect because this is the result if you multiply the area by 3 which does not account for the change to both sides of the rectangle. **Choice B** is incorrect because this is the result if you multiply the area by 6 which is not correct. **Choice D** is incorrect because this value is too large. **Choice E** is incorrect because this value is too large.

6 **Choices A and C are correct.** Based on the given information x must be $470 or $1500 because it is not possible to get the range with the current values.

If x was the largest value, the smallest number, 550, plus the range would give us x which would be $1500. If x was the smallest value, the largest value, 1420, minus the range would give us x which would be $470.

If x was $1500, the order of the numbers would be $550, $750, $1000, $1200, $1420, and $1500. This means the median would be the average of $1000 and $1200 which would be $1100.

If x was $470, the order of the numbers would be $470, $550, $750, $1000, $1200, and $1420. This would mean the median would be between $750 and $1000 which would be $875.

Choice A is correct because it equals one of the medians found. Choice C is correct because it equals one of the medians found.

Choice B is incorrect because it would not work as a median.

7 **Choice A is correct** because if a and b are odd integers, you could plug in values to solve. If a equals 9 and b equals 3, there would be 2 odd integers between them. Plugging this into answer A would get you the answer of 2: $\frac{(9 - 3 - 2)}{2} = \frac{4}{2} = 2$.

Choice B is incorrect because this would not properly relate a and b. **Choice C** is incorrect because this would not properly relate a and b. **Choice D** is incorrect because this would not properly relate a and b. **Choice E** is incorrect because this would not properly relate a and b.

8 **Choice D is correct** because plug in any two values for a and b to see if this rule holds true. Let's say $a = 4$ and $b = 1$, then $f(5) = f(4)f(1)$. Finding $f(5)$ will give you 2^5 which equals 32. You can then find $f(4) = 16$ and $f(1) = 2$. Multiplying these two numbers together does get you 32. This also makes sense algebraically because exponential equations have a common ratio which would allow for this pattern to work every time.

Choice A is incorrect because this relationship does not exist for functions of this type. For example if you use $a = 1$ and $b = 2$, then you would get $f(a + b) = f(1 + 2) = f(3) = \frac{3}{3} = 1$.

Then, $f(a) = f(1) = \frac{3}{1} = 3$ and $f(b) = f(2) = \frac{3}{2}$. $f(a + b) = f(a)f(b)$ is not true because 1 does not equal $3(\frac{3}{2})$ or $\frac{9}{2}$.

Choice B is incorrect because this relationship does not exist for functions of this type. For example if you use $a = 1$ and $b = 2$, then you would get $f(a + b) = f(1 + 2) = f(3) = \sqrt{3}$. Then, $f(a) = f(1) = \sqrt{1} = 1$ and $f(b) = f(2) = \sqrt{2}$. $f(a + b) = f(a)f(b)$ is not true because $\sqrt{3}$ does not equal $1(\sqrt{2})$ or $\sqrt{2}$. **Choice C** is incorrect because this relationship does not exist for functions of this type. For example if you use $a = 1$ and $b = 2$, then you would get $f(a + b) = f(1 + 2) = f(3) = 3^2 = 9$. Then, $f(a) = f(1) = 1^2 = 1$ and $f(b) = f(2) = 2^2 = 4$. $f(a + b) = f(a)f(b)$ is not true because 9 does not equal $1(4)$ or 4. **Choice E** is incorrect because this relationship does not exist for functions of this type. For example if you use $a = 1$ and $b = 2$, then you would get $f(a + b) = f(1 + 2) = f(3) = 3 + 4 = 7$.

Then, $f(a) = f(1) = 1 + 4 = 5$ and $f(b) = f(2) = 2 + 4 = 6$. $f(a + b) = f(a)f(b)$ is not true because 7 does not equal $5(6)$ or 30.

9 **Choice B is correct** because using the known values it is possible to determine the robot's rate as 3 hours to unload 1 shipment by itself.

Find the rate of the warehouse worker by setting up a ratio of shipments per hour. For the worker, their rate would be $\frac{1\ shipment}{6\ hours}$.

Find the combined rate for the worker and the robot to be $\frac{1\ shipment}{2\ hours}$. To get the rate of the robot by itself set up the rate equation $\frac{1}{6}$ + rate of robot = $\frac{1}{2}$. Subtract $\frac{1}{6}$ from both sides to get the rate of the robot to be $\frac{1\ shipment}{3\ hours}$.

Quantitative Reasoning (Hard) Answers & Explanations — Section 5

Therefore the total time it takes to unload 1 shipment is 3 hours.

Choice A is incorrect because this would not match the rate found. **Choice C** is incorrect because this would not match the rate found. **Choice D** is incorrect because this would not match the rate found. **Choice E** is incorrect because this would not match the rate found.

10 **Choice E is correct** because only positive integers will satisfy the expression $|-n + 3| < |n|$ and the only answer that will result in a positive is $n(n + 3)$.

To test possible values for n, plug if $n = 5$ to see if the expression still holds true. $|-n + 3| < |n|$ would become $|-5 + 3| < |5|$ which simplifies to be $|-2| < |5|$ or $2 < 5$, a true statement. On the other hand, if $n = -1$ then $|-n + 3| < |n|$ would become $|-1 + 3| < |-1|$ which simplifies to be $|-2| < |1|$ or $2 < 1$, a false statement.

Now that it is understood that n must be positive, plug into each answer choice to see what results. For Choice E, if $n = 5$ then $(n)(n + 3)$ would be $(5)(5 + 3)$ which is $(5)(8) = 40$, a positive value.

Choice A is incorrect because this would be a negative number. If you plug in $n = 5$ you would get -5. **Choice B** is incorrect because this might be a negative number. If you plug in $n = 2$, you would get $2 - 3$ which is -1. **Choice C** is incorrect because this would be a negative number in some situations. If you plug in $n = 5$, you would get $-5 + 3$ which equals -2. **Choice D** is incorrect because this would result in a negative number. If you plug in $n = 5$, you would get $-5(5 + 3)$ which would be $-5(8)$ which is -40.

11 **The correct answer is 30** because to find out the measure of each exterior angle of the polygon, you first need to find out how many sides the polygon has.

To find this, use the expression sum of interior angles equals $180(n - 2)$ where n is the number of sides.

Plugging in what you know would get you $1800 = 180(n - 2)$. Dividing by 180 would get you 10 and then adding 2 gives you 12 sides.

Every polygon has exterior angles that add up to 360, so divide 360 by 12 to get 30° per angle.

12 **Choice D is correct** because you can set up the average equation to determine the possible values for x. Use the equation average $= \dfrac{\text{sum of values}}{\text{total number of values}}$ to get the equation $80 > \dfrac{45 + 65 + x + x}{4}$. Simplify and then multiply both sides by 4 to get $320 > 110 + 2x$. Subtract 110 from both sides and then divide by 2 to get $105 > x$. This means the largest possible x value would be 104.

Choice A is incorrect because x has to be larger than 75 to get a mean greater than 80. **Choice B** is incorrect because x has to be larger than 80 to get a mean greater than 80. **Choice C** is incorrect because x has to be larger than 100 to get a mean greater than 80. **Choice E** is incorrect because x has to be less than 105.

13 **Choice C is correct** because to find the impact of x input the changes directly into the equation.

A 10% increase in a would be equal to a times 1.10 which would make the equation $x = (1.10a)^2 b$.

A 45% decrease in b would be equal to multiplying b by 0.55. This would now make the expression $x = (1.10a)^2(0.55b)$.

Simplifying the expression would get you the new statement $x = 0.6655 a^2 b$ which means x decreased by 33.45%.

Choice A is incorrect because x did not increase. **Choice B** is incorrect because x did not increase. **Choice D** is incorrect because it is larger than the actual decrease. **Choice E** is incorrect because it is much larger than the actual decrease.

14 **Choices A and D are correct.** From the expression $y^2 = 16$, you can determine that y is either -4 or 4.

Plugging in -4 for y would get you the equation $2.1x + 1.2(-4) = -0.3x + 1.5(-4)$ which simplifies to be $2.1x + -4.8 = -0.3x - 6$. Collecting like terms by adding 4.8 and $0.3x$ to both sides would get you $2.4x = -1.2$. Divide both sides by 2.4 to get $x = -0.5$.

Plugging in 4 for y would get you the equation $2.1x + 1.2(4) = -0.3x + 1.5(4)$ which simplifies to be $2.1x + 4.8 = -0.3x + 6$. Collecting like terms by subtracting 4.8 and adding $0.3x$ to both sides would get you $2.4x = 1.2$. Divide both sides by 2.4 to get $x = 0.5$.

5 Quantitative Reasoning (Hard) Answers & Explanations   Section 5

Choice A is correct because x can equal -0.5. Choice D is correct because x can equal 0.5.

Choice B is incorrect because x does not equal -0.25.
Choice C is incorrect because x does not equal 0.25.

15 **Choice D is correct** because to find the average of a and b, use equivalent average expressions.

The average can be represented as the sum of the numbers divided by the number of items. For the first statement, you can write the average as $\frac{a + b + 12}{3}$.

For the second statement, you can write the average as $\frac{a + b + 12 + 36}{4}$.

The problem states these averages are equal so therefore $\frac{a + b + 12}{3} = \frac{a + b + 12 + 36}{4}$. Cross multiply to get $4(a + b + 12) = 3(a + b + 48)$.

Distribute to get $4a + 4b + 48 = 3a + 3b + 144$.

Subtract over $3a$, $3b$, and 48 to get the statement $a + b = 96$.

Now that you have the sum of a and b, divide by 2 to get the average of 48.

Choice A is incorrect because this is not the correct average of a and b. **Choice B** is incorrect because this is not the correct average of a and b. **Choice C** is incorrect because this is not the correct average of a and b. **Choice E** is incorrect because this is not the correct average of a and b.

Chapter 7
Practice Test #6

IMPORTANT
READ THE INSTRUCTIONS BEFORE BEGINNING THE TEST

1. Take this test under real testing conditions. Put away any distractions and sit in a quiet place with no disturbances. Keep a rough paper, some pencils, and a calculator beside you.

2. Begin with **Section 1** of the test on page 160. Write your essay in 30 minutes.

3. Next, move to **Section 2 - Verbal Reasoning** on page 162.

    ❏ Attempt all questions and note the number of correct answers using the answer key on page 283.

    ❏ If you get fewer than 7 correct, proceed to **Section 4 - Verbal Reasoning (Easy)** on page 268.

    ❏ If you get 7 or more correct, proceed to **Section 4 - Verbal Reasoning (Hard)** on page 272.

4. After that, take **Section 3 - Quantitative Reasoning** on page 265.

    ❏ Complete the section, then check your score using the answer key on page 284.

    ❏ If you get fewer than 7 correct, proceed to **Section 5 - Quantitative Reasoning (Easy)** on page 277.

    ❏ If you get 7 or more correct, proceed to **Section 5 - Quantitative Reasoning (Hard)** on page 280.

5. Complete Section 4 and Section 5, respectively, and note down the number of correct answers you got right in each section.

6. Calculate your **Scaled Score** on page 317 for the test.

7. Review **detailed explanations** for all questions beginning on page 285.

Analyze an Issue
30 Minutes

The best ideas arise from a passionate interest in commonplace things.
Write a response in which you discuss the extent to which you agree or disagree with the statement and explain your reasoning for the position you take. In developing and supporting your position, you should consider ways in which the statement might or might not hold true and explain how these considerations shape your position.

You may start writing your response here

Section 2 - Verbal Reasoning

18 Minutes | 12 Questions

For Questions 1 to 3, for each blank, select one entry from the corresponding column of choices. Fill all blanks in the way that best completes the text.

1. Because of crime distribution data, criminologists can add to their qualitative analysis a quantitative dynamic; this _____ of approaches allows for greater insight.

   - (A) confluence
   - (B) reduction
   - (C) petulance
   - (D) reluctance
   - (E) diaspora

2. He had never ridden a motorcycle before but the notion (i) _____ him. The idea of cruising across the country instilled him with a feeling of freedom he had never experienced before. He had always been (ii) _____ preferring the safety of an office environment to anything else.

Blank (i)	Blank (ii)
(A) vetoed	(D) obdurate
(B) exhilarated	(E) milquetoast
(C) censured	(F) contrarian

3. Music and theater have been (i) _____ for millennia. Even the legendary Athenian tragedies, known for their high drama, utilized choruses that were often accompanied by musical instruments. This tradition has (ii) _____ into the modern age of theater. Some of the most famous stage tragedies of our time express their (iii) _____ through the use of music.

Blank (i)	Blank (ii)	Blank (iii)
(A) intertwined	(D) perished	(G) avarice
(B) antagonistic	(E) glided	(H) aplomb
(C) extraneous	(F) lurched	(I) pathos

For Questions 4 and 5, select one answer choice unless otherwise instructed.

Question 4 and 5 is based on this passage.

The lipid metabolism of ctenophores, jelly-like predatory creatures often found on the ocean's floor, may prove to be instrumental in medical research. Cone-shaped lipids seem to explain how these marine creatures withstand the crushingly high pressures exerted at extreme depths. Having gradually adapted to the environment, ctenophores contain flexible elements in their cellular membrane that appear to serve as scaffolding and maintain the integrity of the cellular matrix despite the surrounding force. Interestingly, high pressure becomes a requirement for survival as they function as removal leads to the animal's disintegration.

Diseases such as Alzheimer's have been correlated with reduced production of such lipids, which are found, to a lesser extent, in the human brain. Consequently, researchers are intrigued about the potential benefits of these findings on human cognitive health.

4. What assumption does the author make about lipid metabolism in ctenophores?

   - (A) Lipids providing structural support in ctenophore cellular architecture have evolved very recently.
   - (B) Cone-shaped lipids in ctenophores have developed to increase cell resiliency in a variety of extreme habitats.
   - (C) Ctenophores require an abundance of cone-shaped lipids to maintain cognitive alertness in high-danger environments.
   - (D) Certain ctenophore lipids present remarkable durability and can be directly applied to patients suffering from brain diseases.
   - (E) The architectural role of cone-shaped lipids in ctenophores may be analogous to the role they play in patients with brain diseases.

5. The information in the passage suggests that which of the following is true?

- Ⓐ Incorporation of ctenophores into the diet of patients with brain diseases staves off cognitive decline.
- Ⓑ Environments with high-pressure climates are linked to an accelerated development of brain diseases.
- Ⓒ Future research in neuroscience will examine the role of diminished lipid production, in terms of loss of cellular integrity, in brain diseases.
- Ⓓ Intercellular pressure in the human brain needs to be examined in lab conditions replicating the habitats of ctenophores.
- Ⓔ The study of deep-sea creature neurological behavior is beneficial for understanding the long-term effects of cognitive impairment in Alzheimer's patients.

For Questions 6 to 9, select the two answer choices that, when used to complete the sentence, fit the meaning of the sentence as a whole and produce complete sentences that are alike in meaning.

6. Although the theory on the conservation of mass was not stated clearly until 1789, it had many _____ in the history of the physical sciences.

- A originators
- B derivatives
- C forerunners
- D antecedents
- E imitators
- F descendants

7. I have been watching this conversation grow more and more _____ and it disappoints me that such otherwise learned and productive people can sit around for an entire afternoon and waste so much time.

- A unreserved
- B vapid
- C insipid
- D insightful
- E sectarian
- F pretentious

8. The distillation process was successful. The new liquid was _____ and odorless.

- A similitude
- B homogeneity
- C unadulterated
- D impure
- E corrupted
- F homogeneous

9. If scales are not _____ properly; scientists cannot measure the amounts of chemicals and other materials with enough precision to ensure the accuracy of or replicate experiment results.

- A conjectured
- B calibrated
- C fissured
- D aligned
- E serialized
- F embroiled

Section 2 - Verbal Reasoning

For Questions 10 to 12, select one answer choice unless otherwise instructed.

Questions 10 to 12 are based on this passage.

There seem to be two literary factions pitted against each other. Those of one class employ their best effort in dissuading young writers from writing; those of another set forth an author's life in glowing colors. **One faction will tell you that half the manuscripts sent to editors are not even accorded the courtesy of an examination unless signed by a well-known name.** Another says that editors are keenly on the outlook for original matter, seizing with avidity anything that promises to make a new element in current literature.

A noted author writes to a young aspirant: "Sweet and natural though your utterance seems to be, let me ask you in the friendliest spirit not to write at all. The toil is great, the pursuit incessant, the reward not outward." To the same young woman writes another equally well-known writer: "Your work is excellent; you can and will succeed."

10. This passage primarily sets out to prove which of the following ideas?

    A) Accomplished writers view work with a critical eye and have differing opinions on the rhythm and cadence in a writer's work.
    B) Authors are opinionated and base their criticism of aspiring writers' works on their own experiences.
    C) The profession of writing is difficult and toilsome, yet can also be rewarding.
    D) The opinions of established writers differ greatly and can be distinguished by their outlook on the perceived difficulty of writing as a profession.
    E) In order to earn money, aspiring authors must make their own decisions regarding how to submit their work to editors so that pessimistic people will not dissuade them from reaching their goals.

11. What is the primary effect of the sentence in boldface type on the passage's overall message?

    A) To indicate the severity with which editors express their opinion of work that does not meet the high standards of publishing companies.
    B) This sentence demonstrates the clout that well-known authors have in the publishing world; without a good reputation, it is very difficult to solicit an editor for advice on completed works.
    C) It indicates the fragility of amateur writers' careers and the detrimental effects that harsh criticism can have on their aspirations.
    D) To explain that editors rudely ignore at least fifty percent of submitted manuscripts without so much as a cursory glance unless the work comes highly recommended by one of their colleagues.
    E) It establishes the opinion of one group of people in the writing business who warn about the regimented approach that editors often take to critiquing unpublished manuscripts.

12. Select a sentence from the passage that provides support for the author's viewpoint that writing is too subjective for one person to determine the fate of an aspiring writer's career.

Section 3 - Quantitative Reasoning

18 Minutes | 12 Questions

1

$$x < 0 < y$$

Quantity A   **Quantity B**
$(x + y)^2$ $(y - x)^2$

- Ⓐ Quantity A is greater.
- Ⓑ Quantity B is greater.
- Ⓒ The two quantities are equal.
- Ⓓ The relationship cannot be determined from the information given.

2

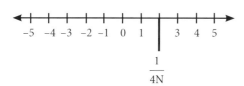

Quantity A   **Quantity B**
N $\frac{1}{8}$

- Ⓐ Quantity A is greater.
- Ⓑ Quantity B is greater.
- Ⓒ The two quantities are equal.
- Ⓓ The relationship cannot be determined from the information given.

3

The aggregate monthly expenditure of a family was $7500 during the first 3 months, $6500 during the next 4 months and $7200 during the last 5 months of a year. Their total savings during the year was $5500.

Quantity A   **Quantity B**
The average monthly income of the family $6950

- Ⓐ Quantity A is greater.
- Ⓑ Quantity B is greater.
- Ⓒ The two quantities are equal.
- Ⓓ The relationship cannot be determined from the information given.

4

$$3y + 6x = 2$$
$$y = -cx + 7$$

The system of equations shown has no solution, where c is a constant.

Quantity A   **Quantity B**
c 2

- Ⓐ Quantity A is greater.
- Ⓑ Quantity B is greater.
- Ⓒ The two quantities are equal.
- Ⓓ The relationship cannot be determined from the information given.

5

A bank is offering an interest rate of 6.0% per annum. How long would it take to earn $1500 if Arnold invested $20,000 in the bank?

- Ⓐ 3 months
- Ⓑ 2 months
- Ⓒ 15 months
- Ⓓ 1.2 years
- Ⓔ 15 years

Section 3 - Quantitative Reasoning

Questions 6 to 8 are based on the following data.

Motor Sales from January-June 2024

Country	Jan	Feb	Mar	Apr	May	Jun	Total
Germany	34	47	45	54	56	60	296
UK	40	44	36	47	47	46	260
France	37	32	32	32	34	33	200
Spain	14	14	14	16	17	14	89
Total	125	137	127	149	154	153	845

Motor Sales of UK according to motor-type, Jan-June 2024

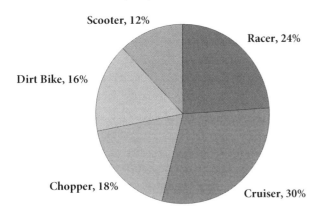

6

For the motor sales of UK according to motor-type, which of the following numbers represents the cruise motors sold from Jan-June 2024?

Ⓐ 30
Ⓑ 31
Ⓒ 47
Ⓓ 62
Ⓔ 78

7

If the racer motorcycle sales from the UK for the month of January to March accounted for 22%, approximately what is the percentage of the sales of this type of motorcycle from April to June?

[   ] %

8

For January motor sales, if scooter sales accounted for 10% of the UK sales, which of the following percentage is accounted for the scooter sales from the total January sales?

Ⓐ 3.2%
Ⓑ 4.2%
Ⓒ 4.5%
Ⓓ 6.5%
Ⓔ 8.2%

9

A cylindrical cup is packed in a 1-liter cube paper box. The cup is in close contact with all the walls of the cube. What is the volume of the cup in terms of π. (Note: 1 liter = 1 dm^3)

Ⓐ $1\pi\ dm^3$
Ⓑ $0.5\pi\ dm^3$
Ⓒ $0.25\pi\ dm^3$
Ⓓ $2\pi\ dm^3$
Ⓔ $0.75\pi\ dm^3$

10

Age	Frequency
10-12	5
13-15	8
16-18	5
19-21	10
22-24	2

The table shows the age of applicants in an English aptitude test. Which of the following numbers could be the median test score for all the students?

Indicate all such numbers.

- [A] 10
- [B] 13
- [C] 15
- [D] 16
- [E] 18

11

The center of a circle lies at the point (8, −5). The point (3, 1) lies inside the circle and the point (−1, 4) lies outside the circle with neither point lying on the circle. If the radius of the circle is the integer value r, how many different values could there be for the circumference of the circle?

- (A) 1
- (B) 2
- (C) 3
- (D) 4
- (E) 5

12

If $|x| - x > 0$ then which of the following must be true?

- (A) $x > 0$
- (B) $x < 0$
- (C) $x = 0$
- (D) $x > 1$
- (E) $x \geq 1$

Section 4 - Verbal Reasoning (Easy)

23 Minutes | 15 Questions

For Questions 1 to 4, select one entry for each blank from the corresponding column of choices. Fill all the blanks in the way that best completes the text.

1. No doubt because of its potential hazards, we tend to think of radiation as something out of the ordinary; in truth, however, radiation is essentially _____, and it is therefore impossible to avoid low-level exposure.

   - (A) ineffable
   - (B) ubiquitous
   - (C) nebulous
   - (D) quiescent
   - (E) foolproof

2. The _____ with which he ate appalled the other guests, who prided themselves on their impeccable table manners.

   - (A) efficacy
   - (B) decorum
   - (C) adroitness
   - (D) temperance
   - (E) alacrity

3. In the story of the "Confessions of Felix Krull, Confidence Man" the young man protagonist, Felix, feigns a serious illness to (i) _____ both his mother and the family physician who is also her lover, that he is indeed very sick. Felix describes the almost intolerable pleasure that his performance brings him saying, "I was beyond beatific, absolutely (ii) _____ with an alternate tension and relaxation necessary to give reality, in my own eyes and others, to a condition that did not exist."

Blank (i)	Blank (ii)
(A) suborn	(D) desultory
(B) cajole	(E) rapturous
(C) inveigh	(F) aberrant

4. The early Chinese made the first unofficial attempts at (i) _____ risk, as they transferred their wares on many different ships. Doing so ensured that the loss of one ship would not destroy their entire inventory. The first use of (ii) _____ insurance, however, belongs to the Babylonians. They had laws that permitted merchants to purchase insurance on their loans in case they were not able to repay it. In the (iii) _____ world of trade, this was often a necessity.

Blank (i)	Blank (ii)	Blank (iii)
(A) alleviating	(D) sardonic	(G) guileless
(B) exacerbating	(E) schematized	(H) portly
(C) annunciating	(F) quiescent	(I) tumultuous

For Questions 5 to 7, select one answer choice unless otherwise instructed.

Questions 5 to 7 are based on this passage.

In 1990 there came a nationwide crackdown on illicit computer hackers, with arrests, criminal charges, one dramatic show–trial, several guilty pleas, and huge confiscations of data and equipment all over the USA. The Hacker Crackdown of 1990 was larger, better organized, more deliberate, and more resolute than any previous effort in the brave new world of computer crime. The U.S. Secret Service, private telephone security, and state and local law enforcement groups across the country all joined forces in a determined attempt to break the back of America's electronic underground. It was a fascinating effort, with very mixed results. The Hacker Crackdown had another unprecedented effect; it spurred the creation, within "the computer community" of the Electronic Frontier Foundation, a new and very odd interest group, fiercely dedicated to the establishment and preservation of electronic civil liberties. The crackdown, remarkable in itself, has created a melee of debate over electronic crime, punishment, freedom of the press, and issues of search and seizure. Politics has entered cyberspace.

5. Which of the following aspects of computer crime is NOT mentioned in the passage?

  Ⓐ Seizure of computer equipment by law-enforcement authorities
  Ⓑ Public discourse about computer crime
  Ⓒ Criminal prosecution of computer crime
  Ⓓ Anti-computer crime legislation
  Ⓔ The goals of the Electronic Frontier Foundation

6. According to the passage, what was true about the 1990 crackdown?

  Ⓐ The crackdown was spear-headed by the federal government.
  Ⓑ The crackdown was considered a success by law-enforcement authorities.
  Ⓒ The crackdown spurred new debate about the prosecution of computer crime.
  Ⓓ The Electronic Frontier Foundation tried to stop the 1990 crackdown.
  Ⓔ The crackdown spurred calls for new laws against computer crime.

For the following question, consider each of the choices separately and select all that apply.

7. According to the passage, which of the following were results of the 1990 crackdown?

  ☐A The creation of the Electronic Frontier Foundation
  ☐B A new focus on political issues within the computer community
  ☐C A temporary decrease in computer-related crime

For Questions 8 to 10, select the two answer choices that, when used to complete the sentence, fit the meaning of the sentence as a whole and produce complete sentences that are alike in meaning.

8. Einstein's discover of general relativity is a major turning point in the history of physics and _____ a full century of further research.

  ☐A stimulated
  ☐B dampened
  ☐C abetted
  ☐D motivated
  ☐E debilitated
  ☐F vitalized

9. Determinism, the notion that reality is independent of how we question or observe it, is the only conclusion that can be reasonably _____ from the classical form of Newtonian physics.

  ☐A imputed
  ☐B drawn
  ☐C ascertained
  ☐D calculated
  ☐E derived
  ☐F assumed

10. Chemical thermodynamics _____ measurements of the thermodynamic properties and the application of mathematical methods to the study of chemistry.

  ☐A entails
  ☐B subsumes
  ☐C constitutes
  ☐D contains
  ☐E involves
  ☐F embodies

Section 4 - Verbal Reasoning (Easy)

For Questions 11 to 15, select one answer choice unless otherwise instructed.

Question 11 is based on this passage.

The newspaper is a private enterprise. Its object is to make money for its owner. Whatever motive may be given out for starting a newspaper, expectation of profit by it is the real one, whether the newspaper is religious, political, scientific, or literary. The exceptional cases of newspapers devoted to ideas or "causes" without regard to profit are so few as not to affect the rule. Commonly, the cause, the sect, the party, the trade, the delusion, the idea, gets its newspaper, its organ, its advocate, only when some individual thinks he can see a pecuniary return in establishing it.

11. Which statement, if true, provides the most strength for the validity of the conclusion?
    - (A) Many religious groups publish newspapers to tell about missionary support.
    - (B) Newspapers are designed to be attractive and interesting for the reader.
    - (C) Newspaper printing is one of the most dependable sources of income because there is always news happening somewhere.
    - (D) The price of newspaper subscriptions has risen 25% in the past 10 years.
    - (E) The new owners of the local newspaper are seeking the most relevant issues facing the community because they hope to increase the number of subscribers.

Questions 12 and 13 are based on this passage.

In an attempt to challenge the exorbitant value placed on material wealth as an indicator of success, exemplified by the ranking of countries by their GDP, sociologists have instituted alternative rankings, one of which focuses on personal happiness. Subjects are asked to assess their level of happiness on a linear scale. These results are then averaged and a list of countries emerges, with European ones often at the top.

However, the very act of assessing oneself with a numerical judgment is a Western concept that is foreign in many countries, especially where literacy is low. Were the survey less culturally biased, it might attain deeper insights about well-being. For instance, not every culture values happiness at the same level as having meaning in life, or even attaining balance and harmony.

12. Which of the following best summarizes the main point of the passage?
    - (A) Limitations in rankings due to biases raise concerns over their use in assessing human conditions.
    - (B) Current ranking systems need revision as they reveal a disputable correlation between the wealth of a nation and the happiness of its people.
    - (C) Sociological surveys require more thorough research on the demographic they target to account for literacy and cultural norms.
    - (D) Happiness rankings should engage a more nuanced approach to avoid cultural bias and acknowledge alternative values.
    - (E) Personal happiness is a more reliable indicator of success and should supplant previously held indicators, such as material wealth.

13. Based on the passage, which of the following could be an alternative explanation for how happiness surveys are culturally biased?
    - (A) Translation of the term happiness could vary from culture to culture, which may be hard to capture accurately in a questionnaire.
    - (B) Well-being itself is a concept that only exists in certain societies around the world.
    - (C) Surveys are developed with the intention of linking wealth with happiness, thereby skewing the results.
    - (D) Surveys were presented to populations whose understanding of linear evaluations may have been opposite to those of the researchers.
    - (E) Researchers only surveyed people in countries with a certain GDP.

Questions 14 and 15 are based on this passage.

For almost a century, Aztec rulers boasted of unparalleled power in Mesoamerica. Each was called a *tlatoani*, meaning the "speaker" perhaps meant in the spirit of noblesse oblige, underscoring the authority bestowed upon them to be the voice of the people and to act in their interests. Similarly, the title referred to representing the empire and communicating with the deities, currying favor through rituals and offerings.

A *tlatoani*, however, rose to power invariably from among the nobles, predominantly from the lineage of predecessors. A Council of Nobles, not common people, ultimately voted for each successor, after weighing each candidate's military prowess and achievements. And yet, far from unassailable figures, public discontent could effectively oust a *tlatoani* who failed to meet expectations.

For the following question, consider each of the choices separately and select all that apply.

14 Which of the following best describes the relationship between the first paragraph and the subsequent paragraph in the passage?

- [A] The first paragraph presents the idea of Aztec rulers representing their people, while the second provides specific historical examples.
- [B] The first paragraph introduces the perceived role of a *tlatoani* as a spokesperson for the people, while the second introduces certain contradictions to the claim.
- [C] The first paragraph describes the duties of a *tlatoani*, while the second elaborates on each duty in detail.

15 Based on the information provided in the passage, which of the following conclusions can be drawn about Aztec social structure?

- (A) The Council of Nobles had no way of changing rulers once they were ordained as spiritual leaders.
- (B) Candidates for succession engaged in corrupt practices to garner favor from the Council of Nobles.
- (C) The Aztecs maintained a stable union and were involved in a few military conflicts.
- (D) Aztec society was tiered, with common people on the lowest rung, holding considerably less power than other classes.
- (E) In Aztec society, it was just as possible for a non-descendant as for a direct descendant of a ruler to be elected.

Section 4 - Verbal Reasoning (Hard)

23 Minutes | 15 Questions

For Questions 1 to 4, select one entry for each blank from the corresponding column of choices. Fill all the blanks in the way that best completes the text.

1. Sensory adaptation occurs when a stimulus that is _____ . When a subject first encounters it, eventually fades from notice, such as the sound of a ticking clock, or cooking smells in a room.

A	negligible
B	equivocal
C	significant
D	imperceptible
E	appreciable

2. While single cell organisms use the cell surface to (i) _____ nutrients from the world outside the system, and to release waste from the organism, multi-celled organisms require a circulatory system and medium of transport for nutrients. Sea-sponges, among the most (ii) _____ animals take advantage of seawater as a medium of transport. As the seawater flows in and out of the organism it delivers nutrients and removes waste.

Blank (i)	Blank (ii)
A annex	D primitive
B procure	E vestigial
C relinquish	F rudimentary

3. Looking back, he was amazed by his own (i) _____. His experienced friends told him that there was no fast way to learn guitar. They said that he would just have to accept a slow progression of skill. But he (ii) _____ this advice every step of the way, pushing his hands as hard as he could. Now that he was starting down the harsh reality of carpal tunnel syndrome, he wished that he had taken their advice.

Blank (i)	Blank (ii)
A pensiveness	D articulated
B reticence	E flouted
C obstinacy	F expanded

4. Fiona was simultaneously (i) _____ by the magic of dreams and turned off by their potential to turn into nightmares. She wondered what they revealed about the human psyche. They were so (ii) _____, yet there had to be some logical impetus for their genesis. She often read books on dream analysis in order to better understand this topic, but the more she read the more she suspected that the purported "experts" in the field were merely (iii) _____.

Blank (i)	Blank (ii)	Blank (iii)
A enraptured	D debonair	G charlatans
B vindicated	E abstruse	H solemn
C denounced	F gentile	I guileless

Section 4 - Verbal Reasoning (Hard)

For Questions 5 to 9, select one answer choice unless otherwise instructed.

Questions 5 and 6 are based on this passage.

The scarcity of diamonds as precious gems lends to their allure, but their provenance is also what makes them contentious. Although the Earth's mantle and crust are replete with these tightly bound carbon prisms, "kimberlites" the volcanic formations that shoot them to the surface seem to have completed their purveyance millions of years ago. Modern-day mining, with notoriously poor working conditions, attempts to uncover the vestiges of these eruptions at great environmental cost, while the sale of conflict diamonds to finance wars raises ethical concerns.

Consequently, labs have started growing "cultured" substitutes using a minuscule seed diamond exposed to a gas enriched with carbon at high temperatures and/or pressures. Although neither ancient nor scarce, synthetic carats still promise a more ethical and sustainable alternative to their primeval counterparts.

5. Based on the information presented in the passage, which of the following conclusions can be drawn?
   - Ⓐ Diamonds would be a far less durable gem if they had not erupted from volcanic structures under high pressure.
   - Ⓑ The appeal of mined diamonds comes from the distinctive marks they receive during the mining process.
   - Ⓒ Lab-grown diamonds cannot be distinguished from their mined counterparts because conditions in the lab match those on Earth during its formation.
   - Ⓓ Diamonds were more easily located in an earlier geological time period when kimberlites were still active.
   - Ⓔ Misconceived notions about the availability of diamonds lead to aggressive mining practices.

For the following question, consider each of the choices separately and select all that apply.

6. Which of the following supports the main argument of the passage?
   - [A] The acquisition of primeval diamonds is complicated by various factors, such as geological processes and modern human practices.
   - [B] Diamonds can be a source of contention based on misconceived notions, which can be resolved with synthetic alternatives.
   - [C] Alternatives to the diamond mining industry are viable in spite of lacking the antiquity of natural diamonds.

Questions 7 to 9 are based on this passage.

The implementation of positive and negative behavioral reinforcements has been questioned by educational professionals and parents alike. Is a system of rewards and punishments, as a means of encouraging desirable behavior and discouraging the undesirable, the paramount method for guiding a child's development and maturity, or a slipshod substitute for fostering long-term self-motivation?

Understandably, parents and educators often face situations where children lack the willingness to perform unpleasant tasks, or certain behaviors may be unwelcome. Rewards, such as stars on the refrigerator, prizes, such as ice cream, or free time often serve as effective incentives for the child to perform or behave along specific expectations. These bolster their extrinsic motivation and demonstrate successful outcomes in the short term.

Findings from longitudinal studies, however, tracing behavioral milestones from adolescence to adulthood, indicate that such reward/punishment systems often fail to instill the intrinsic motivation needed to develop psychological resilience, self-esteem, and a love for learning. Conversely, an approach focusing on the effort exerted over the outcome (applauding the time spent training over goals scored in a match) was shown to foster the intrinsic motivation necessary for developing self-esteem irrespective of goal attainment, as well as a better appreciation of the learning process. Additionally, it conveys to the child that love is not predicated on performance.

7. Based on the passage, which of the following is likely to be the author's perspective on celebrating high grades on a report card?

   (A) Celebrating academic success leads to reinforcing extrinsic motivation and should be avoided, as should any repercussions for failure.
   (B) Celebrating academic success can be as constructive as celebrating failure, as long as emphasis is placed on the effort put into studying, rather than the grades themselves.
   (C) Academic success should be celebrated, while not meeting academic standards should be addressed with negative reinforcements, such as by refusing to purchase things the child desires.
   (D) Academic success should not be celebrated, as it is an outcome, rather prizes should be given after every studying session.
   (E) Celebrating academic success is beneficial for motivating the child, and the greater the reward that accompanies it, the more energetically the child will proceed.

8. What is the primary purpose of the passage?

   (A) To analyze the reward/punishment approach to child-rearing on its merits and drawbacks and present an alternate approach that yields more effective long-term effects.
   (B) To synthesize child-rearing approaches into a comprehensive methodology that improves the way a child's performance is addressed, focusing more on effort.
   (C) To warn parents and educators against choosing a methodology based on instant gratification rather than one designed to ensure long-term outcomes.
   (D) To address the uncertainty that is shared by parents and educators about reacting to the successes and failures of their children and students, respectively.
   (E) To outline a new paradigm of child-rearing that replaces previous ones based on recent behavioral studies on child development.

9. Which of the following could be an alternative explanation for the findings of the longitudinal study discussed in the passage?

   (A) Children in the study inadvertently received external motivation to succeed since emphasis was placed on the importance of academics by the study itself.
   (B) Children who did not receive rewards for performance continued to receive punishments, which had a deleterious long-term effect on motivation.
   (C) Children who did not receive reinforcements interacted less frequently with parents or educators, resulting in more positive results in developing self-motivation.
   (D) Children with parents/educators caring enough to employ new methodologies benefited from a child-centered home/school atmosphere that fostered growth and self-esteem.
   (E) Children who received praise for the time and effort put into tasks received more frequent attention than their counterparts, resulting in higher self-esteem.

For Questions 10 to 12, select the two answer choices that, when used to complete the sentence, fit the meaning of the sentence as a whole and produce complete sentences that are alike in meaning.

10. The differences in symptoms between the autism spectrum disorders and the anxiety conditions (such as obsessive-compulsive disorder) are often so _____ that a patient can go years without receiving a proper diagnosis.

    [A] inconspicuous
    [B] pervasive
    [C] harmless
    [D] debilitating
    [E] subtle
    [F] extravagant

Section 4 - Verbal Reasoning (Hard)

11. The sheer depth of space that must be traversed in order to locate even basic truths about the origins of our universe has rendered _____ reasoning as one of the most effective ways to shirk our empirical handicap.

    A. inverse
    B. deliberate
    C. deductive
    D. inferable
    E. observable
    F. obvious

12. Gang related crime was _____ in that area; even the police were wary about entering after dark.

    A. epidemic
    B. endemic
    C. curtailed
    D. governable
    E. exuberant
    F. prevalent

For Questions 13 to 15, select one answer choice unless otherwise instructed.

Question 13 is based on this passage.

What a given amount of energy will do depends only upon its form, that is, the kind of motion that embodies it. The energy spent upon a stone thrown into the air, giving it translatory motion, would, if spent upon a tuning fork, make it sound, but not move it from its place; while if spent upon a top, would enable the latter to stand upon its point as easily as a person stands on his two feet, and to do other surprising things, which otherwise it could not do. One can, without difficulty, form a mechanical conception of the whole series without assuming imponderables, or fluids or forces.

13. All of the following statements identify assumptions on which the author's argument relies EXCEPT:

    A. The energy that a person spends in throwing an object can be applied to a different object with the same amount of force.
    B. The amount of energy needed to throw an object can be transferred to a different object without hurling the object through the air.
    C. A person who ponders the mechanics of energy can easily comprehend the basic knowledge associated with this subject matter.
    D. It is just as easy to throw a stone as it is to spin a top.
    E. Creating a sound in a tuning fork is as simple as throwing a stone, though may require two people to do so simultaneously.

Questions 14 and 15 are based on this passage.

Tuberculosis (TB) remains the leading cause of death from infectious disease, although treatments successfully resolve most cases. Mortality rates for certain patients over others, however, have confounded researchers. Recent studies in immunology suggest a genetic component may be responsible, particularly in the early inflammatory stages of the disease.

Current research at Rockefeller University is expanding upon the established theory that TNF, a type of cell-signaling protein called a cytokine, plays a role in a patient's capacity to defend against TB. TNF has also long been considered a wide-spectrum pro-inflammatory cytokine, broadly catalyzing the immune response, and is therefore often regulated in treatments of autoimmune diseases. Yet, surprisingly, these recent findings indicate that TNF plays a much narrower role, almost exclusively targeted at protecting the lungs from TB.

For the following question, consider each of the choices separately and select all that apply.

14. Based on the information presented in the passage, which of the following conclusions can be drawn?

    A. Treatments of TB have been based on assumptions about the role of TNF that have recently been shown to be untrue.

    B. Based on recent findings, TNF regulation will now become a central feature in treatments of TB.

    C. Approaches based on TNF modulation previously developed to treat infectious diseases other than TB will have to be reconsidered.

15. Which of the following best describes the relationship between the first paragraph and the subsequent paragraph in the passage?

    A. The first paragraph presents the challenges of researching TB, and the second discusses findings that address those challenges based on research into cytokines.

    B. The first paragraph presents the theory that genetics play a role in TB survival, while the second refutes the theory based on recent findings to the contrary.

    C. The first paragraph presents the idea that genetics may be involved in TB mortality rates, while the second supports that claim and upends a theory about TNF.

    D. The first paragraph presents the idea that genetics may explain varying mortality rates in TB patients, while the second supports the theory with new evidence on TNF.

    E. The first paragraph introduces the genetic factor in the varying mortality rates of TB patients, while the second refutes a previously-held theory about inflammation in TB.

Section 5 - Quantitative Reasoning (Easy)

26 Minutes | 15 Questions

1

$$|3n - 9| = 45$$

Quantity A	Quantity B
n	19

Ⓐ Quantity A is greater.
Ⓑ Quantity B is greater.
Ⓒ The two quantities are equal.
Ⓓ The relationship cannot be determined from the information given.

2

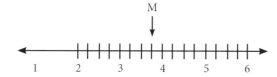

Quantity A	Quantity B
M	$\dfrac{15}{4}$

Ⓐ Quantity A is greater.
Ⓑ Quantity B is greater.
Ⓒ The two quantities are equal.
Ⓓ The relationship cannot be determined from the information given.

3

$a > 0$

Circle A has a circumference of $a\pi$.

Circle B has a radius of $\dfrac{a}{2}$.

Quantity A	Quantity B
Area of Circle A	Area of Circle B

Ⓐ Quantity A is greater.
Ⓑ Quantity B is greater.
Ⓒ The two quantities are equal.
Ⓓ The relationship cannot be determined from the information given.

4

A shop sells two types of pens: A and B. The ratio of the number of pens A to the number of pens B is 5:7. If each pen A costs $3 and each pen B costs $5, and the total revenue from selling all the pens is $1,080.

Quantity A	Quantity B
The number of pens B	150

Ⓐ Quantity A is greater.
Ⓑ Quantity B is greater.
Ⓒ The two quantities are equal.
Ⓓ The relationship cannot be determined from the information given.

5

$$3y - 2x = -9$$
$$3y + ax = 24$$

The system of equations shown has no solution, where a is a constant.

Quantity A	Quantity B
0	a

Ⓐ Quantity A is greater.
Ⓑ Quantity B is greater.
Ⓒ The two quantities are equal.
Ⓓ The relationship cannot be determined from the information given.

Section 5 - Quantitative Reasoning (Easy)

6

At a store, cereal is sold in three sizes. A large box costs the same as three medium boxes or six small boxes. If Emma buys an equal amount of large and medium boxes of cereal for the price needed to buy seventy-two small boxes, how many medium boxes of cereal does she buy?

- A) 4
- B) 5
- C) 6
- D) 8
- E) 9

7

Let X denote a discrete random variable that can take the values 2, 6, 7, and 8. Given that $P(X = 2) = P(X = 6) = \frac{3}{22}$, and $P(X = 7) = \frac{4}{11}$, find $P(X = 8)$. Give your answer as a fraction.

- A) $\frac{4}{22}$
- B) $\frac{6}{22}$
- C) $\frac{4}{11}$
- D) $\frac{5}{11}$
- E) $\frac{8}{11}$

8

Find the least common multiple l.c.m. of the following 3 numbers: 36, 48, 60

- A) 120
- B) 180
- C) 240
- D) 360
- E) 720

9

In a town, it was decided that 600 people would vote in a local referendum. However, $\frac{1}{4}$ of the people were unable to vote due to unforeseen circumstances. The resolution was rejected by the majority. This majority was 40% of the number of votes. How many people in the town finally voted for the resolution and against the resolution?

- A) 150 voted and 450 against
- B) 270 voted and 180 against
- C) 180 voted and 270 against
- D) 450 voted and 150 against
- E) 200 voted and 250 against

10

The average test score for students in Group X is 100. The average test score for students in Group Y is 160. If the combined average score for both groups is 120, what is the ratio of the number of students in Group X to the number of students in Group Y?

Indicate all such answers.

- [A] 4:2
- [B] 5:8
- [C] 4:1
- [D] 8:4
- [E] 10:3
- [F] 20:10

11

A number when divides $(-15)^{-1}$ results $(-5)^{-1}$. Find the number.

- A) 5^{-1}
- B) 3^{-1}
- C) 2^{-1}
- D) 32^{-1}
- E) 5

12

Refer to the pie charts below. The first pie chart shows the percentage of students enrolled in a College Course while the second pie chart shows the percentage of students taking specific Science Courses.

If there are a total of 500 students enrolled, what percent of the total number of students are enrolled in Forensic Science?

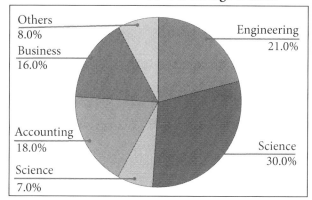

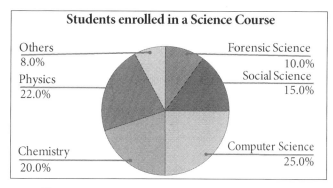

A) 2.0%
B) 2.5%
C) 3.0%
D) 4.5%
E) 5.0%

13

In the xy-coordinate plane, point R lies between the points $(-3, -3)$ and $(2, -3)$, and crosses the y-axis. What is the x-coordinate of point R?

14

Find the coordinates of the point that divides the line joining the points $(-8, 3)$ and $(10, 3)$ in the ratio 4:5 internally.

A) (5, 3)
B) (4, 3)
C) (3, 3)
D) (0, 3)
E) (2, 3)

15

Find the largest value of the two consecutive positive integers sum of whose squares is 365.

Section 5 - Quantitative Reasoning (Hard)

23 Minutes | 15 Questions

1

The average (arithmetic mean) of 70 test scores is 80. The average of 30 additional test scores.

Quantity A	Quantity B
The average of the 100 test scores	85

Ⓐ Quantity A is greater.
Ⓑ Quantity B is greater.
Ⓒ The two quantities are equal.
Ⓓ The relationship cannot be determined from the information given.

2

$$\frac{1}{|x+1|} > \frac{1}{8}$$

Quantity A	Quantity B
x	8

Ⓐ Quantity A is greater.
Ⓑ Quantity B is greater.
Ⓒ The two quantities are equal.
Ⓓ The relationship cannot be determined from the information given.

3

x and y are the numbers in the sequences:
$1^2, 2^2, 3^2, 4^2, x$
$5, y, 45, 80, 125$

Quantity A	Quantity B
x	y

Ⓐ Quantity A is greater.
Ⓑ Quantity B is greater.
Ⓒ The two quantities are equal.
Ⓓ The relationship cannot be determined from the information given.

4

In the y-coordinate plane, the triangle RST is equilateral. Points R and T have coordinates (0, 2) and (1, 0), respectively.

Quantity A	Quantity B
The perimeter of triangle RST	$3\sqrt{5}$

Ⓐ Quantity A is greater.
Ⓑ Quantity B is greater.
Ⓒ The two quantities are equal.
Ⓓ The relationship cannot be determined from the information given.

5

Below is a figure of a regular octagon. Any line segment connecting two nonadjacent vertices is called the diagonal of an octagon.

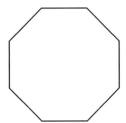

Quantity A	Quantity B
The number of diagonals of the octagon that is parallel to at least one side of the octagon	The number of diagonals of the octagon that is <u>not</u> parallel to any side of the octagon

Ⓐ Quantity A is greater.
Ⓑ Quantity B is greater.
Ⓒ The two quantities are equal.
Ⓓ The relationship cannot be determined from the information given.

6. In a catering team, 4 chefs are needed to prepare for a special event. The team is to be selected from 5 senior chefs and 6 junior chefs. If the selection must include at least 2 senior chefs, how many different ways can the team be chosen?

(A) 200
(B) 210
(C) 215
(D) 230
(E) 245

7.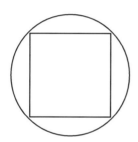

In the figure above, a square is inscribed in a circle with a diameter of 5 cm. What is the area of the square?

(A) $\dfrac{5}{\sqrt{2}}$
(B) $\dfrac{25}{4}$
(C) $8\sqrt{2}$
(D) $\dfrac{25}{2}$
(E) $10\sqrt{2}$

8. In a recent survey, R students were asked whether they eat after 22:00 o'clock. 25 % of the people answered positively and 40 % of the rest were asked, at what time do they get up in the morning? Which of the following expressions represents the number of students who do not eat after 22:00 and were not asked about the time they get up in the morning?

(A) 3R/20
(B) R/10
(C) 5R/9
(D) 3R/10
(E) 9R/20

9. If x and y are both positive odd integers, which of the following must be odd?

(A) $2xy$
(B) xy
(C) $x^y + x^y$
(D) $x^y + y^x$
(E) $x + y$

10. During a certain week, a seal ate 50% of the first 80 smelt it came across, and 30 % of the remaining smelt it came across. If the seal ate 40% of the smelt it came across during the entire week, how much smelt did it eat?

(A) 32
(B) 40
(C) 55
(D) 64
(E) 80

11

If a dealer could get his goods for 8% less while keeping his selling price fixed, his profit, based on cost, would be increased to $(x + 10)\%$ from his present profit of $x\%$, which is

[ ]

12

$(1 - \frac{1}{n}) + (1 - \frac{2}{n}) + (1 - \frac{3}{n}) +$ up to n term will result in _____.

- A) $\frac{1}{2n}$
- B) $\frac{n-1}{2}$
- C) $\frac{1}{n^2}$
- D) $\frac{1}{2n-1}$
- E) $\frac{1}{n}$

13

Suppose you are given the following inequalities:

$2x + 4y \leq 10$

$x - y \geq 2$

$x \geq 0$

$y \geq 0$

Find the maximum possible value of xy.

[ ]

14

The annual percent change in dollar amount of sales at five stores from 2016 to 2018.

Store	Percent Change from 2016 to 2017	Percent Change from 2017 to 2018
A	10	−10
B	−20	9
C	5	12
D	−7	−15
E	17	−8

If the dollar amount of sales at Store A was $800,000 for 2016, what was the dollar amount of sales at the store for 2018?

- A) $727,200
- B) $792,000
- C) $800,000
- D) $880,000
- E) $968,000

15

If $x + y = z$ and $x = y$, which of the following statements must be true?
Indicate all such statements.

- A $x - y = 2z$
- B $x - z = y - z$
- C $x - y = 0$
- D $2x + 2y = 2z$
- E $x = z/2$

Answer Key

VERBAL REASONING

Section 2		
Q. No.	Correct Answer	Your Answer
1	A	
2	B, E	
3	A, E, I	
4	E	
5	C	
6	C	
7	B, C	
8	C, F	
9	B, D	
10	D	
11	E	
12	To the... succeed.	

Section 4 (Easy)		
Q. No.	Correct Answer	Your Answer
1	B	
2	E	
3	C, E	
4	A, E, I	
5	D	
6	C	
7	A, B	
8	A, D	
9	B, E	
10	B, C	
11	E	
12	D	
13	A	
14	B	
15	D	

Section 4 (Hard)		
Q. No.	Correct Answer	Your Answer
1	E	
2	B, F	
3	C, E	
4	A, E, G	
5	D	
6	A, C	
7	B	
8	A	
9	D	
10	A, E	
11	C, E	
12	B, F	
13	E	
14	C	
15	C	

Answer Key

QUANTITATIVE REASONING

Section 3		
Q. No.	Correct Answer	Your Answer
1	B	
2	C	
3	A	
4	C	
5	C	
6	E	
7	26%	
8	A	
9	C	
10	D, E	
11	D	
12	B	

Section 5 (Easy)		
Q. No.	Correct Answer	Your Answer
1	B	
2	C	
3	C	
4	A	
5	A	
6	E	
7	C	
8	E	
9	B	
10	A, D, F	
11	B	
12	C	
13	0	
14	D	
15	14	

Section 5 (Hard)		
Q. No.	Correct Answer	Your Answer
1	B	
2	B	
3	A	
4	C	
5	B	
6	C	
7	D	
8	E	
9	B	
10	D	
11	15%	
12	B	
13	3	
14	B	
15	B, C, D, E	

Analytical Writing   Answers & Explanations   Section 1

Analyze an Issue

The sample essay that follows was written in response to the prompt that appeared in the question.

One tends to think of visionaries as those men and women who can see things that the minds of mere mortals cannot even imagine. Modern conveniences like the telephone and the television seem like miracles. How can a camera take a moving picture on the other side of the world and send it to the television in my little corner of the world? How is it possible that my voice can travel into space and be retrieved by my friend on her phone in the middle of the country? These inventions are, indeed, beyond the ken of the common man who probably can't even fathom where the ideas came from. Other wonders of the modern world, however, do have their roots in objects that we observe every day.

Man has always envied birds. The desire to fly has given rise to myths as old as the ability of man to speak. The most familiar of these myths is populated by the master craftsman, Daedalus and his son, Icarus. Icarus' desire to fly led his father to craft wings made of feather and wax. Daedalus' copied what he could observe of the wings of birds. His only warning to his son was not to fly too close to the sun lest the wax melt and cause the wings to be destroyed. Icarus, enthralled by the freedom of flight, ignored his father's warning and soared higher and higher until he did, indeed, fly too close to the sun. The wax melted, the wings fell apart, and Icarus' plummeted to his death in the sea. In the fifteenth century, Leonardo da Vinci drew plans for a flying device that became the inspiration for the modern helicopter. Some of the earliest planes attempted to imitate the motion of birds' wings. Now that man can actually fly not only around the world but out of it, one must wonder, "Do the birds envy man."

As the birds move in the sky above us, so do the sun, the stars, and the moon. For much of the history of man, the stars and planets were sources of myth and inspired poets, artists and musicians. The earliest ideas about the sun and the stars made the Earth the center of the universe. Later astronomers created the heliocentric theory of our solar system. The first practical use of the stars was for navigation. The longer the scientists observed the heavenly bodies, the greater the desire grew to reach them. When it became possible to measure the distances to the sun, the moon, and other planets, the idea of reaching them became a possibility. Now man has been to the moon, and has set his sights on Mars. The Hubble telescope continues to send back crystal–clear pictures of deep space, and man's fascination continues to grow.

When man looks up, he cannot avoid seeing the birds and the heavenly bodies. They are ubiquitous, and man's envy, fascination, and eventual understanding of them has made incredible journeys possible. The best ideas of the future are likely to come from man's continued passion for commonplace things.

Verbal Reasoning — **Answers & Explanations** — Section 2

1 **Choice A is correct** because "confluence" means a process of merging. This word fits in the context of the sentence because it describes the way that a qualitative approach and a quantitative approach joined together to provide greater insight.

Choice B is incorrect because "reduction" means making a specified thing smaller in amount. This word does not fit in the context of the sentence because neither approach was made smaller. Rather, the approaches were combined for better insight. **Choice C is incorrect** because "petulance" means being childishly sulky. This word does not fit in the context of the sentence because it does not describe what happened with the qualitative and quantitative approaches. They were not being childish but were combined together. **Choice D is incorrect** because "reluctance" means unwillingness to do something. This word does not fit in the context of the sentence because it does not describe what happened with the qualitative and quantitative approaches. They were not being hesitant but were combined together. **Choice E is incorrect** because "diaspora" means the spread of people from their original homeland. This word does not fit in the context of the sentence because the approaches were not being spread. Rather, the qualitative and quantitative approaches were joined together to provide greater insight.

2 **Choice B is correct** because "exhilarated" means very happy or elated. This word fits in the context of the sentence because it describes the feeling the person is getting when thinking about riding a motorcycle. The passage expresses that he feels fondly toward the notion, so this word makes sense. **Choice E is correct** because "milquetoast" means a timid or feeble person. This word fits in the context of the sentence because it describes the way the person has always preferred calm and safe places, like the office, as opposed to exciting activities like motorcycle riding.

Choice A is incorrect because "vetoed" means exercising the right of refusal to allow something. This word does not fit in the context of the sentence because a notion cannot veto a man. This does not make sense. Also, it does not support the meaning of the passage, which is the fact that the man was excited about riding a motorcycle despite his formerly safe life. **Choice C is incorrect** because "censured" means to express severe disapproval. This word does not fit in the context of the sentence because a notion cannot censure a man. This does not make sense. Also, it does not support the meaning of the passage, which is the fact that the man was excited about riding a motorcycle despite his formerly safe life. **Choice D is incorrect** because "obdurate" means stubbornly refusing to change an opinion. This word does not fit in the context of the sentence because it cannot be expounded upon with the phrase, "preferring the safety of an office environment." There is no indication of the man being stubborn. Rather, the passage expresses that he was formerly more timid but is now excited to ride a motorcycle. **Choice F is incorrect** because "contrarian" means a person who opposes a popular opinion. This word does not fit in the context of the sentence because it cannot be expounded upon with the phrase, "preferring the safety of an office environment." There is no indication of the man being oppositional. Rather, the passage expresses that he was formerly more timid but is now excited to ride a motorcycle.

3 **Choice A is correct** because "intertwined" means to twist or connect two things together. This word fits the context of the sentence because it describes the way music and theater are often seen and used together. The remainder of the passage goes on to explain how music and theater have worked together, so this emphasizes their connectedness. **Choice E is correct** because "glided" means to move in a smooth, continuous motion. This word fits the context of the sentence because it describes the way traditional music and theater have continued into the modern age seamlessly. Choice I is correct because "pathos" means a quality that evokes pity or sadness. This word fits the context of the sentence because it describes the way stage tragedies convey particular feelings by using music.

Choice B is incorrect because "antagonistic" means showing hostility toward someone or something. This word does not fit the context of the sentence because it does not accurately describe the relationship between music and theater according to the rest of the passage. **Choice C is incorrect** because "extraneous" means irrelevant or unrelated information. This word does not fit the context of the sentence because it does not accurately describe music and theater. The passage describes these arts as traditions that have continued throughout history. The text does not indicate in any way that these arts are not needed or can be done without. **Choice D is incorrect** because "perished" means suffering an untimely death.

This word does not fit the context of the sentence because it does not describe how theater has carried on over time. This word would suggest that music and theater have died in the modern age. However, the passage is trying to express the opposite. **Choice F is incorrect** because "lurched" means to make an abrupt, uncontrollable movement. This word does not fit the context of the sentence because it does not accurately describe the way music and theater have moved into the modern age. Rather than spasming forward, music and theater have continued on, always being loved and appreciated. **Choice G is incorrect** because "avarice" means extreme greed for material gain. This word does not fit the context of the sentence because it is unlikely that tragic plays would be aiming to express avarice. Rather, they would be attempting to evoke sadness. **Choice H is incorrect** because "aplomb" means having self-confidence in a demanding situation. This word does not fit the context of the sentence because it is unlikely that tragic plays would be aiming to express aplomb. Rather, they would be attempting to evoke sadness.

4 **Choice E is correct** because the passage describes recent findings about cone-shaped lipids, specifically their significance in ctenophores' ability to endure high pressures, as potentially applicable in "medical research." The benefits of cellular flexibility are discussed, followed by the finding that correlated diseases like Alzheimer's with a decrease in such lipid production. As researchers are "intrigued about potential benefits" the assumption is an analogy between lipid function in ctenophore cell architecture and that of human brains.

Choice A is incorrect because the passage refers to the ctenophores "having gradually adapted" to the high-pressure environment, implying this process is thought to have taken place over a long period of time rather than being a recent occurrence. **Choice B is incorrect** because there was no mention of other extreme environments in which the ctenophore could survive. Removal from the particular condition of a pressurized environment, in fact, was said to cause the animal's "disintegration" showing that it lacked the resiliency to survive certain environments. **Choice C is incorrect** because the passage explores the role of cone-shaped lipids in ctenophores in relation to their physical adaptation to oceanic pressure, rather than the need to maneuver in a high-risk environment with other marine animals, which might require cognitive alertness.

Choice D is incorrect because although the passage states that such lipids may provide stability in high-pressure environments, their specific role in human cognition remains unclear. Similarly, it cannot be said that these findings apply directly to neuroscientific research nor to brain diseases in which certain lipid production is lower.

5 **Choice C is correct** because the passage suggests that understanding the architectural function of cone-shaped lipids in ctenophores may lead to "potential benefits … on human cognitive health." Namely, it suggests that the decline of certain lipid production may be a factor in the development of neurodegenerative diseases like Alzheimer's, which is a link that warrants further study.

Choice A is incorrect because the passage does not make a link between lipid production and dietary choices. There is no information presented that would suggest that consuming ctenophores would have an impact on preventing, reversing, or treating the decline of certain lipid production in neurodegenerative diseases. **Choice B is incorrect** because the information in the passage links the loss of cone-shaped lipid production with certain brain diseases. However, it does not correlate to the increase or decrease of pressure in the patient's environment with such diseases. **Choice D is incorrect** because although cone-shaped lipids in ctenophores disintegrate in low-pressure environments, the information in the passage does not suggest that other features of the ctenophore's habitat need to be replicated for research. **Choice E is incorrect** because there is no information in the passage concerning ctenophore behavior as a result of lipid metabolism. The passage focuses solely on its capacity to physically withstand atmospheric pressure in deep ocean habitats.

6 **Choice C is correct** because "forerunners" means something that precedes another thing. This word fits in the context of the sentence because it explains that many theories came before the clear statement of the theory on the conservation of mass. **Choice D is correct** because "antecedents" means one event that precedes another. This word fits in the context of the sentence because it explains that many theories came before the clear statement of the theory on the conservation of mass.

Choice A is incorrect because "originators" means people who initiate or create something. This word does not fit in the context of the sentence because the theory of the conservation of mass did not have many originators, but many events that came before it. Therefore, choices C and D are the best options. **Choice B** is incorrect because "derivatives" means something that is based on another source. This word does not fit in the context of the sentence because the theory of the conservation of mass did not have many derivatives. The theory was not based on something else. Rather, the theory had many events that came before it, making choices C and D the best options. **Choice E** is incorrect because "imitators" means copying the action of another. This word does not fit in the context of the sentence because the theory of the conservation of mass did not have many imitators. The theory was not being copied. Rather, the theory had many events that came before it, making choices C and D the best options. **Choice F** is incorrect because "descendants" means organisms that have originated from particular ancestry. This word does not fit in the context of the sentence because the theory of the conservation of mass did not have many descendants. The theory did not have ancestors or act as an ancestor. Rather, the theory had many events that came before it, making choices C and D the best options.

7 **Choice B is correct** because "vapid" means offering nothing stimulating or challenging. This word fits in the context of the sentence because it provides a reasonable descriptor that explains why the conversation was disappointing. In other words, the conversation was so shallow and wasteful that it was surprising to see learned and productive people engage in it. **Choice C is correct** because "insipid" means lacking flavor or interest. This word fits in the context of the sentence because it provides a reasonable descriptor that explains why the conversation was disappointing. In other words, the conversation was so boring and wasteful that it was surprising to see learned and productive people engage in it.

Choice A is incorrect because "unreserved" means unlimited, open, and without caution. This word does not fit in the context of the sentence because it does not describe the nature of the conversation accurately. The speaker was disappointed in a wasteful conversation that surprisingly came from intelligent people. Therefore, it can be assumed that the conversation was lackluster, not unreserved. **Choice D** is incorrect because "insightful" means having a deep understanding or perspective. This word does not fit in the context of the sentence because it is the opposite of what the speaker is trying to say.

An insightful conversation would be expected from intelligent people. However, the speaker was disappointed in a wasteful conversation that surprisingly came from smart people. Therefore, it can be assumed that the conversation was lackluster, not insightful. **Choice E** is incorrect because "sectarian" means limited in scope or relating to a specific division. This word does not fit in the context of the sentence because it does not describe the nature of the conversation accurately. The speaker was disappointed in a wasteful conversation that surprisingly came from intelligent people. Therefore, it can be assumed that the conversation was lackluster, not focused on a specific sect. **Choice F** is incorrect because "pretentious" means attempting to impress by acting more important. This word does not fit in the context of the sentence because it is the opposite of what the speaker is trying to say. A pretentious conversation might be expected from educated individuals. However, the speaker was disappointed in a wasteful conversation that surprisingly came from such smart people. Therefore, it can be assumed that the conversation was lackluster, not pretentious.

8 **Choice C is correct** because "unadulterated" means complete and not diluted with any other elements. This word fits in the context of the sentence because it describes a distilled liquid that has no odor. It can be assumed that no other elements were mixed with the liquid. **Choice F is correct** because "homogeneous" means consisting of all parts of the same kind. This word fits in the context of the sentence because it describes a distilled liquid that is not contaminated with any other elements. In other words, the liquid was consistent throughout.

Choice A is incorrect because "similitude" means one thing is similar to something else. This word does not fit in the context of the sentence because no two things are being described. Only one single liquid is being discussed and it is not being compared to anything else. **Choice B** is incorrect because although, "homogeneity" has the same meaning as the correct answer, "homogeneous" it is the wrong part of speech for the blank. It does mean all parts are consistent to one another. However, the blank requires an adjective and this word is a noun. **Choice D** is incorrect because "impure" means mixed with foreign matter. This is the opposite of what the sentence is trying to say. This does not describe a liquid that is distilled and odorless. Rather, this word describes a liquid that is contaminated. **Choice E** is incorrect because "corrupted" means to change from good to bad. This word does not fit in the context of the sentence because it does not accurately describe the distilled, odorless, pure liquid. The liquid was not changed from good to bad. It was changed from contaminated to pure.

9 **Choice B is correct** because "calibrated" means an instrument is correctly marked with a scale of readings. This word fits in the context of the sentence because it describes what might be done to a scale so that scientists can make exact measurements. **Choice D is correct** because "aligned" means placing things in a line or in positions that agree with one another. This word fits in the context of the sentence because it describes what might be done to a scale so that scientists can make exact measurements. A scale that is not aligned would not produce accurate results.

Choice A is incorrect because "conjectured" means to form an opinion on something based on incomplete information. This word does not fit in the context of the sentence because it does not describe what might be done to a scale to produce accurate results. A scale cannot form an opinion. Therefore, choices B and D are the best options.

Choice C is incorrect because "fissured" means split into long, narrow cracks. This word does not fit in the context of the sentence because it does not describe what might be done to a scale to produce accurate results. Fissuring a scale would likely break it and produce inaccurate or no results. **Choice E** is incorrect because "serialized" means to publish or broadcast in regular installments. This word does not fit in the context of the sentence because it does not describe what might be done to a scale to produce accurate results. Scales are not typically published or broadcasted. Rather, they are used to measure things. Therefore, choices B and D are the best options. **Choice F** is incorrect because "embroiled" means to involve someone deeply in a conflict. This word does not fit in the context of the sentence because it does not describe what might be done to a scale to produce accurate results. Scales cannot be involved in disagreements. Rather, they are used to measure things. Therefore, choices B and D are the best options.

10 **Choice D is correct** because the passage contrasts two different opinions from established writers about whether aspiring writers should pursue writing. This comparison emphasizes that opinions differ greatly among experienced authors, especially in how they perceive the difficulties and rewards of the writing profession. The passage as a whole explores this divergence in outlook, making Choice D the best summary.

Choice A is incorrect because the passage doesn't delve into specific literary critiques like rhythm or cadence. It's about attitudes toward the profession, not stylistic analysis. **Choice B** is incorrect because the focus isn't on why authors hold their opinions or how they formed them, but rather that their views on writing vary. **Choice C** is incorrect because while writing is described as difficult and possibly successful, the passage does not emphasize both sides equally. The encouragement is less about reward and more about possibility—making D a more accurate summary. **Choice E** is incorrect because the passage provides no practical advice on how to submit work or make money. The focus is entirely on conflicting viewpoints.

11 **Choice E is correct** because this sentence outlines the opinion of the more pessimistic individuals who emphasize the harsh reality of the writing industry. It reflects the viewpoint that manuscripts from unknown authors often go unread, reinforcing the idea that the publishing world can be difficult to break into without connections.

Choice A is incorrect because it expresses a stronger claim than what the passage actually conveys. While the passage notes that editors might not read all submissions, it doesn't portray this as the severity of editorial judgment or rejection of quality. **Choice B** is incorrect because it shifts the focus from industry difficulty to the advantages of being well-known, which is not the primary purpose of the sentence. The line emphasizes the barriers for new writers, not the benefits of fame. **Choice C** is incorrect because it makes an inferential leap by discussing how aspiring writers might emotionally respond to being ignored. The passage doesn't explore emotional effects, only the perceived facts about manuscript reception. **Choice D** is incorrect because it brings editorial intent and emotional judgment into the discussion by calling the behavior "rude." The sentence simply reports what some people believe happens to manuscripts, not to judge editors' actions.

12 "To the same young woman writes another equally well-known writer: "Your work is excellent; you can and will succeed."

This sentence indicates the unreliability of judging a writer's potential on only one opinion. By indicating that the work being judged was written by the 'same' girl, the author establishes a controlled variable. Also, by pointing out that the differing opinion of this same work was that of an 'equally well-known writer', the author of this passage upholds the credibility of both judgments, thus demonstrating the subjective nature of writing and the unreliability of a single opinion.

Quantitative Reasoning — Answers & Explanations — Section 3

1 **Choice B is correct.**

Assign values of *x* and *y* from the given inequality.

x	y	(x + y)²	(y − x)²	
−1	1	(−1 + 1)² = 0	(1 − (−1))² = 4	B > A
−2	1	(−2 + 1)² = 1	(1 − (−2))² = 9	B > A
−3	50	(−3 + (50))² = (47)²	(50 − (−3))² = (53)²	B > A

From the obtained table above, for any value of *x* and *y*, Quantity B is always greater than Quantity A.

Choice A is incorrect because the obtained sum of *x* and *y* is always lesser than the difference between y and *x*. Hence, when the exponent is applied, Quantity B is always greater. **Choice C** is incorrect because the obtained sum of *x* and *y* is not equal to the difference between *y* and *x*. **Choice D** is incorrect because a relationship can be obtained from the given information.

2 **Choice C is correct.**

Based on the number line, $\frac{1}{4N} = 2$. We then solve for *N*.

$\frac{1}{4N} = 2$

$1 = 2(4N)$

$1 = 8N$

$\frac{1}{8} = N$

$N = \frac{1}{8}$, hence, Quantity A is equal to Quantity B.

Choice A is incorrect because based on the obtained value of *N*, Quantity A and Quantity B are equal. **Choice B** is incorrect because based on the obtained value of *N*, Quantity A and Quantity B are equal. **Choice D** is incorrect because a relationship can be obtained from the given information.

3 **Choice A is correct.**

Total expenditure during
the year = ($7500 * 3) + ($6500 * 4) + ($7200 * 5)
= ($22500 + $26000 + $36000)
= $84500

Total income during
the year = total expenditure + total saving
= $84500 + $5500
= $90000

Average monthly income of the family = $\frac{\$90000}{12}$
= $7500

Choice B is incorrect because based on the obtained value of the family's monthly income, Quantity B is lesser. **Choice C** is incorrect because based on the obtained value of the family's monthly income, Quantity A and Quantity B are not equal. **Choice D** is incorrect because a relationship can be obtained from the given information.

4 **Choice C is correct.**

A system of two linear equations has no solution if the lines are parallel. Parallel lines have the same slope and different *y*-intercepts.

Transform the given equations to slope-intercept form, $y = mx + b$.

$3y + 6x = 2$ ———> $y = -2x + \frac{2}{3}$

$y = -cx + 7$ ———> $y = -cx + 7$

Find *c*.

Slope of equation 1 is equal to the slope of equation 2

$-2x = -cx$

$\frac{-2x}{x} = -c$

$2 = c$

Choice A is incorrect because based on the obtained value of *c*, Quantity A is not greater than Quantity B. **Choice B** is incorrect because based on the obtained value of the *c*, Quantity B is not greater than Quantity A. **Choice D** is incorrect because a relationship can be obtained from the given information.

5 **Choice C is correct.**

Using the Simple Interest Formula, fill in the given information from the problem.

Given: R = 6% or 0.06

I = $1500

P = $20,000

I = PRT

$1500 = $20,000(0.06)t

$1500 = $1200t

$t = \frac{\$1500}{\$1200}$

t = 1.25 years

or t = 1.25(12 months) = 15 months

6 Quantitative Reasoning — Answers & Explanations — Section 3

Choice A is incorrect because 3 months is too short for the principal amount to earn $1500 at 6.0% per annum.
Choice B is incorrect because 2 months is too early for the principal amount to earn $1500 at 6.0% per annum.
Choice D is incorrect because 1.2 years is approximately correct but is less than the calculated time. **Choice E** is incorrect because 15 years is too long for the principal to just earn $1500 at 6.0% per annum.

6 Choice E is correct.

The total number of motor sales of UK
from Jan-June 2024 = 260

Percentage of cruiser motortype sold from UK = 30 %

Number of cruiser sold = 260(0.30)
$$= 78$$

Choice A is incorrect because 30 is the percentage and not the unknown number of cruiser sold from UK.
Choice B is incorrect because 31 is the number of scooter sold. **Choice C** is incorrect because 47 is the number of chopper sold from UK. **Choice D** is incorrect because 62 is the number of racer sold from UK.

7 The correct answer is 26%. The percentage of the sales of racer motorcycle from Uk for the month of Jan-March = 22%

The total percentage of the sales of racer motorcycle from Uk for the month of Jan-June = 24%

Let x be the percentage of the sales of this type of motorcycle from April to June

Solution:

% of the sales of racer for the month of Jan-June =

$$\frac{\% \text{ from Jan - March} + \% \text{ from April - June}}{2}$$

$$24\% = \frac{22\% + x}{2}$$

$$22\% + x = 24\% \,(2)$$

$$x = 26\%$$

8 Choice A is correct.

Scooter Sales for UK from January sales = 10%

UK sales for January = 40

Total motor sales for January = 125

Unknown: Percentage of scooter sales for UK January sales from the total motor January sales

Let x be the scooter sales for UK for the month of January.
Solution:
Find x.

x = (Percentage of Scooter Sales for UK for January)(UK sales for January)

$x = (10/100)(40)$

$x = 4$

Percentage of scooter sales for UK January sales from the total motor January sales

= x/Total motor sales for January*100

= 4/125 * 100

= 3.2 $%

Choice B is incorrect because the obtained percentage is 3.2% and not 4.2%. **Choice C** is incorrect because the obtained percentage is 3.2% and not 4.5%. **Choice D** is incorrect because the obtained percentage is 3.2% and not 6.5%. **Choice E** is incorrect because the obtained percentage is 3.2% and not 8.2%.

9 Choice C is correct.

Note that 1 L = 1 dm^3

Volume of the cube box = 1 dm^3

Side of the cube box = diameter of the mug
$$= \sqrt[3]{1}$$
$$= 1 \, dm$$

Height of the mug = 1 dm

Radius of the mug = ½ (1) = 0.5 dm

Volume of the mug = $\pi r^2 h$
$$= \pi (0.5)^2 (1)$$
$$= 0.25 \, \pi$$

Choice A is incorrect because the obtained volume of the mug is 0.25π and not 1π. **Choice B** is incorrect because the obtained volume of the mug is 0.25π and not 0.5π. **Choice D** is incorrect because the obtained volume of the mug is 0.25π and not 2π. **Choice E** is incorrect because the obtained volume of the mug is 0.25π and not 0.75π.

10 Choice D and Choice E are correct. From the given frequency, the total number of applicants is 30. The position of the median is at $(n + 1)/2$, hence, it is at 15.5. Then take the cumulative frequency from the lowest age. The 15.5th value is at the interval 16-18. Therefore, the answers are Option B and Option E.

Choice A is incorrect because it is outside the 16th - 18th position. **Choice B** is incorrect because it is not within the obtained range of 16-18. **Choice C** is incorrect because it is below the obtained range of 16-18.

11 **Choice D is correct** because the distance from the center to point (3, 1) would indicate the least amount the radius could be and the distance from the center to the point (–1, 4) would indicate the greatest amount the radius could be. The formula $d = \sqrt{(x_2 - x_1)^2 + (y_2 - y_1)^2}$ can be used to evaluate both distances.

For the distance between (8, –5) and (3, 1) the equation would be $\sqrt{(3-8)^2 + (1+5)^2}$ which would simplify to be $\sqrt{61}$. This is approximately 7.81.

For the distance between (8, –5) and (–1, 4) the equation would be $\sqrt{(-1-8)^2 + (4+5)^2}$ which would simplify to be $\sqrt{162}$. This is approximately 12.73.

This means the radius can be an integer value between 7.81 and 12.73. That would mean the values 8, 9, 10, and 11 are all possible radiuses, making 4 possible options for the circumference since the circumference equals 2Πr.

Choice A is incorrect because there is more than 1 option for *r*. **Choice B** is incorrect because there are more than 2 options for *r*. **Choice C** is incorrect because there are more than 3 options for *r*. **Choice E** is incorrect because there are only 4 options for *r*.

12 **Choice B is correct** because for a positive number minus another number to be positive, the other number has to be negative. This would mean $x > 0$. For example, if $x = -3$, then the expression $|x| - x > 0$ would be satisfied since $|-3| - (-3) = 3 + 3 = 6 > 0$.

Choice A is incorrect because *x* cannot be greater than 0 because that would not make the statement greater than 0. For example, if $x = 1$ then the equation would be $|1| - 1 > 0$ which is not true. **Choice C** is incorrect because if *x* was zero the statement would be $|0| - 0 > 0$ which is not true. **Choice D** is incorrect because if *x* was greater than 1, the expression would not be true. For example, if $x = 2$, then the statement would be $|2| - 2 > 0$ which is not true. **Choice E** is incorrect because *x* cannot be greater than or equal to 1.

Verbal Reasoning (Easy) — Answers & Explanations — Section 4

1 **Choice B is correct** because "ubiquitous" means present or found everywhere. This word fits in the context of the sentence because it describes the way that radiation is actually common and impossible to avoid despite the fact that most people think of it as something out of the ordinary.

Choice A is incorrect because "ineffable" means too extreme to be described in words. This word does not fit in the context of the sentence because it does not describe radiation based on the rest of the information in the passage. Rather than saying radiation is extreme, the point of the passage is to express that radiation is common, impossible to avoid, and much more ordinary than most people think. Therefore, choice B is the best option. **Choice C** is incorrect because "nebulous" means unclear or in the form of a cloud. This word does not fit in the context of the sentence because it does not describe radiation based on the rest of the information in the passage. The passage does not express that radiation is difficult to understand or cloudy in any way. Rather, the passage is saying that radiation is common, impossible to avoid, and much more ordinary than most people think. Therefore, choice B is the best option. **Choice D** is incorrect because "quiescent" means in a state of inactivity or dormancy. This word does not fit in the context of the sentence because it does not describe radiation based on the rest of the information in the passage. Rather than saying radiation is inactive, the point of the passage is to express that radiation is common, impossible to avoid, and much more ordinary than most people think. Therefore, choice B is the best option. **Choice E** is incorrect because "foolproof" means incapable of being misused. This word does not fit in the context of the sentence because it does not describe radiation based on the rest of the information in the passage. The passage is not trying to express that radiation can't be misused. Oppositely, the passage actually states that it has potential hazards. The point of the passage is to express that radiation is common, impossible to avoid, and much more ordinary than most people think. Therefore, choice B is the best option.

2 **Choice E is correct** because "alacrity" means brisk and cheerful readiness. This word fits in the context of the sentence because it describes the way the man ate so eagerly, which would appall the other guests who showed such control and restraint at the table.

Choice A is incorrect because "efficacy" means an ability to produce a desired result. This word does not fit in the context of the sentence because the man is not producing any result at the table. Rather, he is eating his food in a way that appalls those who are proud of their table manners. Therefore, choice E is the best option. **Choice B** is incorrect because "decorum" means etiquette, or behavior with good taste. This word does not fit in the context of the sentence because it would not explain why the other guests were appalled by the way he ate. If they pride themselves on impeccable table manners and he also showed impeccable etiquette, it is likely that they would be satisfied. **Choice C** is incorrect because "adroitness" means cleverness or skill. This word does not fit in the context of the sentence because the man is not eating in a clever or skilled way. This would not explain why the other guests were appalled by the way he ate. Rather, it can be assumed that he is eating in a way that contrasts with their impeccable table manners. Thus, choice E is the best option. **Choice D** is incorrect because "temperance" means moderation, self-control, and restraint. This word does not fit in the context of the sentence because it would not explain why the other guests were appalled by the way he ate. If they pride themselves on impeccable table manners and he also showed great restraint while eating, it is likely that they would be satisfied.

3 **Choice C is correct** because "inveigh" means to speak or complain about something with hostility. This word fits the context of the sentence because it describes the way he falsely portrays his sickness to his mother and physician. He does not simply act a bit sick but feigns a serious illness and makes others feel that his condition is severe. **Choice E is correct** because "rapturous" means expressing great pleasure or enthusiasm. This word fits the context of the sentence because it describes the way Felix enjoyed the lie he told his mother and his physician. The passage suggests he was proud of his performance and deeply pleased by what he had done.

Choice A is incorrect because "suborn" means to bribe someone to commit an unlawful act. This word does not fit the context of the sentence because Felix is not bribing or inducing his mother and physician to do anything. Rather, he is convincing them that he is very sick. **Choice B** is incorrect because "cajole" means persuading a person to do something via flattery. This word does not fit the context of the sentence because Felix is not convincing his mother and physician to do anything. Rather, he is tricking them into thinking that he is very sick. **Choice D** is incorrect because "desultory" means lacking a plan or purpose. This word does not fit the context of the sentence because it does not describe the way Felix felt about his performance of faking an illness. The passage suggests he is proud and extremely pleased by what he did, not that he lacked a plan or purpose. **Choice F is incorrect** because "aberrant" means deviating from the usual standard. This word does not fit the context of the sentence because it does not describe the way Felix felt about his performance of faking an illness. The passage suggests he is proud and extremely pleased by what he did, not that he did something that departed from the norm.

4 **Choice A is correct** because "alleviating" means making suffering less severe. This word fits the context of the sentence because it describes the mitigation of the risk taken by the Chinese when they shipped goods on many different ships. Previously, if all goods were sent on one ship and the ship was lost, there would be great suffering. However, by shipping on many boats, this risk was alleviated. **Choice E is correct** because "schematized" means arranged into a systematic form. This word fits the context of the sentence because it describes their intentional use of an insurance procedure. It was not a coincidence that they shipped goods on many boats, but an organized act used to protect their inventory. **Choice I is correct** because "tumultuous" means loud and confusing disorder. This word fits the context of the sentence because it describes the world of trade accurately in a way that would explain the need for an intentional act of insurance. Rather than taking a gamble in such an unpredictable and wild world, the Chinese wanted to protect their inventory.

Choice B is incorrect because "exacerbating" means making a problematic situation worse. This word does not fit the context of the sentence because it does not accurately describe what the Chinese wanted to do to the risk of losing their inventory. Rather than making the risk worse, they wanted to find an intentional way to minimize it. **Choice C is incorrect** because "annunciating" means vocally claiming or pronouncing. This word does not fit the context of the sentence because it does not accurately describe what the Chinese wanted to do to the risk of losing their inventory. Rather than vocally stating the risk, they wanted to minimize it. **Choice D is incorrect** because "sardonic" means mocking in a grim way. This word does not fit the context of the sentence because it does not describe what was being done with insurance. The insurance method was not being grimly mocked but was being used in an organized way to reduce risk. **Choice F is incorrect** because "quiescent" means in a state of inactivity or dormancy. This word does not fit the context because the insurance method was not inactive. Rather, it was actively used to reduce the risk of losing inventory. **Choice G is incorrect** because "guileless" means innocent and without deception. This word does not accurately describe the world of trade. The passage does not suggest that trade is particularly honest or innocent; instead, it implies that trade is risky and chaotic, requiring protection through insurance. **Choice H is incorrect** because "portly" means having a stout body. This word does not make sense in the context of the sentence, as the world of trade is not being described physically. The passage describes it as chaotic, which supports the need for risk management—not physical size.

5 **Choice D is correct** because anti-computer crime legislation is not mentioned in the passage. While the passage discusses arrests, trials, guilty pleas, equipment seizures, and debate about electronic rights, it does not reference any new laws being created or passed as a result of the crackdown.

Choice A is incorrect because the passage specifically refers to "huge confiscations of data and equipment all over the USA" which clearly describes seizure by law enforcement. **Choice B** is incorrect because the passage notes that the crackdown "created a melee of debate over electronic crime" pointing to public discourse. **Choice C** is incorrect because it mentions "arrests, criminal charges, one dramatic show-trial, [and] several guilty pleas" all examples of criminal prosecution. **Choice E** is incorrect because the Electronic Frontier Foundation is introduced as being "fiercely dedicated to the establishment and preservation of electronic civil liberties" which describes its goals.

6 **Choice C is correct** because the passage states that "The Hacker Crackdown… has created a melee of debate over electronic crime, punishment, freedom of the press, and issues of search and seizure." This clearly supports the idea that the 1990 crackdown spurred new debate about the prosecution of computer crime.

Choice A is incorrect because the passage describes the crackdown as a joint effort involving "the U.S. Secret Service, private telephone security, and state and local law enforcement groups" rather than being led solely by the federal government. **Choice B** is incorrect because the passage notes that the effort had "very mixed results" indicating that law enforcement did not view the crackdown as a complete success. **Choice D is incorrect** because the passage explains that the Electronic Frontier Foundation was formed after the crackdown, as a response to it, not to stop it: "The Hacker Crackdown had another unprecedented effect; it spurred the creation... of the Electronic Frontier Foundation." **Choice E is incorrect** because there is no mention of new laws being proposed or passed as a result of the crackdown. The focus is on debate and civil liberties, not legislation.

7 **Choice A is correct** because the passage states that the Hacker Crackdown "spurred the creation" of the Electronic Frontier Foundation, which was "fiercely dedicated to the establishment and preservation of electronic civil liberties." This directly supports A as a result of the crackdown. **Choice B is correct** because the final lines of the passage say, "Politics has entered cyberspace" and describe a "melee of debate over electronic crime, punishment, freedom of the press, and issues of search and seizure." This clearly shows that political issues became a new focus within the computer community.

Choice C is incorrect because the passage does not mention a decrease in computer-related crime as a result of the crackdown. It only describes the effort as "fascinating" and having "very mixed results" implying that any reduction in crime was neither clear nor lasting.

8 **Choice A is correct** because "stimulated" means encouraging interest in an activity. This word fits in the context of the sentence because it accurately describes the way Einstein's discovery led to a century of additional research. In other words, the discovery of general relativity induced further studying of the topic. **Choice D is correct** because "motivated" means providing someone with an incentive to do something. This word fits in the context of the sentence because it accurately describes the way Einstein's discovery led to a century of additional research. In other words, the discovery of general relativity induced further studying of the topic.

Choice B is incorrect because "dampened" means making slightly wet. This word does not fit in the context of the sentence because it does not accurately explain how a full century of research relates to Einstein's discovery. The passage does not indicate that anything was made wet. Rather, it expresses that Einstein's discovery led to further research, making choices A and D the best options. **Choice C** is incorrect because "abetted" means encouraging someone to do something morally wrong or illegal. This word does not fit in the context of the sentence because it does not accurately explain how a full century of research relates to Einstein's discovery. The passage does not indicate that anything morally incorrect or against the law was done. Rather, it expresses that Einstein's discovery led to further research, making choices A and D the best options. **Choice E is incorrect** because "debilitated" means making weaker or more infirm. This word does not fit in the context of the sentence because it does not accurately explain how a full century of research relates to Einstein's discovery. The passage does not indicate that the discovery weakened future research. Rather, it expresses that Einstein's discovery led to additional research, making choices A and D the best options. **Choice F is incorrect** because "vitalized" means giving strength or energy to something. This word does not fit in the context of the sentence because it does not accurately explain how a full century of research relates to Einstein's discovery. The passage does not indicate that the discovery gave strength to future researchers. Rather, it expresses that Einstein's discovery stimulated the additional research to take place, making choices A and D the best options.

9 **Choice B is correct** because "drawn" means to make a judgement based on given information. This word fits in the context of the sentence because it accurately expresses what can be done with classical Newtonian physics to produce a conclusion. In other words, the information from classic physics is analyzed and a conclusion is determined. **Choice E is correct** because "derived" means to obtain something from a specified source or concept. This word fits in the context of the sentence because it accurately expresses what can be done with classical Newtonian physics to produce a conclusion. In other words, the information from classic physics is analyzed and a conclusion is obtained.

Choice A is incorrect because "imputed" means naming the blame for something falsely or unjustly. This word does not fit in the context of the sentence because determinism is not being blamed for anything. Rather it is a concept that is drawn based on classic Newtonian physics. Therefore, choices B and E are the best options. **Choice C is incorrect** because "ascertained" means to find the certain answer to something. This word does not fit in the context of the sentence because determinism is not being ascertained or figured out for certain. Rather, it is a concept that is being supposed based on classic

Newtonian physics. Therefore, choices B and E are the best options. **Choice D is incorrect** because "calculated" means worked out via mathematics. This word does not fit in the context of the sentence because determinism is not being calculated and mathematics is not discussed in the passage. Rather, determinism is a concept that is being supposed based on classic Newtonian physics. Therefore, choices B and E are the best options. **Choice F is incorrect** because "assumed" means taking something as true without proof. This word does not fit in the context of the sentence because determinism is not being guessed. Rather, determinism is a concept that is being concluded upon based on the reliability of classic Newtonian physics. Therefore, choices B and E are the best options.

10 **Choice B is correct** because "dulcet" means sweet and soothing. This word fits in the context of the sentence because it accurately describes poems that focus on the topic of love. The poems are later described as evocative and mellifluous, which also supports the idea that the poems were sweet and soothing. **Choice C is correct** because "redolent" means strongly reminiscent. This word fits in the context of the sentence because it describes poems that were created a very long time ago that are still cherished in present day. The author, Rumi, was reminiscing on love.

Choice A is incorrect because "odoriferous" means giving off a smell that is usually unpleasant. This word does not fit in the context of the sentence because it does not describe poems. Poems cannot be odoriferous because they are not tangible. In addition, the passage describes the poems as beautiful love poems, so this word does not align with the remainder of the passage. **Choice D is incorrect** because "fecund" means fertile or producing an abundance of offspring. This word does not fit in the context of the sentence because it does not describe poems. Poems are inanimate things that cannot produce offspring. **Choice E is incorrect** because "restive" means unable to keep still or silent. This word does not fit in the context of the sentence because it does not describe poems. Poems are inanimate things that cannot move or speak. Therefore, they cannot behave in a restive way. **Choice F is incorrect** because "nostalgic" means thinking fondly of a past condition. This word does not fit in the context of the sentence because it does not accurately describe the poems. The poems being discussed were about love, not past times or previous conditions. Therefore, choices B and C are better options.

11 **Choice E is correct** because it addresses the conclusion that all people owning newspapers are more interested in the money than the cause. The fact that the new owners are hoping to increase subscribers (and therefore funds) is the most significant comment. The method of accomplishing an increase in business is based upon relevancy of the content of the paper.

Choice A is incorrect because it just illustrates an example of one reason to print a newspaper. **Choice B is incorrect** because it only offers a detail. It does not address the concern of the profits of the owner. **Choice C is incorrect** because while it addresses some income benefits of printing a newspaper, it does not specifically compare profit with the cause for publishing newspapers. **Choice D is incorrect** because the increased price of subscriptions could help the newspaper owner earn more income. However, the response does not address the income of the owner. It merely states a fact that the price has increased, only showing weak support for the conclusion.

12 **Choice D is correct** because the passage states that the current survey contains Western bias and is also not appropriate where literacy is low, implying it would benefit from a more sensitive approach. It further suggests that a modification of the survey to allow alternative responses, such as "meaning in life" would result in "deeper insights."

Choice A is incorrect because while the passage discusses certain limitations of this particular survey on happiness, it does not suggest that all rankings are inherently limited. In fact, it makes suggestions for improving the survey by broadening its scope and altering its data-collecting methods. **Choice B is incorrect** because the passage does not state any correlation between wealth and happiness (the ranking of European countries at the top notwithstanding). On the contrary, it makes several points against the notion that wealth can be used as an indicator of success. For example, it refers to the "exorbitant" value often placed on material wealth, implying it is unreasonable and deserves to be challenged. **Choice C is incorrect** because while this may be part of the solution to the issue of cultural bias, it is not the best summary of the passage in general. The main idea of the passage is that the happiness ranking needs to be adjusted to accommodate cultural norms and low literacy rates, but it does not discuss how this should be accomplished. **Choice E is incorrect** because while the passage defends the happiness ranking in its effort to supplant one centered on material wealth, that is not the main idea of the passage. By mentioning the ranking's drawbacks, the passage explores the limitations of evaluating solely personal happiness above other qualities of life valued in non-Western cultures. It also makes the suggestion ("were the survey less culturally biased") to improve said ranking to gain "deeper insights" about the human condition.

13 **Choice A is correct** because the passage refers to cultural bias, and language would be one way that cultural bias is transmitted. In particular, this may be the case as a result of translations into languages that may have more than one term for the idea of ´happiness,´ each with a different connotation. Survey-takers may not be responding to the same idea of happiness as the researchers who wrote it originally.

Choice B is incorrect because the passage does not suggest that well-being is a Western concept, even though personal happiness may be. Broader responses to the survey about happiness, such as "meaning in life" and "balance and harmony" show that well-being is not a foreign concept, even though it may be processed differently in different cultures. **Choice C is incorrect** because the passage states that the happiness survey was made "in an attempt to challenge" the notion that wealth equals success. Therefore, the intention is certainly not to link the two. **Choice D is incorrect** because the problem with linear evaluations was based on the fact that they required a certain education level to understand and were also culturally biased in the sense of using metrics to evaluate a state of being. So, while the possibility that they were mistakenly taken to mean the opposite cannot be ruled out, it is not the best alternative explanation to culturally biased survey results. **Choice E is incorrect** because although the passage states that European countries often appeared at the top of the list, it also states that not all countries were Western, and some had a low literacy rate. Therefore, there is no indication that only countries with a certain GDP participated in the survey.

14 **Choice B is correct** because the first paragraph states a *tlatoani* is referred to as the "speaker" reflecting their role as a representative who acts "in [the] interests" of the people. In the second paragraph, this role is challenged, given that rulers come from the "noble class" and are elected by a Council of Nobles, rather than by common people, suggesting the voice and interests of the commoner is not as valued. This raises certain contradictions in the idea of the ruler as a speaker, even though sufficient public discontent can "oust" rulers who "fail to meet expectations."

Choice A is incorrect because the second paragraph provides no examples of a ruler acting as a speaker, rather it explains the election process by the Council of Nobles and the would-be version of "impeachment" based on public outcry. **Choice C is incorrect** because the first paragraph outlines the role of the *tlatoani* as speaker, rather than their duties in general. The second paragraph introduces the election process and ends with how a ruler might lose their title.

15 **Choice D is correct** because the passage emphasized that common people did not participate in elections, also noting rulers came "invariably" from among the nobles. It also mentioned the Council of Nobles that had the power of deciding on the successor. Even though it states that significant public protest was known to have a political impact, even dethroning a ruler, one cannot infer that common people were on equal footing with nobles on an everyday basis.

Choice A is incorrect because the passage states the power that the Council of Nobles had, without referring to the limitations of that power. Therefore, one cannot infer that it was delimited to the election process or that they lacked the authority to depose a ruler seen as unfit. **Choice B is incorrect** because although one can infer there was competition to gain the Council's favor, there is no indication from the passage that corruption was involved. Furthermore, the reference to the concept of *noblesse oblige*, which means the duty of high birth to act benevolently, suggests that corrupt practices were at least not the norm. **Choice C is incorrect** because "military prowess" was cited as a significantly desirable quality in the election process, suggesting that there was ample opportunity to demonstrate military skill and courage in between elections. **Choice E is incorrect** because the passage read that candidates were "predominantly" from the "lineage of predecessors" meaning that the vast majority of rulers shared lineage with their predecessors.

6 Verbal Reasoning (Hard) — Answers & Explanations — Section 4

1 **Choice E is correct** because "appreciable" means large or important enough to be noticed. This word fits in the context of the sentence because it accurately describes a stimulus that initially draws attention, such as the sound of a ticking clock or the smell of something being cooked. However, over time the subject pays less attention to these appreciable stimuli.

Choice A is incorrect because "negligible" means something is so small it is not worth considering. This is the opposite of what the passage is expressing. Rather than something being too small for consideration, the stimuli being described are initially powerful and draw the attention of the subject, such as the sound of a clock or the smell of a room. If a stimulus was negligible, the subject would not be paying attention to it in the first place. **Choice B** is incorrect because "equivocal" means open to more than one interpretation. This word does not fit in the context of the sentence because the stimuli discussed are not being interpreted or analyzed but simply being noticed due to their command. Therefore, choice E is the best option. **Choice C** is incorrect because "insignificant" means too small for consideration. This is the opposite of what the passage is expressing. Rather than something being too small for consideration, the stimuli being described are initially powerful and draw the attention of the subject, such as the sound of a clock or the smell of a room. If a stimulus was insignificant, the subject would not be paying attention to it in the first place. **Choice D** is incorrect because "imperceptible" means impossible to process by a sense or the mind. This is the opposite of what the passage is expressing. Rather than something being too small for processing, the stimuli being described are initially powerful and draw the attention of the subject, such as the sound of a clock or the smell of a room. If a stimulus was imperceptible, the subject would not be paying attention to it in the first place.

2 **Choice B is correct** because "procure" means obtaining something with care and effort. This word fits the context of the sentence because it describes the way single-cell organisms use the cell surface to gather nutrients from the world and release waste. In other words, these organisms must collect and secure their food using the cell surface. **Choice F is correct** because "rudimentary" means limited to basic principles. This word fits the context of the sentence because it describes the limitations of sea sponges. In other words, these incredibly basic organisms take advantage of the flowing seawater to transport their nutrients and waste.

Choice A is incorrect because "annex" means to add a subordinate part. This word does not fit the context of the sentence because no subordinate parts are being added to single-cell organisms. Rather, they are using one of the parts already in existence—the cell surface—to complete the task of gathering nutrients. **Choice C** is incorrect because "relinquish" means to leave behind or give up something. This word does not fit the context of the sentence because nutrients are not being relinquished by single-cell organisms but gathered and secured. The organisms don't want to get rid of the nutrients; rather, they want to procure them. **Choice D** is incorrect because "primitive" means having the style or character of something from a very early stage in evolutionary history. This word does not fit the context of the sentence because it does not describe sea sponges based on the rest of the text. The passage is trying to express that sea sponges are a basic animal that uses the flow of water as their circulatory system, not that they are frozen in an early evolutionary stage. **Choice E** is incorrect because "vestigial" means small or imperfectly developed so that it is not able to function as a larger version would. This word does not fit the context of the sentence because it does not describe sea sponges based on the rest of the text. The passage is trying to express that sea sponges are basic animals that use water flow effectively, not that they are underdeveloped or nonfunctional.

3 **Choice C is correct** because "obstinacy" means the condition of being stubborn. This word fits in the context of the sentence because it describes how the man behaved in the face of his experienced friends telling him to learn guitar slowly. Instead of heeding their advice, he pushed himself to learn faster. Therefore, he behaved in a way that was stubborn instead of allowing himself to be guided by others. **Choice E is correct** because "flouted" means openly disregarded. This word fits in the context of the sentence because it describes what he did to the advice of his experienced friends. Rather than listening to them, he proceeded to engage in the behavior opposite of what they suggested.

Choice A is incorrect because "pensiveness" means a deep and serious thoughtfulness. This word does not fit in the context of the sentence because it does not describe the way he behaved. Rather than deeply and

Verbal Reasoning (Hard) — Answers & Explanations — Section 4

seriously considering the advice of his seasoned friends, he took his own route in a stubborn and careless way. **Choice B is incorrect** because "reticence" means the quality of being reserved or restrained. This word does not fit in the context of the sentence because it does not describe the way he behaved. Rather than restraining or controlling himself as he practiced, he pushed himself to learn quickly and go against the advice of his experienced friends. **Choice D is incorrect** because "articulated" means expressed by putting into words. This word does not fit in the context of the sentence because it does not describe what the man did to the advice of his friends. Rather than articulating their advice, he disregarded it and went about learning guitar his own way. Therefore, choice E is the better option. **Choice F is incorrect** because "expanded" means extending or enlarging something. This word does not fit in the context of the sentence because it does not describe what the man did to the advice of his friends. Rather than expanding their advice, he disregarded it and went about learning guitar his own way. Therefore, choice E is the better option.

4 **Choice A is correct** because "enraptured" means giving intense pleasure to. This word fits the context of the sentence because it describes the way Fiona felt about the magic of dreams. Based on the sentence structure, one can assume that the word in the first clause would have an opposite meaning to the second clause, which describes being turned off by dreams. Therefore, it makes sense that the magic of dreams would bring her intense pleasure. **Choice E is correct** because "abstruse" means something that is difficult to understand. This word fits the context of the sentence because it describes the way dreams can be challenging to interpret. Based on the sentence structure, one can assume that the first blank should convey ambiguity or confusion, contrasting with the second clause that implies logic. Therefore, it makes sense that dreams would seem illogical or difficult to understand. **Choice G is correct** because "charlatans" means people who falsely claim to have special knowledge. This word fits the context of the sentence because it describes the way that the supposed experts on dreams seemed to merely be making assumptions rather than having a concrete understanding of the topic.
Choice B is incorrect because "vindicated" means clearing someone of blame or suspicion. This word does not fit the context of the sentence because it does not describe what the magic of dreams did to Fiona. Fiona is not being blamed for anything. Rather, the magic of dreams is enrapturing her, or bringing her pleasure. **Choice C is incorrect** because "denounced" means publicly declaring something to be wrong or evil. This word does not fit the context because Fiona is not declaring anything about the dreams. Instead, the sentence implies that she finds them alluring or pleasurable. **Choice D is incorrect** because "debonair" means confident, stylish, and charming. This word does not fit the context of the sentence because the sentence contrasts mysterious or confusing dreams with logically explainable ones. Dreams are not being described as confident or charming; rather, they are described as difficult to interpret. **Choice F is incorrect** because "gentile" means not Jewish. This word is irrelevant to the topic of dreams and has no logical place in the sentence. **Choice H is incorrect** because "solemn" means serious and dignified. This word does not fit the context of the sentence because it fails to convey the idea that the so-called experts were pretending to know more than they actually did. The passage suggests deception, not dignity. **Choice I is incorrect** because "guileless" means innocent and without deception. This word does not fit the sentence because it contradicts the implied criticism of the experts. The sentence implies that they were misleading or uninformed, not honest and sincere.

5 **Choice D is correct** because the passage states that millions of years ago, volcanic formations called kimberlites shot diamonds up to the surface from the Earth's mantle and crust. It goes on to say that "modern-day mining" tries to "uncover the vestiges" of those eruptions. As vestiges mean trace amounts of something left over after a period of time, it can be concluded that, previously, the existence of diamonds on the surface was far less scarce.

Choice A is incorrect because the passage does not link the durability of diamonds with the process by which they surfaced (eruptions from "kimberlites"). In addition, it states that diamonds already existed in the Earth's mantle and crust, so they formed before the eruptions "shot" them to the surface. **Choice B is incorrect** because the passage states that the "allure" of diamonds comes from their "scarcity." There is no suggestion that mining itself leaves perceptible marks on the diamonds, but rather that it has an adverse impact on the environment, and indirectly on local populations. **Choice C is incorrect** because although the "cultured" diamonds are said to be cultivated under high heat and pressure, it is not stated that these conditions replicate those of the Earth when it was forming. **Choice E** is incorrect because the passage alludes to misconceived notions about the scarcity of diamonds in contrast to their abundance underneath the Earth's surface. However, it also states that their presence ("vestiges") on the surface is limited. So, while their scarcity on the surface may lead to more aggressive mining practices, these are not linked to misconceived notions about scarcity, but rather to an awareness of it.

6 **Choice A and C are correct** because the main argument of the passage is that primeval diamonds are increasingly problematic, and therefore, cultivated ones provide an alternative, despite lacking the prestige of old age. The first paragraph discusses the reasons for the scarcity of diamonds and the complications that arise in finding them due to inactive kimberlites on one hand, and concerns over mining (working conditions, the financing of war, environmental cost), on the other. The second paragraph explains how synthetic diamonds offer a viable alternative, even though the "allure" of scarce precious gems cannot be duplicated by "neither ancient nor scarce" substitutes.

Choice B is incorrect because the misconceived notions are not the source of contention, which is rather what is known about mining practices. Furthermore, the second paragraph points to the "promising" ability of lab-grown diamonds to address the problems raised in the first, not to disabuse misconceived notions.

7 **Choice B is correct** because the passage does not state that celebrations are inherently unconstructive, providing the example of "applauding" training time. It states, however, that irrespective of outcomes (academic success or failure), the effort should be emphasized. For example, in the training example, one should celebrate time dedicated to training "over goals scored in a match."

Choice A is incorrect because the passage does not suggest that successes and failures should be altogether ignored ("applauding" time spent in training). Rather, it presents the idea that rewarding progress based only on the outcome is less constructive than supporting effort. It suggests that an approach focused on effort encourages a deeper appreciation for the process itself, which serves to "foster the intrinsic motivation necessary for developing self-esteem irrespective of goal-attainment." **Choice C** is incorrect because the passage discourages both positive and negative reinforcements that are outcome-based. Therefore, withholding desired purchases would be part of the "rewards and punishments" system that, according to the passage, will "fail to instill the intrinsic motivation needed to develop psychological resilience, self-esteem, and a love for learning." **Choice D** is incorrect because the passage does not discourage celebrations ("applauding" time spent in training). It shifts the focus of the celebration on process more than outcome to "foster the intrinsic motivation necessary for developing self-esteem irrespective of goal-attainment." However, given the importance of intrinsic versus extrinsic motivation, a system of prizes after every study session may be unconstructive as it falls into the category of implementing "rewards and punishments" approach.

Choice E is incorrect because it goes directly against the premise of the passage, which challenges the notion that providing rewards to encourage performance is a constructive approach for, among other things, instilling the intrinsic motivation "necessary for developing self-esteem irrespective of goal attainment."

8 **Choice A is correct** because the passage analyzes the positive and negative aspects of the reward/punishment approach in order to present an effort-based approach that it claims to be more effective. The second and third paragraphs refer to the rewards/punishments system with its positive ("effective incentives for the child") and negative ("fail to instill … intrinsic motivation") aspects. The third paragraph ("conversely…") then offers an alternative approach, "shown to foster the intrinsic motivation necessary" for developing important psychological traits.

Choice B is incorrect because the passage only analyzes the reward/punishment approach, rather than a number of different approaches, which would be needed to develop a synthesis of child-rearing approaches. Also, it presents an alternative way to address performance, focusing on effort, which is far from developing a comprehensive methodology. **Choice C** is incorrect because the primary purpose is to present an effort-based methodology based on the analysis of the rewards/punishment approach and its shortcomings. Although the rewards/punishments approach is referred to as a "slipshod substitute" for more effective methods, thereby warning parents of its inadequacy, the primary purpose is the discussion of the alternative approach, rather than the warning. **Choice D** is incorrect because while the passage starts by expressing the concerns and the uncertainty over what approach to take, the primary purpose goes beyond this by presenting one that has been shown to have more effective results over the long-term, as it was able to "foster the intrinsic motivation necessary…" **Choice E** is incorrect because the passage discusses the drawbacks of an approach focusing on outcomes in comparison to one that focuses on effort. It does not present a new paradigm of child-rearing, which would be an entirely new theoretical framework that encompasses more than one alternative approach.

9 **Choice D is correct** because the passage mentions the importance of "self-esteem" and feeling loved by children in general. It is conceivable that a household or educational center that is willing to implement new approaches is one that deeply cares for the children and so, provides a more nurturing environment for growth irrespective of which approach specifically is implemented.

Choice A is incorrect because the study would equally affect children in both groups, the one with the rewards/punishment system as well as the one with the alternate approach. Therefore, this would not be an explanation for the beneficial long-term results appearing more in one group than the other. **Choice B** is incorrect because the passage refers to both rewards and punishments as being part of the same "reward/punishment" system. Therefore, the study group that was not to receive rewards similarly would not have received punishments. **Choice C** is incorrect because the passage does not establish a link between parental or educator's attention and a child's motivation. It does mention the importance of conveying to the child that "love is not predicated on performance" which suggests that less attention is unlikely to yield positive results. **Choice E** is incorrect because the passage does not state that praise for effort should occur more or less frequently than rewards or punishments for outcomes. Thus, it cannot be concluded that the amount of attention given is affected necessarily by the approach used.

10 **Choice A is correct** because "inconspicuous" means not clearly visible or attracting attention. This word fits in the context of the sentence because it describes the slight differences between these two categories of mental conditions. Because the differences are so difficult to notice, many people go years without receiving the correct diagnosis. **Choice E is correct** because "subtle" means so precise that it is difficult to describe. This word fits in the context of the sentence because it expresses the slight differences between these two categories of mental conditions. Because the differences are so difficult to notice, many people go years without receiving the correct diagnosis.

Choice B is incorrect because "pervasive" means an unwelcome effect spreading widely through an area. This word does not fit in the context of the sentence because it does not describe the slight differences in symptoms between these two conditions. Rather than being an unwelcome and spreading effect, these differences are very small and difficult to pinpoint. This makes choices A and E the best options. **Choice C** is incorrect because "harmless" means unable to cause damage or offense. The passage does not express in any way that either of these conditions are harmless to individuals. This word does not fit in the context of the sentence because it does not describe the slight differences in symptoms between these two conditions. Rather than being unable to cause harm, these differences are small and difficult to pinpoint. This makes choices A and E the best options. **Choice D** is incorrect because "debilitating" means making something weak or infirm. This word does not fit in the context of the sentence because it does not describe the slight differences in symptoms between these two conditions. Both conditions could be described as debilitating to an individual, but this does not explain how the conditions relate to one another. Rather than the degree to which they make the individual weaker, these differences are small and difficult to pinpoint. This makes choices A and E the best options. **Choice F** is incorrect because "extravagant" means exceeding what is appropriate financially or resourcefully. This word does not fit in the context of the sentence because it does not describe the slight differences in symptoms between these two conditions. Rather than being inappropriately expensive (which would not make sense when discussing symptoms of a mental condition), these differences in symptoms are very small and difficult to pinpoint. This makes choices A and E the best options.

11 **Choice C is correct** because "deductive" means provable by deriving conclusions based on reasoning. This word fits in the context of the sentence because it describes the nature of the reasoning that must be used in order to understand truths about the origins of the universe. In other words, conclusions based on reasoning must be derived in order for these truths to be discovered. **Choice D is correct** because "inferable" means derivable through the use of drawing conclusions and reasoning. This word fits in the context of the sentence because it describes the nature of the reasoning that must be used in order to understand truths about the origins of the universe. In other words, conclusions based on reasoning must be derived in order for these truths to be discovered.

Choice A is incorrect because "inverse" means something contrary to nature or reversed. This word does not fit in the context of the sentence because it does not accurately describe the reasoning that must be used in order to understand truths about the origins of the universe. The passage does not express that anything must be reversed or that an opposite must be drawn in order to understand these truths. **Choice B** is incorrect because "deliberate" means done consciously and intentionally. This word does not fit in the context of the sentence because it does not accurately describe the reasoning that must be used in order to understand truths about the origins of the universe. The passage does not express that anything done very intentionally or explicitly in order to understand these truths. **Choice E** is incorrect because "observable" means able to be noticed or discerned. This word does not fit in the context of the sentence because it does not accurately describe the reasoning that must be used in order to understand truths about the origins of the universe. The passage does not express that anything must be observed or visually analyzed in order to understand these truths. **Choice F** is incorrect because "obvious" means clear, self-evident, and easily understood. This word does not fit in the context of the sentence because it does not accurately describe the reasoning that must be used in order to understand truths about the origins of the universe. The passage does not express that these truths are apparent. Rather, these truths require deductive reasoning to discover.

12 **Choice B is correct** because "endemic" means something negative is occurring regularly in a population year round. This word fits in the context of the sentence because it describes the way crime was always existing in the area, leading to the police officers' fear. **Choice F is correct** because "prevalent" means widespread in a particular area. This word fits in the context of the sentence because it describes the way crime was always existing in the area, leading to the police officers' fear.

Choice A is incorrect because "epidemic" means an outbreak of disease that spreads quickly throughout a community. This word does not fit in the context of the sentence because the sentence describes crime in a way that suggests it always exists in the area. Rather than occurring in one single outbreak, crime is a consistent condition that characterizes the region. **Choice C** is incorrect because "curtailed" means to impose a restriction on. This word does not fit in the context of the sentence because the sentence does not suggest that the crime was decreasing or being restricted. Rather, it is suggested that crime in the area is always existent, leading to the police officers' fear. **Choice D** is incorrect because "governable" means something is capable of being controlled or managed. This word does not fit in the context of the sentence the sentence suggests that the crime in the area is so out of control that even the police are afraid. **Choice E** is incorrect because "exuberant" means filled with lively energy and excitement. This word does not fit in the context of the sentence because it does not describe crime that is so severe it leaves the police with fear. Rather, the crime could be described as endemic or prevalent, meaning it is always around in the area.

13 **Choice E is correct** as it is the only choice that does not accurately represent an assumption relied upon by the author. Mentioning how many people it would take to conduct two actions is irrelevant to this passage, as is the implied simplicity of creating a sound and throwing a stone, which is also what this choice discusses.

Choices A and B are both assumptions that deal with the idea that a person is able to expend his or her energy in a way that is accurate to the needs of the experiment and that the situation surrounding these actions (making noise, throwing objects) is not brought on by external motivators other than gathering data. **Choice C** represents the assumption made clear by the author's assertion that a person can, without difficulty, form a mechanical conception of the whole series without assuming imponderables" which based on the generalization that this type of thought process is easy for anyone—a fact that may not be true amongst certain groups of people who are perhaps uneducated or young. **Choice D** also incorrectly assumes that a person throwing a stone can expend his or her energy just as easily to apply that force to spinning a top, which relies on the basis that every person has the skill and ability to apply energy in this specific way.

14 **Choice C is correct** because the passage indicates that it was previously thought the role of TNF was "broadly catalyzing the immune response." It is also clear this theory underpinned the approach to certain treatments, such as its regulation in "treatments of autoimmune diseases." However, the newly discovered evidence indicates that TNF "plays a much narrower role, almost exclusively targeted at protecting the lungs from

TB" which means that other treatments based on TNF modulation will have to be reconsidered.

Choice A is incorrect because the assumptions shown to be untrue, specifically about TNF playing a wider role and "broadly catalyzing the immune response" do not change the accepted theory that TNF "plays a role in a patient's capacity to defend against TB." Therefore, they do not necessarily alter its role in treatment. **Choice B** is incorrect because the passage does not challenge the "established theory" that TNF plays a key role in TB survival. The new evidence is likely to have implications on other diseases, where TNF has been shown to be less involved than previously thought. However there is no indication in the passage that treatments of TB need be necessarily affected by these findings.

15 **Choice C is correct** because the first paragraph states that studies in TB "suggest a genetic component" in varying mortality rates. The second paragraph supports this claim by referring to research that is "expanding upon the established theory" that certain components in the immune system, namely TNF cytokines play "a role in a patient's capacity to defend against TB." However, the second paragraph then states that recent findings show that "TNF plays a much narrower role" than previously thought. Instead of being "wide-spectrum" and "broadly catalyzing" the immune response, it is very "targeted" a fact that upends, or refutes, a previously held theory about the role of TNF in general.

Choice A is incorrect because although scientists have been "confounded" by the varying mortality rates, it doesn't indicate that researching the disease is in itself a challenge. The second paragraph, far from addressing any challenges, introduces new ones for medicine in general by stating that previous theories on TNF are incorrect and need to be revised. **Choice B** is incorrect because while the first paragraph presents the role of genetics, the second further supports the claim by stating that current studies are "expanding on the established theory" which means it is still considered valid. The theory that is refuted is about the extent of TNF's role in immune response beyond TB and in general. **Choice D** is incorrect because while the first paragraph presents the role of genetics in TB mortality rates, the purpose of the new evidence on TNF presented in the second paragraph is not to support that theory, which is already accepted ("expanding on the established theory" that "TNF plays a role in a patient's capacity to defend against TB"). The new evidence challenges the theory that TNF plays a larger role in immune response ("...recent findings indicate that TNF plays a much narrower role"). **Choice E** is incorrect because while the first paragraph does introduce the genetic factor in TB survival rates, the second refutes a previously-held theory on the role of TNF in immune response, as it used to be "considered a wide-spectrum pro-inflammatory cytokine." The role of inflammation in TB, however, has not been challenged. Current studies are building on the (accepted) idea that TNF is a pro-inflammatory cytokine that "plays a role in a patient's capacity to defend against TB."

6 Quantitative Reasoning (Easy) Answers & Explanations Section 5

1 **Choice B is correct** because the obtained values of n are 18 and –12.

Apply the absolute rule: If $|u| = a$, $a > 0$ then $u = a$ or $u = -a$

$3n - 9 = 45$	or	$3n - 9 = -45$
$3n = 45 + 9$	or	$3n = -45 + 9$
$3n = 54$	or	$3n = -36$
$n = 18$	or	$n = -12$

Choice A is incorrect because Quantity A is less than Quantity B. **Choice C** is incorrect because Quantity A is not equal to Quantity B. **Choice D** is incorrect because a relation can be obtained from the given information.

2 **Choice C is correct** because based on the number line every increment represents ¼. M is located at 3 ¾. Quantity B can be converted into a mixed number and 15/4 is the same as 3 and 3/4. This makes Quantity A and Quantity B equal.

Choice A is incorrect because Quantity A and Quantity B are equal. **Choice B** is incorrect because Quantity A and Quantity B are equal. **Choice D** is incorrect because it is possible to determine the exact values of Quantity A and Quantity B.

3 **Choice C is correct** because the obtained area for Circle A and Circle B are equal.

Find the Area of Circle A.

From the given circumference of Circle A, let's first find its radius.

$$C = 2\pi r$$
$$a\pi = 2\pi r$$
$$\frac{a\pi}{2\pi} = \frac{2\pi r}{2\pi}$$
$$r = \frac{a}{2}$$
$$A = \pi r^2$$
$$A = \pi(\frac{a}{2})^2$$
$$A = \pi(\frac{a^2}{4})$$

Find the Area of Circle B.

$$r = \frac{a}{2}$$
$$A = \pi r^2$$
$$A = \pi(\frac{a}{2})^2$$
$$A = \pi(\frac{a^2}{4})$$

Hence, Quantity A is equal to Quantity B.

Choice A is incorrect because Quantity A is not greater than Quantity B. **Choice B** is incorrect because Quantity B is not greater than Quantity A. **Choice D** is incorrect because a relation can be obtained from the given information.

4 **Choice A is correct** because the obtained value of pen B is approximately 151 pieces.

Solution:

Let A be the number of pens A sold.

Let B be the number of pens B sold.

Let's set up the ratio of each pen.

$$\frac{A}{B} = \frac{5}{7}$$

This can be further expressed as $A = \frac{5}{7}B$

Let's set up the revenue equation.

Each pen A costs $3 and each pen B costs $5. The total revenue from selling all the pens is $1080. Thus:

$$3A + 5B = 1080$$

Substitute $A = \frac{5}{7}B$ into the revenue equation.

$$3(\frac{5}{7}B) + 5B = 1080$$
$$\frac{15}{7}B + \frac{35}{7}B = 1080$$
$$\frac{50}{7}B = 1080$$
$$B = 1080(\frac{7}{50})$$
$$B = 151.2$$

Choice B is incorrect because Quantity B is less than Quantity A. **Choice C** is incorrect because Quantity A is not equal to Quantity B. **Choice D** is incorrect because a relation can be obtained from the given information.

6 | Quantitative Reasoning (Easy) Answers & Explanations   Section 5 | 6

5 **Choice A is correct** because if a system of equations has no solution then it means the two lines are parallel and have the same slope. Rearrange the equations into slope intercept form to determine their slope. The first equation in slope intercept form is $y = \frac{2}{3}x - 3$. The second equation in slope intercept form is $y = -\frac{a}{3}x + 8$. The slope of the first expression is $\frac{2}{3}$ and the slope of the second equation is $-\frac{a}{3}$. Since the slopes should be equal, set up the expression $\frac{2}{3} = -\frac{a}{3}$ and solve for a. Through cross multiplication you will get $-3a = 6$. Divide by -3 to solve and get $a = -2$. -2 is less than 0 so Quantity A is greater than Quantity B.

Choice B is incorrect because Quantity B equals -2 which is less than 0. **Choice C is incorrect** because a does not equal 0. **Choice D is incorrect** because it is possible to solve for a.

6 **Choice E is correct** because the obtained number of medium boxes is 9.
Assign values.

    Let S be the cost of a small box.

    Let M be the cost of a medium box.

    Let L be the cost of a large box.

Analyze the given statements.

    $L = 3M$ - A large box costs the same as 3 medium boxes.

    $L = 6S$ - A large box costs the same as 6 small boxes.

Express M in terms of S.

    $L = L$

    $3M = 6S$

    $M = 2S$

Calculate the cost of the 72 small boxes.

    Total cost = 72 S

Let x be the number of large boxes Emma buys. She buys an equal number of large and medium boxes.

    The number of medium boxes is x.

Find the total cost of the large and medium boxes.

    Cost of large boxes = x (L) = $x(6S)$

    Cost of medium boxes = x (M) = $x(2S)$

    Total cost of medium and large boxes = $x(6S) + x(2S) = x(8S)$

Set the total cost equal to the cost of 72 small boxes and solve for x.
$$x(8S) = 72S$$
$$x = \frac{72S}{8S}$$
$$x = 9$$

Choice A is incorrect because 4 is fewer than the obtained number of the medium of boxes. **Choice B is incorrect** because 5 is fewer than the obtained number of the medium of boxes. **Choice C is incorrect** because 6 is not the obtained number of the medium boxes. **Choice D is incorrect** because 8 is not the obtained number of the medium boxes.

7 **Choice C is correct** because the obtained value of $P(x = 8)$ is $\frac{4}{11}$.

We know that in the Probability distribution, $\sum_i P(x = x_i) = 1$.

x_i	2	6	7	8
$P(x = x_i)$	$\frac{3}{22}$	$\frac{3}{22}$	$\frac{4}{11}$	?

$\sum_i P(x = x_i) = 1$

$P(x = 2) + P(x = 6) + P(x = 7) + P(x = 8) = 1$

$\frac{3}{22} + \frac{3}{22} + \frac{4}{11} + P(x = 8) = 1$

$\frac{3}{22} + \frac{3}{22} + \frac{8}{22} + P(x = 8) = 1$

$\frac{14}{22} + P(x = 8) = 1$

$\frac{7}{11} + P(x = 8) = 1$

$P(x = 8) = 1 - \frac{7}{11}$

$P(x = 8) = \frac{4}{11}$

Choice A is incorrect because 4/22 does not equate to 1 when added to the other given probabilities. **Choice B is incorrect** because 6/22 is just the sum of $P(x = 2)$ and $P(x = 6)$. **Choice D is incorrect** because 5/11 does not equate to 1 when added to the other given probabilities. **Choice E is incorrect** because 8/11 does not equate to 1 when added to the other given probabilities.

6 Quantitative Reasoning (Easy) Answers & Explanations   Section 5

8 **Choice E is correct** because the obtained lcm of the three numbers is 720.

Find the multiples of the numbers.

36, 72, 108, 144, 180, 216… 720…

48, 96, 144, 192, 240… 720…

60, 120, 180… 720…

Choice A is incorrect because 120 is not a multiple of 36 and 48. **Choice B** is incorrect because 180 is a multiple of 60 only. **Choice C** is incorrect because 240 is a multiple of 48 and 60 only. **Choice D** is incorrect because 360 is a multiple of 36 and 60 only.

9 **Choice B is correct** because the obtained value of the total voters is 450 of which 270 voted and 180 rejected the resolution.

Find the number of people who were unable to vote.

Number of people unable to vote = Total number of people(percentage of unable to vote)

Number of people unable to vote $= 600(\frac{1}{4})$

Number of people unable to vote $= 150$

Find the number of people who were able to vote.

Number of people who were able to vote = Total number of people - # of people unable to vote

= 600 − 150

= 450

Find the number of voters who rejected the resolution.

# of people who rejected the resolution = # of people who were able to vote(% of who rejected)

= 450(0.40)

= 180

Find the number of voters who voted for the resolution.

# of people who voted for the resolution = # of people who were able to vote − # of people who rejected the resolution

= 450−180

= 270

Hence, 270 voted and 180 were against the resolution.

Choice A is incorrect because the total number should be 450 instead of 600. **Choice C** is incorrect because the number of those who voted should be greater than the number of those who rejected the resolution. **Choice D** is incorrect because the total number should be 450 instead of 600. **Choice E** is incorrect because the total number should be 450 instead of 500.

10 **Choices A, D, and F are correct** because the following ratio is simplified to 2:1.

Assign values.

Let A be students in classroom A.

Let B be students in classroom B.

Combined average of students for both classroom is

$120 = (100A + 160B)/(A + B)$

$120 = (100A + 160B)/(A + B)$

$120A + 120B = 100A + 160B$

$120A - 100A = 160B - 120B$

$20A = 40B$

$\frac{A}{B} = \frac{40}{20}$

$\frac{A}{B} = \frac{2}{1}$

Hence, the ratio is 2:1.

We see that Choices A, D, and F are all in a 2-to-1 ratio.

Choice B is incorrect because 5:8 is not in a 2-to-1 ratio.
Choice C is incorrect because 4.1 is not in a 2-to-1 ratio.
Choice E is incorrect because 10:3 is not in a 2-to-1 ratio.

11 **Choice B is correct** because the obtained is 3^{-1}.

Let x be the number such that

$(-15)^{-1} \div x = (-5)^{-1}$

Use the property of exponents to find x.

$-\frac{1}{15} \div x = -\frac{1}{5}$

$-\frac{1}{15}(\frac{1}{x}) = -\frac{1}{5}$

$-\frac{1}{15x} = -\frac{1}{5}$

$-15x = -5$

$x = \dfrac{-5}{-15}$

$x = \dfrac{1}{3}$ or $x = 3^{-1}$

Choice A is incorrect because the base is incorrect. Should have been 3 instead of 5. **Choice C** is incorrect because the base is incorrect. It should have been 3 instead of 2. **Choice D** is incorrect because the obtained answer is not a whole number but a fraction. **Choice E** is incorrect because when -15 is divided by 5, it won't result in 5.

12 **Choice C is correct** because the obtained value of the percentage of students who took Forensic Science is 3.0%

Find the number of students who took a Science course.

# of students who took a Science course = 500(0.3)

# of students who took a Science course = 150

Find the number of students who took Forensic Science.

# of students who took Forensic Science = 150(0.1)

# of students who took Forensic Science = 15

Find the percentage of students who took Forensic Science from the total number of students.

% of students who took Forensic Science = $\dfrac{15}{500}(100\%)$

% of students who took Forensic Science = 3.0%

Choice A is incorrect because 2.0 % is below the obtained percentage of students in Forensic Science. **Choice B** is incorrect because 2.5 % is close to the obtained value of the percentage but not an accurate value. **Choice D** is incorrect because 4.5 % is more than the obtained percentage of students in Forensic Science. **Choice E** is incorrect because 5.0 % is more than the obtained percentage of students in Forensic Science.

13 The correct answer is **0** because it lies between the given points and crosses the *y*-axis.

Plotting the given points in the *xy*-coordinate plane gives us a horizontal line with the equation $y = -3$. Point R lies on the horizontal line and crosses the *y*-axis, hence, point R is at (0, −3). The *x*-coordinate of point R is 0.

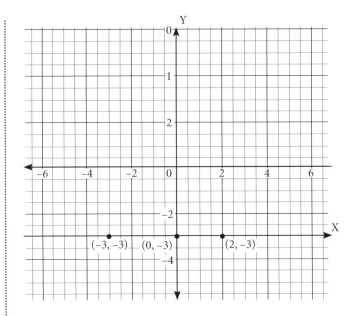

14 **Choice D is correct.** Let's find the coordinates of the point that divides the line segment joining (−8, 3) and (10, 3) in the ratio 4 : 5 internally using the section formula.

$$\dfrac{mx_2 + nx_1}{m+n}, \dfrac{my_2 + ny_1}{m+n}$$

where $(x_1, y_1) = (-8, 3)$

$(x_2, y_2) = (10, 3)$

Ratio $m : n = 4 : 5$

Apply the values to obtain the *x* and *y* coordinates.

$x = \dfrac{4(10) + 5(-8)}{4 + 5}$

$x = \dfrac{40 - 40}{9}$

$x = \dfrac{0}{9}$

$x = 0$

$y = \dfrac{4(3) + 5(3)}{4 + 5}$

$y = \dfrac{12 + 15}{9}$

$y = \dfrac{27}{9}$

$y = 3$

Hence, the point is (0, 3).

Choice A is incorrect because (5, 3) is not the obtained point at which the ratio is 4 : 5. **Choice B** is incorrect because (4, 3) is not the obtained point at which the ratio is 4 : 5. **Choice C** is incorrect because (3, 3) is not the obtained point at which the ratio is 4 : 5. **Choice E** is incorrect because (2, 3) is not the obtained point at which the ratio is 4 : 5.

15 **The correct answer is 14.** Let x be the first integer and $x + 1$ be the second integer.

Set up the equation.

$$x^2 + (x + 1)^2 = 365$$
$$x^2 + x^2 + 2x + 1 = 365$$
$$2x^2 + 2x + 1 = 365$$
$$2x^2 + 2x + 1 - 365 = 0$$
$$2x^2 + 2x - 364 = 0$$
$$x^2 + x - 182 = 0$$
$$(x - 13)(x + 14) = 0$$
$$x = 13 \text{ and } x = -14$$

We disregard the negative value of x.

The first consecutive number are $x = 13$ and $x + 1 = 13 + 1 = 14$.

Hence, the largest value of the consecutive positive integer is 14.

6 Quantitative Reasoning (Hard) Answers & Explanations — Section 5

1 **Choice B is correct** because the obtained value of the mean of 100 scores is 83 which is lesser than Quantity B.

Let's determine the total sum for the 70 test scores.

Total sum of the initial 70 scores = 70 × 80 = 5600.

Let's determine the sum of the additional 30 test scores.

Total sum of the additional 30 scores = 30 × 90 = 2700.

Find the total sum of all test scores combined.

Total sum of all 100 test scores = 5600 + 2700 = 8300

Find the average of the combined 70 test score and 30 test score.

Total average = $\frac{8300}{100} = 83$

Choice A is incorrect because Quantity A is less than Quantity B. **Choice C** is incorrect because Quantity A and Quantity B are not equal. **Choice D** is incorrect because there is a relation between the given information.

2 **Choice B is correct** because the obtained value of x is less than 8.

Let's rewrite the inequality.

From the given inequality, it implies that $\frac{1}{|x+1|}$ is greater than $\frac{1}{8}$. This means that $|x+1|$ must be less than 8 because the reciprocal function decreases as its argument increases.

We obtain,

$|x+1| < 8$

Solve the inequality.

$-8 < x + 1 < 8$

$-8 - 1 < x < 8 - 1$

$-9 < x < 7$

Hence, Quantity B is greater than Quantity A.

Choice A is incorrect because Quantity A is lesser than Quantity B. **Choice C** is incorrect because Quantity A and Quantity B are not equal. **Choice D** is incorrect because a relation can be determined from the given information.

3 **Choice A is correct** because Quantity A is greater than Quantity B.

Find the value of x.

The given series is in the form n^2.

Hence, $1^2, 2^2, 3^2, 4^2, x$

$1^2, 2^2, 3^2, 4^2, (4+1)^2$

$x = (4+1)^2$

$x = 5^2$

$x = 25$

Find the value of y.

$5, y, 45, 80, 125$

The given series is in the form $5(n)^2$.

$5, y, 45, 80, 125$

$5(1)^2, 5(2)^2, 5(3)^2, 5(4)^2$

$y = 5(2)^2$

$y = 5(4)$

$y = 20$

Hence, $x > y$.

Choice B is incorrect because Quantity B is less than Quantity A. **Choice C** is incorrect because Quantity A is not equal to Quantity B. **Choice D** is incorrect because a relation can be determined from the given information.

4 **Choice C is correct** because Quantity A and Quantity B are equal.

Let's find the distance between point R and T using the distance formula

$d = \sqrt{(x_2 - x_1)^2 + (y_2 - y_1)^2}$.

Plug the coordinates (0, 2) and (1, 0).

Find the distance between point R and T using the distance formula

$d = \sqrt{(1-0)^2 + (0-2)^2}$

$d = \sqrt{1^2 + (-2)^2}$

$d = \sqrt{5}$

Since the triangle RST is an equilateral, the 3 sides have equal length.

Hence, $3 \times \sqrt{5}$ or $3\sqrt{5}$.

6 Quantitative Reasoning (Hard)   Answers & Explanations   Section 5

Choice A is incorrect because Quantity A is not greater than Quantity B. **Choice B** is incorrect because Quantity B is not greater than Quantity A. **Choice D** is incorrect because a relation can be determined from the given information.

5 **Choice B is correct** because more diagonals are not parallel to any of the sides of the octagon.

Find the total number of diagonals in an Octagon where $n = 8$.

Number of diagonals $= \dfrac{n(n-3)}{2}$

Number of diagonals $= \dfrac{8(8-3)}{2}$

Number of diagonals $= \dfrac{40}{2}$

Number of diagonals $= 20$

Find how many diagonals are parallel to any side.

As shown in the figure, two diagonals (in dotted) are parallel to a side of a regular octagon.

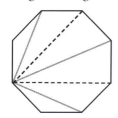

So, for each vertices of the octagon, there are $8 \times 2 = 16$ diagonals parallel to a side of a regular octagon.

However, there were counts of duplicate diagonals. We divide the number by 2.

Number of unique diagonals parallel to a side $= \dfrac{16}{2} = 8$.

To find the number of diagonals that are not parallel to any side.

Number of unique diagonals not parallel to a side $= 20 - 8 = 12$.

Hence, Quantity B is greater than Quantity A.

Choice A is incorrect because Quantity A is not greater than Quantity B. **Choice C** is incorrect because Quantity A and Quantity B are not equal. **Choice D** is incorrect because a relation can be determined from the given information.

6 **Choice C is correct** because the obtained value of the combination is 215.

Take note of the condition that "at least" 2 senior chefs are selected.

Case 1: Selected 2 senior chefs and 2 junior chefs.

Case 2: Selected 3 senior chefs and 1 junior chef.

Case 3. Selected 4 senior chefs and 0 junior chefs.

Let's analyze each case using the combination formula.

Case 1:

Choosing 2 senior chefs from 5:

$$\binom{5}{2} = \dfrac{5!}{2!(5-2)!} = 10$$

Choosing 2 junior chefs from 6:

$$\binom{6}{2} = \dfrac{6!}{2!(6-2)!} = 15$$

Total combination: $\binom{5}{2} \times \binom{6}{2} = 10(15) = 150$

Case 2:

Choosing 3 senior chefs from 5:

$$\binom{5}{3} = \dfrac{5!}{3!(5-3)!} = 10$$

Choosing 1 junior chef from 6:

$$\binom{6}{1} = \dfrac{6!}{1!(6-1)!} = 6$$

Total combination: $\binom{5}{3} \times \binom{6}{1} = 10(6) = 60$

Case 3:

Choosing 4 senior chefs from 5:

$$\binom{5}{4} = \dfrac{5!}{4!(5-4)!} = 5$$

Choosing 0 junior chefs from 6:

$$\binom{6}{0} = \dfrac{6!}{0!(6-0)!} = 1$$

Total combination: $\binom{5}{4} \times \binom{6}{0} = 5(1) = 5$

The total number of different ways 2 choose a team of 4 with at least 2 senior chefs is 215.

6 Quantitative Reasoning (Hard) Answers & Explanations Section 5

Choice A is incorrect because 200 is not the obtained value of the combinations. **Choice B** is incorrect because 210 is not the obtained value of the combinations. **Choice D** is incorrect because 230 is not the obtained value of the combinations. **Choice E** is incorrect because 245 is not the obtained value of the combinations.

7 **Choice D is correct** because the obtained area of the square is $\frac{25}{2}$

The diameter of a circle is the diagonal of the square. The square forms a 45-45-90 triangle. The diameter of the circle becomes the hypotenuse of the triangle (formed when the square is cut along its diagonal).

Use the pythagorean theorem to find the side of the square.

$c^2 = a^2 + b^2$

$5^2 = a^2 + a^2$

$5^2 = 2a^2$

$a^2 = \frac{5^2}{2}$

$a = \frac{5}{\sqrt{2}}$

Find the area of the square.

$A = s^2$

$A = \left(\frac{5}{\sqrt{2}}\right)^2$

$A = \frac{25}{2}$

Choice A is incorrect because it is the value of the side of the square and not area. **Choice B** is incorrect because the denominator is incorrect. **Choice C** is incorrect because $8\sqrt{2}$ is not the obtained area. **Choice E** is incorrect because $10\sqrt{2}$ is not the obtained area.

8 **Choice E is correct** because the obtained answer is 9R/20.

Let R be the number of students asked.

Number of student who do eat at 22:00 = 0.25R

Find the number of students who do not eat at 22:00.

Number of students who do not eat at 22:00 = 1 − 0.25R = 0.75R

Find the number of students who were asked what time they got up.

Number of students who were asked what time they got up = (0.40)(0.75)R = 0.30R

Find the number of students who do not eat after 22:00 and were not asked about the time they get up in the morning.

Number of students = 0.75R − 0.30R = 0.45R

Convert the 0.45R to a fraction.

$0.45R = \frac{45}{100}R = \frac{9}{20}R$

Choice A is incorrect because 3R/20 is not the correct expression of the obtained answer. **Choice B** is incorrect because R/10 is not the correct expression of the obtained answer. **Choice C** is incorrect because 5R/9 is not the correct expression of the obtained answer. **Choice D** is incorrect because 3R/10 is not the correct expression of the obtained answer.

9 **Choice B is correct** because it satisfies being odd.

The product of two odd integers is always odd.

Let x and y be positive odd numbers.

For any positive odd number, $x = 2a + 1$ and $y = 2b + 1$

$xy = (2a + 1)(2b + 1)$

$xy = (4ab + 2a + 2b + 1)$

$xy = 2(2ab + a + b) + 1$

This can be in form $2k + 1$, which is odd.

Choice A is incorrect because $2xy$ will result in an even number. xy is always odd, when multiplied by 2 becomes an even number. **Choice C** is incorrect because $x^y + x^y$ it results in $2x^y$ where x^y is always odd but when multiplied by 2 becomes even. **Choice D** is incorrect because $x^y + y^x$ are odd individually but become even when added. **Choice E** is incorrect because the addition of two odd numbers is always even.

10 **Choice D is correct** because the obtained answer is 64.

Let S be the total smelt the seal came across during the week.

It ate 50% of the first 80 smelt it came across means

Number of smelt eaten in the first 80 = 80 × 0.50 = 40 *smelts*

The remaining smelts would be S − 80 *smelts*.

The seal ate the 30% of the remaining smelts.

312 | *Practice Tests for the GRE*

6 Quantitative Reasoning (Hard) Answers & Explanations — Section 5

Number of smelt eaten from the remaining = $0.30(S - 80)$

Number of smelt eaten from 1st 80 and remaining = $40 + 0.30(S - 80)$

Find the total number of Smelt eaten based on the overall percentage.

Total number of smelt eaten = $0.40S = 40 + 0.30(S - 80)$

Solve for S.

$$0.40S = 40 + 0.30(S - 80)$$
$$0.40S = 40 + 0.30S - 24$$
$$0.40S - 0.30S = 40 - 24$$
$$0.1S = 16$$
$$S = 160$$

The total number of smelt eaten is 40% of the total smelt. Hence, $0.40 \times 160 = 64$

Choice A is incorrect because 32 is only half of the obtained value. **Choice B** is incorrect because 40 is fewer than the obtained value. **Choice C** is incorrect because 55 is not the obtained value. **Choice E** s incorrect because 80 is too much of the obtained value.

11 **The correct answer is 15%.** Let C be the current cost price of the goods.

Let C' be the new cost price of the goods.

Let S be the selling price of the goods.

Let x be the old profit of the goods.

Let x' be the new profit of the goods.

Profit is equal to the selling price – cost price. $x = S - C$

Profit percentage is $x = \dfrac{S - C}{C}(100)$

Solving for S would be $S = C\left(1 + \dfrac{x}{100}\right)$

The cost price is decreased by 8%, the new cost price would be $C' = C(1 - 0.08) = 0.92C$

The selling price is the same, find the new profit.

$$x' = S - C' = S - 0.92C$$

Substitute $S = C(1 + \dfrac{x}{100})$ into the equation of the new profit.

$$x' = C(1 + \dfrac{x}{100}) - 0.92C$$
$$x' = C(0.08 + \dfrac{x}{100})$$

Percentage of the new profit is Profit percentage is

$$P' = S - \dfrac{S - C'}{C'}(100)$$

$$\text{New Profit Percentage} = \dfrac{C\left(0.08 + \dfrac{x}{100}\right)}{0.92C} \times 100$$

$$\text{New Profit Percentage} = \dfrac{x + 8}{0.92}$$

Find the increase in Profit percentage

New profit percentage is $(x + 10)\%$

$$\text{New Profit Percentage} = \dfrac{x + 8}{0.92} = x + 10$$

Solve for x.

$$\dfrac{x + 8}{0.92} = x + 10$$
$$x + 8 = 0.92(x + 10)$$
$$x - 0.92x = 9.2 - 8$$
$$0.08x = 1.2$$
$$x = 15$$

Hence, the current percentage is 15%.

12 **Choice B is correct** because the obtained sum of the series is $\dfrac{n - 1}{2}$

$$(1 - \dfrac{1}{n}) + (1 - \dfrac{2}{n}) + (1 - \dfrac{3}{n}) + \text{ up to } n \text{ term}$$

Write the general term.

k-th term can be written as $(1 - \dfrac{k}{n})$.

Find the sum of the series.

$$S = \sum_{k=1}^{n} (1 - \dfrac{k}{n}).$$

$$S = \sum_{k=1}^{n} (1) - \sum_{k=1}^{n} \dfrac{k}{n}.$$

$$S = n - \dfrac{1}{n}\left(\dfrac{n(n+1)}{2}\right)$$

$$S = n - \dfrac{n + 1}{2}$$

$$S = \dfrac{n - 1}{2}$$

Choice A is incorrect because $\dfrac{1}{2n}$ is not the obtained sum of the series. **Choice C** is incorrect because $\dfrac{1}{n^2}$ is not the

Quantitative Reasoning (Hard) Answers & Explanations — Section 5

obtained sum of the series. **Choice D** is incorrect because $\frac{1}{2n-1}$ is not the obtained sum of the series. **Choice E** is incorrect because $\frac{1}{n}$ is not the obtained sum of the series.

13 **The correct answer is 3** because it is the obtained maximum value of xy.

Let's find the feasible region by combining all the shaded regions from the inequalities.

First, locate the vertices of the region by finding the intersection between the inequalities.

- Rewrite the inequalities $2x + 4y \leq 10$ and $x - y \geq 2$ in terms of x.

$$2x + 4y \leq 10$$
$$2x \leq 10 - 4y$$
$$x \leq \frac{10 - 4y}{2}$$
$$x \leq \frac{10 - 4y}{2}$$
$$x \leq 5 - 2y$$

This represents the region on or below $x = 5 - 2y$

$$x - y \geq 2$$
$$x \geq 2 + y$$
$$x \geq 2 + y$$

This represents the region on or below $x = 2 + y$

- Find the intersection between $x = 5 - 2y$ and $x = 2 + y$.

$$5 - 2y = 2 + y$$
$$-2y - y = 2 - 5$$
$$-3y = -3$$
$$y = 1$$
$$x = 5 - 2(1)$$
$$x = 3$$

The intersection between the inequalities is (3,1).

- Find the intersection between $2x + 4y \leq 10$, $x \geq 0$, $y \geq 0$.

Substitute $x = 0$ into the equation.
$$2x + 4y = 10$$
$$2(0) + 4y = 10$$
$$4y = 10$$
$$y = \frac{5}{2}$$

The intersection is $(0, \frac{5}{2})$.

Substitute $y = 0$ into the equation.
$$2x + 4y = 10$$
$$2x + 4(0) = 10$$
$$2x = 10$$
$$x = 5$$

The intersection is (5, 0).

- Find the intersection between $x - y \geq 2$, $x \geq 0$, $y \geq 0$.

Substitute $x = 0$ into the equation.
$$x - y = 2$$
$$(0) - y = 2$$
$$y = -2$$

$(0, -2)$ is not an intersection because the value of y is negative.

Substitute $y = 0$ into the equation.
$$x - y = 2$$
$$x - 0 = 2$$
$$x = 2$$

The intersection is (2, 0).

- The obtained intersections are $(3, 1)$, $(0, \frac{5}{2})$, $(5, 0)$, $(2, 0)$.

- Determine which among the intersections satisfies the given inequalities.

Intersections	$2x + 4y \leq 10$	$x - y \geq 2$
(3, 1)	$2(3) + 4(1) \leq 10$ $6 + 4 \leq 10$ $10 \leq 10$ TRUE	$3 - 1 \geq 2$ $2 \geq 2$ TRUE
$(0, \frac{5}{2})$	$2(0) + 4(\frac{5}{2}) \leq 10$ $0 + 10 \leq 10$ $10 \leq 10$ TRUE	$0 - \frac{5}{2} \geq 2$ $-\frac{5}{2} \geq 2$ FALSE
(5, 0)	$2(5) + 4(0) \leq 10$ $10 + 0 \leq 10$ $10 \leq 10$ TRUE	$x - y \geq 2$ $5 - 0 \geq 2$ $5 \geq 2$ TRUE
(2, 0).	$2(2) + 4(0) \leq 10$ $4 + 0 \leq 10$ $4 \leq 10$ TRUE	$x - y \geq 2$ $2 - 0 \geq 2$ $2 \geq 2$ TRUE

6 Quantitative Reasoning (Hard)   Answers & Explanations   Section 5 6

- The obtained intersections are (2, 0), (3, 1), (5, 0). Evaluate xy at each intersection.

  At (2, 0): $xy = 2(0) = 0$

  At (3, 1): $xy = 3(1) = 3$

  At (5, 0): $xy = 5(0) = 0$

Hence, the obtained maximum value of xy for the given inequalities is 3.

14 **Choice B is correct** because the obtained answer is $792,000.

Let's look at the table for store A

Percentage change from 2016 to 2017 is 10%

Percentage change from 2017 to 2018 is –10%.

Starting sales for 2016 is $800,000.

Percentage change from 2016 to 2017 is 10% increase which means that's 110% of the initial sales.

Percentage change from 2016 *to* 2017 = $800,000 (1.1) = $880,000.

Percentage change from 2017 to 2018 is –10% which means the sales is 90% of the sales in 2017.

Percentage change from 2017 *to* 2018 = $880,000 (0.9) = $792,000.

Choice A is incorrect because $727,200 results from an incorrect application of the percentage changes. **Choice C** is incorrect because $800,000 is the 2016 value and does not account for the changes in the following years. **Choice D** is incorrect because it includes the 2017 value ($880,000) and the correct 2018 value ($792,000) but confuses the two. **Choice E** is incorrect because $968,000 and $880,000 do not reflect the correct percentage changes for Store A.

15 **Choice B, C, D and E are correct** because upon careful examination, these statements are true.

Find the simplest numbers that satisfy the given conditions

$x + y = z$ and $x = y$.

Let's choose $x = 2$, and $y = 2$, hence $z = x + y = 2 + 2 = 4$.

Analyze each choice with the given values of x, y and z.

Choice A: $x - y = 2z$

            $2 - 2 = 2(4)$

               $0 \neq 8$ FALSE

Choice B: $x - z = y - z$

            $2 - 4 = 2 - 4$

            $-2 = -2$ TRUE

Choice C: $x - y = 0$

            $2 - 2 = 0$

              $0 = 0$ TRUE

Choice D: $2x + 2y = 2z$

            $2(2) + 2(2) = 2(4)$

                 $8 = 8$ TRUE

Choice E: $x = z/2$

            $2 = 4/2$

              $2 = 2$ TRUE

Choice A is incorrect because it contradicts the conditions $x + y = z$ and $x = y$.

Know Your Scaled Score

This table can be used to calculate your scaled score. Use a pencil to note down your scores for each section.

Input the number of questions you got right for both sections and add them in the adjacent columns. To get your scaled score for each section, refer to the table on page 317. Lastly, add both sections' scaled scores to get your total score for all tests.

If you attempted the Easy Section, check your scaled scores in the Verbal/Quantitative (Easy) column.

If you attempted the Hard Section, check your scaled scores in the Verbal/Quantitative (Hard) column.

	Verbal Reasoning		Quantitative Reasoning	
	Section 2 (Number of correct answers)	Section 4 (Number of correct answers)	Section 3 (Number of correct answers)	Section 5 (Number of correct answers)
Total				
Scaled Score				

SCALED SCORE TABLE

Raw Score	Verbal (Easy)	Verbal (Hard)	Quantitative (Easy)	Quantitative (Hard)
27	160	170	160	170
26	159	170	159	167
25	158	168	157	164
24	157	166	155	162
23	156	165	154	161
22	155	163	153	159
21	154	162	152	158
20	153	161	151	157
19	153	160	150	155
18	152	159	149	154
17	151	158	148	153
16	150	157	147	153
15	149	156	146	152
14	148	155	145	151
13	147	154	144	150
12	146	153	143	149
11	145	153	142	148
10	143	152	141	147
9	142	151	140	146
8	141	150	139	145
7	139		137	
6	137		136	
5	135		135	
4	133		133	
3	130		131	
2	130		130	
1	130		130	
0	130		130	

Made in United States
Orlando, FL
19 September 2025